Talking Back
to
The New York Times

Talking Back
to
The New York Times
Letters to the Editor,   1851—1971

Selected and Edited
with an Introduction by
KALMAN SEIGEL

QUADRANGLE BOOKS
New York/Chicago

A New York Times Company

Table of Contents

Acknowledgements

Every anthology or collection of writing is of necessity the product of many hands. This collection of letters is no exception.

I am, of course, grateful to the hundreds of letter writers for their interesting, provocative and thoughtful contributions to the letters pages of *The Times*. Others whose efforts deserve my gratitude are Mildred Liebowitz, my erstwhile colleague in the letters department of *The Times* for her counsel, direction, wisdom and encyclopedic knowledge; Gray Peart and Paul Greenfeder of *The Times* library for their helpfulness in unearthing material; the staff of *The Times* morgue for its cooperation; John B. Oakes, editor of the editorial page of *The Times*, for his belief in a strong letters page; and my daughters, Ann Goodman and Carolyn Shanoff for their helpful suggestions and manuscript review.

I am particularly indebted to one person, who more than any other, put this book on paper and carefully nurtured it through long days and nights, weekends and weeks of exhausting manuscript preparation—my wife, Lillian. To her I owe a special debt of gratitude for her effort and dedication.

For permission to reprint the letters, acknowledgement is made to the letter writers; to those now deceased, acknowledgement is made to their executors and heirs. To those letter writers I could not reach, I also make acknowledgement. For permission to reprint the letter from the late W. E. B. Du Bois acknowledgement is made to Mrs. Shirley Graham Du Bois, and for the letter from Lord Russell, acknowledgement is made to the estate of Bertrand Russell.

KALMAN SEIGEL

Talking Back
to
The New York Times

I·Introduction

"This is true liberty, when freeborn men speak free."—EURIPIDES

On a Monday early in February, 1971, the letters to the editor page of *The New York Times* carried correspondence from Senator Sam J. Ervin of North Carolina on amending the Senate's filibuster rules, a discussion of New York's traffic snarls, revenue sharing, Israel and Vietnam. On the following day Vice President Spiro T. Agnew shared the letters page with several New Yorkers, a professor from Philadelphia and a New Jersey woman on current topics just as varied and urgent.

The letters page of *The Times* has been variously described as a battlefield for ideas, a forum for serious discussion of public issues and a safety valve through which the public's capacity for indignation can find expression in a harmless, but useful way. Perhaps the letters page is all of these. Together, they add up to an opportunity for a reader to "talk back" to a paper, to promote honest debate and discussion, to initiate ideas and to make real the promise of a democratic dialogue.

Letters to the editor are a highly valued part of every responsible newspaper and one of its most interesting and widely read features. They are a critical function of the editorial page and provide the public access to the press and editors an opportunity to discover what their readers are thinking and saying.

As a newspaper feature, letters are as old as American journalism itself. Readers in the early 18th century attacked the establishment. Then, as now, they aired novel ideas for a better life, fought City Hall, denounced an editorial and pleaded special causes.

When Adolph S. Ochs became publisher of *The Times* in 1896 he wrote in an announcement on the paper's editorial page: ". . . to make the columns of *The New York Times* a forum for the consideration of all questions of public importance, and to that end to invite intelligent discussion from all shades of opinion." In 1931 he told a journalism student at Columbia, "A paper with principles and ideals has a bounden public duty to present every side of a question. Only in this way can a constructive and worthwhile public opinion be formed." Sixteen years later Mr. Ochs' view was echoed in the report of the Commission on Freedom of the Press.

"All the important viewpoints and interests in society," the Commission said, "should be represented in its agents of mass communication. The giant units can and should assume the duty of publishing significant ideas contrary to their own, as a matter of objective reporting, distinct from their proper function of advocacy." Unless this is done, the report warned, "the unchallenged assumptions of each group will continue to harden into prejudice. The mass medium reaches across all groups; through the mass medium they can come to understand one another."

Since World War II the number of letters written to American newspapers has risen dramatically. Estimates, and they are only that, put the current number of letter-writers in the nation at 8,000,000. This new lively interest in letters is not easily explained, but a series of upheavals following the war stirred readers enough to write in greater numbers than ever before. Among these were the climate of fear and repression of the early fifties, the sit-ins in the South, Cuban missile crisis, the assassinations, revolt on the campus, the Black revolution, the walk on the moon, Vietnam, problems of the cities and the deteriorating quality of life.

Other factors are the existence of an increasingly literate and concerned readership and an undeniable and growing need to discuss complex issues in a disturbingly complex time. Add also a mounting frustration with what many regard as an immovable establishment, a lengthening alienation from traditional institutions and a sense of loneliness. For many a desperate need to communicate is met by a readily available listener—the editor.

Letters and letter-writers are indigenous to those countries where democracy and egalitarianism have been cherished ideals. In Great Britain and the United States, for example, where letter-writers abound and an attentive hearing is given to writers, the correlation is clear. But while both countries have a common base for the interest in letters, there are substantial differences in subject, style, appreciation and attitude.

There is nothing in the daily press of the United States comparable in any great degree to the letters in *The Times* of London. The homogeneity of the British, their gift of articulation and their appreciation of the odd or different permits, even encourages, a kind of letter rarely seen regularly in the American papers.

All Britons can read with equal pleasure and understanding about the special problems, adventures and frustrations of a fellow-Briton. In the United States sharply felt sectional differences and a generally heterogenous melting-pot population make much less likely a national, uniform reaction to the problems, adventures or frustrations of a fellow-American. There are some issues on which the nation does stand as one, but they do not include the simple, homely personal variety that binds the British.

American letters have special qualities of their own. They are more energetic, passionate, earthy and driving than most in the British press, and while less graceful in style, they have more vitality than many of the letters published abroad. They also tend to exhibit an anger and frustration that is so unlike the sort of gentle remonstrance that in letters in the British Press not only effects change, but even makes the target of their jibes like it.

The years since World War II have been vintage years for *The Times'* letters department. The 40,000 and more letters that now arrive annually make an incomparable mailbag. Whose mail can rival mine for diversity, passion, brilliance, hate, humor, invective, punditry, inventiveness and pathos? What a vivid reflection of history can be seen through the candid correspondence of the readership, and what an opportunity to indulge every man's foible for reading other people's mail!

The letters to *The Times* are most often serious, thoughtful contributions to the daily dialogue on major issues, prepared with care, knowledge and often after thorough research. They are also puffs of emotion composed in white heat. They are sometimes irate, sometimes silly, puckish, trivial and ponderous. They are, as much as any other index, an accurate measure of ourselves.

In number and content they tell with barometric accuracy the political, social, economic and psychological weather in this country and abroad. It is not uncommon for the letters page of *The Times* to give space simultaneously to a head of state explaining a nation's position, a Nobel laureate challenging construction workers on patriotism and a subway commuter asking only respite from the city's din, dirt and danger.

Letters also give insight into our capacity for indignation—a capacity that is fortunately alive and high. Letters are valuable as a source of news, as leavening for editorial writers who tend to be oracular, as a reminder to news professionals to hone their writing and thinking. They also affirm a paper's hospitality to opinions and attitudes different from its own.

A new appreciation of letters in providing access to the press is yet another reason for the increasing interest in this form. At present letters

5

are the center of controversy in a growing debate over coercive publishing—mandating through legislation the right of reply. This has put lawyers and newsmen in opposite corners of the ring on still another issue. Critics as well as defenders of the press look more and more to letters as an avenue through which minority groups can reach the press. Letters are also finding a place in radio and television. Broadcasters have been airing excerpts from listeners' letters while seeking a format for the electronic media as effective as the letters columns in newspapers.

"The voice of the exile, his pen is his word:
and were't not letters, I should not be heard."
Ovid.

In everyday's mail there are always a number of surprises—forecasts from astrologers, requests from foreign students for funds, inquiries about pets with strange illnesses, religious and inspirational messages, requests for aid in finding lost relatives, errant husbands, and obscure companies, challenges to the editor to demonstrate "guts" by seeing issues as the writer sees them, and a variety of solutions to national and world problems, usually simplistic but altogether sincere.

While letters can and do tell us what our readership is thinking, they are not necessarily the most accurate index to the division of opinion. Readers are far more prone to write against something than for it—to condemn rather than to praise. As a result editors must be wary of letter writing campaigns, which can give a distorted picture of sentiment on an issue, and of minorities, whose numbers may be small, but whose voices are often disproportionately loud.

Who writes letters to the editor? Everyone does. Surprisingly there is little formal research information available, although one study of about 10,000 letters shows that men wrote 46 per cent of all letters to the editor and women 37 per cent—the others were not identifiable. Of the letters attributable to men, 23 per cent came from clergymen, 21 per cent from lawyers, civic leaders and minor officials, 18 per cent from active politicians, 15 per cent from secretaries of organizations, 12 per cent from disgruntled public servants and 11 per cent from publicity-seekers. Among the women letter writers, 42 per cent of those who wrote were spokesmen for various movements and groups, 28 per cent were teachers, 16 per cent were working women and 14 per cent were housewives.

A 1964 study, published in the *Journalism Quarterly*, indicated published letter-writers were mostly elderly and middle-aged, predominantly well-educated; male by a three-to-one ratio; of all occupational levels; residents of the area in which the publishing newspapers circulated; extremely well-read, and remarkably conscious of their voting privilege.

A study of the letters received at *The Times* in the past three years shows somewhat similar results. Men outnumber women as letter writers, and the most prolific writers are doctors, lawyers, university faculty, government officials, businessmen and students. Among women, the most frequent letter-writers are professional women and housewives.

The motivation behind letter writing is generally evenly divided between personal and civic considerations. Some feel they can affect the course of events through their letters directly, or by helping through their letters to mold opinion. Some write because they feel certain things must be said. Others write because of a need for catharsis, for "getting it off my chest."

Lonely people write out of a need to communicate—even if it is with nothing more than a nameless, faceless, impersonal editor. Those who feel anger, frustration and sometimes hate, attack their private windmills with long, handwritten screeds, in colored inks, or blurred carbons beyond even the most sympathetic comprehension.

All letter writers have great pride of authorship and defend every word fiercely. Writers with some experience accept editorial discipline with grace and understanding. Others, moved sufficiently by events to perform the conscious act of writing, feel they have something important to say and place on the paper the responsibility for providing the forum in which to say it. They also feel the frustrations of the limits which the papers must impose, and the result is a host of problems to which an editor must bring tact, skill and understanding.

In selecting letters for publication in *The Times* we are guided by simple ground rules. Good letters are generally brief, clearly written, pegged to the news, free of vituperative attack, issue-oriented, and offer constructive informative comment or criticism.

Letters to the editor have always had an important place in *The Times*. The first letter to the editor appeared five days after the paper's first issue on Sept. 18, 1851. Letters continued to appear frequently, but on an irregular basis until Mr. Ochs assumed control on the paper. He sensed the importance of a diversity of judgments and informed views and assigned to letters an increasing importance and prominence as part of the paper's editorial page.

In 1931 letters were brought together in a fixed position under a standing headline on the right side of the editorial page. John B. Oakes, present editor of the editorial page, believes strongly in a good letters column. He feels it is one of the paper's great responsibilities in helping to form well-grounded opinion. Believing *The Times* had an obligation to print a larger percentage of the letters it receives, he sought

7

and obtained expanded space for letters in 1970 when the daily letters space was doubled.

In selecting the letters for the daily and Sunday letters pages from the 100 to 150 received every day, we try to give voice to a variety of positions and issues crying for exposure, to opinions that differ with the paper's editorial stand and to rebuttals and dialogue with previously published letter-writers.

All letters are read, screened and recorded as to issue and position. Anonymous letters are ignored. So are obscenities and obvious cranks which account for a relatively small part—some 10 or 12 per cent—of the daily mail. Letters signed with pseudonyms are considered, but rarely used. (If the quality of the letter is high and the reason to protect the writer's identity good, the letter will be considered for publication.) Open letters, letters addressed to public officials and those offered elsewhere simultaneously or generally circulated are not considered for publication at *The Times*. The identification or background of letter-writers is included where it is germane to indicate to the reader special expertise or special interest. *The Times* does not solicit letters, nor does it pay for the letters it prints.

Letters that are not used—and this accounts for some 93 out of every 100 letters received—are acknowledged with a series of forms. Since the forms bear my name as letters editor, I have become the target of every disappointed letter-writer and my personal mail has grown from a rill to a river. To juggle Israelis and Arabs, conservatives and liberals, landlords and tenants, new left and old right, Democrats and Republicans, students and police, ambassadors and embassy representatives, is to walk a treacherous path. When I draw critical comment from both sides, I feel I haven't been all wrong.

The letters page of *The Times* is a target for propagandists and special pleaders, for trial balloons from government officials and for unorthodox ideas from everyone who sees himself as the possessor of the world's residual wisdom. Editors must be constantly alert to mail from pressure groups, from professional letter-writers and from organized letter-writing campaigns. The last-named are easy to spot. They generally come from the same area and betray themselves by similarity of phrasing. Professional letter-writers tend to hog short letters space. They are discouraged by imposition of a limit, generally two a year for a single writer, maintained in an effort to achieve as broad a base of participation as possible in the letters page.

Libel laws and standards of good taste apply to letters just as they do to news. And letters editors often have to react to news developments just as swiftly as do news editors. On occasion newsbreaks between the time the letter was put in the page and the time the page goes to press have affected a letter's message.

The letters page of *The Times* tries to reflect a balance on most issues. On highly controversial subjects where the mail on one side is preponderantly heavy, the ratio used gives a clue to, not an exact reflection of, the numbers received on each side. On highly controversial issues on which the paper has taken a stand, weight is given to positions opposed to *The Times*' editorial policy.

The letter to the editor is more than idle epistolary chatter. It is the reader's lance as he tilts with City Hall. It is his passport to a community of interest with his fellow man, or an arena of controversy in which he can test his thinking with those who differ. It is his town meeting in print, his approach to a purer form of participatory democracy.

The Times' letters have made news, reflected history, helped right some wrongs. Above all, they have given the voices of quiet expression and honest persuasion to masses of men and women in a world that shouts more, but listens less. In the letters that follow the identifications and associations of the letter writers are those applicable at the time the letters were written.

Out of the mailbags that are opened daily at *The Times*, here is a sampling of letters that over the last 120 years have given substance and form to the dialogue of free men.

II·Some Landmark Letters

The first letter to the editor of *The Times* appeared on September 23, 1851, five days after the then New York *Daily Times* began publication. Characteristically, it voiced a complaint—about the dreary provincialism of the citizens of Philadelphia as contrasted with the lively enterprise and industry of New Yorkers.

But letters and letter-writers were not destined to play the sole role of a scold. They soon reached a new level and became a vehicle upon which many men of history rode. As much as any other form of expression, newspaper letters made it possible for national and world leaders to participate in a direct, sometimes personal way, in the dialogue of their times.

The letters that follow reflect some of the history of the last century through the comments of the men and women who helped make it—from the debate about prisoners of war in 1865 to the debate over the publication by *The Times* of the Pentagon papers in 1971.

11

Philadelphia

To the Editors of *The New York Daily Times:*

I thank you for the spirit of your notice of Philadelphia in this morning's *Times*. As a Philadelphian, of unmixed descent through many generations, having my home, affections, interests and hopes in Philadelphia above every other spot, I thank you for the just rebuke which you have administered to that class of her citizens whose occupations, means and example control her fate. A frequent visitor to New York during the last 20 years, I have marked with shame and sorrow the splendid contrast, which the enterprize and consequent progress of this city, have presented to the penny-wise caution and slow motions of my own. That Philadelphia has increased vastly in wealth and population, that her people are worthy and industrious, as a mass; that she has noble institutions of benevolence and science; that she will continue to hold her relative place among the capitals of the Union, there can be no doubt. Nature favors her so bountifully in many respects that the stupidity of Baotia and the vices of Sodom could hardly prevent her advance in material greatness. But nature is not seconded by her people. The leaven of a few generous and far–seeing spirits is not sufficient to raise the mass. Two influences control her—one, that of prescriptive place-men and pot-house politicians; the other, that of old fogies. The former care for nothing but the maintenance of a municipal system which keeps them in power and in pocket: the latter for nothing that puts a penny at risk, adds a mite to taxes, or contributes to her dignity and beauty as a metropolis. I am not ignorant of the difficulties which Philadelphia has had to contend with; of her immense losses in the financial revulsions commencing in 1837, when she was debtor of the East and the creditor of the South and West, and was thus the scapegoat of the Union. Nor do I overlook the fact that her port is somewhat remote from the sea. But these drawbacks are no apology for blind indifference or niggardly opposition to increasing her wealth, consequence and attractions.

The construction of the Central Railroad from Philadelphia to Pittsburgh, and the establishment of a line of propeller steamers to Liverpool, are enterprises equally creditable and important. But they are only a tithe of what should have been done since New York made the Erie Canal, and Atlantic steam navigation was proved practicable. On the latter agent of trade, Philadelphia should have been the first instead of the last to seize. It annihilates the delays of her seaward intercourse, with other ports at home and abroad, and would have suggested to any wide-awake community its instant adoption. But our good easy merchants doze over the idea for 11 years, and then wake up to the construction of two or three vessels which screw their way across the ocean in 14 or 15 days, while a score of Boston and New York ships are paddling over in nine or ten. Any community afflicted with such 11th-hour spasms and partial paralysis, cannot hope to compete with a vigilant, daring and vigorous neighbor. If the spirit of New York and Philadelphia were exchanged, the Hudson and the Bay would not save the former from the latter's competition. It is the character of the New York people not less the geographical advantages of the port, which have raised this city to its present unrivaled position. I say unrivaled advisedly, for although Philadelphia may have four-fifths as many inhabitants, with the assurance of a steady and rapid increase in numbers and means, yet it is idle to compare the general aspect of the two cities. The present wealth and energy, and the future magnificence of the one, destined to cast both London and Paris in the shade, are unmistakable. The condition of the latter, fair as may be, seems to demand some other assurance than that of the mere senses, to justify a similar hope. We would rather witness the dust and mud of Broadway, with its business and bustle, than the Quaker neatness and the Quaker quiet of most Philadelphia thoroughfares. Our second fiddle may be a very good one—better than any other perhaps—but still it is but a second fiddle.

I have trespassed on your columns much farther than I intended, stating a few of many, not more welcome, truths, for the digestion of philo-Philadelphians. If we wish our city to emerge from provincialism, we must emulate the features of all great capitals. Until we adopt a more adventurous, prompt and liberal system of trade; until we have streets divested of flat, dead brick walls, sprinkled with bits of marble; until we have hotels built for the purpose, and not patched-up old houses; until we have theatres and other places of amusement commodious and elegant, to entice and retain the presence of strangers; until the city is governed for its own sake, and not for the selfish purposes of small-souled millionaires and needy office–holders; until, in a word, we reject old fogyism of every type, and not only follow, but hold up the new lights of money-making and money-spending, living for something else than bonds and mortgages secured by architecture equally monotonous and tasteless—then and not until then, may we have unmingled cause to be proud of Philadelphia.

VISITOR
New York, Friday, September 19, 1851

13

Surrender of General Lee

To the Editor of *The New York Times*:

There seems to be a general misunderstanding, both among our people and some of our editors, with reference to the terms of surrender granted by Gen. Grant to the "Army of Northern Virginia."

In his letter of the 8th inst. to Gen. Lee, Gen Grant says: "Each officer and man will be allowed to return to their homes, not to be disturbed by the United States authority, so long as they observe their parole and the laws in force where they reside."

It is assumed that these terms grant an unconditional pardon for all past offences against the "civil law" to the officers and men belonging to the surrendered army. A little consideration will show this cannot be so. Gen. Grant, seeing through the endeavors of Gen. Lee to entangle him in the meshes of diplomatic interviews in relation to a general peace, refused to treat with him in a "civil" capacity, and only offered the terms of a victorious and magnanimous soldier to a brave enemy. By surrendering to the military power, Gen. Lee and his army became simply "prisoners of war"; as much so in their homes in the South as if they were shut up in some huge Fort Lafayette. Gen. Grant evidently remembered that the army of Pemberton, paroled by him at Vicksburgh, was kept in a state of perfect organization by being formed into "a paroled camp." On this occasion he provided that the officers and men should "be allowed to return to their homes"—thus totally breaking up the rebel army. This "allowing," in military language, is equivalent to a command; so that these prisoners can go to "their homes," there to remain, unless allowed by express permission of the military authorities to go elsewhere.

The military law in relation to "prisoners of war" is the same, whether the prisoners are under parole or under actual duress; and in either case they are entitled to personal protection, as much against the "civil law" as against an armed mob. This protection, it is to be presumed, is what Gen. Grant means when he says they shall "not be disturbed by the United States authority so long as they observe their parole," &c.

Military law is supreme only when the civil law is inoperative; and where success follows military operations, can only, in a country like ours, be temporary. Nevertheless, all pledges made or privileges granted by virtue of military law, while it is the controlling power, must be respected by the civil law when it reassumes its supremacy. It follows from this principle, that although the whole South may return to its allegiance, and the States and United States authorities may be in full exercise of their civil functions, the "Army of Virginia" is not amenable to them, but still remains under the protection of military law. It may be the policy of our government to continue to hold the officers and men of this army as "prisoners of war" forever; or at least till the last one of them has passed from this earth. No punishment could be more severe than this, and no guaranty so efficacious to prevent their formenting future discord. The military punishment for breaking a parole, is death, and no member of the "Army of Northern Virginia" can ever free *himself* from the parole which he has given.

Should, however, the government prefer to subject them to the action of the civil law, it has only to declare "the officers and men of the Army of Northern Virginia exchanged, and released from their paroles." From the moment it does this, all promises made by Gen. Grant at the time of surrender will have been fulfilled; and the members of that army, ceasing to be "prisoners of war" become once again ordinary citizens, and, as such, are fully amenable to the civil authorities. The idea seems to prevail that, because the South has no prisoners to exchange, this army can never be released. Any government has the right to free its prisoners at any time; and it has often been done as an act of policy, or for the very purpose of restoring the supremacy of the civil power.

It is evident, therefore, that the terms granted to Gen. Lee and his army do not in the slightest degree affect their future responsibility to the civil authorities. Time only and the calm judgment of the American people will show what punishment will be meted out to them.

While it is becoming in a great nation to temper justice with mercy, it behooves the controlling powers for the time being to remember the duty they owe to posterity, and to fulfill that duty by placing the stamp of eternal infamy upon those parricidal brows who, while the sworn supporters of their country, used their best endeavors to destroy it.

"Then and Now"
New York, Thursday, April 13, 1865

Ovation to Rebel Leaders

To the Editor of *The Times:*

One of your correspondents proposes an ovation in this city to the rebel Gen. Lee. This is surely in the progressive spirit of the age. It is far ahead of the requirements of the Christian religion. But let us go further. Let us also give an "ovation" to the other chieftains, who presided over and dispensed "Southern hospitality" to our sons and brothers in Libby prison, at Andersonville, and at Salisbury. I am not sure that *all* of them, like Lee, had been educated and fed at the nation's expense at West Point, and had, like him, taken an oath before Almighty God to support the Constitution, but they are at least of the "chivalry" and of the "Sunny South."

ZOUAVE
April 12, 1865

Shafter's Army Must Come Home At Once

To the Editor of *The New York Times*:

There are moments when the public is so possessed with one overwhelming feeling that men are ready for united and decisive action. Is it not so with us today?

We have read with deepest indignation the scathing letter of Col. Roosevelt and the no less forcible utterance of the division and brigade commanders through their round robin to Gen. Shafter, and most significant of all is the action of Gen. Shafter in making public these letters. It must mean that the General commanding in Cuba, a professional soldier, trained to silence and obedience has taken this unprecedented step because he has appealed in vain to those whose duty it is to protect our soldiers, and now, as a last desperate resort he appeals to the public.

Shall we stand by and see our army die through official incompetency? Shall we not by a mass meeting of the citizens make a united protest? Shall we not join with us the great body of medical experts to answer the official plea that convalescent patients can be better moved into Cuban mountains than to some North Atlantic beach?

We believe that we have the facts before us and that the citizens are capable of judging and acting. Every hour passed amid malarial miasma is laden with death for our gallant soldiers. Let the body of American citizens speak with the power which as never yet been resisted, nor can be, when we speak as one man.

If the Government has not transports enough, let us show for our own army the same solicitude that we have maintained for our Spanish prisoners. Charter steamships and the companies will promptly respond, and will take pride in bringing our enfeebled but still spirited soldiers to the North under better sanitary conditions and with greater comfort than our Government vessels have done.

16

But we must act speedily, Mr. Editor. Your paper and all the leading papers can help the public to make known its will. We are not carping at the Administration. We wish to give it all the help we can, but where it fails egregiously we must make it feel that it is our servant and not our master

C.

New York, August 5, 1898

Criticism of the President's Speech

To the Editor of *The New York Times*:

President Wilson has at last openly spoken his mind. His address in the Senate is nothing short of a colossal pronouncement. It is one of the greatest and truest conceptions ever expressed in words. If enacted it would revolutionize the policy of every government on earth, and would create new ones. It would bring the world as near to a permanent brotherhood of nations as it seems possible to conceive. When he states that one of the conditions necessary for this country to enter into a world league of peace is that all government must be by the consent of the governed, he strikes a startling blow for world democracy—as bold as it is timely.

When he advocates the independence of Poland "and that henceforth inviolable security of life, of worship, and of industrial and social development should be guaranteed to all peoples who have lived hitherto under the power of Government devoted to a faith and purpose hostile to their own," he would remove the yolk of foreign power from the neck of the little nations and set them free according to their kindred desires. The fulfillment of this idea would free Belgium, Serbia, Rumania and Montenegro, pass back Alsace and Lorraine to France, its rightful owner, and free Italia irredenta and reform the Balkan states on natural national lines. Within this part of the President's message the Allies could attain their full territorial peace demands. This is "peace without victory," simply because it is just.

There is no victory in justice, and that is what the Allies are fighting for. The address is as much pro-Ally as it is anti-German, but, above these two, it is pro-American and pro-justice. As for America, the Wilson idea is revolutionary, and for that reason it will bear the fullest discussion, but I venture to predict that, under anything like the conditions

17

he names, it will find overwhelming favor. In this historic address President Wilson has spoken the noblest and most worthy word for the greatest as well as the smallest nation—the richest as well as the humblest human being on the face of the earth. This utterance will stand in the full light of all time.

CIVILIZATION
New York, January 24, 1917

Was Loss Paper or Real?

To the Editor of *The New York Times:*

I have a feeling that fewer persons are affected by the stock market drop than one would infer from the figures, just as fewer persons were affected by the previous rises. I am judging by my own situation. Among the stocks I happen to own are some that suffered the greatest losses last week, such as Tel. and Tel., American Tobacco, Union Pacific and Western Union, but my income from them remains the same as before.

As far as I am concerned a group of men, technically known as the Stock Exchange, gets together and decides that my Tel. and Tel. stock is worth $310 a share, and I experience a momentary glow of elation. A few days or weeks later they get together and decide that it is worth only $232, and I have a feeling of disappointment, also momentary. It is unlikely that the slump will affect the continued use of the telephone or that the company will be unable to continue to pay the $9 a share. I bought my stock at an average price of $98 a share, so even at the present low—or high, according to the point of view—it is worth more than double what I paid for it.

Doesn't it seem probable that mine is the situation of a great majority of holders of this and other good stocks? That they have merely lost some of their spectacular gains, but their stocks are still quoted at and worth more than they paid for them?

It seems to be the practice to compute the total loss in such a recession and multiply it by the total number of shares outstanding, and imply that somebody or the country has lost that vast amount. Headlines last week said that the loss was about $4 billion. In Monday's market only 87,100 shares of Tel. and Tel. were traded in. That is a very small percentage of the 13,203,093 shares outstanding. How many of the holders of these shares have actually lost anything? I am just where I was a few weeks ago. When Tel. and Tel. first crossed 232 I thought that was pretty good, and I still think so now that it has receded to 232, and I felt the same about American Tobacco when it first touched 196, Union Pacific when it first touched 240, and Western Union when it first touched 191. My profits the last few weeks have been paper profits, and my losses last week are paper losses, and one cancels the other.

It reminds me of the farmer who told a neighbor that Josh Stebbins had offered $200 for his horse.

"Josh Stebbins ain't got two hundred dollars."

"Yes, I know, but ain't it a good offer?"

EARNEST ELMO CALKINS
New York, October 29, 1929

Keynes On Recovery

To the Editor of *The New York Times:*

I should be grateful if you would allow me to supplement briefly the article from my pen which you published on June 10; in particular by a more exact computation of the rate of the net loan expenditure of the American Treasury. The United States budget is, of course, by no means so heavily unbalanced, including a substantial sinking fund ($600 million) for the redemption of debt, while a considerable proportion of the emergency expenditure is represented by more or less valuable capital assets, much of it being merely refinancing and the substitution of one document for another. I believe, however, that the following table gives a fairly accurate impression of the rate of government expenditure not covered by taxation, which gives rise to new purchasing. These totals are arrived at by taking a three months' moving average (so that the figure against any month is the average for that and the two preceding months) of the expenditures which clearly lead to new incomes, plus the excess of payments to farmers in any month over the corresponding processing taxes (or minus the deficiency), plus a half of the advances which in the first instance increase liquidity rather than new purchasing:

1933	$1,000,000	1934	$1,000,000
September	102	January	369
October	123	February	422
November	158	March	435
December	231	April	348
		May	311

The statistics for the first half of June indicate that the figure for June calculated on the same basis will be in the neighborhood of $300 million. Nor, on the information available, should I expect the three months' moving average to fall appreciably below $300 million for the present, while there is some hope of an increase by the late summer.

Admittedly there is at the present time some recession in factory output in the United States, due partly to seasonal influences, partly to the falling away of government expenditure as shown in the above table and partly to business optimism in the first quarter of 1934 having encouraged industry, particularly in the case of textiles and automobiles, to provide for a somewhat larger effective demand than is in fact maturing today. But I should doubt if this recession will go very far, since a mere continuance of the present rate of government loan expenditure should gradually provide more stimulus than has yet been experienced. For the public have not unnaturally used much of their first increment of income to repay debts of all kinds rather than to keep rolling the ball of new purchasing.

Both in the United States and in England I have found a tendency to overestimate the extent of the British recovery up to date as compared with the American recovery. One has to remember, of course, that your recovery started from a much lower point than ours. There is also the difficulty that the only satisfactory American index of employment is confined to industrial employment in factories and does not include building, transportation or distribution. It is possible, however, to arrive at certain broad conclusions. In both countries a peak of unemployment was reached in January, 1933. Since that date the increase in the number of men employed in Great Britain as shown by our own statistics is almost exactly 10 per cent, two-thirds of this improvement having occurred in 1933 and one-third in the first five months of 1934. There can be no doubt that the percentage improvement in the United States greatly exceeds this. Factory employment shows an increase exceeding 40 per cent between January 1933, and May 1934; and it would, I think, be generally agreed that a more comprehensive index would show an improvement in excess of 25 per cent. Even more notable is the increase in the factory payrolls, which have increased over the same period by fully 70 per cent. I should suppose that the American national income must have increased by at least 12 to 15 per cent in 1933 and probably by a further 12 to 15 per cent in the first half of 1934—which is a colossal achievement in the time.

Different authorities will differ in their estimates of the relations of cause and effect. But the above figures may perhaps help all alike to see the matter in a more accurate perspective. The exaggerated improvement during the first three months of office of the new administration, based almost entirely on psychological excitement and not on real factors, which was inevitably followed by a steep recession, has tended to obscure the extent of the ground gained over the period up to date, taken as a whole.

If we take the average of the pre-boom years 1923–25 as 100, the schematic picture, which I see in my own mind, of the rate of progress of the American economy toward normal, after smoothing out the excessive rise and subsequent fall in the middle of 1933, is, very broadly, as follows:

	1933	1934
First quarter	63	79
Second quarter	67	83
Third quarter	71	"
Fourth quarter	75	"

I feel that the maintenance of existing policies might continue this rate of a quarterly rise of four points during the rest of 1934. But I cannot see how 1935 can achieve a figure of 95 and better unless the United States enjoys the two advantages which mainly explain the measure of improvement achieved in England—namely, a large reduction in the long-term rate of interest and a high degree of activity in the building industry.

J. M. KEYNES
London, June 23, 1934

The Late Emmy Noether

To the Editor of *The New York Times:*

The efforts of most human beings are consumed in the struggle for their daily bread, but most of those who are, either through fortune or some special gift, relieved of this struggle are largely absorbed in further improving their worldly lot. Beneath the effort directed toward the accumulation of worldly goods lies all too frequently the illusion that this is the most substantial and desirable end to be achieved; but there is fortunately, a minority composed of those who recognize early in their lives that the most beautiful and satisfying experiences open to humankind are not derived from the outside, but are bound up with the development of the individual's own feeling, thinking and acting. The genuine artists,

21

investigators and thinkers have always been persons of this kind. However inconspicuously the life of these individuals runs its course, none the less the fruits of their endeavors are the most valuable contributions which one generation can make to its successors.

Within the past few days a distinguished mathematician, Professor Emmy Noether, formerly connected with the University of Goettingen and for the past two years at Bryn Mawr College, died in her fifty-third year. In the judgement of the most competent living mathematicians, Fraeulein Noether was the most significant creative mathematical genius thus far produced since the higher education of women began. In the realm of algebra in which the most gifted mathematicians have been busy for centuries, she discovered methods which have proved of enormous importance in the development of the present-day younger generation of mathematicians. Pure mathematics is, in its way, the poetry of logical ideas. One seeks the most general ideas of operation which will bring together in simple, logical and unified form the largest possible circle of formal relationships. In this effort toward logical beauty spiritual formulae are discovered necessary for the deeper penetration into the laws of nature.

Born in a Jewish family distinguished for the love of learning, Emmy Noether, who, in spite of the efforts of the great Goettingen mathematician, Hilbert, never reached the academic standing due her in her own country, none the less surrounded herself with a group of students and investigators at Goettingen, who have already become distinguished as teachers and investigators. Her unselfish, significant work over a period of many years was rewarded by the new rulers of Germany with a dismissal, which cost her the means of maintaining her simple life and the opportunity to carry on her mathematical studies. Farsighted friends of science in this country were fortunately able to make such arrangements at Bryn Mawr College and at Princeton that she found in America up to the day of her death not only colleagues who esteemed her friendship but grateful pupils whose enthusiasm made her last years the happiest and perhaps the most fruitful of her entire career.

ALBERT EINSTEIN
Princeton University, May 1, 1935

Seeking to Preserve German Cultural Freedom

To the Editor of *The New York Times:*

Frequent mention has recently appeared in the American press of the German Academy in New York, an offspring of the American League for German Cultural Freedom; it has also been stated that I have joined this fully organized body. May I state briefly the reasons for the sympathy with which I have welcomed this idea and which have moved me to collaborate in its realization?

We are living in an age which, among some potent disadvantages, possesses the virtue that it leads our experience back to the roots of things—to fundamental truths, fundamental facts, and again renders noteworthy the eternal realities of which we have more or less lost sight because of their very obviousness. One such simple truth—a truth to be experienced as new and deserving of new expression—is that the spirit must be free if it is to possess any interest or evoke any curiosity.

A regimented, commanded, terrorized spirit is not worth a shot of powder; it will not tempt a dog from the hearth. It is a nonentity about which no one will bother because it does not deserve any confidence; because it lacks every prerequisite of true creativeness, of human relationship to the universal spirit, and because it cannot clear itself of the suspicion that all of its utterances are the products of evasion, of compliance and of oppressed makeshift. That is completely unavoidable. It has nothing to do with political polemics; it is a simple fact which even those who have brought it about cannot gainsay. Freedom and spirit are one and the same thing. Free spirit is a pleonasm and unfree spirit is a contradiction in terms. A "Life of the Spirit" in the compulsory service of a political power concentration, under the dictatorial thumb and in dictatorial leading-strings, is devoid of all moral credit; it exists only in quotation marks.

I do not believe that the statement of this plain fact places me in contradiction with the better part of my colleagues who live in Germany. I have sufficiently retained contact with my country not merely to surmise but to know that the paralyzing effect of the totalitarian demands of the ruling party upon the cultural life is felt there as deeply as abroad. Often enough have I heard from German mouths the disconsolate assurance that it is unthinkable and impossible that any life-giving values can grow on that soil. The one astounding fact is that the great majority of German intellectuals did not realize this in advance, but instead contributed greatly to the creation of the forces which are about to deprive Germany in the world of all its creative strength.

But in the last analysis those who could regard otherwise than as intolerable the intrusion into the cultural life of the nation of standards of measure and of value so foreign to it and, out of their deepest instincts, did not reject the complete absorption of German cultural life into the authority of the State (apart from the spiritual and moral quality of any State demanding such subjugation) could not have been Germans. The protest which arises within me against such coordination, against such harnessing of culture to the political chariot, seems to me, at least, genuinely German and entirely normal. German culture has never been geographically confined to the Reich. To the extent to which German culture transcends beyond the borders of the Reich ethnologically and linguistically, its conception is higher than that of the State. That is Germanic freedom. No president of an official chamber of culture can subdue it.

To profess the conviction that it is desirable, nay, necessary that there remain alive a tradition of German culture outside of the sphere of dictatorship—a sphere controlled by men unfamiliar with the prerequisites of spiritual creativeness—is forbidden the German intellectual living in Germany on pain of life and limb.

Fundamentally, the task of affirming this does not belong to us emigrants. It is the task of the world to proclaim this—of that world which cannot forget the sympathy and gratitude with which it time and again welcomed the questing and creative German spirit in the days of its moral autonomy and self-responsibility. It must be the profound concern of that world to safeguard, support and sustain that spirit in so far as it is still effective in freedom abroad, but deprived of the support of the State and oppressed and condemned at home.

One observes, not without emotion, that the world has by no means failed to cherish that memory and that good will not only by words but by action. Of that fact the American Guild for German Cultural Freedom, its organization, the illustrious personalities composing it and the decisive understanding which its endeavors promptly met in American public opinion, furnish abundant evidence. Its program, to state it generally, aims to mitigate as much as possible the difficulties under which the culturally productive German emigrants (excepting a few favorably situated individuals of prominence) must do their work, that is to say, to help the young generation which has not yet made a name for itself in its difficult struggle, without permitting that help to scatter and exhaust itself in individual cases. It was soon perceived that this program could not be carried out without the active cooperation of the emigrated bearers of German culture themselves. They are the ones who must actually build up the movement by means of which the values that the German spirit has made precious to the world may be preserved, further developed and

24

transmitted to future generations. Out of this realization was born the idea of the German Academy.

It is conceived as a representative, practical and effective coalition of all the spiritual, artistic and scientific forces of the German nation which are compelled nowadays to serve Germany, and thereby humanity, abroad, because of the intolerance of a totalitarian State which denies freedom of conscience and of the spirit at home. The significance of such an organization is obvious. It achieves unity, concreteness and force for what would otherwise be diffuse, scattered among individuals without either a joint will or a joint vision. It offers the German artists and scientists who have been exiled and scattered among many nations that united support which spiritual workers in other countries possess at home. Comprised of all types of cultural productivity, of artists in marble and on canvas, men of letters, musicians, scholars in many fields, the academy will be able to create a perspective of the totality of German intellectual work outside of the Reich. It will be able to erect a bridge not only between the German culture of yesterday and the German culture of tomorrow but also between the spiritual life of Germany and that of other peoples.

The higher duty of the academy will also serve as a protectorate over the threatened German intellectual wealth. But its function will not exhaust itself merely in being representative. The academy will have a European senate, through which the connection between the academy and the American guild will be maintained. This senate will administer and dispose of the funds which the American guild will place at the disposal of the academy. It will make proposals to the officers of the guild concerning the award of stipends, subventions, advances to publishers and the award of prizes with which outstanding achievements of the German cultural emigration will be recognized and brought to the notice of the world.

The senate, moreover, will have to conclude agreements with European and American publishing houses, music institutes and art galleries concerning the publication, production or purchase of the works which will be produced under the protection and with the assistance of stipends awarded by the academy and which may earn prizes. The academy hopes also to create a permanent nuclear public for the works of exiled German intellectuals by uniting the friends of German culture in German and English cooperative book societies.

One should not forget that Germany is greater than the Reich, and that outside of the borders of the Reich there live 35,000,000 people whose intellectual and spiritual life takes place more or less decisively within the German language. It would be improvident to leave this whole

25

part of the German-thinking and German-understanding world exclusively to the destructive influences of Berlin's Propaganda Ministry. It is possible to create counter-influences. To maintain another tradition of German culture may perhaps be designated as the principal aim of the academy, profoundly important because in this way, through the medium of the German people living abroad, succor can be brought to the finer forces which have undoubtedly still survived in Germany and a salutary influence exerted upon the people of the Reich itself.

A European secretariat of the American guild and of the German Academy connected with it has been established in London and has assumed its duties. It reports that very soon a new meeting of the board of directors of the American guild will take place, at which the questions concerning the budget for the current year, the legal constitution of the European senate of the academy, membership, division of work and the immediate program will be decided upon. It is rumored also that in the course of the winter the members of the academy are to be called to Geneva for a general session, at which the general secretary of the American guild, Prince Hubertus zu Loewenstein, will report concerning what has been accomplished and what it is planned still to accomplish.

I have written in such detail about this matter because my heart says yes to it and my good wishes are with it—the wishes of a German to whom it would be a heavy blow if the word German should become, without any mitigating connotation, merely another name for threats of war, coercion of the spirit and of other peoples.

Whoever feels beholden to the German spirit for the free contributions which the general culture of the world has received from it will not withhold his moral and material support from the German Academy in New York.

THOMAS MANN
Zurich-Kuessnacht, Switzerland, December 1, 1936

Trotsky On Russia

To the Editor of *The New York Times:*

Your Moscow correspondent in a dispatch on the foreign policy of the Kremlin, in *The New York Times* of Nov. 12, affirms that this policy is dictated by Marxist doctrine. Mr. Gedye reiterates insistently: "They are Marxists first, last and always." Thus he agrees completely with his evaluation which the heads of the Kremlin are giving themselves and which is necessary for them in order to sustain the reputation of their international agency, the Comintern. It is impossible, of course, to enter here into a discussion upon the Kremlin's "Marxism." However, there are more concrete affirmations in Mr. Gedye's dispatch which I cannot pass over.

"The leaders," writes Mr. Gedye, "have not adopted the theory of Leon Trotsky of 'permanent revolt' and the view that socialism in one country is impossible. Far from that, they are as convinced as ever that Lenin was right."

These two sentences contain, mildly speaking, two misunderstandings. Lenin never propagated the theory of socialism in one country. On the contrary, he affirmed constantly that the ultimate fate of the social order of the U.S.S.R. depends completely upon the fate of international capitalism. Permit me to refer to my *History of the Russian Revolution* (Vol. III, pp. 378–418), where, I dare believe, it is proved irrefutably that Lenin stood on the conception directly opposed to that which is now ascribed to him by the Kremlin.

Even after the death of Lenin in the Spring of 1924, Stalin still continued to explain in his compilation, "Problems of Leninism," how and why Lenin considered it impossible to construct a Socialist society in a single country. Only in the next edition of the same book in the Fall of 1924 did Stalin, moved by practical and not theoretical considerations, radically change his position on this not unimportant issue. Following this turn, the Kremlin made an attempt to force Lenin to change his conception too. Mr. Gedye unfortunately supports this attempt.

Not less erroneous is the assertion concerning the theory of "permanent revolt" allegedly subscribed to by me. The theory of "permanent revolution" (not "revolt"), started from an analysis of the class relationships in Czarist Russia, reached the conclusion that the democratic revolution in Russia must lead inevitably to the conquest of power by the proletariat and thus open the era of Socialist revolution. I don't believe that the latest events have refuted this theory promulgated at the beginning of 1905. In any case, it has nothing in common with the theory of "permanent revolt," which seems to me simply nonsense. The totalitarian press of Moscow more than once of course has represented my views in a caricatural form. Mr. Gedye obviously has assimilated this caricatural presentation.

I must say in general that nowhere are the foreign correspondents so persistently and successfully worked upon as in Moscow. In the past years we have observed how some American journalists systematically induced American public opinion into error by their articles upon the "most democratic constitution in the world," upon the Kremlin's profound sympathy for the democracies, upon the Kremlin's not less profound hatred for Hitler, and so on.

As a result of such information the latest turns of the Kremlin took the public by surprise. In a country where the books devoted to the history of the party and the revolution, the historical plays, historical films, historical paintings are nothing but consciously fabricated falsifications, the foreign correspondent should provide himself with a good deal of critical distrust if he really wishes to inform public opinion in his own country and not simply maintain friendly relations with the Kremlin.

Permit me to utilize this occasion for another correction. Several times I have encountered the allegation that Lenin characterized Trotsky as the "most clever member of the Central Committee." I am afraid that this translation originated also from one of the too trustful Moscow correspondents. The word "clever" in this context has an ironical, a somewhat debasing connotation of which there is not a trace in the so-called Testament of Lenin. "Samly sposobniy," the exact Russian words used by Lenin, can be translated into English as "most able," but in no case as "most clever."

LEON TROTSKY
Coyoacan, Mexico, November 20, 1939

Compromise for Palestine

In view of the conference of Arab states in Cairo, the following proposal by the president of the Hebrew University in Jerusalem has special interest.

To the Editor of *The New York Times:*

The year 1945 will probably be a year of fateful decision for the world, and it behooves those of us who are concerned for the fate of the Holy Land to offer constructive suggestions, if we have any. It is clear that Palestine will not be constituted as either an Arab state or a Jewish state. It is clear also that the White Paper of 1939 offers no hope for future peace development.

It is therefore necessary to seek compromise, and the first task of all men of good-will is to teach and preach compromise and to elaborate such forms of compromise as they believe to be reasonable and practicable.

The very idea of compromise—the word itself—has been made abhorrent to too many of the inhabitants of Palestine. Their political education has not yet taught them that political compromise is the very breath of life of the Western democracies.

I have talked with many Jews and many Arabs during my 22 years in Palestine. Upon this basis I venture the assertion that a compromise can be found which will be acceptable to the ordinary Jew and the ordinary Arab. The compromise I speak about is one upon the basis of which no Arab leader could again get Arabs to revolt and "take to the hills," and no Jewish leader could get Jews to put pressure upon the rest of the world. The compromise I speak about is not easy to work out and does not offer a solution overnight. But it is a reasonable answer and is possible of being put into practice.

This compromise contains a number of elements, each of which requires careful study and detailed elaboration. On some points this has been done, on others not. What I shall attempt here is but a cursory glance.

There are three worlds interested in Palestine—Jewish, Christian and Moslem. For this reason any answer to the Palestine question must have interreligious and international character. Politically, the international background may be said to consist of three main factors—the United Nations, the union of Arab states now coming into being, and the Jewish people.

A Middle East Regional Council, the setting up of which by the United Nations, one is bound to assume, would have specific functions in relation to Palestine, and for this purpose its Palestine section would consist of representatives of these three international bodies. The Jewish representatives would be chosen by a reconstituted and strengthened Jewish Agency. The Regional Council would be responsible for security and armed forces, and it would act as the final authority in disputes on basic issues.

This Regional Council would have its seat preferably in Jerusalem. Jerusalem is the Holy City of these three great monotheistic faiths. A historic mission will be fulfilled if Jerusalem can be made increasingly the seat of interreligious, international organizations.

The administration of Palestine should be on a binational basis— namely, parity between Jews and Arabs in government, so that neither would rule the other. It is not easy anywhere in the world to work out administrative machinery for a multinational council. The most successful example is, of course, Switzerland, which has been at peace for generations. But though practical binational constitutions are difficult to achieve, they are not impossible. Some plans have been prepared in this direction, and it is essential that the aid of experts and men of experience be enlisted in this basic task.

One way of meeting some of the difficulties is to give the Middle East Regional Council the power of appointing a High Commissioner and a few additional key men who are neither Jews nor Arabs. How long such an arrangement would continue would depend on how a binational constitution for Palestine worked generally.

Partition of the country? But that is a compromise that settles nothing. All it will do is to create two irredentas, irreconcilable and activist, on either side of the borders. That is the way to never-ceasing warfare, the kind that made the Balkans a byword. Partition also mutilates and cripples the living Jewish conception of the land of Israel, the Holy Land. Partition, furthermore, reduces the area available for Jewish settlement in Palestine. Partition may appear to be a rough and ready way of cutting the Gordian knot, but this surgical operation would kill the patient. If there be no mangling by partition, there is a chance of bringing the diseased body to health, even though this task be difficult and long drawn out.

If partition were carried out because of a declaration by some statesmen concerning a Jewish state or commonwealth, that would be nothing short of misfortune.

A fruitful way of compromise is to seek a solution in the whole of Palestine which will commend itself as reasonable to the ordinary Jew and Arab and to Christians everywhere, even if some political leaders do not acquiesce. The one or the other among these leaders may have engaged themselves deeply in state solution on either side—have burned their bridges behind them. That may be regrettable but is not irreparable. Their peoples can be trusted to recognize a reasonable, feasible compromise when they see one.

But one should be quick to add that a break ought to be made now with the present system in Palestine, where there are hundreds of British officials of all kinds in posts which could be filled satisfactorily by Jews and Arabs. Aside from the higher British salaries, which are an unnecessary burden on the budget of this small country, what is of fundamental importance is that the presence of so many British officials deprives the population of its natural right to participate more fully in its own government. If mistakes are made they should be made by the population. That is the way in which political responsibility is taught and learned.

I speak not only of the large number of lesser government posts in districts and municipalities but more especially of higher offices. No Jew or Arab is a district commissioner, head of a department, president of a court or a member of the executive council of government.

It is time that a substantial beginning be made in this direction. There are certain departments where having an Arab or a Jewish head would present no insurmountable difficulty. In offices where complications at the moment are too great, Jews and Arabs can be appointed as deputies and thus prepare themselves for a more normal future.

A very great additional advantage in appointing Jews and Arabs to responsible positions without further delay would be the creation in this way of a corps of men of two communities who would learn to know and respect one another through being engaged upon essential tasks for the good of their common country, Palestine. This would be a potent means of bridging the chasm which constantly widens between Jews and Arabs and between them and the British.

If it be asked what non-Palestinians are to be appointed by the Regional Council, I would answer that they be preponderantly British, for the following reasons: first, it is impossible to disregard the fact that of all the United Nations the British have had and now have more important interests here than any others.

Secondly, the British have greater administrative experience, and though one cannot say that they have been over-successful in Palestine, still, under the proposed new dispensation it would be reasonable to suppose that they would propose to the Regional Council some of their best men.

Thirdly, since international administration has nowhere been effective, one nation has to be entrusted with the main burden of administration. Whereas the Regional Council should be responsible for the major policy, the chief responsibility for actual administration as sketched here must be committed to one of the United Nations.

It is hardly necessary to point out that the Regional Council is something far different from the Mandates Commission, which has but advisory powers, and that the position of Great Britain as the tutelary administrator is very different from that of Great Britain as the ruler of Palestine.

Jewish immigration, which is a large crux of the situation, should be permitted up to parity; that is, up to one-half of the population. Present official figures show that there are more than 500,000 Jews and more than a million Arabs in the country.

Nazi persecutions have massacred so many hundreds of thousands of Jewish men and women that it is thought there may be only about one and a half million left in all Europe outside Russia and the non-invaded countries. For tens of thousands emigration is a crying physical and spiritual need. The young almost without exception want to come to the new life of Palestine.

If, as Dr. Weizmann has advocated particularly, immediate stress be laid upon bringing into Palestine as many as possible of the 100,000 children who may be left, all too many without parents, then the whole Jewish and Christian world and—I make bold to say—much of the Islamic world would back such a project. It might be more practical if formulated thus: the tempo of immigration to Palestine is to be dependent upon the economic capacity of Palestine to absorb new immigrants. A generous and gallant attempt to rush immigrants into the country regardless of the economic situation would result in catastrophe.

One task of the Regional Council would be to determine and help develop the economic absorptive capacity of the country from time to time. Jews have already proved that this capacity is far greater than has been believed, and if given a fair chance they will increase this through patience, love and self-sacrifice. But this should not be their task alone. The Regional Council should work out and be responsible for the development of a plan for the whole country—Jews and Arabs alike.

Immigration up to parity would free the Jews from the minority status which is theirs in other parts of the world. It would not, however, produce a Jewish majority and therefore would not upset the political balance in Palestine.

One often hears the question asked: What about Jewish immigration after parity has been attained? In the first place, in order to maintain parity, Jews would have the right to additional immigration each year to make up for the difference between the lower Jewish birth rate and the higher Arab birth rate. But more important than this, our whole argument is based on the conviction that if there be a number of years of cooperation between Jews and Arabs and peaceful development of the habitants, the chances are that further understanding between Jews and Arabs as to number would be achieved.

I have been trying to outline some of the terms of a reasonable, feasible compromise which I am convinced the two peoples interested can safely accept, even though many of their leaders may not be able to do so.

Yet no compromise comes to pass by itself. This or any other compromise must be labored for. The time has come for this. Time is passing quickly and the opportunity must be seized. For this reason the establishment of an Arab union at this juncture is of the greatest importance.

Nations are now to have a responsible address to whom they themselves and others can be referred: and as to the Palestine problem the chances for compromise are thus made much brighter because discussion is lifted out of the narrow parochialism of Palestine politics and put on the higher and wider plane of international interests.

I have shared hope for many years that a political union of the autonomous lands of Palestine, Trans-Jordan and Lebanon might be effected. I have hoped for this because it would be a step forward in Arab unity generally and this is sooner or later a historical necessity, and an Arab union would be the cornerstone union in the Middle East generally. All of this seems to me to offer greater possibilities for Jewish-Arab understanding and an atmosphere of mutual confidence.

But whatever momentary form an Arab union is to take when the time is ripe, it is not yet too late for Jewish leaders and Arab leaders to come together to discuss possible compromise—this or any other. Arab union and Jewish Agency—let them find ways of meeting informally and then officially. If they meet, a compromise can be found.

In order to hammer out compromise, ground is to be prepared. Leaders must be given a chance to adjust their minds, the hearts of two peoples must be softened, statesmen in whose hands decisions rest must be persuaded, political theorists and economists must be called in. Time is running short and there is much work to do.

What a task before the British and others to make up for lost opportunities and to bring two peoples together? I do not share the theory that the British have deliberately held them apart. But the British have not really exerted themselves, certainly never systematically and as matter of major policy, to bring the two peoples together.

An Egyptian Arab recently put forward the following considerations, "Civilization," he said, "began in large measure in the eastern Mediterranean including Egypt, Babylon and Greece.

"The wheel of history has now come to a full turn, and the new civilization of which mankind is in such desperate need can find its beginnings here again. Two of us together, Arabs and Jews can do it. We need each other. We Arabs do not need your money so much as your great experience and your great schooling. Let us sit down together and view our problem from this larger point of view. Numbers and machinery are certainly of importance and we must extend ourselves to the full in order to work out satisfactory arrangements.

"We can do this only if we look upon such arrangements as ancillary to the main spiritual problem of finding our soul again. Together we can develop this important part of the world for the benefit of mankind. This has become again a center of communication—not caravans and camels any more, but airplanes and lorries carrying men and goods and ideas. Have we not leaders of large enough outlook and enough courage to face this task?"

His question is indeed the basic question.

JUDAH LEIB MAGNES
Jerusalem, Feb. 15, 1945

33

Yalta Vote Formula Upheld

To the Editor of *The New York Times:*

The Yalta formula for voting in the Security Council represents a statesmanlike solution of a knotty problem. There has been a tendency to oversimplify that problem and to believe that it could be dealt with by applying the maxim that no nation should be the judge of its own case. That maxim is applicable where a case is being judged by previously determined law. It is not applicable to the decision of what principle shall govern political action. That is a quasi-legislative decision, and legislative processes normally permit interested voters, through their representatives, to determine what the law shall be.

Chapter VIII of the Dumbarton Oaks proposals contemplates that the Security Council shall deal both with what it calls "justiciable" disputes and those which are non-justiciable. Justiciable disputes are disputes which can be determined in accordance wtih a pre-existing body of law. Under the provisions of Paragraph 6 of Section A of Chapter VIII, justiciable disputes will normally be referred to the Permanent Court of International Justice. Also, where disputes are partly justiciable and partly non-justiciable the Security Council can get advice from the Court with reference to the justiciable aspects of the dispute.

Clearly to the extent that a dispute is justiciable an interested party ought not to have veto power. That is where we can properly invoke the maxim that no person should sit as judge in his own case. The voting formula agreed to at Yalta embodies that principle. Under it, a party to a dispute cannot vote on determining whether or not the dispute is justiciable or upon its reference to the Court and, of course, the party to the dispute has no power to control or veto the decision of the Court itself.

In addition to dealing with disputes which are justiciable, the Security Council, as we have seen, will have to act in relation to disputes which at present are non-justiciable. That action would be political rather than judicial. Perhaps those acts will serve as precedents to build up a body of international "common law" so that we shall see a constant increase in "justiciable" disputes and a constant diminution of the disputes which can be settled only by political action. So long, however, as the action to be taken is, in essence, political and liable to be influenced by political expediency, then we cannot rigidly apply the doctrine that an interested party is disqualified from voting.

It may be noted that the formula agreed to at Yalta closely conforms to the recommendation of the Cleveland Church Conference of last January, where it was proposed that "non-voting" should apply only when a member's case "is being judged in accordance with predetermined international law."

Of course, the result of the Yalta formula is that a permanent member can prevent the Council deciding under Chapter VIII, Section B to invoke force against it. That will be of little practical disadvantage, because the organization will not dispose of force quotas adequate to coerce a great power. There will be affirmative advantage in permitting the Council to proceed under Section A without necessarily having to invoke force under Section B. If condemnation of a great power under Section A would obligate the Council to go on to attempt to coerce that power, then the practical result would be a great reluctance to condemn. For the time being we shall have to rely primarily upon moral restraints upon the great powers.

The important thing is to have an international agency which can study world disputes and courageously lead moral restraints upon the great powers, great or small, whose conduct conflicts with generally accepted standards of justice and decency.

The foregoing considerations, while they support the Yalta formula, do suggest the importance of some changes in the Dumbarton Oaks proposals. The Security Council should be bound to standards of justice rather than mere expediency. Only if this is made explicit and mandatory will we achieve the desired development of international law and an increase in the disputes which are "justiciable."

Also, the procedure for amending the Dumbarton Oaks proposals should be liberalized. The proposed voting formula is one of several provisions which ought to evolve into something better. Yet it can never be changed without the unanimous consent of the permanent members, and there can never be any change in the five states which initially become permanent members. When we are dealing with an instrument which all recognize will require frequent amendment, we ought not to give each of five nations a veto power in perpetuity.

JOHN FOSTER DULLES
New York, March 6, 1945

35

Problems of Africa

To the Editor of *The New York Times:*

Now that the silence of the press and of liberal thought on Africa and its problems has broken briefly, may I venture to stress the critical importance of these matters.

Since the First World War, Africa has been appealing to the world for hearing and redress, in clear logic and modern phrase. With disappointing unanimity, the world has refused to listen, the press has failed to notice and forward-thinking people have been content to remain ignorant.

In 1915 the Congress of British West Africa, attended by representatives of chiefs, professions and business from four colonies, made a plea for democratic institutions, which deserves to be called a great document.

During the San Francisco conference, the Non-European Unity Committee of The Union of South Africa addressed "A Declaration to the Nations of the World," to which neither our free press nor any member of the conference paid the slightest attention.

Dr. A. B. Xuma, a native practicing physician of Capetown, president of the African National Congress of South Africa, now in New York, writes:

"We Africans of South Africa protest and oppose the incorporation of Southwest Africa into the Union. The Africans of Southwest Africa have no share in the Government and therefore are no party in the incorporation negotiations. South Africa itself denies political and economic rights to her 8 million Africans. Eighty-three per cent of the land is reserved for 2 million Europeans only: less than 17 per cent for 8 million Africans. Only 40 per cent of African children are accommodated in mission schools; there are no Government schools for African children. . . . Ninety-five per cent of the African prison population is imprisoned for discriminatory regulations used against Africans only. . . . African trade unions are not recognized. Africans are excluded from skilled work. In short, Africans are underfed, underpaid, undereducated, underemployed, poorly housed and poorly and indirectly represented. . . ."

The Cameroon Native Council, over the signature of Etia Moume Leopold, appealed to the United Nations in October, 1946, to be placed under United Nations trusteeship.

In Sierra Leone, Nigeria, Rhodesia and South Africa strikes against alleged starvation wages, aggravated by sharply rising prices, have been made but neither the world press nor philanthropy has made an adequate effort to inquire into cause and results.

All these matters are not isolated phenomena. They are part of a definite policy, originating in South Africa and in its daughter state Kenya, to separate African colonialism from Asiatic and perpetuate in Africa that slavery, serfdom and exploitation of labor and materials which the wiser world is trying to abolish as the one and only path to democracy. In 1923 the plan was enunciated in a pamphlet published in Nairobi, "The Thermopylae of Africa."

This plan developed during the First World War by the capture of German East Africa; was pushed further in the Second World War in the attempt to put Kenya and its leaders over Ethiopia. It still persists in the refusal to give Ethiopia access to the sea, by depriving her of Eritrea, and seizing Ogaden, its granary; by garrisoning Ethiopia with British soldiers and airmen, and by the proposed transfer of British military bases to East Africa.

I am calling attention to all this, not simply as a plea for Africa, but as a warning to the United Nations. Is it possible to build one world, free and democratic, on the foundation of a continually enslaved Africa? Of an Africa, whose labor at 20 cents a day is in direct competition with the free labor of the world?

Finally, what shall 15 million Negroes in the United States, many more than the population of the Argentine, and of Belgium and Holland combined, do to secure recognition of their rights as human beings at the hands of the peoples of the world? They are in majority disfranchised. Their disfranchisement in the South makes democracy unworkable in the nation and a third party movement impossible. Their rights of travel, domicile, use of public facilities, and right to work are widely infringed. Five thousand of them in 50 years have been lynched by mobs without trial and no lyncher has been punished because as the Attorney General of the nation admits, the law gives him no adequate ground on which to prosecute.

Is this the way to build a new world? Is even the atomic bomb of greater importance than the freedom and manhood of 200 million black men?

W. E. DU BOIS
New York, Nov. 8, 1946

Irish Partition

To the Editor of *The New York Times:*

Surely a minimum requirement from a correspondent in Europe is that he give right names to places and communities. Your correspondent, Herbert L. Matthews, did not do so when he wrote the other day: "Strong reaffirmation of Ulster's loyalty to Britain and her determination to maintain the partition of Ireland was made by Sir Basil Brooke." Now the partition of Ireland is relatively a minor problem, but correct information about it should be in order. And as Eire is one of the sixteen nations who are about to form a European group, the relations between Britain and Eire, the degree of cooperation and good-will between them, become something appreciable in a European settlement.

Mr. Matthews' use of the name "Ulster" gives a wrong impression. Ulster is the northern Irish province; it consists of nine counties; of these six have been arbitrarily cut off to form a separate government, thus making for Irish partition. Of the six cut off, two counties have every right to do what they want to do—put themselves under an Irish government. They are prevented from doing this by the rigor of a police state.

To Irish people "Ulster" denotes the most famous part of Ireland— the scene of the national epic, of Saint Patrick's foundation, and the homeland of the northern princes who fought for the independence of Gaelic Ireland. To speak of "Ulster" as Sir Basil Brooke, the head of the government of the six counties, and as Mr. Matthews does, as completely alienated from Ireland is a way to make numbers of Irish people furious. "I care not if my life be for the span of a day and a night," says the Ulster hero, Cuchulainn, "if my deeds are spoken of by the men of Ireland." Even in pagan times the unity of Ireland was gloried in.

That ideological differences, Protestantism and Catholicism, give doggedness to northern isolationism is well known. These differences go back to the 17th century and are due to immigration, to settlement after conquest, and the deliberate making of a barrier between Gaelic Ireland and Gaelic Scotland.

That the community whose origins go back to this are fine men and women who have done well on the land and created large-scale industries is also well known. But, however respected, they are a minority—a minority that is outnumbered in the province of Ulster itself, and no minority has a right to destroy the unity of a country—a unity that is the case of Ireland is ancient and deeply felt. An ideological difference could have been used to destroy the unity of Belgium and Holland. But if this had been done by German domination, how horrible it would have seemed to people who are complacent about Irish partition.

38

Of course the ideological differences would have to be recognized and safeguards found for Ulster Protestantism. It is a good thing for a country to have ideological differences within its unity. If this were done, Northern Ireland would benefit. It has to be a police state to hold down a minority that is a high percentage of the population. And like every police state the six counties cannot be anything except static.

Then, too, the position of a poor relation always appealing for funds and protection is not a fitting one for the Northerners, who are by nature upstanding men and women. Eire with its exceptional solvency could raise large loans to help in the development of their land and industry. It should be noted, too, that the hydroelectric potential is in Eire, and the six counties would help to modernize many Northern industries.

To return to the ideological differences, I could see that in Eire no difference is made by the Government between Catholics and Protestants —there has been a Protestant President—but I recognize that Protestants in the north, with their homogeneity and their strong sectarian bias, are in a very different situation from Protestants in the rest of Ireland; a really statesmanlike effort would have to be made to discover ways and means of preserving their agrarian, religious, social and industrial security.

PADRAIC COLUM
New York, April 20, 1948

Antiquity of Hebrew Scrolls

To the Editor of *The New York Times:*

A news story published in *The New York Times* on March 4 refers to an article by Prof. Solomon Zeitlin of Dropsie College, Philadelphia, questioning the antiquity of the ancient Hebrew scrolls which were recently discovered by Bedouins in a cave in the Judaean desert. Since this is one of the most important finds in recent times, and of great interest to Bible students, I hope you will grant me a little space for comment.

Dr. Zeitlin questioned the date and authenticity of the scrolls and based his comments on the preliminary reports by Prof. Millar Burrows and Dr. John C. Trever, who were at the American School of Oriental Research in Jerusalem when the Syrian Metropolitan of St. Mark's Monastery in Jerusalem brought to them the scrolls which were in his possession. The cause of scholarship would have been served better had Dr. Zeitlin withheld his comments until a substantial portion of the manuscripts had been published, together with photographs and facsimiles.

Since I was the first to identify them and the only one who has had the entire group of scrolls in his hands, it may be appropriate for me to comment on Dr. Zeitlin's remarks.

When I was shown the first fragments of this find I was skeptical of their authenticity, as one should be with every object of antiquity which is not found in the course of an archaeological exploration or excavation. I came to the conclusion, however, that this was a discovery of the greatest importance, the authenticity of which could not be disputed. I based my opinion, first of all, on the form of the written characters, which I recognized to be of the period preceding the destruction of Jerusalem by the Romans (about the year 70 of the Christian era).

When I was able to examine parts of these scrolls my opinion was strengthened. This opinion was shared by several of my colleagues on the staff of the Hebrew University, specialists in the Hebrew language and the Bible. May I point out that several American scholars, thoroughly familiar with paleographic problems and with the literature of this period, among them Prof. W. F. Albright of Johns Hopkins University, Profs. H. L. Ginsberg and Saul Lieberman of the Jewish Theological Seminary, accept this point of view.

It is true that this is an unexpected find. We all had been of the opinion that the climate of Palestine renders impossible the preservation of organic matter such as papyrus or leather. Fortunately, these manuscripts were found in a relatively dry area of Palestine. They were wrapped in cloth and covered with a thin coat of a substance containing bitumen and wax and stored in earthenware jars.

May I be allowed here to add that there are passages in the writings of the Church Fathers, Hieronymus and Epiphanius and others, according to which a similar discovery consisting of Biblical Hebrew and Greek manuscripts was made in the year 217 C. E. in the vicinity of Jericho, just a few miles from the cave where these latest scrolls were found. The Greek version of the "Book of Psalms" from this discovery was used by Origenes for his edition of the Hexapla.

Professor Zeitlin points out that an examination of these jars is necessary to the determination of the antiquity of the find, and he expresses regret that "we do not have the jars in which the Bedouin stated the scrolls were found." Dr. Zeitlin is misinformed. He points to the failure of the Syrian Metropolitan to purchase the jars from the Bedouins as proof that their antiquity is suspect. The reason for this apparent failure is simple: I had bought them for the university four months before and they are in our possession.

E. L. Sukenik
Professor Palestinian Archaeology and Director of Museum of Jewish Antiquities, Hebrew University, Jerusalem
New York, March 8, 1949

The French in Cochin China

To the Editor of the *New York Times:*

May I be allowed to submit some observations concerning your editorial of May 23 "France Acts on Cochin China"?

You write that "a free ballot in Cochin China showed a disposition to join that (Vietnam) projected government." This statement is distant from the facts. The decision to join a future Vietnamese state was made by a newly elected Assembly of Cochin China. But that Assembly itself has been elected under such conditions that its representative value is open to question. The system was complex and it would not be possible to discuss it in brief detail. But here are the final figures: Out of a population of roughly 5 million Cochin Chinese and Europeans, 5,775 only, i.e., a fraction more than one-thousandth, were voters. Only 1,175 cast their votes and 4,600 did not vote.

Your paper alludes to a twofold opposition to the present French Government's policy, that of the Communists and the one you describe as "colonial die-hardism." I cannot but feel that this description is unfair so far as it applies to the Gaullist opposition. Our friends in the House did oppose the project, but not on the ground you suggest. The Gaullist spokesman, Rene Capitant, a representative of the left-center, made the following statement: "We sincerely and really want a united Vietnam; that is, incorporation of Cochin China to the Vietnam."

He pointed out, at the same time, that the Cochin Chinese Assembly could not represent the opinion or will of the population. He also observed that the Vietnamese state does not exist, and that it seems unwise to surrender a territory to a "future" state, which may mean to surrender it, in fact, to the Communist chieftain Ho Chi-Minh.

That is why M. Capitant's project, which was defeated by the House, did authorize the incorporation of Cochin China to the Vietnamese state, but under the condition that an agreement be concluded between the

French Republic and that state. This is no "die-hardism," but clear-headed statesmanship. I do not think that anybody in Cochin China, nor for that matter in the United States, would enjoy seeing that territory turned over to the Communists. Mao Tse-tung has Shanghai. Why should we give Saigon to Ho Chi-Minh?

JACQUES SOUSTELLE
Secretary General, Reunion of the French People
Paris, May 28, 1949

Loyalty in Washington

To the Editor of *The New York Times:*

The present charges against the Department of State have not in my view deserved much attention. But the very widespread notice they have received prompts me to make certain comments.

First, this is most emphatically not the proper way in which to insure loyalty of government employes. If that had been the real purpose of the accuser, he would have used the fully developed and tested procedure of the executive branch of the Government, under which charges are investigated and weighed by men of both parties and unimpeachable integrity. Any constructive result which may eventuate from the present charges would have been achieved far more surely and effectively by use of the existing procedures. The fact that the accuser has wholly ignored this well-established method indicates that his interest is of a different character.

Second, no matter what else may occur, the present charges have already spattered mud upon individuals of the highest integrity, and in the present state of the world the denial cannot always overtake the accusation. It should by now be wholly clear that indiscriminate accusations of the sort are doubly offensive; they damage the innocent, and they help protect the guilty. For if the accuser is so stupid as to connect a man like Ambassador Jessup with communism, are not all such accusations made suspect?

Third, and more important by far, the method of the present charges directly and dangerously impedes the conduct of the foreign affairs of our Government. It creates abroad a feeling that we are frightened and suspicious of each other; it diverts our attention, at home, from the genuine and pressing problems of our foreign affairs; it requires of many high officials that they desert their proper duties in order to prepare and deliver such extensive replies as that of Mr. Jessup. Not one of these effects would have resulted from a disinterested study of the loyalty of any suspected State Department employes; each of them is the direct result of the manner in which these charges have been made.

Fourth, it seems to me quite clear that the real motive of the accuser in this case is to cast discredit upon the Secretary of State of the United States. This man is not trying to get rid of known Communists in the State Department; he is hoping against hope that he will find some. Fortunately, the Secretary of State needs no defense from me. No one who knows his extraordinary record of able and disinterested public service can believe that he is in any danger from these little men. It is already obvious that in any test of personal confidence the men of honor, in both parties, will choose to stand with the Secretary.

But there is more at stake in the matter than the rise or fall of individuals. What is at stake is the effective conduct of our foreign policy.

Every Secretary of State, second only to his President, and alone among appointive officers of the Government, stands before the world as the representative of the United States of America. No man who holds this office can fail to feel the extraordinary responsibility he carries for service to the country and its peace. No man has a greater right to ask the sympathetic support and the cooperation of his fellow citizens, and none is more properly exempt from the ordinary trials of politics. The man who seeks to gain political advantage from personal attack on a Secretary of State is a man who seeks political advantage from damage to his country.

The American Government, led by the President and the Secretary of State, is currently engaged in a major effort to give leadership to the country in a time of changing international conditions and grave world tension. This effort will require as part of our democratic process widespread and earnest public consideration of the great problems now before us, so that the ultimate decision will surely reflect the basic steadiness and faith of our people. In such public consideration there is always room for honest differences, but now, as for many years past, the formulation of foreign policy most urgently demands an adjournment of mere partisanship.

This is no time to let the noisy antics of a few upset the steady purpose of our country or distract our leaders from their proper tasks. This is rather a time for stern rebuke of such antics and outspoken support of the distinguished public servants against whom they are directed.

HENRY L. STIMSON
Huntington, L.I., March 24, 1950

43

Meaning of Apartheid

To the Editor of *The New York Times*:

It will be known to many of your readers that Kent School, Connecticut, offered to Stephen Ramasodi, a pupil at St. Peter's School, Rosettenville, Johannesburg, the opportunity to complete his education at Kent School.

This was, as you know, the chance of a lifetime. Stephen, who is 16 years old, would have been, to my knowledge, the first African boy from our country to enjoy such an opportunity. His father, who is a faithful member of the same Church that maintains both St. Peter's and Kent School, and is also headmaster of a large African school in Pretoria, was willing that his son should have this opportunity. Mr. Ramasodi considered both the pros and the cons and decided that whatever the consequences might be, his son should accept this lifetime chance.

It was the South African Government which determined otherwise. First the South African police refused to issue the certificate of character without which your country would not allow Stephen to enter. The Department of the Interior would not grant a passport without this certificate. This department also consulted the Department of Native Affairs, which is responsible for the African people of the Union.

Finally, the headmaster of St. Peter's School informed the authorities that he would have to give the facts to the press and the public. This stung the Minister of Native Affairs into immediate action. He replied that he would not be intimidated by persons whom he took to be agitators, and meantime the Department of the Interior stated that the passport had been refused on the grounds that it was not in Stephen's true interests to allow him to go to America.

Many Americans have no doubt tried to understand the true meaning of the Bantu Education Act, which act places all African education under the Minister of Native Affairs. One at least of the real meanings of this act is to be seen in this action of the Minister. One true meaning of apartheid is clearly indicated here.

Americans are often told that apartheid means the creation of separate racial societies, all pursuing their own ways of life, all enjoying the impartial benevolence of the state, all proceeding, unimpeded, to their several destinies. This rosy view omits the darker implications of apartheid. The myth of racially separate societies existing harmoniously side by side is exposed. This harmony can only be achieved when all of these societies are subservient to one dominant society—that of Afrikaner nationalism. It is not justice that is being pursued by our Government but domination.

44

At what stage in the development of African society will an African father be allowed to accept for his son an American scholarship of this kind? The answer is never. I hope that no American is deceived into thinking that this step was taken merely because Stephen was a child. It was taken because Stephen's father was considered to be a child also. That is one of the meanings of the Bantu Education Act. Like many other acts of this Government, it gives much that is better and withholds all that is best.

I do not pretend that all African people are equipped by tradition and education to participate fully in the life of a Western and industrial society, but they want to be, they try to be, and they attain success in many of their endeavors. They want nothing more than to participate in the life of the Family of Nations. They want nothing more than to understand the world in which they live, and to see it if they can. It is this deep and passionate desire that our Government thwarts continually, ultimately in vain, it is true, but immediately with intolerable consequences to human individuals.

The State Information Office of the Union will no doubt try to defend this unjust act. I do not know how many Americans and Europeans will be convinced by their arguments, but I assure you, sir, that they will not convince one single African on the continent.

ALAN PATON
Kloof, Natal, South Africa, August 4, 1955

Population Planning

To the Editor of *The New York Times:*

Birth control, family planning and population limitation are most important in any effort to bring real peace in the world. Less population will bring less war. Fewer people means more peace. Population planning through Government health and welfare departments will both improve the health, welfare and happiness of children, mothers and families and provide the essential foundations for world peace.

Leaders of Asian nations which I visited this year have learned this lesson. They are acting on this belief. Government officials, as well as voluntary agencies, scientists, teachers and preachers are responding to the message about birth control which I took to them 25 years ago. Prime Minister Nehru of India and Premier Kishi of Japan are in the forefront of this leadership toward peace through birth control.

India alone has budgeted and appropriated for this program the amount in rupees equal to 10 million United States dollars in the present five-year plan. No fewer than six times, the Indian Government officials have indicated and suggested to our country that aid from us in this program would be most welcome.

Our United States was struggling along behind, finally coming to realize that population planning must be part of our Government policy. The Draper Report recommended to President Eisenhower that the United States, as a matter of Government foreign policy, should help other nations which request such aid.

Then a few dozen Roman Catholic Cardinals, Archbishops and Bishops gathered and proclaimed an edict to the effect that the United States Government cannot give such recommended aid.

President Eisenhower embarked on his world-wide junket, announced to promote peace. Before he departed he crippled his entire project by stating that birth control is "simply none of the Government's business." He says it is a religious matter. How the President came to hold such an opinion is open to analysis and study.

The President's short comments about birth control do not state the problem fairly and are far short of being well-informed about the path toward world peace today. The fact is that Government health departments are active in such population programs which the President denies to them. They are giving funds, spreading advice and conducting research to wipe out epidemic and other killing diseases.

In so acting, without attending to the population-balancing factor of birth control, our Government is increasing the population pressures against peace and bringing ever closer the population "explosion" and World War III.

Clear-headed thinkers of impartial scientific outlook have realized that such Government policies of increasing population by reducing the death rate must be balanced sensibly by practices reducing the birth rate.

A majority of the people in the United States hope that our country and our Government will give emergency aid to the countries in need who ask our assistance, including birth control information, family planning advice and population research assistance. Only a minority oppose this plan for world peace. The short-sightedness of the Roman Catholic hierarchy in this country shows in their bold assault upon the Draper committee's report about a medical and welfare project for the well-being of the entire world.

Most Roman Catholic church members do not fight the program of birth control. The records show that those members use this path to planned, wanted, happy children and better families, as well as world peace, just as much as do Protestants, Jews and persons of no religion. They of course use in some cases the official Roman Catholic, Pope-approved method of (unreliable) "safe-period" or so-called "rhythm." But in addition, they quite frequently use the same, better methods that other family planners use, labeled by the Pope, "artificial means" of birth control.

This dogmatic attitude about their special religious belief as controlling their personal and official conduct through life is all right for Roman Catholics in the United States, but their edicts and bulls should not be allowed to stifle the basic American freedom of people who are not adherents to the Roman faith.

Today our United States Government needs to listen to the voice of a majority of its voters. We believe the majority want proper medical care and aid to be given the sick, undernourished, troubled people—children, mothers and families everywhere in the world. Birth control and contraceptive practices are a medically recognized part of current ethical healing.

The majority of this nation sincerely hope the President will revise his statement upon the basis of more information than he had at hand when he announced this unfortunate position for our Government.

MARGARET SANGER
Tucson, Ariz., Dec. 28, 1959

The writer, founder and first president of the American Birth Control League, was President Emeritus of the International Planned Parenthood Federation.

Electing a Catholic

To the Editor of *The New York Times:*

The American voter has been asked to believe in effect that the Catholic keeps his political life and his moral and religious life rigidly separated, confining each, as it were, on an island, with an unnavigable body of water in between. This Catholic wasn't taught to make, let alone live by, so facile a dichotomy.

The American voter must distinguish between the practical and the theoretical objections against electing a Catholic to the Presidency. Nothing could be clearer than that the practical case is, given our present horizons, virtually nonexistent. It is just plain foolishness to suggest either that President Kennedy would move to curtail religious freedom, or that the Vatican would want him to do so.

If anything—we are dealing now in probabilities—he is likely to go the other way, even to the point of injustice. Senator Kennedy's stand on parochial schools—in which he goes further than many Protestants— I for one consider to be archly separatist and anti-Catholic in effect.

But the theoretical question is not answered so readily. Every Catholic is himself bound to regard with reverence papal generalizations, even those that deal directly with political and economic affairs, and is bound, where the Pope speaks formally in his role as pastor, to submit to his teaching authority in matters of faith and morals.

The President of the United States was never a mere administrator of the national or Congressional will: but in the past thirty years he has become the principal and continuing initiator of policy. A faithful Catholic President would not be morally free to initiate policies clearly condemned by the Church. And under certain circumstances he would not be free to execute national policies even if the responsibility for their initiation lay elsewhere.

Is this an alarming state of affairs? I for one say it is far from being that; it is most reassuring to men of all faiths that a President should have moral moorings that can ride out the passionate and anarchistic tidal waves that sometimes wreck whole nations.

I should remind those who are fond of constructing the abstract conflict and then holding it up for the public to gaze at in horror that all civilized men acknowledge laws that are prior to political laws.

That much at least was posited at Nuremberg, whatever the merits of the legal arguments, and a fresh affirmation is being made for us by the Government of Israel, as it prepares the case against Adolf Eichmann.

Mr. Eichmann did not have the right to follow Hitler's orders when those orders were to go out and commit genocide; and it made no difference whatever that in Hitler the supreme political authority was vested. Beware the man who says he is not governed by a higher law than that formulated by his constituents.

What needs, then, to be understood, I think, is that by renouncing the political mandate in the event of conflict, a Catholic President would almost certainly be taking the more enlightened course; the same course which, most probably, properly instructed Protestants and Jews would also take under similar circumstances.

For Catholics it is a certitude, for others it should be the operative presumption, that the Catholic Church will over the years maintain a more reliable moral equilibrium than can be presumed by any single nation (let the vainglorious among us remember what happened in our time to Russia, to Germany, to Japan, to Italy): and that therefore, on that unknown, unforeseeable day when nation X might well find itself fighting a hot moral war with the Vatican, the chances are that the Vatican will be right.

WM. F. BUCKLEY, Jr.
New York, Oct. 7, 1960

Urban Violence Discussed

To the Editor:

The advice recently given members of a Catholic Diocese in Brooklyn to stay at home after dark and the castigation of members of the Jewish community who are voluntarily patrolling a lonely area of the city at night are evidence of the confusion which increasingly complicates the discussion of urban violence. It is time that we disentangle the issues: the danger of crime, the danger of riots, and the role of the police—so that we can deal realistically with each kind of problem as it actually exists.

The first problem is that of crimes committed by individuals or small groups against solitary and usually anonymous victims. The commission of such crimes is encouraged by empty streets, poorly patrolled parks and subways and unguarded entrances, passages and elevators.

The answer to this problem is not fewer but more people out in public places at all hours. To persuade responsible, God-fearing people to remain indoors in the evenings is to turn streets and public places into a frightening no-man's land for disturbed and alienated teenagers, dope addicts and pathological criminals. For the prevention of crime we need well-lit streets where responsible citizens are willing to walk at any hour, going about their own business but conscious of the needs of others. In lonely neighborhoods we also need supplementary patrolling—by radio cabs, for example, which can provide the police with inexpensive checkpoints.

The second problem is that of flaring tempers and the danger of panic and violence when members of different social groups converge in very limited space and overcrowding prevents unimpeded movement. The answer here is better and more carefully implemented planning to direct the flow of crowds by diverting part of the crowd (as we do during parades), staggering hours, preventing traffic blocks and giving continuous attention to points where rioting may occur.

49

We also need carefully demonstrated methods of dealing with incipient riots—not only for the police but also for teachers taking children on outings, guards in public places, guides, bus drivers and subway guards. Ways of spotting trouble and summoning help could be demonstrated over television so they would become part of our common awareness.

The third problem of public safety stems from our tendency to treat the police as if they were just members of the "other team" in a game of cops and robbers. This is a game we all played as children and one which is played out daily in various forms on television, but it is poor preparation for city living.

As long as we continue to see the police as the natural enemies of law-abiding citizens and lawbreakers alike, we shall continue to struggle helplessly with the multiple effects of low trust, diffuse hostility and defeatist attitudes.

The basic difficulty is that we do not face the necessity of organizing over-all protection for a whole city population in different but definable situations. The role of the police is a crucial one; and without trust in the police there can be no order.

With too small a police force, the police will inevitably be subjected to undeserved blame. But with an adequate force, trained to protect the potential murderer as well as the potential victim, we have some hope of controlling a dangerous and frightening situation which is damaging to the city and the country and the hopes of people everywhere in the promise of a democratically organized world.

A responsible police force—the enemies of crime and danger and the protectors of all people—depends on trust and is an essential safeguard of trust in a complex society.

MARGARET MEAD
New York, June 18, 1964

Owen Lattimore Warns of Disaster in Asia

To the Editor:

The tragedy deepens. President Johnson's generosity and humanity carry conviction. But he has accepted the distorted policy of previous administrations. Not a word to show that the people of North and South Vietnam are one people, fighting a civil war, though other nations are involved on both sides.

50

Instead we are told once more that Hanoi manipulates the Vietcong and Peking manipulates Hanoi. China is presented as the Great Menace looming behind Vietnam, as Japan once depicted Russia as the Great Menace looming behind China. Most fatal of all, America is exhorted to accept the mission, once claimed by Japan, to impose order in China.

Our march toward doom recalls that of Japan in the 1930's. Then Japan's slogan was the Co-Prosperity Sphere—and co-prosperity was to be whatever Japan said it was. Today we proclaim a Free World—and free is to be whatever we say is free.

Then Japan had set up in Manchuria a regime without popular support (though it fielded an army, under Japanese advisers), which Japan said represented the "kingly way." Today we act from behind a Government in South Vietnam which is without popular support, though it can line up some collaborators and can keep an army in the field, under American advisers. We say it represents the Free World.

Then Japan would not permit reunion between Manchuria and the rest of China because Nanking was "not sincere"—which meant that it would not knuckle under. Today we will not permit union between North and South Vietnam because Hanoi has not acknowledged that it has "got the message"—the message to knuckle under.

Then Japan was consolidating Chinese nationalism under a pressure that made sure that, in the end, nationalism under Communist leadership would triumph over nationalism without Communism. We are doing the same thing.

Then it was essential to the Japanese calculation that China and Russia would not be able to compose their differences. Today we have made that our own calculation.

Then the Japanese Government, armed forces and university experts had more hard-fact information about China than any other country. They kept assuring the world that they knew what they were doing, that they were saving not only China but the rest of Asia from Communism (the domino theory of those days), and that other countries ought to accept Japan's judgment. But though the Japanese based their analysis on more known, tested, catalogued facts than anyone else could cite, they misunderstood what was going on and misjudged the essentials that make history.

It is the same with us today. We know the facts, we pile up the facts, we cite the facts, we turn on Kremlinologists and Pekinologists to expound the facts—and yet we don't realize what's going on, we don't know what the score is, we are misjudging what goes into the making of history.

In the end, goaded by the failure of their creeping barrage of bombing and terror to numb the "lesser breeds without the law," the Japanese advanced to the final escalation: they bombed another country. Is that to be the end, or the beginning of the end, for America too?

Is the next Pearl Harbor to be an American bombing of China? Is that the meaning of the smooth, cold, authoritative, hypnotically evasive voices of McGeorge Bundy, Dean Rusk, Robert McNamara, and the imperfectly civilianized Gen. Maxwell Taylor?

One difference between Japan then and America now is that we are more free to protest. We must use that freedom. Between here and the Pacific Coast I have heard and read enough to know that many have been ahead of me in raising their voices and many of them are more influential than I.

But unless we all unite in a great outcry of horror, repudiating this obsessed policy of doom, we shall not waken from the nightmare in time.

OWEN LATTIMORE
New York, April 8, 1965

The writer, a former adviser to Chiang Kai-shek, is Professor of Chinese Studies at The University, Leeds, England.

French in Indochina

To the Editor:

C. L. Sulzberger's editorial page column of Feb. 25 somewhat lacks the serenity and even urbanity which I have come to associate with him. But the point which concerns us here is whether such a war as that in Vietnam can be lost by debate and whether—as Gen. Maxwell Taylor said, and Mr. Sulzberger says is true—the French lost the Indochina war in Paris, not in the field.

The hard and brutal fact is the French lost the Indochina war in the field. One year before the battle of Dienbienphu the ratio between French and Communist forces had finally dropped to 1.2–1 in a situation where (as is visible today) a 5–1 ratio even with all the firepower in the world gives rise to little optimism, and 10 or even 20–1 is considered a useful superiority level.

By that time also (spring 1953) the Vietminh had conquered all of Tonking (North Vietnam) shy of the Red River Delta, a fortified "enclave" in which the French controlled 1,800 villages out of 5,000. All of northern Laos had fallen to Giap in one swift offensive.

52

In South Vietnam an unbroken expanse of Vietminh territory existed from a few miles south of Danang to almost the gates of Saigon save for yet another French "enclave" in the mountain plateau area. Beyond the Mekong Delta, Camau Peninsula and the whole Cardamom Mountain chain of Cambodia were in Vietminh hands.

The French Army had failed in every one of its offensives in which it attempted to "find, fix and destroy" the enemy—although it, too, could point to reassuring casualty statistics. A 25,000-man stab into the northern hinterland netted a few hundred dead in late 1952; an airborne attack on the Chinese border in 1953 found a few tons of weapons but no troops; a 20,000-man operation near Hue brought in 76 weapons.

By 1954 the French Army had lost 1,500 officers (including over 1,100 platoon commanders) and was exhausted—even without the Dienbienphu disaster. No French politician did that: the war did it, because it's that kind of war.

In fact, year after year, the Communists and a few of their associates excepted, the French Parliament voted the credits for the war and voted for the reinforcements which could be squeezed out of a weakened postwar France.

I have read every parliamentary debate on Indochina since 1945, and they make instructive reading as bewildered but honest men were faced, on one hand, with glowing reports that the war was being won and, on the other, with new requests for more funds and troops. Even when the United States made available to the French in 1953–54 almost unlimited funds and, in many fields, more equipment than they could usefully handle, the war was not being won on the battlefield.

The only political limitation on the French Army was, that it could not, after 1950, use draftees in Vietnam until the much-maligned Mendes-France, after Dienbienphu threatened to use two divisions with draftees from France. And considering that the French, like King Canute, were fighting the combined waves of Vietnamese nationalism and Communism, a Parisian show of unity or even the sending of draftees would have made little difference.

It is rather curious, finally to see observers who, for two decades, have berated the French Army for all sorts of true or imagined failings, now resort to the German "stab-in-the-back" myth to club their own opposition here. Surely there must be better arguments than that to justify the war in Vietnam.

BERNARD B. FALL
Washington, Feb. 23, 1966

Separatism in "Black Power"
Seen by Roy Wilkins

To the Editor:

A few months ago the slogan "Black Power" was introduced into the civil rights struggle. Since then it has created alarm and confusion among Americans, of all races and has made it plain that civil rights groups differ not only in strategy and tactics but also in objectives.

It is therefore appropriate at this juncture in history to state—or, more accurately, to restate—the fundamental principles which have guided the N.A.A.C.P. since 1909. Our objective now as then is the full participation of Negro Americans, without discrimination, in all phases of American life.

During these six decades we have employed many methods to achieve that objective. If these methods have any single common denominator, it is that they have always been nonviolent. Today nonviolence is stridently challenged on the premise that Negroes must defend themselves when attacked. But the right of Negroes and of all others to self-defense is not truly an issue. The N.A.A.C.P. has always defended this right.

What we oppose is the doctrine that Negroes should stand in armed readiness to retaliate and deal out punishment on their own. The record of unpunished murders of Negroes and civil rights workers makes this position emotionally understandable, but its fruit would be disastrous. As private vigilante vengeance, it would inevitably breed white counter-vigilantism and would furnish a pretext to any law officer wishing to "crack down" on Negro protest.

A more serious issue is posed by the slogan "Black Power." No matter how often it is defined, this slogan means anti-white power. In a racially pluralistic society, "Black Power" has to mean that every other ethnic group is the antagonist. It has to mean "going it alone." It has to mean separatism.

We of the N.A.A.C.P. will have none of this. We have fought unceasingly for genuine pride of race and for the inherent nobility of equal citizenship. We deny that racial dignity requires the ranging of race against race.

We are Americans as well as Negroes. While we will fight to defend this country, we are also determined to improve it. I urge every American to help us in the historic struggle by supporting the N.A.A.C.P. Such

54

support is a vote against all forms of racism; it is affirmation of the principles for which N.A.A.C.P. stands.

Roy Wilkins
Executive Director
National Association for the Advancement of Colored Peoples
New York, Oct. 7, 1966

Poland's Anti-Jewish Campaign

To the Editor:

Some days ago the world observed the 25th anniversary of the Warsaw ghetto uprising, when 40,000 Jews took up arms in a doomed effort to combat the Nazi forces. This was surely one of the glorious chapters in the annals of martyrdom and heroic resistance to tyranny. What irony and tragedy that at this moment virulent anti-Semitism is being revived on Polish soil soaked with the blood of millions of Jews. The wave of anti-Jewish hysteria in Poland is being whipped up by potent reactionary forces in the regime and exploited as a weapon in a power struggle, a scapegoat for popular discontent, a smoke-screen for economic and political ills, an instrument to stifle progressive reforms demanded by the intelligentsia and students. The close link between anti-intellectualism, anti-liberalism and anti-Semitism is once again tragically demonstrated.

On March 8 thousands of Warsaw University students demonstrated for freedom of expression, fair trials and an end to censorship. These demonstrations spread swiftly to other universities throughout the country, and were met by police violence and arrests.

It is universal knowledge that the outbreak of students' demonstrations was due to the suppression by the authorities of public performances of "Dziady," the masterpiece of Mikiewicz, Poland's greatest poet. Will the music of Chopin be next to be prohibited from being heard in public? The political ideology of Chopin and his friend Mickiewicz was identical.

Since then Poland has been undergoing a massive systematic course of purge and propaganda whose central feature has been its undisguised anti-Semitism. The Jewish community of 18,000, many elderly or ill, is accused of disloyalty and browbeaten into self-abasement. Dozens of distinguished Jewish academics, artists, writers and intellectuals of international repute are called alien to Poland, charged with being spiritual instigators of the student movement, expelled from the Communist party and dismissed from their positions.

55

Scores of students are arrested. All, intellectuals and students alike, are named and are pointed out as Jews. Many hundreds of others less prominent are also being purged more quietly but not less efficiently.

Most shocking is that all this is being done to the accompaniment of a vast propaganda campaign which has charged the country's atmosphere fearfully. Jews are accused of being "cosmopolitans, national nihilists, members of an international Zionist conspiracy, Zionist lackeys of 'Western imperialism'." Jewish philanthropic organizations which have poured millions of dollars into the economic and social rehabilitation of war-torn Poland are accused of conspiracy, sabotage and espionage at the behest of international Zionism and Western imperialism.

The moral nadir of this campaign is the falsification and distortion of the facts of Jewish martyrdom at the hands of the Nazis, the obscene denigration of the Jewish victims of mass murder.

This is the brutal lexicon used by Stalin and his anti-Semitic purges of 1948–52 and in the infamous doctors' plot he concocted in January 1953. It is, tragically, the very language that has been revived in the Soviet Union since the Arab-Israel War last June, in an ominous propaganda campaign against the Jewish people. This is the policy and the propaganda now taken over and carried further by the Polish authorities.

I appeal to the leaders of Poland to cease this outrage. I appeal to world public opinion to rally to the defense of the Polish intelligentsia and Polish Jewry.

ARTUR RUBINSTEIN
Paris, April 16, 1968

The writer is the well-known concert pianist.

Nixon's Vietnam Policy Backed

To the Editor:

In your lead editorial of Nov. 17 "Demonstrating Against the War" you conclude: "The responsible course for war foes is to focus their energies on more manageable forms of protest—for example, political action directed at members of Congress . . ."

Surely the most responsible course for "war foes"—and surely that term includes all of us—is to focus on finding out what the issue is, if, indeed, there is one. No one, including your esteemed selves, has yet proposed a quicker and more practicable manner of ending our participation in the war than that being followed by the President—the steady withdrawal of American forces and the steady strengthening of Vietnamese forces.

General MacArthur was ordered on Dec. 14, 1945, to return as expeditiously as possible all our 3 million Japanese prisoners of war in China. With an average haul of 800 miles and all Japanese ships at his disposal, this task took him 14 months.

The logistics of moving a half million men and a mountain of war material 8,000 miles, to say nothing of the impediment (should we press the panic button) of the one million refugees who fled the Communists from the North, would be formidable.

If there is a better plan than the President's let's hear it.

DEAN ACHESON
Washington, Nov. 17, 1969

Slaughter in Songmy

To the Editor:

Many Americans are justifiably horrified by reports of mass executions of civilians in Vietnam. The most recent incident at Songmy, or "Pinkville," in Quangngai Province now centers around two servicemen, Lieut. William Calley and Staff Sgt. David Mitchell, who stand accused of murder. Experience in Vietnam and Quangngai Province as journalists has led us to write this letter in hopes of dispelling two possible misapprehensions; that such executions are the fault of men like Calley and Mitchell alone, and that the tragedy of Songmy is an isolated atrocity.

We both spent several weeks in Quangngai some six months before the incident. We flew daily with the F.A.C.'s (Forward Air Control). What we saw was a province utterly destroyed. In August 1967, during Operation Benton, the "pacification" camps became so full that Army units in the field were ordered not to "generate" any more refugees. The Army complied. But search-and-destroy operations continued.

Only now peasants were not warned before an air strike was called in on their village. They were killed in their villages because there was no room for them in the swamped pacification camps. The usual warnings by helicopter loudspeaker or air-dropped leaflets were stopped. Every civilian on the ground was assumed to be enemy by the pilots by nature of living in Quangngai, which was largely a free-fire zone.

57

Pilots, servicemen not unlike Calley and Mitchell, continued to carry out their orders. Village after village was destroyed from the air as a matter of *de facto* policy. Airstrikes on civilians became a matter of routine. It was under these circumstances of official acquiescence to the destruction of the countryside and its people that the massacre of Songmy occurred.

Such atrocities were and are the logical consequences of a war directed against an enemy indistinguishable from the people.

ORVILLE SCHELL
JONATHAN SCHELL
Berkeley, Calif., Nov. 19, 1969

Anthony Eden Urges Conference on Southeast Asia

To the Editor:

I write to express agreement with the suggestion in your March 26 editorial that the time has come for "a broader, high-level Geneva-style meeting to seek a comprehensive settlement as at the 1954 conference."

Laos and Cambodia are sincere in their search for neutrality. And it is to the long-term advantage of the great powers concerned in the future of Indochina, the United States, China and the Soviet Union, that this neutrality should be respected and upheld.

They should therefore meet now with the other members of the 1954 conference to reestablish the neutrality of the two countries before these are finally eroded by the fighting in Vietnam. This last should, of course, also form part of the conference agenda and a supreme effort be made to secure a comprehensive and guaranteed solution of·the Indochina war.

Admittedly the difficulties are formidable, but the alternative of a widening conflict is a warning signal which every influential capital should heed before it is too late.

AVON
Boston, March 26, 1970

Lord Avon (Anthony Eden), former Prime Minister of Great Britain was co-chairman of the 1954 Geneva Conference on Far Eastern Affairs.

Invitation To Workers

To the Editor:

I want to talk to the New York construction workers. They will know what I'm saying. I grew up on the streets of Brooklyn, in a tough Irish-Italian-Polish neighborhood. I talk Brooklynese.

I march with the students, and I think that the construction workers should be marching with the students. What happens to me doesn't matter. One Nobel laureate has already been killed. That was Martin Luther King. What happens to the kids—their kids, my kids—matters very much.

So I want to talk to them. Any time, any place. How about it?

GEORGE WALD
Nobel Laureate in Physiology and Medicine
Cambridge, Mass., May 10, 1970

Mr. Agnew's Stand

To the Editor:

The basic issue raised by my criticism of recent statements by Joseph Rhodes Jr. seems to elude you. At issue is the ability of Mr. Rhodes to perform the job assigned—that is impartially to collect and evaluate the facts about campus unrest.

Mr. Rhodes has already reached some stunning conclusions without a factual investigation. Among other things, he proclaimed that "Governor Reagan was bent on killing people for his own political gain." You apparently did not consider that statement indicative of disqualifying bias.

Ask yourselves, gentlemen, and answer honestly—what would your editorial reaction have been if a conservative person on a panel investigating police deaths from left-wing militant action stated, "Ralph Abernathy was bent on killing people for his own political gain"?

Of course, we know Mr. Abernathy would not do that; but we also know that Governor Reagan would not do that. The question is would you or would you not then have felt that such an extreme and unwarranted conclusion by a member of a quasi-judicial body was reason to demand his resignation?

SPIRO T. AGNEW
Washington, June 18, 1970

Re-escalating the Vietnam War

To the Editor:

So low is the credibility of an American President today that Richard Nixon can mislead and lull the American public in the very process of telling them exactly what he means to do, and doing it.

Confident that he will not be believed by Americans, Mr. Nixon has promised that he will keep as many United States troops in Vietnam as are needed by our Saigon "allies" until Hanoi and the National Liberation Front meet his conditions for a "just peace," which amount to their concession of defeat. In other words, large numbers of United States troops will remain in Vietnam so long as he is in office.

Again hoping to be heard by Hanoi but tuned out by most Americans, he has threatened repeatedly to re-escalate the war when his Vietnamese opponents resist this prolonged American occupation, as they are virtually sure to do. He has acted steadily upon these threats. We should believe him.

Moreover, except for the recent renewal of the bombing of North Vietnam (launched with a replay of the Tonkin Gulf "reprisal"), each of his escalations—the invasion of Cambodia, expansion of United States air attacks throughout Laos and Cambodia, and now a ground incursion deep into North Vietnam—has demonstrated that he will not be bound by restraints that limited even the massive though ineffective "pressures" applied by Lyndon Johnson.

His spokesmen pointedly refuse to admit any limit at all to the violent measures he feels free to use without consulting Congress, or is willing to justify as "protecting the lives of American troops."

Thus, current U.S. attacks are only warnings of what the North Vietnamese can expect from their continued "obduracy" after United States troops are reduced to their semipermanent levels, probably between 100,000 to 200,000 men. Remaining measures, long urged by the military (and in some cases by Nixon himself) include mining Haiphong, interference with Soviet shipping and interdiction attacks along the Chinese border and the destruction of Hanoi and Haiphong.

The recent abortive commando raid foretells even "limited" invasions of North Vietnam. What else could have been the contingency plan for rescuing the "search and rescue" team itself, if it had been pinned down last weekend? When all such measures fail, a full-scale invasion aimed at Hanoi, or the threat and possible use of nuclear weapons, could be "contingencies" whose time has come.

Nixon's clearly announced and demonstrated strategy entails not only prolonging but vastly expanding this immoral, illegal and unconstitutional war.

American casualties may decline, unless we invade the North. Yet the price of thus protecting Nixon from his fear of charges, borrowed from his own past, of "losing Indochina to Communism," will be millions more refugees and hundreds of thousands of more dead in Indochina, many more thousands of American dead, and the moral degradation of our country.

To refuse any longer, wishfully, to believe that Nixon really means what he says and does, or to fail to resist his policy, is to become an accomplice.

DANIEL ELLSBERG
Senior Research Associate
Center for International Studies, M.I.T.
Cambridge, Mass., Nov. 26, 1970

This letter has been endorsed by a group of Massachusetts Institute of Technology faculty members headed by Dr. Salvador Luria.

Secrecy and Passage Into the Quagmire

To the Editor:

A sense of outrage, like a poor knife, gets dulled by use, and such has been the effect for many of us of Vietnam. But mine has been usefully sharpened again by the Pentagon Study, and, as usual, personal experience helped.

In 1964, with numerous others, I campaigned across the country for the Johnson-Humphrey ticket. I was, by then, considerably concerned over our Vietnam involvement. I spoke principally of the need for military restraint, of the irresponsibility of Senator Goldwater's talk about unleashing the Air Force.

All this became an unpleasant matter for reflection a few weeks later when, as it then seemed, the Administration changed its mind. One now discovers that the plans for the bombing already existed and were awaiting an excuse that would, if necessary, be manufactured.

It follows that, to the knowing, those of us who were making the speeches were patsies serving usefully because of our ignorance. I do not reflect on such trickery with relish. I hope that all who were similarly involved have a like reaction.

But if one can contain his personal anger, there are further lessons.

61

What we have learned is that a small group of professionally assured, morally astigmatic and—a point to be emphasized—intellectually myopic men had undertaken deliberately to mislead the Congress, the public and the people of the world at large as to their intentions and, so far as might be possible, as to their actions.

They would largely have escaped criticism if *The Times,* in an action which belies much that is said about the modern institutionalized press, had not ripped away the protecting shroud. Whatever the plea, the primary effect of the present court action is to protect what is still undisclosed of this mendacity and duplicity.

But this is not all. The further lesson is that we can no longer afford the secrecy which protects such conduct of our public affairs, for against whom is such secrecy employed? It was not employed against the Government of North Vietnam. The papers are replete with references to our desire to make clear our intentions to that Government, and the worse our intentions seemed, the better.

Professor Walt Rostow is associated with more signals than an old-time telegrapher. Much consideration was given to informing the Soviets and the Chinese.

It was for protection from the Congress, our own people and our friends that this secrecy was employed, as the most casual reading of the papers will make clear. And the thing it protected, above all, was the freedom to make catastrophic mistakes.

For if the public had known that the Administration was seeking a Gulf of Tonkin Resolution in the spring of 1964, or had plans to bomb North Vietnam that autumn, or intended putting in large numbers of troops with a combat mission in the spring of 1965, there would have been a vigorous and bruising debate.

Foreseeing and fearing such a debate, the Administration might well have reconsidered the action. Or, in the wake of the debate, it might have been forced to do so. And in the course of the debate the very great question which—as the papers show, none of the strategists (George Ball apart) ever sought to ask—would have been asked. That is: Where does this policy lead us? It was secrecy that made possible our silent and unhampered passage into the quagmire.

It was part of our founding wisdom that public power, whether guided by good sense or, as in this case, by stupidity, must be subject to the hard test of public discussion. In these last years we've allowed soldiers and civilian strategists—the most bizarre of authorities to entrust with such a matter—to divert us with the doctrine that because the Communist countries do not have public debate on public decisions, neither should we.

Let us now accept the lesson. What may work for the Communists works disaster for us. The worst policy is one made in secrecy by the experts.

Our safety lies, and lies exclusively, in making public decision subject to the test of public debate. What cannot survive public debate—as the experience of Vietnam shows—we must not do.

JOHN KENNETH GALBRAITH
Cambridge, Mass., June 16, 1971

Comment on Pentagon Study

To the Editor:

Not since the Presidency of John Adams has any administration so instinctively distrusted the exercise of freedom of speech and of press by the American people as the present one.

That is why it rides roughshod over constitutional limitations on wiretapping. That is why it recommends the use of police force against even peaceful demonstrations. That is why it seeks to intimidate the networks when they tell the truth about the war or the Pentagon. That is why it now seeks to muzzle the press.

Its reaction to criticism is, like that of John Adams, not argument or explanation but censorship and coercion, and its reaction to the Bill of Rights, that it is a tiresome anachronism that should be swept aside.

Thus the hysterical argument of irreparable damage to national defense, when the only irreparable damage is to the reputation of this and past administrations. Thus Secretary Rogers' astonishing statement that publication of the papers by *The Times* ". . . is going to cause a great deal of trouble."

This is precisely the objection that the Government of George III had to the disclosures of the Hutchinson letters by Benjamin Franklin.

The Bill of Rights was not written into the Constitution in order to protect governments from "trouble," but so that the people might have a legitimate method of causing trouble to governments they no longer trusted.

HENRY STEELE COMMAGER
Amherst, Mass., June 17, 1971

63

Reaction to Pentagon Studies

To the Editor:

It is unfortunate that a great newspaper that stands for the rule of law and the preservation of representative government should arrogate to itself a function that Congress has said belongs to the Government, not to the press. That is, the responsibility for classifying and declassifying public documents.

We all know that there is a tendency to over-classify Government documents and to be too cautious about declassification. However, I can think of no rational basis for turning the declassification process over to the gentlemen of the press.

The *Chicago Tribune* would have declassified the Yalta papers before the ink was dry. Other publications would have declassified the Government's personnel security files, including, perhaps, the dossiers full of unevaluated information in the F.B.I. files.

If the only standard were whether or not American lives would be endangered by the declassification, as is suggested by *The Times* statement on the Vietnam papers, certainly the crop estimates of the Department of Agriculture would not have to be a carefully guarded secret until some mere Government official decided that it was appropriate to publish the data.

The minutes of the Federal Open Market Committee could be published on the following day with no threat to human life. Many law journals would doubtless find the deliberations of the Supreme Court justices fascinating material for publication.

The high officials of *The Times* seem to be suffering from the delusion that they are the final arbiters of right and wrong in this country. They would be the first to scourge any paper that published material from confidential files that *they* thought ought to remain confidential.

A little more humility from *The Times,* a little more respect for the law would be in order.

REED J. IRVINE
Silver Spring, Md., June 16, 1971

64

Vietnam Papers

To the Editor:

Roger Fisher (Op-Ed June 22) advises *The Times* to concede the Government's power to prohibit press publication of information that it classifies as confidential, and to throw itself upon the Government's discretion not to prosecute, or to punish lightly, this act of "civil disobedience." I trust *The Times* and the rest of the press will defend more determinedly the freedom which the Constitution assures it on behalf of all of us.

Professor Fisher urges, first, that "the Government should be able to classify as Secret or Top Secret documents involved in the confidential planning of high military and political strategy." He argues, second, that "there should be no different rule for the one who knowingly receives and passes on Government secrets than there is for the one who first takes them."

We may concede the first point. But the second does not follow. It is a very different proposition.

It is one thing for the Government to decide what internal information it needs to keep confidential, to instruct those it entrusts with the information—mostly its own officers and employes—to preserve that confidence, and to penalize them if they breach it.

It is quite another thing to punish dissemination of the information by someone who is in no way accountable to the Government. The Government may be legally entitled to keep its own secrets, if it can. It is not entitled to make the rest of us keep them, least of all the press.

There is an analogy in the contemporary efforts to minimize the effect of news coverage and comments on criminal trials. Courts may order the active participants in the process—attorneys, police officers, etc.—not to reveal or discuss evidence before trial, at the risk of committing contempt of court. But if a court were to try to punish a newspaper for publishing what someone nevertheless has revealed, it would surely run afoul of the First Amendment.

The Government's right to keep its confidences, and its power to punish outsiders who disseminate information once the secret is out, are two different constitutional issues. Precisely between them runs, I believe, the line drawn by the First Amendment.

HANS A. LINDE
University of Oregon
Eugene, Ore., June 22, 1971

65

Vietnam Documents

To the Editor:

The decision of *The Times* to publish lengthy excerpts and, in some instances, the full text of highly classified U.S. Government documents relating to the development of U.S. policy in the Vietnam war, raises many issues. *The Times,* supported by other media, insists that the real issue here is the freedom of the press as guaranteed in the First Amendment to the Constitution.

While this principle may be involved, it is by no means the primary one. More crucial is the question as to whether, regardless of the highest motivation and the most sincere conviction, any individual or organization in the American community can take it upon itself to breach the security of the U.S. Government or conspire to violate the law of the land with impunity.

Were this question to be answered affirmatively, the result would inevitably be to create complete chaos within the executive branch of the Federal Government and seriously inhibit or render virtually impossible the effective conduct of foreign relations.

Can any reasonable person expect the Israeli Premier, for example, to feel secure in her conversations with the President or Secretary of State, if the possibility exists that her views will be read in *The Times* or other American newspapers within a few days?

Would U.S. negotiators ever be able to guarantee that secret conversations held with American officials would remain privileged? I think not.

Another important issue which *The Times* disclosures raise and to which thoughtful Americans, official or private, must address themselves promptly is how to insure that in the case of future crises like Vietnam both the Congress of the United States and the American people are kept adequately informed by the President so that they may fulfill their responsibilities intelligently. Only if this is done can any Administration hope to gain public understanding and support for its policies and avoid crises of confidence.

HENRY B. COX
Chicago, July 1, 1971

III•Black Revolution

The struggle of the Negro for equality is perhaps the most important social revolution in 20th-century America. His efforts for equality in employment, education, housing, human dignity and the myriad amenities of simple living continue.

A large chapter in the history of this revolution is being written, a chapter about integration in the North and South, Martin Luther King Jr. and his philosophy of non-violence, the riots in Detroit, Newark and Los Angeles, the emergence of Black Panthers and the schism in black ranks. It is being written in part as "people history" in letters to *The Times* by those who made it happen. The letters contain a rich lode on the black revolution and the Negro's struggle for equality in the last 25 years.

Passage of FEPC Bill Urged

To the Editor of *The New York Times:*

Concerning your editorial "The FEPC Problem" in your issue of Jan. 24, you state: "If the bill could actually accomplish what its proponents believe it will, we would have no hesitation in urging that it become law with the least possible delay."

Obviously neither the FEPC Bill nor any bill which is now, or will come before the Congress, will accomplish 100 per cent performance. But the word "what" suggests such a performance. The fact that the Federal Constitution has been amended some nineteen or more times shows that it did not accomplish 100 per cent performance. But if the Founding Fathers had refused to support the Constitution on the grounds that it was not infallible and complete we would today be unable to predict what the course of the nation would be. What bill or law is without its Achilles' heel?

"If its swift passage could be made a rebuke to Senator Bilbo and others who propose to filibuster against a vote, there would be another argument in its favor," you observe. But how can its swift passage be effected? Certainly not by tenuous reservations, but with the support of powerful voices, such as *The New York Times*, which cannot successfully be accused of wild-eyed demogoguery.

Supporting your reason for refusing to back Senator Chavez's measure, you state: "The act would apply to every employer or labor union with more than a handful of employes or members in interstate or foreign commerce in any State, territory or possession of the United States." I don't see anything wrong with this. The National Labor Relations Act and the Railway Labor Act apply to businesses with a so-called handful of employes, and these acts have the same scope of territory as FEPC. However, in order to remove the grounds for this criticism, representatives of the National Council for a Permanent FEPC met in conference with the Senators leading the fight for the bill and agreed upon increasing the number of employes involved from six to 25.

You add that "an FEPC order, if sustained, could in theory be enforced by the Federal courts, with contempt penalties, and any wilful interference with the commission or its agents or agencies could be punished by imprisonment and fines." But this is not different from the procedure of other administrative agencies such as the Interstate Commerce Commission. Federal Trade Commission, the Fair Labor Standards Act, Securities Act and the National Labor Relations and Railway Labor Acts. These Federal administrative agencies have been reasonably successful.

68

"We do not believe this act would be enforceable in any state or community where the dominant opinion runs strongly against it," your editorial points out. Undoubtedly the law would encounter difficult problems of enforcement in certain areas where dominant opinion runs strongly against it, but that is no valid reason for not passing the bills. Dominant opinion ran strongly against the National Labor Relations Act in the South. It still does. But I am sure you would not advocate repealing the act for this reason.

Who does not remember the terrorism against labor unions in Harlan County, Kentucky, and other boss-ridden, open-shop sections of the country?

If this logic were to prevail, it would justify abolishing the Thirteenth, Fourteenth and Fifteenth Amendments to the Federal Constitution, for the dominant sentiment runs strongly against them throughout the South.

You go on to say: "Discrimination is always hard to prove, because it involves the subjective question of intent." I doubt that modern psychology will sustain this position. While it is true discrimination is hard to prove, it does not follow that it involves the question of subjective intent. You are confusing prejudice with discrimination. Prejudice, racial, religious or national is subjective, and involves intent. It is an emotion or feeling, a state or attitude of mind. It is an inner condition.

Not so with discrimination. Discrimination, racial, religious or what not, is an objective practice, which can be seen, heard and felt. For instance, discrimination against workers through the blacklists, yellow-dog contracts and company unions was stopped by the Wagner Act. But this does not mean that the prejudice against, and hatred of, the workers by the employing class are any less. FEPC is not designed to abolish prejudice but to eliminate discrimination. The law cannot compel Protestants to love Jews, but it can stop hoodlums from smearing synagogues with swastikas. Federal legislation may not be able to make Senator Bilbo embrace Representative Adam C. Powell but it can stop mobs from lynching Negroes. Laws can prevent residential segregation through restricted covenants and Jim Crow in transportation.

"It will have to be created by education," you insist. Certainly education is a basic factor in preparing the way for the enactment of legislation of any kind. But this does not indicate that in order to make public opinion favorable to FEPC classes and tracts on anthropology should be held and distributed. While there is no objection to this form of education it doubtless would involve astronomical time to register any visible change on FEPC or any other issue in the interest of minorities.

It appears that there is an unwarranted distinction between the processes of education and legislation. The fact is legislation is a form of

69

popular education. It tends to dramatize an issue which educates the people. The fight for FEPC legislation brings into public focus a concrete socio-economic question, which is debated and discussed pro and con in schools, churches, trade unions, business clubs, barber shops and on street corners. But this exchange of ideas on FEPC in the arena of public discussion would not obtain and have the vital interest and enthusiasm were there no bills before Congress. This form of education is a living, dynamic force. It conforms to the principle of the progressive school of education of learning by doing.

A. PHILIP RANDOLPH
Co-Chairman, National Council for a Permanent FEPC
New York, Jan. 25, 1946

Restricted Enlistments Criticized

To the Editor of *The New York Times:*

The War Department recently announced, according to *The New York Times* of Aug. 6, that new demands to fulfill draft requirements would be necessary because of a decline in enlistments during July.

Why have enlistments declined? Because, among other reasons, of the stoppage of Negro enlistments.

Why have Negro enlistments been stopped? Because the Army is hewing to the line of limiting Negroes to their proportion in the nation's population—roughly 10 per cent.

This artificial limitation flies in the face of all social, economic and military history. It is a well-known fact that in all other democratic countries, during peacetime, the ranks are filled with persons from the lower economic levels.

The Army could easily fill its requirements through admitting all persons applying from the lower economic brackets. In normal times these persons would be predominantly Southern whites and Negroes from all sections of the country.

But our American Army, which now finds itself armed with the most powerful weapon in history, feels itself obliged to interfere with this natural process of recruiting by applying artificial restrictions based on racial grounds.

There is food for reflection here. What hope is there for a better world dominated by an army armed with an atomic bomb, but restricting its membership artificially on the basis of one of man's most primitive social deficiencies: racial prejudice?

HORACE MANN BOND
President Lincoln University
Lincoln University, Pa., Aug. 7, 1946

Negro Ban Protested

To the Editor of *The New York Times:*

The Jim Crow restrictions in the theatres in Washington, D.C., are anachronistic and scandalous. As one of my Washington friends said to me the other day, "They are relics of the time when Washington was considered a sleepy old Southern town. Nobody seems to have informed the theatre-owners that this has become a great, cosmopolitan capital."

There is no local law or ordinance imposing these restrictions. It is a matter of custom or tradition, variously interpreted. The situation is complicated and confusing but, as I understand it, the following policies prevail:

In the National Theatre Negroes are permitted on the stage but not in the audience. In Constitution Hall they are permitted in the audience but not on the stage (except occasionally at benefits). At the Uline Arena Negroes are admitted to prizefights but not to such intellectual entertainments as the "Ice-capades." Billy Rose recently cancelled an engagement of "Carmen Jones" at this arena because of this policy.

The Lisner Auditorium of George Washington University is a modern, well-equipped theatre which has recently become available from time to time for commercial productions. The first play booked there is the Playwrights' Company production of Maxwell Anderson's "Joan of Lorraine," starring Ingrid Bergman.

There was no question in the minds of the Playwrights' Company of any racial discrimination in the sale of tickets and, undoubtedly, a proportionate number of the tickets have gone to Negroes. However, the authorities of the university decided that the Lisner Auditorium must conform to the general practice in Washington theatres and refuse admission to Negroes.

Washington is an important unit in the economy of the theatre. It is what is known as "a great show town." The audiences are exceptionally

71

intelligent and the press generous in the support it gives to the theatre as an institution.

However, the revenue to be derived is poor compensation for the injury done to the conscience of American citizens for this continuance of injustice in our national capital.

I believe that only a small minority of the people of Washington want this to continue. And there is surely no law compelling that minority to go to the theatre if they object to the presence of Negroes under the same roof.

Therefore, I believe that it is the duty of all of us who work in the American theatre—actors, playwrights, producers—to protest against this intolerable situation by agreeing that we shall keep our productions out of Washington until the ban against Negroes is abolished.

ROBERT E. SHERWOOD
New York, Oct. 26, 1946

School Decision Discussed

To the Editor of *The New York Times:*

To those millions of us who spent our youth in segregated Negro schools of the South and know the psychological and spiritual damage of segregation, the unanimous decision of the Supreme Court outlawing secregation in the public schools does much to heal a deep wound.

I think I can now understand for the first time how my great-grand-father felt when he, a former slave, read the Emancipation Proclamation. I can also understand now why there was not more bitterness among the freed Negroes when slavery was ended. When a deep wrong to the human spirit has been righted, there is no need for forgiveness. Both wronged and wrongdoers have weathered the catastrophe and found new levels of spiritual strength.

Personal vindication, however, dwindles before the magnificent universal stature of the court's decision. On May 17, the United States stood taller and with greater dignity in the eyes of the world than at any other time in the twentieth century.

No lawyer or student of democracy who has followed closely the legal efforts to eliminate racial segregation and discrimination can read the court's recent decision without realizing the tremendous power which a lone individual dedicated to a principle can wield upon history. In this moment of our nation's triumph in a principle of human rights too much tribute cannot be paid to the memory of Justice John M. Harlan, a former lecturer at Howard University School of Law and a former justice of the United States Supreme Court.

In 1883 that court struck down the Federal Civil Rights Act of 1875 in the "Civil Rights Cases." The purpose of the act was to prohibit racial discrimination in all places of public accommodation, travel and amusement throughout the United States. In an eight-to-one decision the court declared that the act was unconstitutional. Justice Harlan wrote the lone dissenting opinion.

Again, in 1896, when the court adopted the "separate but equal" doctrine in its 8 to 1 decision in *"Plessy* v. *Ferguson,"* now partially overruled by the present court, Justice Harlan wrote the lone dissent.

His reasoning in both dissenting opinions was substantially the same: that the intent of the Thirteenth and Fourteenth Amendments was not only to abolish slavery and guarantee citizenship with all its privileges to the newly freed Negroes, but also to wipe out all "badges of inferiority and servitude" which the degrading experience of slavery had imposed upon them. He rejected the "separate but equal" doctrine in all its implications, warned the court of the great injustice that was being done to an entire race by branding it as inferior, and predicted the widespread discrimination which would result from the court's decisions.

In the public school cases, at least, the substance of Justice Harlan's dissent in *"Plessy* v. *Ferguson"* has become the unanimous opinion of the Supreme Court. Is it too early to suggest that his vision was also correct when he wrote his dissenting opinion in the "Civil Rights Cases"? Is it too much to predict that we will find, in the light of history and overwhelming psychological and sociological authority, the Civil Rights Act of 1875 is still constitutional and in force?

PAULI MURRAY
New York, May 19, 1954

The writer, an attorney, is the compiler of "States' Laws on Race and Color."

Extending Compulsory Association

To the Editor of *The New York Times:*

It seems highly desirable and not at all paradoxical that white people of the South who are possessed of funds should now become generous contributors to the campaign chest of the National Association for the Advancement of Colored People.

This work should go on for the benefit of Northern as well as Southern whites. The march of progress must not be confined to the primary and high schools, where the only beneficiaries will be the children of parents who lack the means to pay for a private and select education. Logic and justice require that the blessings of indiscriminate and compulsory association be extended to all schools whatever, as well as to all restaurants, hotels, motels, apartment houses and "nice" real estate developments, throughout the broad land.

Have we not been told many times that "the cure for the evils of democracy is more democracy"? As who should say, the cure for pneumonia is more pneumonia; the cure for choking is strangling.

The North is entitled, no less than the South, to this renewed and unceasing and adequately financed effort from the N.A.A.C.P.; and the results will undoubtedly be at least as noble as those of the similarly reasonable and persistent crusade for prohibition.

All of us are entitled to this fulfillment as we complete the process from a representative federal republic, our status in the dark old days, to the sunrise of a gutter democracy.

MITCHELL RAWSON
New York, May 18, 1954

Problems in Harlem

To the Editor of *The New York Times:*

The recent trouble in Harlem has highlighted the problems of this community. While they can be described as racial, they are also problems of the city's newest immigrant groups, the Negroes and the Puerto Ricans.

My work as a City Councilman has indicated to me that a fairly large number of individuals and families have collapsed as viable human beings in Harlem. Largely a rural people, they are unable to compete for a living in our highly developed urban environment.

Because of this, on June 21, 1957, I introduced a resolution in the

City Council requesting the Mayor to appoint what would have amounted to a Point Four commission for the city. Among other things the commission would:

Make a complete social inventory of the people who live in the city in order to evaluate their economic, social and cultural resources.

Evaluate the effectiveness of the public and private agencies in curing social maladjustments and in developing the potential of the city's inhabitants so that they may achieve social and economic mobility and contribute more to the city.

Develop a creative welfare program designed to help low-income groups to help themselves by developing native capacities, in place of a program which is largely old-fashioned alms-giving.

One example of a job only half done by the city of its failure to assist in the development of its human resources while spending hundreds of millions of dollars, is seen in its construction of many mammoth housing projects. While they are absolutely necessary, all the city has done is to stuff them full of people and then sit back.

The city has ignored the fact that some of the tenants in low-rental developments are culturally deprived. They cannot get ahead on their own steam. If the city does not remedy this condition, it will merely have transferred its slums from the back streets to magnificent modern structures.

The first function of the Point Four commission would be to find out how well our newest immigrants are adjusting to their urban environment. It would also find out their ability to hold their families together, to compete for better jobs, to raise their living standard and to train their children to compete for a living; the school achievements of the various elements of our population and the reasons for a lack of achievement; the amount and the causes of middle-class flight from the city; and the amount of crime and juvenile delinquency, but more importantly, their nature and causes.

One thing the city could do immediately to alleviate conditions in Harlem and other similar sections of the city would be to assign to them its best teachers, policemen and other civil servants. Too often those sections of the city which need the best services and facilities are given the worst.

Although there are many responsible leaders in Harlem working for its betterment, it is a hunting preserve for demagogues who sell their phony racist and political potions for their own purposes.

Rackets, such as the numbers game, are run fairly wide open in Harlem. The police cannot stop gambling so they join the gamblers. Under these circumstances many citizens, particularly the hoodlum element,

75

lose respect for both the law and its enforcers. Nevertheless, in spite of this condition Harlem is better policed today than in years.

It will require a basic job in human engineering to solve some of Harlem's deep-rooted social problems and improve the lot of its people. The task is so large that only the city can do it, and it will no doubt need financial aid from the Federal Government. The time has come, however, for the city to do more about it than to hold another meeting of leading citizens to talk some more about the same problem.

EARL BROWN
City Councilman
New York, July 19, 1959

Attack on Status Quo

To the Editor of *The New York Times:*

Doesn't anyone understand what is going on? The reason there is violence in parts of our benighted South is simply that there are many Americans who find the status quo intolerable.

Would our allies prefer that we kept our so-called prestige undamaged by ignoring a situation which is immoral, and one which, thanks to the efforts of organizations such as the White Citizen's Council, is simply throwing excelsior on the fires of Communist propaganda? Our allies condemn the violence *per se* without, it appears, taking into consideration the fact that it is also Americans, both white and black, who are fighting for the rights of other Americans regardless of color.

The majority of white Southerners seem to be in large part fighting mainly for the repeal of the 20th century. But they do not represent the United States except in so far as the rest of the country condones segregation and discrimination in schools, housing and social intercourse. To that extent we must bear the same burden of guilt.

To a Christian or a Jew there should not be even the ghost of a question as to what must be done—"Peace is not the absence of tension, but the presence of justice," in the South, the rest of the United States and the world.

EVA COFFIN
(Mrs. William Sloane Coffin Jr.)
New Haven, Conn., May 24, 1961

76

Distrust in Africa

To the Editor of *The New York Times:*

Like a cold wind the news from Alabama is blowing through Africa. Our rural and townspeople are shivering before this new evidence that even the undisputed achievements of the black man in the West cannot protect him from the stigma of color—even in the United States of America, the land which has claimed to be the champion of anti-colonialism and the rights of man.

Many of my friends in Central Africa are saying, How can we trust the United States of America? Her offers of friendship and help are not really true. She wants us to be friendly to her but is not prepared to prove her friendship to us. Is it not true that in the United States of America men and women of our color have won respect and fame as doctors, lawyers, teachers, business men, scientists, soldiers, airmen, etc.? Did not a black man first stand alone with Commander Peary at the North Pole in 1907? Has not our brothers' blood flowed with the blood of white Americans in the defense of freedom and the rights of man? And yet, in this same country, men and women are suffering because their skin is black. How can the United States of America speak for us in Africa?

Our hearts beat like yours, America. Oh, Alabama, be brief, be quick for once.

GODWIN A. MBIKUSITA LEWANIKA
Member of Parliament for Luangwa
Kitwe, Northern Rhodesia, May 25, 1961

For Equal Job Opportunity

To the Editor of *The New York Times:*

I have read with a great deal of interest your news article of June 18 and your editorial of June 19 concerning the alleged controversy within the President's Committee on Equal Employment Opportunity. I do not propose to promote a controversy where in my opinion none exists, but I would like to state for the record my concept as to the legitimate objectives of the committee and the direction which I believe it is taking.

Controversy, like beauty, is frequently in the eye of the beholder. The facts are that people involved in different aspects of a program are quite likely to put heavier emphasis on that with which they are the most familiar. In this sense, it is easily possible to interpret as controversy supplementary programs which are actually working toward the same objective and which do not fundamentally conflict.

As far as I am concerned, the objective of the committee is to insure equal employment opportunity for all of our citizens without regard to race, creed, color, or national origin. This goal is based upon considerations of both wisdom and morality.

I believe that it is the positive obligation of the committee to attempt to reach that goal by all legitimate means and under no circumstances should progress toward that goal be impeded by procedural arguments.

The committee operates a compliance program, and, as I have said frequently, we mean business. It is the policy of this Administration that no man or woman be denied the opportunity of competing for a job because of considerations of ancestry that are irrelevant to merit. I believe the record establishes beyond a doubt that despite our limited staff we have made long strides toward achieving this goal.

Unfortunately, there are limitations upon such a program. We cannot legally impose sanctions except in the fields of Government employment and employment related to Government contracts. Therefore, our committee has sought to go beyond the policing functions of the Executive Order and to build other positive programs which will speed progress toward our goal. I would describe the committee's activities as follows:

1. In the first place, we operate a compliance program which requires strict observance of the unswerving policy of this Government that Federal employment and work related to Federal contracts be made available on the basis of equal opportunity regardless of race, creed, color or national origin.

2. Then, we operate a voluntary program which seeks to enlist employers in positive affirmative steps to broaden the portals of equal opportunity. (It should be emphasized that these voluntary programs do not relieve employers of their obligation to comply with the Executive Order.)

3. Next, we are actively negotiating with America's trade unions (which can be reached only indirectly by the Executive Order) agreements to take affirmative steps to promote nondiscrimination.

4. Finally, we are seeking to persuade people in the local communities to tackle one of the most important forms of discrimination—denial of access to the training that qualifies a man to compete for a job on a basis of equality with his fellow man.

I do not regard any of these programs as competing with each other. In fact I would welcome suggestions for more programs. We must rid ourselves of the notion that there is one simple solution to this highly complex problem. We must adopt the psychology of giving a hearty welcome to every step that promotes progress and every tool that will bring justice and equal opportunity closer to a reality.

Justice has been long delayed by abstract procedural arguments. People are entitled to fair play and equal treatment now—while they can still enjoy its benefits—and it is my intention to sponsor any and every legitimate form of action that will produce results.

LYNDON B. JOHNSON
Washington, June 19, 1962

Anti-Negro Bias in Unions

To the Editor of *The New York Times:*

The hierarchy of the A.F.L.–C.I.O. suggest that local autonomy and established rules limit the action of the organization's national officers in dealing with discrimination against Negroes in some of its unions. This means asking a large and long-suffering group of people, who have waited over 100 years for this implementation of the Emancipation Proclamation, to accept patience and fortitude in the one place that should have little patience and much fortitude with respect to the resolution of an issue that might very well shape the future of the entire world.

The A.F.L.–C.I.O. had little difficulty in finding the necessary machinery to oust Communist-dominated and racket-ridden unions. To determine, as it has, that the same machinery cannot be used to oust unions that practice racial discrimination is not only a convenient rationalization but is also antithetical to the basic tenets and high principles of trade unionism.

HENRY MAYER
New York, Nov. 20, 1962

Discrimination in Unions

To the Editor of *The New York Times:*

Henry Mayer, in his letter published Nov. 23, takes the American Federation of Labor and Congress of Industrial Organizations to task for failing to oust local unions practicing racial discrimination. His argument is based on the premise that since the A.F.L.–C.I.O. expelled racket-

79

ridden unions and the old C.I.O expelled Communist-dominated ones, the same punishment should be exercised once again.

Mr. Mayer fails to understand that the A.F.L.–C.I.O. is interested in eliminating segregation and discrimination and not in just meting out punishment.

Obviously discrimination is as bad as corruption. But it is a different kind of disease requiring a different kind of cure. Corruption and Communist domination of unions begin at the top and eat down into the very heart of the union by destroying democratic processes. The exercise of discrimination or segregation, on the other hand, begins at the bottom in the rank-and-file, who reflect the mores of their communities and the prejudices of their fellow citizens. It exists in part by the very exercise of the democratic process.

The cure for corruption-dominated unions was expulsion, for this was the only way to insure that the rank-and-file recognized the systematic, cynical corruption of their union by men who had betrayed their trust. Expulsion from the House of Labor proved to these members that the corruption was real, and their reaction has been in many cases to form new, clean unions and to throw out dishonest leaders.

Discrimination, on the contrary, exists despite the opposition of trade union leaders, and expulsion would only weaken the hand of these leaders who are actively working to eliminate the twin evils of segregation and discrimination. Expulsion would not eliminate discrimination in a local union; it would allow it free rein, and the leaders who oppose discrimination would be powerless to change the situation.

Expulsion would be the easy route; it would cure nothing. We have taken the tougher route of working inside the labor movement to bring about abolition of bias. The great bulk of our unions have signed commitments to wipe out racial barriers in membership and in jobs. The federation also supports fair employment practices legislation under which it would be illegal for employers of unions to discriminate. The road we follow is the only dependable one for achieving a trade union movement true to the very principles to which Mr. Mayer refers.

WILLIAM F. SCHNITZLER
Secretary-Treasurer, American Federation of
Labor and Congress of Industrial Organizations
Washington, Nov. 28, 1962

Dealing With Race Bias

To the Editor of *The New York Times:*

The Constitution is the fundamental document that limits the power of government and distributes that limited power between central and parochial governments. The Constitution is also used as a "counter" in arguments over a proposed course of action. This dual nature of the Constitution must be kept firmly in mind when considering the current debate over the Administration's proposals for civil rights legislation.

When dealing with problems facing the nation as a whole the central government normally uses one of the granted national powers. On the assumption that the best vehicle for exercising national power is the commerce clause, the proposed approach is through that clause. It is to be expected that those who oppose this effort to end racial discrimination in commercial activity will claim that the Federal Administration is engaged in an invalid invocation of the power of the central government.

It is bootless to argue that the Founding Fathers did not anticipate the use of the commerce clause for such a purpose as insuring open accommodations in hotels, restaurants and stores. Of course they did not. But the Founding Fathers did visualize a central government dealing with national problems and they provided the commerce clause as one means of handling national problems.

Over the years we have used the commerce clause to solve national problems of a traditional commercial nature. But we have also used the same clause to solve national problems not traditionally considered commercial in nature. Witness the Mann Act forbidding interstate transportation of women for immoral purposes and the Dyer Act making it a Federal crime to transport a stolen automobile across a state line.

The United States Government is constitutionally justified in using the commerce clause to its fullest extent to solve the problem of racial injustice arising out of commercial activities. It is proper for people to oppose the Administration's proposal on the grounds that the need to eliminate racial injustice is not great enough to justify interference with a man's use of his own property. It is a smoke screen to assert one's opposition by appeal to the Constitution.

It is likewise appropriate to suggest that the Federal Government ought to use its power under the 14th Amendment on the ground that thereby some activity not involving intercourse among the states could be covered. It is not constitutionally significant to argue that the 14th Amendment should be used because the problem of racial injustice is a moral matter and not a matter of commerce.

The point is that the United States Constitution was designed to create a nation with a government that could cope with national problems. Racial injustice is clearly a national, indeed an international, problem today.

The power to deal with this problem resides in the Federal Government. Those who invoke the Constitution in the name of states' rights are throwing up a smoke screen to hide behind. Presumably they do not care to argue that they approve of racial discrimination.

GEORGE D. BRADEN
Schenectady, N.Y., July 25, 1963

Local Encouragement

To the Editor of *The New York Times:*

We deplore the brutal affront to constitutional guarantee in Birmingham. Such open disregard for the right to redress grievances is a flagrant abuse against any segment of this citizenry. Open defiance on the part of Governors and other officials of the states of Mississippi and Alabama only gives encouragement and official endorsement to killings, bombings and illegal arrest.

We feel that had something been done by the Federal Government to curtail the defiance of Gov. Ross R. Barnett and Lieut. Gov. Paul B. Johnson of Mississippi, this tragedy would not have occurred.

CHARLES EVERS
Field Secretary, N.A.A.C.P.
Jackson, Miss., Sept. 16, 1963

Busing Pupils Opposed

To the Editor of *The New York Times:*

I resent the possibility that my child may be forced to ride a bus to school. I deliberately purchased my home because of its proximity to an elementary, junior and senior high school, despite necessary sacrifices, so that my child might walk to school. Surely my high tax rate should guarantee me some degree of protection and rights.

MILLICENT MAURER
New York, Feb. 13, 1964

Reports Mississippi Complies With Laws

To the Editor:

In your columns recently appeared news articles describing action of the Mississippi Economic Council and the Mississippi Manufacturers Association urging that all Mississippians make adjustments to abide by the Civil Rights Act.

In our state we are going through a transition period. We are experiencing reluctance and in some cases bitterness, but the changes are taking place under the leadership of those who realize that Mississippi is part of the United States of America and must comply with court orders and laws. During this period we ask of our fellow Americans their patience and understanding, instead of criticism and condemnation.

In Mississippi we have laws prohibiting boycotts, and stiff penalties are provided for any persons who conspire to restrain trade. We buy and enjoy many products produced in your area, and we hope that citizens in your state will continue to buy and enjoy those products that we manufacture or process in Mississippi. For your information; our plants and factories provide employment for citizens of both races.

The Mississippi State Sovereignty Commission is a state agency created by the Legislature with the Governor as ex officio chairman.

ERLE JOHNSTON Jr.
Director
Mississippi State Sovereignty Commission
Jackson, Miss., Feb. 5, 1965

Commission's Stand Against Civil Rights

To the Editor:

As one who recently worked in Mississippi as a post-graduate intern for the Law Students Civil Rights Research Council, I was extremely interested in a letter written by Erle Johnston Jr., director of the Mississippi State Sovereignty Commission, published Feb. 18.

I think that when he described the Sovereignty Commission he should have mentioned that, as he himself recently testified in a hearing arising out of the challenge to the five Mississippi Congressmen, the function of the Sovereignty Commission has been to give money to the White Citizens Council and to "investigate" Negro voter registration drives.

The Commission, a state agency, used taxpayers' money to support lobbying, both in Mississippi and in other parts of the country, against the 1964 Civil Rights Act. If white Mississippians are as anxious to bring meaningful change, as Mr. Johnston suggests, they should start by abolishing the Mississippi State Sovereignty Commission.

WILLIAM G. KOPIT
New York, Feb. 18, 1965

Voting Inequities in Northern States

To the Editor:

Public discussion of the remedies for the excessive representation in the Congress to those states which deny Negroes the suffrage too often disregards some stubborn facts of history.

Self-interest has made it easy for the Northern states—or some of them—to forget that Section 2 of the 14th Amendment requires that when any state chooses to deny resident American citizens of 21 years of age who have not been convicted of crime, the right to vote for state or national officers, its representation in the Congress shall be reduced in the proportion which such excluded citizens bear to the whole population of the state. This provision was unquestionably intended to penalize those states which prefer not to adopt universal suffrage as their rule of government.

If, at long last, a systematic effort is going to be made to enforce the principles of the 14th Amendment against such states as Alabama and Mississippi, would it not be well for those other states which have not yet accepted the principle of universal suffrage either now to adopt that principle or acknowledge their willingness to pay the designated price for retaining literary and other qualifying standards?

Those Northern states which do not want to pay the price fixed by the Constitution have, of course, justification for their insistence that such offenders as Alabama and Mississippi are infected by a more malignant iniquity than that which contaminates them. The exclusions that prevail in the North are not, in general, unlawful exclusions, maintained in violation of the 15th Amendment's absolute prohibition of racial discriminations in voting.

Though that is so, it none the less would seem appropriate and politic for any state which contemplates demanding a reduction in the repre-

sentation of states that deny Negroes the suffrage to put its own principles and practices in constitutional order before pressing for the
enforcement of the second section of the 14th Amendment against others.

MARK DEW. HOWE
Cambridge, Mass., March 13, 1965

'Asp', Not 'Wasp'?

To the Editor:

In his July 21 column on balanced ethnic tickets Tom Wicker observed that John Lindsay's fusion drive includes a Jew, a Catholic and a
"wasp."

Although it is doubtful that anthropologists (and Shinto-worshipers)
could ever agree upon what constitutes an Anglo-Saxon, there can be
no gainsaying the fact that members of this worthy breed are assumed
to be white. No one, it is reasonable to conclude, has ever heard of a
black Anglo-Saxon or a yellow Anglo-Saxon.

It is therefore suggested that the designation "asp" would be far more
appropriate. And if Anglo-Saxon Protestants are disposed to take issue
with the proposal, let them come up with something better.

JAMES D. CLARK
Cleveland Heights, Ohio, July 22, 1965

Black Power and Political Awakening

To the Editor:

"Black power" is an articulated hope; its object is the entrance of the
lower-class Negro into American society via the route of practical politics.

When lower-class politics flourished, the Negro was disfranchised. Today, politics is not only white, but also middle class. The lower-class
Negro is thus excluded from meaningful participation on two counts.

His consequent powerlessness is manifested in an array of Negro
"leaders" over whom he has no control—they neither represent him nor
are responsible to him. The constituencies of these "establishmentarians"
includes everyone but lower-class black people.

85

Politics is the interaction of self-interested groups in an effort to determine the distribution of social benefits. As such, it is of vital concern. How can the lower-class Negro gain political influence? How can he acquire representatives who not only speak for him but who are responsible to him?

Black power is one method—organization of black people in heavily Negro areas for achieving specific political goals. In the South, the method would be a third party on a local level; in the North, bloc pressure within the existing party structure.

This is not "racism in reverse." To say this demonstrates either a lack of information or a willingness to distort the facts. Black power is a political, community-oriented movement that seeks an individual—not separate—place in America's pluralistic society. It does not, like racism in general, thrive on hatred and insult. It is not, like white racism in particular, responsible for lynchings or violation of the rights of large numbers of human beings.

This is the end of the civil-rights movement, and consequently, of nonviolence. Nonviolence, a tactic used on mass demonstrations, has never denied a man the right to protect his home and family. As mass demonstrations generate little political power, they will be phased out. Nonviolence will as a tactic become irrelevant.

Civil rights was a middle-class, libertarian movement, aimed at America's conscience; it was made simple by easily recognizable enemies and issues—Jim Clark, "Freedom Now," and so forth.

The Negro movement, of which black power is a phase, recognizes that true liberty is not only freedom from restraint but possession of power. It is a political awakening of black people, a sophistication realizing that in politics there are no easily defined issues, no friends or enemies—only power and self-interest.

I wish to join Floyd McKissick in assuring whites that no one plans a Mau Mau uprising or slave revolt. What specific program he plans for implementation of black power I await. But I am sure it will show a realization that in our society standing is not determined by charity or conscience; that is a lesson we have learned from American political history.

HAROLD A. McDOUGALL
Managing Editor
Harvard Journal of Negro Affairs
Cambridge, Mass., July 12, 1966

Black Power Rejected

To the Editor:

It is regrettable that a 20-odd-year-old organization like CORE (with a commendable record heretofore) has now changed its slogans, tactics and leadership to such an extent that I do not believe that the majority of Americans, truly dedicated to the cause of civil rights, can support the organization.

It is unfortunate that CORE's leader, Floyd McKissick, could possibly believe that our President and Vice President are reacting to civil rights developments in a "racist" fashion. Truly we Negroes would be a "doomed group" insofar as civil rights were concerned if Mr. McKissick's ill-advised utterances at his recent press conference were true.

May I say that I believe in the sincerity of the Executive branch of our Federal Government and am indeed happy for the articulation of Dr. Martin L. King and Roy Wilkins, as well as your editorial of July 7 on the futility of the concept "black power."

ALMA C. J. MORMENT
Clinical Social Worker
New York, July 8, 1966

Negroes' Critical View of Integration

To the Editor:

Last winter it was Julian Bond who symbolized the whites' refusal to play by their own rules if those rules led ultimately to anything faintly resembling "black power." The latest example is Congressman Adam Clayton Powell. Outside of the political sphere a parallel drama was enacted over Cassius Clay who, because he dared to doff the obsequiousness which is traditionally expected of Negro sports champions, was subjected to unprecedented exclusion from major American boxing circles.

It is my opinion that the appearance of "black power" on the civil rights stage, far from being the cause of the increasing disenchantment with the Negro as suggested in the recent news series by Gene Roberts (*Times*, Sept. 19), is rather a convenient excuse which many whites are seizing upon to shed a vogue with which they have never felt comfortable. Perhaps, as Roberts suggests, we are entering a second post-reconstruction period in which new barriers to Negro progress will again be erected across our nation.

What the significance of such a reactionary trend would mean for the United States only the most foolhardy would dare to predict. Roberts concludes his news article with the fearsome thought that Negroes may well be confined to their ghettos by white police power, and that we might "rock along that way for a generation or so." Perhaps only coincidentally the same issue of *The Times* carried W. V. Shannon's editorial page column entitled "On Negro Separatism," which also concluded on a note of "apartheid."

As a Negro, I feel no better equipped than others to predict what the failure of the "melting-pot" theory of American culture will ultimately mean. The mood of the Negro, and of the world generally, is hardly such as to permit the institution of apartheid in America or even a return to the *status quo ante*.

On the other hand, *The Times*'s comment is quite correct in observing that the Negro's disillusionment with integration as a goal is burgeoning rapidly. Not only does it appear to be unachievable; its very desirability is being increasingly subjected to a critical Negro eye.

To cite only a single example; the racist aspects of the Vietnam war. The cavalier manner in which America employs the most barbaric techniques against the Vietnamese people is a growing topic of discussion among Negroes (and all other colored peoples) who have never forgotten that it was Japan, not Germany, upon whom the atom bomb was dropped. At the same time, the disproportionate numbers in which Negro troops are being used in the war is becoming increasingly apparent and resented in the ghettos also.

Although perhaps regrettable, it is certainly not impossible that the American Negro may ultimately decide that the two-car garage and color TV society of white America is really not worth integrating into after all. But it is unlikely that apartheid will be an acceptable alternative for him. Nor is he likely to be willing to "return to Africa," leaving the United States to the mass of white immigrants who arrived a century or more after he did.

Partition? It's still taboo to speak of it in respectable circles, but there is already whispered talk of "which states" and of possible political alliance with the country's conservatives to achieve this end. All of which does not add up to a very promising prospect for the coming decade or two.

ROBERT S. BROWNE
Teaneck, N.J., Sept. 19, 1966

New Living Pattern for Negro

To the Editor:

Fortunately for most Negroes living in the urban areas of the North, the present debate over the social merits of segregated Negro living versus integrated Negro living seems almost totally irrelevant to the outcome.

As I read the abundant evidence, urban Negroes of the Northern cities are shaping their own pattern; and it is neither a pattern of huddling segregated in the 50-year-old slums of these cities nor a pattern of losing themselves by diffusion in the white-dominated neighborhoods of the suburbs. Instead, the crowded Negro ghetto of the central city is thinning and spreading.

In the spread, however, white-dominated areas are being overleaped and new nuclei of Negro neighborhoods are appearing in the suburbs. Most of the suburban neighborhoods that Negroes are managing to enter are old, consisting of middle-income housing that has passed its prime.

In one respect, therefore, Negroes are simply repeating the choice of other identifiable minorities over the past century. Like the Swedes, the Germans, the Italians, the Armenians, and the Jews, they are finding better neighborhoods; yet finding them where they and their children will be somewhat protected against the subtle or brutal slights and discriminations that accompany the process of out movement.

The white community, meanwhile, tends to draw back from the edges of the suburban areas in which the Negroes are managing to gain a foothold, thereby creating new opportunities for more Negroes to enter.

Those who would like to see the Negro families of our Northern cities massed in a tight and manageable nucleus in the old central city slums are pursuing a will-o'-the-wisp; and those who would like to see the Negroes indistinguishably dispersed among the whites are no more realistic. The forces that are leading Negro families to find their own living patterns seem to me to be too strong to be affected much by exhortation and urging in either of these directions.

While the Negroes are finding a response to their living needs which is similar to that of so many groups before them, there are at least two differences between the Negroes' efforts and those of the earlier groups. First, Negroes do not seem to be able to find suburban housing quite rapidly enough to follow the inexorable and irreversible outbound movement of the job market. Second, because urban living space today is so much less densely exploited than it has been in decades past, the geographical boundaries where Negro and white neighborhoods meet are much more extensive than was the case for the earlier outmoving groups.

89

If there is an issue of public policy here, as there certainly is, it is that of helping Negroes to achieve their self-contrived solution more expeditiously and more painlessly than they now seem able to do. This calls for many things, including help in the search for housing closer to the suburban labor markets, and family rent supplements that can be spent wherever the housing can be found.

But it is chimerical to think of "solutions" that lock Negroes in the central cities slums or of solutions that merge them indistinguishably into neighborhoods dominated by the whites.

RAYMOND VERNON
Cambridge, Mass., Dec. 18, 1967

The writer was the director of the New York Metropolitan Regional Study from 1956 to 1959 and is the author of several books on the city.

Importance of Swahili

To the Editor:

I would very much like to know the basis for the condemnation by *The New York Times* of the plan to teach Swahili in a New York City high school. There were no specific reasons given in your recent editorial. No attempt was made to analyze sociologically, psychologically, or educationally the reasons why *The Times* regards the introduction of this language as "a prime example of how not to improve the educational opportunities of the city's Negro youngsters."

Since the writer of the editorial has probably had little or no trouble with his own self-identity, it is perhaps asking too much to expect him to understand why we firmly believe that anything that can make a contribution toward improving the badly eroded self-image of black people is legitimate and relevant.

There is nothing "fashionable, sentimental and emotional" about introducing into the curriculum a language with which black children can identify. There is nothing artificial, manufactured or pseudo-nationalistic about enabling a black student to see himself among the courses he can take just as a white student sees himself when he sees among his choices French, German, Spanish, Italian, Hebrew or Norwegian (all languages taught in the New York City public schools).

Swahili is one of the most important of the several hundred African

90

languages. I fail to see the irrelevance of teaching it with world events developing as they are.

When you speak of a flight from reality, I suggest very strongly that you examine your own view of the world around you.

ROY INNIS
New York, Dec. 27, 1967

Mr. Innis wrote as Associate National Director of the Congress of Racial Equality.

Every American Shares Guilt

To the Editor:

The murder of Martin Luther King is an unspeakable tragedy. It is a tragedy for which all Americans must be held guilty who, when Negroes were lynched, civil rights workers murdered, and white juries and judges found the murderers not guilty, stood by and did nothing.

The law, the church and all other institutions in the South have for the most part existed and continue to exist in relation to the Negro to keep him in his "proper place." That place has been conceived by Americans generally and by Southerners in particular, as outside the brotherhood of man and beyond the rights and privileges available to anyone with a white skin.

Where are the murderers of Medgar Evers, of the three civil rights workers, of the Unitarian minister beaten to death in Selma, of the Detroit mother shot to death on the Lowndes county highway, of the little girls bombed to death in Birmingham? The calendar of crimes against the Negro is endless. The South has sanctioned the murder and institutionalized the maltreatment and sequestration of Negroes for more than 350 years.

The murder of Martin Luther King is a tragic consequence of that long history of brutality toward the Negro. Martin Luther King's murder constitutes yet another evidence of the widespread disease that affects the majority of white Americans: the racism that is the expression of deep insecurities and even more profound confusions as to what it means to be a human being.

There is no "race problem," there is no "Negro problem," but there is a sick white man problem, and he is the Negro's problem as well as humanity's challenge.

Unless we recognize this sickness for what it is and do what is required

91

to set ourselves in order, we shall go on committing these crimes against humanity, and fail to recognize that we are as responsible for the death of one of humanity's greatest leaders, Martin Luther King, as if we had pulled the trigger ourselves.

ASHLEY MONTAGU
Princeton, N.J., April 4, 1968

The writer was responsible for drafting the first UNESCO Statement on Race, and is author of "Man's Most Dangerous Myth: The Fallacy of Race."

Negro Anti-Semitism

To the Editor:

I read Mr. Kovach's Oct. 23 article on Negro anti-Semitism in *The Times*, and I would say, after all, why should we segregate anti-Semites? Is there really a difference between white and colored anti-Semites?

More, of course, is involved than the fear of property deterioration, sloppy neighborhoods or interracial marriage. Negro anti-Semitism is a symptom of the dilemma of the American middle class. Again, wealth or middle-class status is no longer the goal in itself. Instead, these classes are afflicted with the fear of displacement.

Negro anti-Semitism takes into consideration all the Negroes' own resentment. Anyone who has ever succeeded loses his first "friend." It is much easier to believe that one has pulled himself up by his own bootstraps.

And the Jew was indeed the Negro's first friend, almost from the day the Negro was allowed a friend. The Jew was the first white man to grant the newly liberated Negro some degree of humanity. In the most rigid days of segregation Jewish peddlers began to sell the Negroes on credit and the Jew was the first white man to sell a Negro an insurance policy. But when most of the Christian-owned stores warned Negroes: "Don't touch unless you buy," the Jewish merchant allowed the Negro to try on the dress or the suit or the hat.

Elderly Negro women have told me that when the Jew "collector man" came around she insisted that the children see the book with their name on the account sheet, "Mr. and Mrs. Isaac Jones." These were the days in the Southern Christian society when if the Negroes purchased even a plug of tobacco it was put on the account sheet of the farmer or landowner for whom he worked.

There is no doubt there are Negro anti-Semites, and that as the Negroes escape the margins of society there will probably be many more Negro anti-Semites. And as Negroes enter the open society they may find the Jew a terrible burden. As his "first friend," the Jew must forever remain identified with the Negro status of racial inferiority. Fellowship with the Jew will prove no bargain for the Negro. The Jew knew him "when."

Basically, however, Negro anti-Semitism is peripheral to the whole subject, the main issue. Whether some Negroes are or are not anti-Semites bears not at all upon whether the Negroes achieve first-class citizenship and that their children are uninhibited and unimpeded by segregation and discrimination.

The Negro lawyers who have walked in and out of the American courtroom during these last twenty years have made the Constitution of the United States a living document. The struggle has convinced Americans and continues to convince them every day that the Constitution means just what it says. Thus we Jews have achieved a great victory, without even being exposed to the firing line.

Basically, however, a Negro anti-Semite is about as convincing as a Jewish white supremacist.

HARRY GOLDEN
Editor, the *Carolina Israelite*
Charlotte, N.C., Oct. 24, 1968

Blacks and Africa

To the Editor:

Many people who read of the unfortunate confrontation which occurred on March 22 following Tom Mboya's speech at the Countee Cullen Library in Harlem were deeply confused.

They had difficulty understanding why black Americans who are struggling for freedom in this country would verbally attack a revolutionary African leader who urged them to continue their struggle and not to abandon it by returning to Africa.

It is important to understand the dynamic that is involved here, since it bears heavily upon the relationship of all black Americans to their native soil—which is America.

The vast majority of Negroes profoundly desire social change in this country. They have a vision of freedom and equality which was articulated by Martin Luther King Jr. and which has not been destroyed despite centuries of suffering and daily indignities.

93

There have been major setbacks in the struggle for justice. Our society has not made the vast investment in resources required if black people are to have a full life in this country. Thus a small percentage of Negroes have lost faith in America. They argue that since equality is impossible within the larger society, one should opt out and establish separate institutions, and that one should be prepared ultimately to return to Africa.

This is a form of frustration politics that is far removed from reality. Africa has become for these Negroes an illusion which Mr. Mboya destroyed by reminding them that they are Americans, and that their identities have been forged in bitterness and suffering on this soil.

I think Mr. Mboya is to be congratulated for his forthright political analysis. He has rightfully directed our attention to the social problems in the United States.

And while he recognized the great influence that the creative protest of American Negroes has had in Africa, as well as the tremendous effect the African independence movement has had on the self-image of black people in this country, he has understood that Africa and America are separate nations, and that Negroes, though drawn toward one by ancient heritage, are the citizens of the other by birthright and experience.

And they cannot deny that citizenship without doing untold damage to their identity as black men and as human beings.

BAYARD RUSTIN
Executive Director
A. Philip Randolph Institute
New York, March 31, 1969

Racist Mother Goose

To the Editor:

Now that Mother Goose has been withdrawn with apologies from circulation as being "racist," how long will it be before the "Merchant of Venice" and "Ivanhoe" also are requested to disappear along with "Little Black Sambo," a little classic, beloved by all children and no more related to Harlem than the Eiffel Tower? What rot. And how tragic to allow this point of view to be emphasized.

ALICE R. H. DOERMANN
New York, April 3, 1969

Blacks' Lack of Power

To the Editor:

Recent actions of black students, and black militants in general, reveal a basic misunderstanding of the nature of power. Threats, arms, and destruction of property are accoutrements of power. But they do not represent true power. True power has an economic, political, technological, and, in a more limited sense, a moral basis.

Black Americans are not only a numerical minority but also a politically and economically deprived minority with no access to the technology of modern weapons. The limited success of the black militant has been due less to "black power" than to the reluctance of those in authority to bring "white power" to bear against him. Concessions have been made largely for political and moral reasons, but the white community is now in the process of demanding that these concessions come to an end.

Powerlessness and passivity for 350 years in the face of insult has produced a psychological need for the black American to create a more satisfactory image of himself. The militant has chosen to prove his manhood by projecting the image of the warrior. The development of black militancy is historically logical; however, it sets a series of incorrect priorities and tends to be self-defeating.

The basic problem which we black people face is to get ourselves together politically, economically, and psychologically. This problem cannot be solved if we waste time and effort by acting out the role of a warrior against the white establishment.

MORRIS JOHNSON
Bronx, N.Y., April 23, 1969

White-Black Income

To the Editor:

The rapidity or slowness with which the gap between white and black income is closing is increasingly more a matter of regional industrial growth or stagnation and cultural lags rather than racism and discriminatory patterns, whose intensity is assuredly declining.

The median income of black families in the central cities of the United States expressed as a per cent of the median income of white families reached an all-time but extremely modest high of 68 in 1967, compared to 61 in 1959.

However, in the western sector of the nation, the 1967 ratio of black family income to white within those thirteen states was 84 per cent, a spectacular rise from the 65 per cent of 1959. In the twelve North Central states, the 1967 figure was 75 per cent, compared to 68 in 1959, and in the 17-state South, the ratios were 62 and 52 per cent. Only in the Northeast did the Negro ratio decline, dropping from 69 per cent in 1959 to 68 per cent in 1967.

The thesis of this letter is substantially reinforced when the 1967 and 1959 median income of white families in the Northeast are used as the basis of comparison to Negro family income in the other three areas of the nation.

In 1959 the median income of Negro families in the West was 72 per cent of the median income of white families in the Northeast, but soared to 91 per cent in 1967. For the North Central states, the ratios were 74 and 82 per cent, and in the South, 50 and 63 per cent.

Expressed as a per cent of the 1967 median income of black families in the Northeast, Negro families in the West stood at 134 per cent, 121 per cent in the North Central states and 93 per cent in the South. The comparable figures for 1959 were 105, 107 and 72 per cent. Negro families in all three regions registered larger increases relatively and absolutely than in the Northeast.

Finally, median income of white families in the South caught up to and surpassed the Northeastern white family in 1967. The Southern advantage in 1967 was $124, compared to a disadvantage of $360 in 1959.

Only half-facetiously, Horace Greeley should be updated to read: Go West, young black man, and go South, young white man.

NICHOLAS KISBURG
Legislative and Research Director
Teamsters Joint Council 16
New York, April 13, 1969

Indebted to Rockefeller

To the Editor:

In 1909 the Rockefeller Sanitary Commission, well endowed with John D. Rockefeller money, tackled the hookworm problem in the South and elsewhere, and eventually cleared it up pretty well. They may even have contributed toward the well-being of the family of James Forman, who last Sunday disrupted the Riverside Church services, and among other animadversions, accused the Rockefellers of exploiting his people. *Sic transit.*

Oscar Baron
Yonkers, N.Y., May 5, 1969

Asking Reparations

To the Editor:

I have just read in your newspaper about the outrageous intrusion at Riverside Church on May 4, when a representative of the black militants demanded reparations.

If the question of reparations is going to be raised, then justice demands that there also be reparations to those who have been and are being injured by a proportionately small segment of the black population.

I refer not only to the businessmen ruined by looting and rioting, but also to the thousands and thousands of innocent victims of savagery. Most of these felonies are not reported in the newspapers—simply because, I imagine, it is so repetitious.

My family came to this country in 1634 and helped to build it from the very beginning. My husband's family has also made its contribution. He himself has paid heavy taxes for fifty years, done the work of two men day after day, given jobs to many people, and been of great value to his community. Recently he was twice attacked by hoodlums in broad daylight—the second time he was seriously injured. No amount of money could begin to make up for the anguish and pain he and his family suffered. But he has also sustained a loss in his business.

Reparations? Where shall I send *our* bill?

Ruth de Menezes
San Francisco, May 5, 1969

97

James Forman's Message

To the Editor:

The controversy surrounding the method of delivery of James Forman's message at Riverside Church should not obscure some real and very basic questions:

Why Riverside? Maybe because it was founded by John D. Rockefeller, to many whites and blacks a symbol of the white power structure in America. It is old, prestigious, borders Harlem and includes a number of middle-class blacks among its parishioners.

There is the legitimate concern of many as to whether the church, because of its nontaxable privileges, should be exempt from payment of taxes on funds in excess of those necessary for the maintenance and growth of its institution. It is common knowledge that some church organizations control extensive real estate holdings and investments, which, if taxed on all profits above operating costs, might very well provide income, in New York City alone, equal to the total New York City budget of about $6 billion. If these funds were voluntarily channeled into the numerous areas which constitute the "urban crisis," the role of the church might more rapidly improve the human condition and plight of many of those it purports to serve.

Let not our white, middle-class sense of propriety divert our attention from the truths, symbolic and practical, that Forman dramatically drove home. Frankly, I regret I was not present to share with him an expression of his moment of moral conscience and truth. Those who left the church offended might be the very ones who might have benefited most from his unorthodox participation in the liturgy.

The black community is well aware that it can no longer survive by spirit alone—but requires a larger slice of the bread of white America.

(RABBI) A. BRUCE GOLDMAN
Jewish Chaplain
Columbia University
New York, May 6, 1969

Rights of Black Panthers

To the Editor:

While I deplore as misguided and self-defeating the Black Panthers' recourse to arms, there can be no question that they have a right to keep and bear arms under the Second Amendment to the Constitution, as well as the right to assemble, speak and publish under the First Amendment.

And while every person who hopes for civil harmony and order must feel a tremendous sympathy for police officers who are insulted and provoked by verbal abuse as well as by physical threats, the case of two Black Panthers killed in Chicago raises again a question of police response which has broad constitutional overtones largely ignored by the public.

It seems to be widely accepted that police officers, in the course of fulfilling their duties, may on occasion be forced to "shoot to kill" a suspect or person they believe to be engaged in committing a crime or about to commit a crime. The question should be asked whether this view is not in direct conflict with the Fifth Amendment of the Constitution which states that no person shall be deprived of life, liberty or property, without due process of law.

When a police officer kills an individual in such a situation he is acting as prosecutor, judge, jury and executioner all in one short moment of time. Of course, the right of self-defense extends to police officers as to all citizens; but even self-defense need not involve killing.

Modern police methods and equipment yield a variety of highly effective ways to restrain or prevent actions of suspects without resort to this ultimate violation of due process. Our courts and law enforcement officials should consider establishment of the principle that police officers should never shoot to kill; that police methods should always insure the right of due process.

I think it highly unlikely, with police techniques now available, that such a rule would render law enforcement any less effective than it now is. On the contrary, because of the greater trust and respect it would engender for police officers, I believe it would increase their effectiveness significantly. But, more important, it would help re-establish the concept of rule of law, which has been so central in our country's history.

RICHARD B. ANGELL
Birmingham, Mich., Dec. 21, 1969

Mr. Angell wrote as Chairman and Professor, Department of Philosophy, Wayne State University.

99

Right To Bear Arms

To the Editor:

In a letter concerning the Black Panthers there occurred this statement: ". . . there can be no question that they have a right to keep and bear arms under the Second Amendment to the Constitution. . . ." There can indeed be a question.

The Second Amendment to the Constitution does not grant any absolute right to American citizens to keep or bear arms; it merely forbids Congress or the President to interfere with their doing so. But it leaves the states free to restrict the possession and use of firearms in any way they see fit, for the whole Bill of Rights applies solely to the national Government.

Those who proposed and voted for the first ten Amendments did not fear oppression by their state governments, but there was considerable fear that those who had drafted the Constitution, in their zeal "to form a more perfect union" might have established a too powerful central Government, which might become tyrannical and attempt to deprive the people of their natural rights.

It was to guard against this possibility that the first ten Amendments, limiting the powers of the central Government, were passed by the first Congress and ratified by the states. That these Amendments limited the powers of only the central Government was well understood at the time and remained unquestioned until the end of the Civil War.

The Civil War Amendments, however, and especially the 14th Amendment, opened up avenues through which at least some of the rights which had been protected in the Bill of Rights against infringement by the central Government could also henceforth be protected from infringement by the states.

Using these avenues the Supreme Court, especially in this century, has been able to cast the mantle of protection from state infringement about some of the rights mentioned in the original Bill of Rights.

The Court has not, however, attempted to cover with this mantle of protection *all* the rights mentioned in the first ten Amendments. I can recall no case in which the Supreme Court has attempted to prevent infringement by states of the right to keep and bear arms.

Therefore, Black Panthers and other citizens as well have no constitutional right to keep or bear arms in violation of laws which states have made or may make in the future restricting or abolishing such a right.

HAROLD W. THATCHER
Forty Fort, Pa., Dec. 30, 1969

Pampered Black Panthers

To the Editor:

Now that Leonard Bernstein has started the ball rolling I suppose that it will be quite fashionable among New York's beautiful people to extend invitations to the poor, oppressed Black Panther party propagandists.

On the basis of past events we shall soon witness the birth of local Rent-a-Panther organizations. For those who preach and practice the new "encounter" and "group therapy" games, an evening of anti-Establishment vituperations seems just right to bring out the *mea culpa* in all.

Just what this country needs—another outlet for unreasonable and unreasoned criticism. It's quite obvious that the Panthers will gladly welcome another soapbox from which to espouse their philosophy.

HARRY W. PORTER 3D
Fort Lee, N.J., Jan. 15, 1970

Black Panthers' Legal Aid

To the Editor:

As a civil libertarian, I asked a number of people to my house on Jan. 14 in order to hear the lawyer and others involved with the Panthers 21 discuss the problem of civil liberties as applicable to the men now awaiting trial, and to help raise funds for their legal expenses.

Those attending included responsible members of the black leadership as well as distinguished citizens from a variety of walks of life, all of whom share common concern on the subject of civil liberties and equal justice under our laws.

The outcome of the Panther 21 trial will be determined by the judge and jury. That was not our concern. But the ability of the defendants to prepare a proper defense will depend on the help given prior to the trial, and this help must not be denied because of lack of funds.

It was for this deeply serious purpose that our meeting was called. The frivolous way in which it was reported as a "fashionable" event is unworthy of *The Times,* and offensive to all people who are committed to humanitarian principles of justice.

FELICIA M. BERNSTEIN
New York, Jan. 16, 1970

101

The Moynihan Memo

To the Editor:

The Moynihan Memorandum on the Status of Negroes is a superb parody of the meretricious cant which no doubt ends up on any President's desk. I am concerned, however, that President Nixon, burdened as he is with so many weightier matters, may take it seriously.

ANTHONY TOWNE
Block Island, R.I., March 3, 1970

Moynihan's Critics

To the Editor:

Do the civil rights leaders who signed the statement attacking the "benign neglect" memorandum really believe their approach to improving the lives of poor blacks will do more for them than Dr. Moynihan's? They call upon a morally and politically confused and divided nation to act directly in favor of the interests of Negroes—and this at a time when a majority of the electorate has only recently demonstrated it prefers to support Presidential candidates who promise nothing to Negroes.

Dr. Moynihan seeks, in a dark time, to define policies which assist the poor and deprived and which can simultaneously win support in an Administration and Congress which reflect a conservative electorate.

The Family Assistance Program, of which Dr. Moynihan was the principal mover, and which he helped make the policy of a conservative Administration, will put billions into the hands of black poor, working and nonworking. It has gone as far as it has—further than anyone dreamed possible—because it is not standard liberal or civil rights legislation. No civil rights legislation could have done as much for the black poor—even if it could have been passed, or, if passed, enforced.

Why cannot the civil rights leaders look behind the phrase to the policies Dr. Moynihan has fought for in this Administration? Do they really think Negroes and other deprived groups would be better off if he were not in it?

NATHAN GLAZER
Cambridge, Mass., March 6, 1970

The writer is the author, with Daniel P. Moynihan, of "Beyond the Melting Pot."

'Fantasy of Black Life'

To the Editor:

The hyperbole of that darling of the press, Daniel Patrick Moynihan, on black progress fast is being surpassed by the incredible statements in his support by his zealous coterie.

The latest case in point is the letter of Prof. James Q. Wilson. Mr. Wilson informs us that while in 1960, 8 per cent of blacks had incomes over $10,000, 21 per cent have such incomes today. This is a statement that must make even Mr. Moynihan's Celtic imagination boggle.

Presumably, Mr. Wilson is talking about black family income, but he does not say so. This is quite a different matter. How different can be seen by the stark fact that it takes three wage earners in a black family to earn the median income of almost $8,000 that a single white wage earner makes.

Professor Wilson goes on to agree with Mr. Moynihan that what is wrong is not the "race problem" in the United States, because "when most members of (the black) race are making great gains some are making no gains at all." This is a fantasy of black life in the central cities and the countryside where these Americans are overwhelmingly to be found.

To stick to the data, one-half of black families still earn less than the income the Bureau of Labor Statistics tells us is required as a minimum adequate level of living. Moreover, there is no evidence that attainment of a high school diploma has any influence on that income.

One could go on to wage statistics, but what is most disturbing is that a scholar of Professor Wilson's repute should make such slovenly use of data. It may never be understood by Professors Moynihan and Wilson and others of their persuasion that when academics of their public reputation represent and interpret socially sensitive data in ways that are certainly open to question—and it is doubtful that they would submit in scholarly presentation to the judgment of their colleagues—their impulses are bound to be widely seen among blacks as racistic.

LISLE C. CARTER JR.
Ithaca, N.Y., March 17, 1970

IV·Atomic Bombs and Missiles

The explosion of the atom bomb on Hiroshima in 1945 ended a war, but filled a nation with horror. It marked the beginning of an agonizing reappraisal by man, who now knew he had the power to destroy himself. The shock and revulsion induced by knowledge of the bomb were soon temporarily muted by discovery that the Soviet Union also had the devastating weapon.

The efforts of men and governments to avoid a suicidal arms race in favor of a program of disarmament hold the world's attention. Strategies, proposals, efforts to control testing and the hazards of radioactive fall-out evoked a heavy mail from scientists, statesmen and citizens. The continuing debate over missiles and the overkill strategy of the Pentagon raised serious questions among readers of *The Times*, who put them to Washington and the rest of the country in the letters columns of the newspaper.

Inches of progress—the seabed treaty and non-proliferation pact —were widely hailed. There is hope in the promise of the Strategic Arms Limitation Talks. Every turn in the long, difficult road to disarmament has been mapped by *The Times*' readership in its letters to the editor.

Bomb Stirs Mixed Feelings

To the Editor of *The New York Times:*

The destruction of Hiroshima by an atomic bomb fills me with horror. Sixty per cent of the city was destroyed and presumably 60 per cent of the population—men, women and children—were killed. There was no pretense of precision bombing for military purposes and the notice that the city was to be bombed contained no statement to anticipate such a hideous result as occurred. It is a stain upon our national life.

Neither Germany nor ourselves used poison gas, nor have the Japanese done so except in isolated instances, if then. Here was a device far more deadly and far more indiscriminate than poison gas and it has probably wiped out 60 per cent of the 300,000 people of that city. If the use of this terrible power can be confined to war personnel and war material all right; but if it will result in the killing of 100,000 women and children, it is all wrong.

When the exhilaration of this wonderful discovery has passed we will think with shame of the first use to which it was put.

WM. CHURCH OSBORN
Garrison, N.Y., Aug. 8, 1945

Disposal Suggestion

To the Editor of *The New York Times:*

Science has reached to the fringe of the universe and stolen the secret of life inviolate since the beginning of time.

Let us thank God the larceny was ours and not our enemies and then dump the whole thing into the middle of the Atlantic or the Pacific, whichever is deeper.

Man is too frail a being to be entrusted with such power as atomic energy possesses.

WILLIAM H. FANNING
Shoreham, Vt., Aug. 8, 1945

Atomic Test Queried

To the Editor of *The New York Times:*

The recent editorial, "The Atomic Bomb Tests" in *The Times* contains statements which should be clarified. I believe a correct understanding of the situation leads to the conclusion that the tests should not be held.

Let us agree first that the huge initial cost of the ships to be used in the tests has nothing to do with the argument. Only a tiny fraction of them will be destroyed and they are certainly just about worthless now anyway.

Let us also waive the argument about the international implications of the tests. I am not competent to comment on them, though it is my own belief that further "showing off" of the atomic bomb at this time is in poor taste, to say the least.

Let us see, then, whether the scientific values of the tests are sufficient to justify the cost and the risks. You state that "there were no scientists in the area—at Hiroshima and Nagasaki." I happen to know personally several excellent scientists who were either in the bomb-carrying plane or an accompanying plane on one or both of these missions, and I know others who made extensive surveys on the ground shortly afterward. What happened when these two bombs went off is no scientific secret. Good measurements and good observations were made.

You also state that "the New Mexico tests were on a small scale." I thought everyone knew by now that there is no such thing as a small-scale atomic bomb. Scientifically speaking, these tests were on a big scale. The most brilliant scientific talent of the country was concentrated on the New Mexico tests. Oppenheimer, Bacher, Bethe, Bainbridge, Rossi, Kistiakowski, Weisskopf, and a host of other top men planned and carried out these tests. Not one of these men is involved in the Bikini tests. They are all back at their peacetime university positions, and so are most of their key assistants. Clearly, there is no assurance that the Bikini tests "will answer with scientific accuracy many of the still unanswered questions." On the contrary, many young scientists who are participating are discouraged about learning anything at all on tests which have been so hurriedly organized and which must be carried out under such difficult conditions. I think it is safe to dismiss as negligible the scientific value of the tests.

What, then, about the military value? You state "the tests in the Pacific would provide clarification of the use of the atomic bomb as a military weapon." Any scientist can tell you right now that neither an air nor a surface burst is a sensible way to use an atomic bomb against ships. Here again you are in error by describing the second test as an "underwater" rather than a "surface" test. A real underwater test (e.g., 2,000 feet under)—which might be effective, or at least would teach something new—has not yet been scheduled. What of value can be learned from an experiment in which a weapon is incorrectly or wastefully used? We know that an air burst will damage well-built structures over an area of about three or four square miles. The fleet in the Bikini tests, it is reported, will be spread out over 100 square miles. Clearly, only three or four out of ninety ships will be damaged. Dr. Hans Bethe has already stated in the April *Science Illustrated*, "We can expect no sinking of capital ships, perhaps not even of destroyers."

You say, "If the tests are as destructively successful as the atomic scientists believe they will be, they should be a necessary reminder of the fearfulness of this new weapon." Precisely the opposite is true. The atomic scientists do not believe the tests as planned will be destructive against naval targets at all. They anticipate already the screaming headlines, "Atomic Bomb Fails to Sink Fleet." The public reaction will be that the atomic bomb is not so bad after all, and there are many people who will encourage such a reaction. Thus positive harm rather than good will result from the test. Why not ask now rather than later the pertinent question of who wants to waste an atomic bomb on a fleet anyway when it can destroy a whole city?

If we really want a test which, as you say, "will clarify the current Navy-Air controversies as to whether navies . . . are obsolete," why not ask atomic bomb experts what kind of a bomb they would design and how they would use it if the objective was to destroy a fleet rather than a city. Give them a year or two to design the weapon and to set up the tests and the measurements. Then and only then will the tests clarify rather than confuse this issue.

L. A. DuBridge
Rochester, N.Y., April 25, 1946

The writer is Professor of Physics at the University of Rochester, and was formerly director of the Massachusetts Institute of Technology Radiation Laboratory in Rochester.

Atomic Tests Defended

To the Editor of *The New York Times:*

In a letter to *The New York Times* of May 5 Dean L. A. DuBridge of the University of Rochester criticized the forthcoming atomic bomb tests on the grounds that

(1) The tests will be of little value scientifically because adequate data were secured from the previous bomb explosions.

(2) Top nuclear physicists are not serving in the Task Force.

(3) The wide spacing of the target vessels will result in an unimpressive amount of damage to them and will accordingly produce a false sense of security in the minds of the public concerning the significance of an atomic attack.

(4) The tests will have no military value since it is not sensible "to waste an atomic bomb on a fleet anyway when it can destroy a whole city."

His letter serves to highlight a point of view which has been expressed from time to time and which, it seems to us, rests on a misunderstanding of various aspects of the coming atomic bomb tests.

We cannot agree that "good measurements and good observations were made" of the earlier explosions of such quantity and quality as to render further experiments unnecessary. The scientific data obtained from those tests leave much to be desired. At the time of the New Mexico tests the scientists themselves were in almost complete agreement that, had more time been available and had they been able to make closer estimates of the pressures and radiation intensities to be expected, they could have obtained a much larger amount of valuable data. Indeed, it would have hardly been possible to obtain all the information that is scientifically required in one experiment, which was also the first one in an absolutely new field.

Although it is true that two or three scientists observed the explosions over Japan, the fact is that visual observations alone are not at all suited to providing the numerical data needed for an adequate analysis of such an explosion. Furthermore, these scientists were able to transport with them and to operate only a very few instruments. They were consequently unable to obtain any photograph of technical value or, most important, any numerical data on radiation intensity. While considerable information was obtained some time later by United States technical men inspecting Hiroshima and Nagasaki, these men agree that the story they have been able to piece together is far from complete. A majority of the inspection teams did not reach these cities until three to six weeks after the explosions, by which time much of the information, particularly the medical information, had become greatly obscured.

In short, we know relatively little about the radiological and blast effects in air of an atomic bomb explosion and can estimate only very roughly the radioactivity and shock effects that may be produced in the ocean. Even if we knew all these things, our most competent scientists and naval constructors could only make very incomplete estimates of the effects of air blasts and water shocks of such great violence and so widely extended area and duration on ships and their equipment. Nor are the facts on ship damage obtainable from scale tests alone, although such facts are vitally needed to strengthen existing ships and improve future design.

It is true and in fact entirely proper that, as Dean DuBridge states, the majority of the Los Alamos nuclear physicists have returned to their universities and to the training of the nuclear physicists of the future. But it is also a fact that a large number of first-class men are still connected with the Manhattan Project. Assembling the entire or even a major portion of the original Los Alamos group once more for a military test would be a major interruption of our scientific life which could hardly be justified in peacetime.

It should perhaps also be pointed out that the principal purpose of these tests is the carrying out of a wide variety of measurements, the great majority of which call for technical rather than theoretical skill. The Task Force's complement of roughly 1,000 scientists, engineers and technicians is peculiarly well fitted for this work. Indeed it is essential that the tests be completed while this group is still at full strength. These men are accustomed to field operations and the equipment supplied them for these tests is magnificent. There is no doubt that they will obtain much data of a type and scope that was not, and could not have been, obtained from the previous explosions, and which the armed forces feel is vital and unobtainable in any other way.

Dean DuBridge's comment concerning the wide spacing of the target vessels suffers from the fact that the exact spacing to be used has not been announced. For example, he states that the target vessels will be dispersed over an area of 100 square miles. Actually more than a score of the vessels, including many of the largest, will be concentrated in a central area of approximately one square mile, and nearly all the vessels will be grouped within a total central area of approximately ten square miles.

It should be further noted that while we anticipate a number of sinkings and a good deal of severe damage, one of the major purposes of the test is to obtain scientific data and detailed information on all grades of damage. Also, many measurements will have to be made which require as a platform ships at a greater distance that are definitely not sunk.

The deep underwater test (incapable of execution at this time but definitely planned for 1947) will do a different type of damage than either of the bursts planned for this year. Regardless of over-all damage comparisons, it is only by means of an air burst that the full effects of the various lethal radiations can be determined. Although the air-burst test is generally applicable, particularly to ships in harbors which are ordinarily relatively shallow, the deep underwater test applies principally to ships steaming in open sea. Here the separation of the ships could of course be increased to such an extent that a single bomb would seriously affect only one or two of them.

The contention that atomic bombs would be used against cities rather than "wasted" on fleets is perhaps true in the case of a user country which already has an unmatched fleet; but any country which is inferior to us in naval strength might well regard our large and far-flung Navy as a logical target.

It seems to us that the information to be obtained in the forthcoming tests is vital to increasing the defensive strength of the Navy.

RALPH A. SAWYER
JOHN VON NEUMANN
Princeton, N.J. May 7, 1946

The writers are, respectively, Technical Director of Joint Task Force One, and Scientific Adviser to Joint Task Force One. In addition, Dr. Sawyer is Professor of Mathematics, Institute for Advanced Study, Princeton.

General Disarmament Asked

To the Editor of *The New York Times:*

What concrete proposals can be made to meet the situation created by the atomic explosion in the Soviet Union? We are faced with crucial alternatives. To us it seems that in the last analysis the possible courses of action reduce themselves to two: Either an atomic arms race that can only lead to unthinkable disaster, or an effective program for universal disarmament.

It is desirable that the citizens of our country consider this situation and try to suggest solutions that are practical. In view of this the Women's

International League for Peace and Freedom urges that serious consideration be given to the following recommendations:

Recognizing that disagreement on means of controlling large-scale atomic energy production has been the chief cause of the deadlock in the Atomic Energy Commission, we recommend that all nations agree to stop simultaneously and at once the production of atomic bombs and, for the time being, the stockpiling of atomic fuel until further research reveals ways of using large-scale production of atomic energy for peaceful purposes and until adequate international control has been achieved.

Recognizing that nations under constant threat of war may be unwilling to eliminate from their arsenals such a decisive weapon as the atomic bomb and that, in any case, international security cannot be secured by the elimination of any one weapon alone, we recommend that, in conformity with the U.N. resolution of Dec. 14, 1946, the elimination of all weapons of mass destruction (atomic and other bombs, biological and chemical weapons) and the reduction of conventional armaments be considered as one problem and that means be sought at once to achieve general disarmament.

Recognizing that effective international agreements on disarmament must have the force of binding law, we recommend that they be enforced by a system of inspection to be initiated in all nations simultaneously under the authority of the U.N. and by a world police force capable of arresting individual violators and bringing them to trial before the World Court.

Recognizing the demonstrated value of disinterested mediation in international disputes, we recommend that a permanent board of mediation be set up by the U.N. to operate in all disputes between member states, including all disputes about the program for general disarmament.

A preliminary step in the direction of securing international agreement might very well be acceptance of the proposal of the Indian delegation to the United Nations to charge the Commission on International Law with the task of dealing with this matter.

EMILY GREENE BALCH, Honorary International President
GERTRUDE C. BUSSEY, International Co-Chairman
OLIVE I. REDDICK, Chairman, Policy Committee, U.S. Section
GLADYS WALSER, U.N. Observer for U.S. Section
ANNALEE STEWART, President, U.S. Section
Washington, Oct. 6, 1949

112

Government for Peace

To the Editor of *The New York Times:*

The scientists predicted right. Russia has had an atomic explosion, perhaps a bomb, and all the world knows it. For the moment, at least, another wave of fear has swept over mankind.

When the bomb was dropped on Hiroshima, killing 80,000 innocent human beings, the world was stunned. For the first time in history it was realized that man had at last unleashed such forces in nature that he could destroy himself.

One would have thought that the discovery and inevitable development of such forces would have been sufficient to bring into being such an overwhelming unity for action as would weld all men together under heroic leadership to abolish war. Instead of such leadership, what have we witnessed? The governments and statesmen are deadlocked. They have little to offer but military preparedness, armed alliances and negotiation, none of which has ever yet contributed to the essential solution of the problem of war and peace.

Theodore Roosevelt, when he left the Presidency and took a hunting trip in the African jungle, wrote a book of experiences. There are some striking sentences in his introduction in which he describes a lion attacking a herd of zebras. He tells how they fled in an agony of terror until the lion had seized one of them. And then, when the survivors were out of danger, they almost instantly stopped running and resumed their browsing and grazing, just as though they had not been at the point of death only a few minutes before.

After Hiroshima, men including their leaders, dashed about and cried out in their consternation and terror. But soon they were occupying themselves with their daily concerns, browsing and grazing in their own private preserves, just as though the terrible danger did not still hang over their heads.

That was our first call to reality. Russia's acquisition of the bomb is the second call.

Are these two calls enough to arouse us at last to compel our governments to stop playing with palliatives and get to the heart of the problem?

The peace problem is nothing but the substitution of reason for force, right for might, law for war. That means that sooner or later we must establish a government over the nations with the power to enforce world law with every legislative, judicial and police power necessary to maintain peace.

113

The monster of war must be dethroned and the majesty of law must be enthroned. This is the immediate and paramount issue before every one of us.

HAMILTON HOLT, GEORGE C. HOLT
Woodstock, Conn., Oct. 3, 1949

Strategy of Defense

To the Editor of *The New York Times:*

This statement is the product of a deep apprehension over the present strategic position of the United States. It is addressed to questions of military strategy and to these alone. We emphasize that we do not regard military defense as the only or even the first source of security of the United States. That security we regard, first of all, as depending on the economic strength and political cooperation of the free world. These latter are the first tasks of American policy.

We are concerned here with military policy, not as a means of preparing for war, but as a means of gaining time during which economic and political efforts may help create the situations out of which lasting peace may emerge.

We believe that our present strategic position is founded on a misplaced faith in atomic weapons and strategic bombing. This system of defense seems to us, for reasons we shall set forth below, to impair the moral and physical strength of the United States in the present period and to evade the true requirements of national security. We believe that the United States must move beyond its present central reliance on atomic warfare and must accept the costs in money and inconvenience involved in such a shift in policy. These costs are to be measured against the loss of American moral position in the free world, the invitation to limited aggression inherent in the present strategy, and the possibly catastrophic dangers to ourselves and civilization in an atomic war.

We believe that the civilian may properly speak on questions of national defense. While the plans for defense cannot be the property of all citizens, an important distinction is to be drawn between essentials and details. It is the details that must remain secret. The fundamental problems are the proper concern of all; and it is to such fundamentals that this statement is applied.

The power which forces the United States to adopt a posture of defense is the Soviet Union. We make no estimate as to the immediacy of the Soviet threat to the security of the United States and Western Europe. For present purposes we assume the danger, and the corresponding need for Western military strength sufficient to deter Soviet aggression. The difference between a deterrent force and one that accords absolute security in the event of actual aggression must be emphasized. In case of actual war, the nation can have only the single objective of overwhelming superiority; but the prevention of war is a different undertaking and there is room for argument as to the size and nature of the effort required. The present defensive position of the United States depends heavily on its possession of atomic weapons coupled with faith in strategic bombardment. This has been made evident in the recent controversies over the roles of the several services and in the allocation of defense appropriations. It is implicit in the size and distribution of our ground forces—the fact that at present the United States has about ten divisions, few of which are fully manned and equipped—and in the subordinate role assigned to tactical air power.

This defense plan, with its emphasis on atomic weapons and strategic air power, has been misleadingly attractive to the American people and Congress. It has promised us all great economies in financial outlay, in manpower, and in political inconvenience. We believe that this plan has been shaped less by a dispassionate view of the United States in the world than by political factors, including the ebb and flow of interservice rivalry.

However, it is less important to allocate responsibility for present strategy than to assess its consequences. These, we believe, raise questions which go to the roots of the position of the United States in the world.

1. United States strategy today is not well equipped to deal with problems of limited aggression. We accept the view that the essential deterrent to all-out Soviet attack is the conviction that such attack would provoke a general war with the United States. But there are degrees of Soviet pressure short of open military aggression; and to this form of limited aggression—such as sponsorship of "revolution" or of guerrilla operations in independent countries—the United States may have no effective response except an atomic war. This condition may invite the extension of techniques of guerrilla warfare and internal revolt in marginal areas in the confidence that such local activity would incur only local risks.

2. The predominant reliance by the United States on atomic warfare may weaken the morale and confidence of our European allies. Unless we have substantial ground, naval and tactical air forces available to supply immediate help in the event of Soviet aggression, our allies may be the less disposed to make the necessary efforts and sacrifices to

115

prepare for such an ordeal. Yet their present strength and their will-to-resist are important elements among the factors which can deter Russian aggression and avert war. Anything that weakens the will-to-resist of our allies therefore jeopardizes the peace we are striving to maintain.

3. The present reliance by the United States on the threat of the bomb is continuing indication to the world that American military strategy accepts the principle of mass destruction of human life. This can only lead to a damaging misconstruction of American motives and character and to resentment of American power. It has already contributed to the conviction that the United States is a dangerous ally and has strengthened the search for neutrality or some other form of immunity as between the United States and Russia.

4. To the extent that the United States has placed extensive reliance on the bomb, it has become more difficult for the United States to accept agreement restricting the use of atomic weapons. Such an agreement today would, in effect, constitute unilateral disarmament. To the degree that it has liberated its own defense strategy from its present central commitment to atomic weapons, the United States will be the more free to press for international control of atomic energy as part of a general system of disarmament. In the meantime, if control of atomic energy, with genuine inspection and safeguards, is impossible, the United States has no alternative but to continue to build up its atomic strength for the certainty of retaliation is probably the major deterrent to atomic warfare.

5. The peacetime defects of our present strategy are matched by equally serious defects in time of war. There may be the hope, however faint, that in case of war both sides may hesitate to initiate the use of atomic weapons, through fear of the inevitable retaliation. But there is not the slightest ground for hope that mutual fear may thus spare the world if either side is dependent on atomic weapons as its main instrument of war.

Atomic war has no clear limits. If the battle should be joined in Western Europe, the Red Army could be subjected to direct atomic attack only at the expense of blotting out the people and the cultural heritage which the North Atlantic Pact has committed us to defend.

The employment of the bomb on Russian soil, whatever its immediate military advantages, would complicate vastly any post-war rehabilitation of the Russian nation. And, now that the bomb is no longer a United States monopoly, Americans must recognize their own exceptional vulnerability to this weapon.

Our population and our industry are highly concentrated; our main cities are easily accessible by air and water. We are dependent on intricate and fragile systems of communication and transport. As a people we are not accustomed to the shock of military catastrophe. Moreover, where our vulnerability is relatively great, that of Britain is virtually total. An atomic war would almost certainly result in the obliteration of our closest ally. It is one of the tragic contradictions of our time that American strategy has organized the science and technology of the nation around weapons which, when imitated abroad, are potentially most dangerous to itself and its friends.

From the standpoint of its desire to achieve moral leadership in world affairs, the United States can ill afford a strategy which commits it in advance to warfare of mass slaughter on both sides—which might doom it to the fearful choice between world-wide mass destruction, on the one hand, and outright military defeat, on the other.

The emphasis on the weakness of the present strategy is justified if only to stimulate, the search for alternatives. We assume that responsible members of our military establishment have this problem constantly in mind; but, inasmuch as military decisions must be circumscribed by political considerations, we believe that the problem will benefit from public discussion.

It seems clear that important alternatives have so far been set aside, not on their merits, but because of the strategic commitment to and the popular faith in atomic weapons. The danger of exclusive or even predominant reliance on the atomic alternative must now be clear.

The question of the kind of conventional military force which would supplement the bomb as a deterrent is one the American people must now face. The development of an adequate ground army, the strengthening of our tactical air wing, the supply and logistic components, including the provision for air transport, the development of anti-submarine and other specialized naval forces, the use of the draft—all these problems pose questions not easily answered.

But these questions, we believe, must be answered if the United States policy is to be liberated from its present overwhelming dependence on atomic warfare. We call upon our political and military leaders to explore these issues with the American people.

DUNCAN S. BALLANTINE, MCGEORGE BUNDY
SAVILLE P. DAVIS, MARTIN DEUTSCH, J. K. GALBRAITH
WILLIAM R. HAWTHORNE, JOHN E. SAWYER
ARTHUR M. SCHLESINGER JR., CHARLES H. TAYLOR
JEROME B. WIESNER, JERROLD R. ZACHARIAS
Cambridge, Mass., April 26, 1950

The signers are members of the faculties of Harvard University and the Massachusetts Institute of Technology.

117

Proposal to Disarm Discussed

To the Editor of *The New York Times:*

Your June 8 editorial entitled "A Disarmament Plan" attacks a resolution which ten other Congressmen and myself introduced into the Senate and House. I was not a little puzzled when I read your words of warning. I thoroughly agree with them, as do my co-sponsors. As a matter of fact, in our resolution, we tried to bend over backward in repudiating the very evils you so rightly condemn.

You say, for instance, that "to agree to a one-sided disarmament plan now would be national suicide." We heartily agree with you. For this precise reason, our resolution stresses again and again that if our nation is to disarm, there must be effective and certain guarantees (through inspection and other means) that Russia will also disarm in the same degree and under the same conditions.

You observe that making ourselves impotent while Russia remains powerful would be the height of folly "and would bewilder and dismay our European allies." Once more, and of course, we heartily agree with you. That is why we took great pains to underscore the imperative necessity for world-wide, foolproof safeguards against bad faith in any agreement controlling weapons.

If these conditions are observed—and only then—we ask that all countries take the money they would otherwise have spent on weapons and give it instead to a United Nations fund—where it would be used for constructive purposes throughout the world. Given the necessary safeguards and methods of enforcement, this proposal should grip the imaginations of people everywhere and make dramatically clear the sincerity and ardor with which Americans seek a just peace.

Our resolution also calls for an immediate session of the United Nations General Assembly to consider international control over weapons. Surely you favor, rather than oppose, U.N. debates on this subject. If they lead to an acceptable agreement, mankind will have taken the first step on the road to salvation. If the debates lead to nothing, we Americans will at least have tested one more possibility; at least we will have continued to discharge our moral duty to strive tirelessly, hopefully and positively for peace with justice.

I wonder if a re-reading of our resolution will not persuade you that it not only bespeaks common sense but voices America's conscience as well.

BRIEN McMAHON
Chairman, Joint Committee on Atomic Energy
Washington, June 9, 1950

Using the Atom for Peace

To the Editor of *The New York Times*:

The forthcoming United Nations-sponsored International Conference on the Peaceful Uses of Nuclear Energy, which will convene in Geneva on Aug. 8 of this year, could well mark the beginning of a new era of international cooperation.

This conference will mark the first time since the ill-fated United Nations discussions of 1947–48 that scientists and engineers from both sides of the "Curtain" will sit together in an attempt to arrive at an understanding on questions of a purely technical nature. Indeed, if the conference can manage to avoid becoming entangled in irrelevant political problems, there is every reason to hope that there may emerge a blueprint for future international collaboration in the development of nuclear energy.

The events leading up to the organization of the conference augur well for its success. President Eisenhower's original proposal for the pooling of resources and efforts in the field of nuclear power was enthusiastically received abroad. The resolution calling for the organization of the conference passed through the United Nations in an unaccustomed display of unanimity with a minimum of wrangling over details.

The delegates to the meeting at which the conference agenda was agreed upon were scientists of international repute who according to all reports had little difficulty in agreeing upon an agenda.

Provided the delegates are well selected and provided their instructions are sufficiently broad to allow uninhibited scientific discussions, we can be sure that much of significance will emerge in the conference sessions. But can we be sure that this last condition will be met?

The field of nuclear power is still beset, in many countries, by a broad and unnecessary network of restrictions on the release of information. If the Geneva conference is to be a success, these restrictions must be removed. The United States can and should take the lead in removing the barriers to the free flow of information.

No new legislation is required for such action on our part. The Atomic Energy Act of 1954 permits the Atomic Energy Commission to throw open the field of nuclear power. The law leaves the means and the timing to the discretion of the commission. The Geneva conference provides an unexcelled occasion for such action by the commission.

It is becoming increasingly evident that the field of nuclear power is well on the way toward becoming an "unclassified" field. The pressures of American industry, anxious to participate in a field of such obvious promise, are already making themselves strongly felt in this direction. In an article in *The New York Times* of Feb. 20 Professor Whitman, head of the M.I.T. Chemical Engineering Department, is stated to believe "that there is a strong feeling that within a year or so all but a small percentage of secret data on weapons will be declassified." What better time than now?

It is said that the budding American nuclear power industry would be subject to unfair competition from foreign industries if all of our knowledge, acquired at such great expense, were released. But at least at this stage, when American industry has not yet made many significant contributions to the field of nuclear energy, this knowledge belongs to all the American people.

It has been further argued that this would be, on our part, a unilateral action which would only be meaningful if it were followed by similar actions on the part of other nations. What, we are asked, will be gained if other nations do not follow suit?

Leaving aside all questions of propaganda, it does not seem at all likely that such an action would remain unilateral for even a short time. For if a nation with such a great fund of knowledge in this field were to release its information other nations could not fail to follow.

Furthermore, there is every reason to believe that such a general de-classification of the field of nuclear power would result in a net gain for us, as well as for other nations. We have no reliable information on Russian progress in the field. But there is every indication that the British are at least as, if not more, advanced in the field of nuclear technology as we. Under these conditions the general removal of security barriers can only result in accelerated progress in all countries.

Finally, we have recently been assured by spokesmen for the Atomic Energy Commission that a significant amount of information is scheduled to be released, through the normal channels, for the Geneva conference. So, it may be argued, no special action is necessary. However, to release information piecemeal is by no means the same as to throw open the entire field, even though the same information may be involved in both procedures.

In the former case workers outside the security barrier have every reason to believe that something is still being held back. Under such circumstances the psychological barriers are so great that it is practically impossible to hold a free and uninhibited discussion.

Actually, nothing short of a general declassification of the entire field of nuclear power can assure success at Geneva.

The United States has a great stake in the success of this conference. We have been its initiator and, until recently, its main proponent. The world will regard our actions in this field as a real test of the sincerity of our proposals. If this conference should be a failure, a serious blow will have been struck against the possibility of coexistence and survival. Success, on the other hand, will arouse new vigor in those who seek a way out of the impasse in which the world now finds itself.

BERNARD T. FELD
Cambridge, Mass., March 8, 1955

The writer was associated with the Manhattan Project. Now Associate Professor of Physics at the Massachusetts Institute of Technology, his present field of research is high-energy nuclear physics.

Uses of Atomic Science

To the Editor of *The New York Times:*

Readers who scan our newspaper headlines or have read Bruno Pontecorvo's statement might, at times, feel doubt enter their minds and believe that we only pursue destructive aspects of atomic energy. Let me hasten to correct this impression by mentioning the following fact, which has not been emphasized enough.

Our scientific journals contain thousands of detailed articles on medical, biological, archaeological and technical uses of atomic science and on new advances acquired through it in all basic sciences. This new knowledge is disseminated for the benefit of all the world.

In contrast, the Russian journals in all those years, in spite of their propaganda, do not contain one single technical article on these peaceful uses of atomic energy. All we know for sure about the Russians is that they have exploded a few bombs.

S. A. GOUDSMIT
Upton, N.Y., March 2, 1955

The writer, co-discoverer of the "spin of the electron," was detailed by the War Department as chief of Scientific Intelligence Mission in Europe. He is now a senior physicist at Brookhaven.

Control of Nuclear Tests

To the Editor of *The New York Times:*

On Jan. 14 an excellent letter appeared in your columns urging that economic aid to distressed or backward areas be administered by the United Nations instead of being used as a bait in the economic phase of the cold war between the United States and the U.S.S.R. The suggestion is far too sane and sensible to be adopted, no doubt. But even to consider it gives a hint of the better world we would live in were such a procedure possible.

I think it is well to put beside this suggestion another one. If only the tests of nuclear weapons with which Russia and the United States now terrify each other were put under the direction of the U.N. we would have another powerful factor in the world situation working toward peace instead of war.

We know too well that under the world's present temper neither of these processes, the relief of misery or the development of destructive power, can be put entirely into the hands of international order, where in a reasonable world they would belong. But just at this time, with many nations, especially in the tumultuous Near East, clamoring for aid, and with a new test series of explosions announced, one step in the right direction could be taken: the United States could propose putting the great flood-control plan on the Nile under the administration of the United Nations and at the same time invite the U.N. to administer the atomic tests set for this spring in the Pacific.

Such a step would by no means solve the problems of putting all world relief or all world armament control into the hands of an international agency. But it would be a bold move in that direction. And the millions who live in misery, the millions who live in terror, would glimpse for a moment the sort of world their hearts desire.

PENNINGTON HAILE
New York, Jan. 13, 1956

Determining Fallout

To the Editor of *The New York Times:*

Whether or not the radioactive fallout is likely to reach the minimal harmful level is a problem discussed in many quarters. I want to point out that we do not know where this level is. The main experiments on this line have been conducted on mice or fruit flies. If conducted well and over long periods they may give an exact answer to what the permissible limits are for mice or fruit flies, but will have no validity for man simply because man is neither a mouse nor a fruit fly.

Nobody can be more convinced than I am of the unity of living nature and, as I often have pointed out, there is no fundamental difference between "cabbages and kings." This pertains to the basic principles but not to the subtler biological reactions involved in problems of human health and disease.

I also want to point out a fallacy of statistics. If, for instance, incidence in leukemia would rise by a small fraction, say .1 per cent, this may seem insignificant indeed. But, .1 per cent may mean, in time, 1,500 cases. Fifteen hundred dead children, laid out in a row, would look different from the number .1 per cent, and I suspect that if the children of those who think the number .1 per cent insignificant would be among the 1,500, they would arrive at a different evaluation.

I know that those who shape national policies have to weigh one chance against the other and may have to balance the .1 per cent against millions of lives lost in a possible war. But maybe the human intellect can find a way to peace which does not lead over the dead bodies of children.

ALBERT SZENT-GYORGYI
Woods Hole, Mass., March 31, 1958

The writer is Director of the Institute for Muscle Research. He was Nobel Prize winner in 1937 in physiology and medicine.

Genetic Menace of Tests

To the Editor of *The New York Times:*

I have read with interest the letter from Drs. J. Laurence Kulp, Wallace S. Broecker and Arthur R. Schubert in your issue of May 2. In this letter they say that my statement that carbon 14 represents "a far more serious long-term menace than all other radioactive by-products of an atomic explosion" is incorrect and that carbon 14 will contribute only a minor fraction of the radiation produced by strontium 90 and cesium 137.

In fact it is their statements that are incorrect. When the cumulative dose to the entire population over the total lives of all isotopes is considered, the radiation from the carbon 14 produced by bomb tests is found to be considerably larger than the amount attributed by the Atomic Energy Commission to other isotopes and the number of defective children that can be predicted to be produced by the radiation from carbon 14 is far greater than the number predicted for the other isotopes.

In his 1956 paper on radioactive fallout Dr. W. F. Libby pointed out that neutrons released in the explosions of nuclear weapons in air react with nitrogen nuclei to make carbon 14; he said that "fortunately this radioactivity is essentially safe because of its long lifetime and the enormous amount of diluting carbon dioxide in the atmosphere."

Perhaps because of a feeling of reassurance engendered by this statement and others by Dr. Libby, I did not make any calculations of the genetic and somatic effects of the carbon 14 produced in the testing of nuclear weapons until last month.

Dr. Libby gave additional information about carbon 14 in his March 27 address in Lausanne, including a statement about the amount of carbon 14 generated per megaton, with fusion and fission weighed as they had actually occurred; this amount is 7.4 kilograms, about seven times the amount that he had reported in 1956 for a pure fission weapon. He states that a considerable part of the carbon 14 (which I estimate as two-thirds) falls back as calcium carbonate, the rest of it entering the reservoirs of which the biosphere is a part.

At the present time the concentration of carbon 14 in the atmosphere has been increased by the bomb tests to a value of 10 per cent greater than its former value. As carbon dioxide dissolves in the ocean, this percentage will ultimately decrease if the bomb tests are discontinued.

I shall calculate the effect of carbon 14 on the basis of the following assumptions: The rate of bomb testing is 30 megatons a year. One-third of the generated carbon 14 is released to the atmosphere. There is moderately rapid equilibrium with a large reservoir, including the ocean, with normal content 74,000 kilograms of carbon 14. The mean life of carbon 14 is 8,070 years; the normal amount of carbon 14 in the human body produces a gonad exposure of 0.0015 roentgen a year, as stated in 1956 by Dr. Libby.

The effect of a single gonad exposure of 0.1 roentgen for a world population equal to that at present is to cause ultimately a total of 380,000 seriously defective children (gross physical or mental defect, stillbirth, childhood death) plus 700,000 embryonic and neonatal deaths. This estimate was made by Prof. James F. Crow, a member of the National Academy of Sciences—National Research Council Committee on Genetic Effects of Atomic Radiation, in his testimony before the Congressional subcommittee on radiation on June 4, 1957; the population of the world, which has increased by over one billion during the last hundred years, will continue to increase and will have an average value during the next 10,000 or 20,000 years such that there will be five times as many children born as at present.

A straightforward calculation based on the above assumptions leads directly to the conclusion that one year of testing at the standard rate of 30 megatons a year (two 15-megaton bombs, similar to the one detonated by the United States on March 1, 1954) will ultimately be responsible for the birth of 230,000 seriously defective children and also for 420,000 embryonic and neonatal deaths.

We may compare these numbers with the number caused by the other isotopes. The official estimate given in the 23rd Semi-Annual Report of the Atomic Energy Commission is 2,500 to 13,000 seriously defective children a year of testing. I think the number may be somewhat higher, but the statement is justified that carbon 14 is a far more serious long-term genetic menace than the other products of atomic explosions.

The bomb tests carried out so far (including 1958, which is starting off as a bad year) can be estimated to correspond roughly to five 30 megaton years. Accordingly we may say that the predicted effect of the carbon 14 released in these bomb tests will be to produce about one million seriously defective children and about two million embryonic and neonatal deaths, and that the predicted effects of the other isotopes will be somewhat smaller.

As other people have pointed out, these numbers will represent a minute fraction of the total number of seriously defective children and of embryonic and neonatal deaths during coming centuries. But I feel that each human being is important, and that it is well worth while to calculate the numbers of individual human beings who will be caused to suffer or to die because of the bomb tests, rather than to talk about "negligible effects," "undetectable increase," "extremely small fraction."

LINUS PAULING
Pasadena, Calif., May 8, 1958

The writer won the Nobel Prize in Chemistry in 1954. He is head of the chemistry division and director of the Gates and Crellin Laboratory of the California Institute of Technology and a former president of the American Chemical Society.

125

Soviet Test Plan Examined

To the Editor of *The New York Times:*

The Russian proposal made on March 19 at Geneva is a major step forward in the negotiations for cessation of nuclear weapons tests. Provided the details can be satisfactorily cleared up it seems to me a suitable basis for a treaty.

In regard to furthering research on detection, the Russian proposal seems to me very well balanced. If we concluded now a complete agreement banning all tests, the Russians might not have much incentive to improve the detection system. With a time-limited moratorium on small tests, however, it would be very much in their interest to improve the methods of detecting small tests as quickly as possible.

Conversely, if the ban were limited to large explosions without any moratorium on small ones, then the United States might not have much incentive to change this status quo. The moratorium would provide such an incentive because it is very much to our interest to make the duration of the unmonitored moratorium as short as possible. Just as we want to have an assurance that the Russians will want to improve the system, so they need an assurance that we will have the same desire.

No international agreement can be entirely foolproof. It must always be partly based on faith in the other party's good intentions. The only thing that technical methods of inspection can do is to reduce the area in which one needs to rely on good faith. This is accomplished by the present Russian compromise proposal: The area of faith is reduced in scope to small, underground explosions, and in time to a few years.

This seems to me an entirely acceptable risk. The Russians have shown that they are just as anxious as we are to reach a workable agreement, satisfactory to both sides. And even in the unlikely case that they should violate the moratorium, would this be so catastrophic?

We have already a large variety of nuclear weapons of low yield and small size. The Russians are probably substantially behind us in this area. Underground tests require considerable time of preparation, especially if a country has never carried out such a test, and even more if they have to be done in secret and in violation of a treaty.

It seems to me very unlikely that within the limited duration of the moratorium the Russians could shift the balance of military power even in the restricted area of small nuclear weapons.

Obviously the United States will have to seek further clarification of the Russian proposal. In particular, we must be assured that the Russians will permit an adequate number of on-site inspections, and liberal criteria for initiating them.

126

Furthermore, the duration of the moratorium will have to be negotiated. But if these and other details can be satisfactorily cleared up, the Russian proposal seems to me to give a good basis for an agreement on test cessation at rather small risk.

The risks in the continued and intensified arms race are immeasurably greater.

HANS A. BETHE
Ithaca, N.Y., March 23, 1960

The writer was formerly director of the theoretical physics division of the Los Alamos Scientific Laboratory. Now Professor of Physics at Cornell University, he has written widely in his field.

Toward Agreement on Tests

To the Editor of *The New York Times:*

The current test ban negotiations at Geneva offer the United States the hope and opportunity to minimize somewhat, through agreement with the Soviet Union, the threat of destruction inherent in the arms race. Such an agreement might be a step toward further agreement, and toward the creation of a political climate in all countries encouraging to technical, diplomatic and political inventiveness aimed at preventing the wild spread of atomic and other weapons of mass destruction.

Given the advantage a police state has in secrecy, and the fear of many Russians at having outsiders wandering about, the concessions the Soviet negotiators have made at Geneva are important. Not to seek to take advantage of them means, on the one hand, the risk of strengthening the cadres in the Soviet Union and of course in China, which never did believe it was possible to reach a *modus vivendi* with the "capitalist" powers; and, on the other hand, to confirm the domination of American foreign and defense policies by the military, the Atomic Energy Commission and their respective civilian satellites.

In this desperate situation, the specter of Munich is repeatedly raised, and any effort at rapprochement is denonunced as appeasement—or put off until that halcyon but ever-receding day when we shall be in a "position of strength," strength here being defined in purely military and hence inevitably self-defeating terms.

The analogy with Hitlerism is fallacious (as analogies from earlier wars usually are) not because the Soviet Union is a people's democracy,

127

but because Khrushchev is not a madman. Moreover, to be unwilling to accept the uncertain risks of nuclear warfare is not weakness, but requires the courage not to fear being thought cowardly.

Reliance on deterrence leads in all countries to a garrison state, and to an alleged defense of values that, in a jingoistic milieu, become less and less worth defending—and, in military terms, less and less technically defensible. President Eisenhower's last months of office should not be frittered away in stalling tactics at Geneva, supported by those who hope that his successor, not being a general, will be still more vulnerable to pressures from the military, and to the fear of being thought "soft" on communism.

DAVID RIESMAN
New York, March 27, 1960

*The writer is the author, among other studies, of "The Lonely Crowd."
He is Henry Ford II Professor of Social Sciences at Harvard University.*

Dangers in Test Ban

To the Editor of *The New York Times:*

May I comment on your editorial of June 19 "To Test or Not to Test." The issue is extremely critical and there is need for the greatest accuracy in presenting it.

The editorial cites the total explosive yield from the devices tested by the Russians, the British and ourselves and, on the basis that most of this amount was "accounted for" by the United States, concludes: "These figures indicate that on the basis of tests alone, and hence in knowledge and technology in respect to the design of nuclear weapons, from the largest city-destroying hydrogen bombs to the smallest tactical weapons, the United States is way ahead of Russia."

I submit that this reasoning is faulty. There is no correlation between the total numbers of tons of test yield and the relative progress in respect to weapons design.

You said: "While clandestine underground tests are possible, these are limited to rather small bombs and are very costly and cumbersome. There is no clear evidence that any such tests have taken place, and there is very small likelihood that enough of them could have taken place to catch up with us."

There are a number of fallacies here. Clandestine underground tests

128

are not limited to "rather small" bombs. Explosions great enough to prove design for quite large weapons can be tested clandestinely. Nor is the cost of tests likely to be a deterrent to a nation intent upon clandestine testing.

It is true that there is no "clear" evidence of Russian testing since the Russians have taken care that to date no on-the-site inspection has been possible. But it is totally mistaken to say that "there is very small likelihood that enough of them (tests) could have taken place to catch up with us."

During each year there are about 200 seismic shocks recorded as centering within Soviet territory, any of which could be caused by quite substantial tests. The number of shocks which are annually registered that could be caused by smaller and "decoupled" tests is several times greater than 200. Whether this has afforded Russia opportunity to "catch up with us," only time will tell. To assert that there is "small likelihood" of this is not supportable.

It ought not to be overlooked that clandestine testing has been uniform Soviet practice from the first. They did not announce their tests in 1949 and 1951, and announced their test in 1953 only after we had detected it. Their subsequent tests have been detected, and nearly always announced, by us. Our tests have been announced by us, usually in advance.

The editorial concludes with the observation that "the President should be guided by the consideration that the possible disadvantage is not resuming the tests would be outweighed by the sure disadvantage of giving Russia the chance to catch up with us. . . ."

This certainly does not represent the reported and informed opinions of the members of the Atomic Energy Commission nor those attributed to members of the Joint Congressional Committee on Atomic Energy. The fact is that if we do not resume testing we would be relying upon nothing more substantial than Communist good faith to restrain them from testing.

It will be recalled that President Eisenhower publicly expressed his impatience with Soviet tactics after fourteen months of fruitless negotiations. While he was willing to continue the conversations in a spirit of seeking to reach a safeguarded agreement, he announced that we had resumed our freedom to continue nuclear weapons testing whenever we might see fit to do so.

In the autumn of 1960 the President had reached the conclusion that the time had come to terminate the moratorium and to resume our tests, either underground or in outer space, no radioactive contribution to the atmosphere being involved.

In expressing this conviction to various members of his Administration, however, he observed that since the effects of such an order would necessarily extend beyond his Administration, it would be more proper to leave the incoming President a free hand.

The strong reservations which I had about the consequences of a moratorium on testing linked to negotiations with the Soviets were expressed in detail before a subcommittee of the Senate Foreign Relations Committee on April 16 and 17, 1958, and on subsequent occasions.

I believed and stated that a nation determined to violate an agreement not to test could probably conceal tests of nuclear weapons. Some scientific opinion, then to the contrary effect, was revised during the ensuing year as a result of the test series known as Hard Tack.

Nothing short of freedom of inspection is meaningful and the proposed token inspections are probably worse than none because of the false impression of security which they would convey to the Free World.

LEWIS STRAUSS
Washington, June 19, 1961

The writer was formerly chairman of the Atomic Energy Commission.

Our Resumption Opposed

To the Editor of *The New York Times:*

The U.S.S.R. has given us a fateful opportunity to take command of the search for peace and to convince the world once and for all of our humane intentions. If it is true, as President Kennedy says, that we already have a nuclear arsenal fully capable of devastating the U.S.S.R., then could we not announce our own refusal to resume nuclear testing for an indefinite period? Such a deed would give dramatic content to our words in behalf of peace, and would also give us the moral right to ask the U.N. for a resolution calling upon the U.S.S.R. pointedly to reverse its shocking decision.

This would be one of the great gambles of our history, but such a gamble must sooner or later be made if we are to realize our twin goals of survival and freedom. Let us think long and hard before we match their shocking decision with one of our own.

CLINTON ROSSITER
Ithaca, N.Y., Sept. 1, 1961

Edward Teller Advocates Testing

To the Editor of *The New York Times:*

The development of nuclear explosives in the United States was steady and rapid between the years 1945 and 1958. In 1958 the moratorium made further experimentation impossible and brought our development effectively to a halt.

Our knowledge of Russian developments between 1945 and 1958 is sketchy and unreliable. But what little we know is sufficient to indicate clearly that in 1958 our advantage had not been very great. Thus there cannot be any doubt about the speed and vigor of the Soviet development.

From the fall of 1958 to September, 1961, we have knowledge that the Russians did not detonate any major nuclear explosive in the atmosphere. We also know that they could have performed nuclear explosions underground without being detected. We now know that they have been very greatly interested in the further development of nuclear explosives. It is therefore plausible to assume that they have persevered in secret underground testing.

There can be no doubt that the series of explosions in the fall of 1961 had been thoroughly prepared. This series must have resulted in considerable additional progress. Thus there is ample possibility, even a considerable probability, that Soviet nuclear explosives are now superior to those in our possession.

Under these conditions it is essential that work on our nuclear explosives should receive adequate support. The most essential requirement is a well-planned, continuous effort. No great progress will result from a crash program of short duration.

Many of the essential questions can be answered by underground experimentation. Some answers can be obtained only with the help of atmospheric tests. Furthermore atmospheric testing would give us much needed speed and flexibility. These tests need not result in any considerable increase in world-wide fallout.

Actually the danger of such fallout, if any, is quite small compared to the obvious and imminent danger of Soviet power.

It is only by continued strength that we can safeguard the peace. With-

131

out the development of nuclear explosives in the coming months and years our strength will be inadequate.

EDWARD TELLER
Berkeley, Calif., Nov. 3, 1961

The writer, Professor of Physics at the University of California and Associate director of its Radiation Laboratory, was concerned with the planning and production of the atomic and hydrogen bomb.

Use of Atomic Weapons in Vietnam

To the Editor:

Hanson Baldwin's May commentary upon Senator Barry Goldwater's reference to the use of nuclear weapons for denuding trees of their foliage is keyed to an article in the *Air University Quarterly Review,* spring issue 1960. In that article Gen. Frederic H. Smith Jr. states:

"A nominal-yield weapon . . . would break branches from trees to an effective diameter of 15,000 feet. Trees stripped of leaves and stem breakage would extend out to approximately 22,200 feet, leaving little or no cover to enemy forces."

From this some might erroneously conclude that a nominal bomb (of Hiroshima power) would expose for interdiction an area of 55 square miles and that nuclear weapons could be successfully employed for "tree stripping" in operations against the Vietcong.

General Smith's thesis is in violent disharmony with the official data on nuclear weapon effects. For example, on page 346 of the "Effects of Nuclear Weapons" (Fig. 7.66) there appears a photograph of an area 1.25 miles from Ground Zero at Hiroshima. Trees in this photo are intact, no limbs are broken and leaves are in place.

I have a considerable file of Hiroshima photos and it is remarkable how durable a tree is when exposed to an A-explosion. In part this is explained by the ability of a tree to "roll with the punch," to its firm anchoring and to its shape as presented to a shock wave.

If we consider the searing effect of an A-bomb, I believe that General Smith has failed to distinguish between the thermal damage record at Hiroshima and at Nagasaki. The target area at Hiroshima was dry and ripe for generating a fire storm. This actually occurred and much of the central city core was burned out. Naturally the trees were denuded.

At Nagasaki there was no fire storm and the results were quite different. I have a photo of the area 2,100 feet south of Ground Zero where the leaves of a chestnut tree exhibit thermal scarring but are intact. The leaves are neither stripped nor broken.

Naturally, the dense foliage of rain forests in Vietnam would be far less vulnerable to searing, and the probability of a fire storm would be very low due to the high water content of the leaves. Limb breakage would be expected, of course, but plenty of cover from unburned foliage would probably remain.

It is considerably more significant, however, to weigh the other effects of the bomb, especially the penetrating nuclear radiation. The lethal radius to soldiers hiding in a forest would be about three-quarter mile— or more than that for removal of the foliage. Thus the real effect of the bombing would be to kill troops with nuclear weapons.

The Goldwater nuclear approach would be more effective against the troops than the trees. It would follow that such action would involve quite large numbers of nuclear bursts and escalation into nuclear war would be risked.

Senator Goldwater's reliance on General Smith as an "expert" witness still leaves him way out on a limb.

RALPH E. LAPP
Alexandria, Va., May 28, 1964

The writer, an atomic physicist and onetime science adviser to the War Department General Staff, is the author of "Kill and Overkill" among other books.

Offensive Missile Race

To the Editor:

In Robert Kleiman's column on the editorial page of Oct. 9 ("MIRV and the Offensive Missile Race") he clearly notes a danger which might arise if either the United States or the U.S.S.R. were to replace a large fraction of its single-warhead ICBM by MIRV's (Multiple, Independently targetable Re-entry Vehicles) of accuracy sufficient to destroy enemy missiles in their hardened silos.

Self-delusion seems possible even among powerful nations; and particularly with a light ABM to absorb any surviving missiles, a nation with a MIRV'ed ICBM force might imagine that it could destroy its opponent's ICBM's in their silos and so not be struck in return. It would

133

indeed be valuable to reach an effective agreement to prevent such an arms race.

In truth, the safety of submarine-launched ballistic missiles cannot be threatened in this way, and some bombers can be launched on radar warning of attack, so that a reasonable level of deterrence may persist even if MIRV's are widely deployed. In addition, thousands of MIRV's are required to constitute a real preemptive threat, so that even the ICBM component of deterrence will not vanish with the MIRV production.

The very possibility of MIRV's and the long delay involved in building either more offensive forces or a defense of our ICBM force have compelled (if not persuaded) Secretary McNamara to initiate the deployment of a defense of Minutemen to be effective against Soviet missiles by perhaps 1973. The very fact of this decision evidently implies that the Secretary does not believe that the bombers, the Polaris and the Poseidon alone constitute an adequate deterrent. But even in such circumstances cheaper means of Minutemen defense would seem acceptable and even desirable, to be available at least as early as would be the proposed Minutemen defense.

One such means of making the Minutemen invulnerable to a full-scale Soviet attack (and to destroy a significant portion of our 1,000 Minutemen force would require a very large-scale attack) is to create a relatively inexpensive warning system employing a long-range radar or other means, together with a procedure for determining within a few minutes whether more than, say 500 warheads were in flight or had exploded in the Minutemen fields.

If such a threat were detected and verified, the Minutemen force could be fired, and the knowledge of this strategic reaction would surely constitute as great a deterrent against large-scale attack by the Soviet Union as did the existence of our ICBM's before MIRV's. This solution would persist independent of any MIRV's or other penetration aids used by the Soviet Union and would thus seem to be useful indefinitely.

Since this option would be available to us at any time, it should not be necessary to spend scarce money this next year on A.B.M. to defend the Minutemen.

R. L. GARWIN
New York, Oct. 13, 1967

The writer, Professor of Physics at Columbia University and Director of the IBM Watson Laboratory, is a member of the Defense Science Board and the National Academy of Sciences.

Arms Control

To the Editor:

The lead editorial of Oct. 19, "The Campaign: Arms, Safety," give the impression that the Eisenhower Administration, including Vice President Nixon, had little interest in arms control.

The facts are that every arms control agreement which the Kennedy and Johnson Administrations were able to reach originated during the Eisenhower Administration. In August 1957 the United States submitted to the United Nations Subcommittee on Disarmament a program which included among other matters provisions for test suspension, nonproliferation and outer space controls.

Even the idea of strategic missile negotiations which the Czech invasion blocked was conceived during the Eisenhower Administration. Foster Dulles in a speech on July 22, 1957, said, "It is possible to bring under effective control the future development of major means for the transmission of destructive weapons to their targets. In this connection certain kinds of weapons, as for example intercontinental ballistic missiles, deserve particular consideration." It may be of interest to note that Dulles said in this speech, "because the negotiations might lead to a treaty, the Senate's disarmament subcommittee, of which Senator Humphrey is chairman, is being kept fully informed."

In this speech Foster Dulles also said, "We are willing to cooperate in the working out of a system which would insure that outer space missiles would be used exclusively for peaceful and scientific purposes. The use of outer space is still sufficiently experimental to make it possible to assure that future development in this new area of knowledge and experimentation will be for the benefit of mankind and not for its destruction."

In view of this record and the fact that Mr. Nixon was an active and responsible leader in the Eisenhower Administration, it hardly seems accurate to describe him as "Richard-come-lately on nearly every major proposal and program in this vital area of disarmament and arms control."

As to the editorial's reference to "The Dulles line about 'massive retaliation.' " it may be of interest to note that Dulles as early as 1958 had solemnly and on two occasions put the Joint Chiefs, the Secretary of Defense and the Service Secretaries on formal notice that in his judgment the concept of massive retaliation, while useful in its day, had a very short life expectancy and that it was important and urgent to de-

135

velop strategic doctrine to replace it as well as new weapons systems needed to support it.

GERARD SMITH
Former Assistant Secretary of State and
Director of the Policy Planning Staff
Washington, Oct. 21, 1968

'No' on Nonproliferation

To the Editor:

One of the first matters of importance for the new Administration is Senate consideration of the so-called "Treaty on the Nonproliferation of Nuclear Weapons."

The nonproliferation treaty is intended to prevent nuclear powers from giving or selling nuclear weapons to nations which presently do not have them, and ostensibly would prevent the non-nuclear nations from ever obtaining them.

However, the treaty is looked upon with suspicion by our allies in Western Europe. By pressuring nations such as Germany and Italy to sign it against their will, the United States will harm the cause of Western unity.

Ratification of the nonproliferation treaty would increase the danger of the United States becoming involved in a major war, since it would result in demands from non-nuclear nations for American protection against nuclear aggression. It would thus double our opportunities to get involved in someone else's troubles. Also, a security treaty with one country or group of countries would result in alienation of the United States from the country or group of countries left out of the security pact. Thus the treaty is actually a step toward war, rather than toward peace.

This would not seem to be an opportune time for the United States to signify that we are willing to disregard the promises broken by the invaders of Czechoslovakia. Ratification of the treaty while invading troops remain in occupation of Czechoslovakia would debase the meaning of all treaties and would suggest an attitude of tolerance toward those nations that are prone to regard treaties as scraps of paper.

Since changes, and presumably improvements, were indicated during the recent elections, one improvement would be to delay or discard, and to not ratify, a faulty nonproliferation treaty.

F. Edmund Ryder
Manville, N.J., Jan. 26, 1969

For Nonproliferation

To the Editor:

The nonproliferation treaty was attacked in a letter from F. Edmund Ryder. The main arguments were that the treaty would "harm the cause of Western unity" and "increase the danger of the United States becoming involved in a major war."

It would be difficult to imagine an event that would be more disruptive of Western unity, as well as destabilizing to the strategic balance of forces between NATO and the Warsaw Pact, than the acquisition of nuclear weapons by a non-nuclear NATO member. Since it would add to the stability of the nuclear weapon *status quo* in Europe, the nonproliferation treaty could open up new opportunities for steps toward unity in Western Europe.

Moreover, the nonproliferation treaty does not extend existing United States defense commitments. In addition to our obligations under the United Nations Charter, we are already committed by treaty to defend 40 non-nuclear-weapon nations against armed aggression. If some of these 40 nations acquired nuclear weapons of their own in the future, it would clearly increase the risk of our involvement in a war in which the decision to use nuclear weapons was outside United States Control.

Mr. Ryder's letter overlooks the fact that in a few years civil nuclear-power programs in several non-nuclear-weapon nations will be producing fissionable material sufficient for the manufacture of hundreds of nuclear weapons a year. The international safeguards system in the nonproliferation treaty would provide assurance that these fissionable materials were not diverted to use in nuclear weapons programs. Without the treaty, the growth of civil nuclear-power programs to meet our needs for more electric power and less air pollution would be accompanied by a substantial increase in international tensions.

Therefore President Nixon is to be commended for his decisions to support the nonproliferation treaty and to continue United States efforts

137

to prevent the further spread of nuclear weapons and to achieve other measures of nuclear arms control.

MASON WILLRICH
Professor of Law
University of Virginia
Charlottesville, Va., Feb. 1, 1969

Threat of A.B.M.

To the Editor:

It is being argued that Congress should approve the antiballistic missile appropriation so that this system can be used in bargaining with the Soviet Union at the coming arms limitation talks.

In reality, as a bargaining counter the A.B.M. would be of no value or of negative value.

Neither the "thin" nor the "thick" proposed A.B.M. systems could hope significantly to reduce the catastrophic damage our country would suffer in the event of a heavy Soviet attack. However, the great sacrifice of money, skilled manpower and resources we would have to make in order to deploy it would certainly degrade our national life, weaken our economy and exacerbate our domestic problems.

Therefore, the deployment of an American A.B.M. is not something with which to threaten the Soviet Union. On the contrary, if we assume it is the Soviet goal to cause the United States a maximum amount of trouble, we should expect their encouragement to build the heaviest, most expensive anti-ballistic missile system possible.

Incidentally, since the A.B.M. was "sold" to the Defense Department and the President in 1967 on the grounds that we needed it primarily as a defense against China, why do its proponents now say they would abandon its deployment if Russia would agree on an arms limitation?

GEORGE McGOVERN
U.S. Senator from South Dakota
Washington, Feb. 22, 1969

MIRV Tests Opposed

To the Editor:

Most of the commotion about the deployment of the Sentinel A.B.M. system is misplaced. Sentinel or even a thicker system will not disrupt the strategic balance with the Soviet Union and may have desirable effects.

Much more to be deplored is the Administration's continuance of MIRV (multiple independently targeted re-entry vehicles) testing at a time when further offensive increases here and in the Soviet Union may make all fixed land-based forces vulnerable to a surprise attack.

If MIRV testing is to be stopped, it must be stopped almost at once; otherwise both sides will have to credit the other with an operational capability which could be deployed in secret. If the tests can be stopped now or in the next two or three months, however, neither side would count on such a capability, and our existing Minuteman stocks would be sufficient for deterrent purposes.

Further, the need to develop large-scale mobile capabilities (on land or sea) as a rejoinder to MIRV could be avoided.

This underscores the need for prompt initiation of the strategic talks with the Russians to stop testing. Ideally, one would also wish to see a freeze and later reduction of existing offensive missile stocks. If this cannot be agreed to, a limited buildup of A.B.M. on each side would be permitted.

Such a buildup could not reduce casualties in either the United States or the Soviet Union to some very low figure; but it could make significant inroads on the absurdly high prospective fatality tolls (100 to 125 million each) now calculated on both sides.

RICHARD ROSECRANCE
Berkeley, Calif., March 7, 1969

The writer was formerly Political-Military member of the Policy Planning Council, Department of State.

Nixon Lauded on A.B.M.

To the Editor:

As a former assistant to a series of Secretaries of the Air Force, I protest the spate of spurious logic pouring into print and inundating the airwaves on the subject of the antiballistic missile system. The scientists, the social commentators and the political hacks all say that setting up a Sentinel system will provoke the Russians and escalate the arms race, and that the presence of A.B.M. sites will imperil the neighboring residents; furthermore, that it will do no good.

There are now 63 reported A.B.M. sites around Moscow alone. Has this provoked us into escalation? If missile interceptor systems are valueless, why has Russia with far less economic riches than have we, wasted its substance on useless toys?

Has the presence of hundreds of Nike Zeus missiles and launchers surrounding our population centers visibly endangered the residents or provoked the Soviets? The Nike Zeus has a thermonuclear warhead, but most people I know were glad to see them around.

Probably one reason for the vocal distrust of the present A.B.M. plan was the ridiculous justification given for its predecessor under the Johnson Administration—that it would be built to counter any Chinese threat. That really was balderdash.

The Nixon-Laird Sentinel system is designed to protect our own ICBM launching sites and nothing more. And it is essential. The Russians have pinpointed our sites as we have theirs. If the Soviets know that they can knock out our retaliatory weapons on their first strike we have obviously lost all deterrent power. If they know that they cannot do so, the stalemate remains. Admittedly, the situation may reasonably be designated a balance of terror, but this is better than no balance at all.

It is my considered opinion that President Nixon has looked to the best advice obtainable and, acting thereon, has taken a reasoned, balanced and courageous stand.

FREDERICK AYER, Jr.
Washington, March 21, 1969

Issues in SALT

To the Editor:

It was with great interest that I read in your Nov. 11 issue a news article by your Washington correspondent John Finney on Soviet-American talks in Helsinki.

I should like to point out that hopes for the success of this preliminary meeting are fully shared in the Soviet Union. There is one common truth for our epoch saying that the future of peace largely depends on whether our powers agree to begin gradually to bury their war hatchets.

I think the confidential atmosphere in Helsinki is a good thing. Making public contradictions which inevitably arise at the stage of drawing up an agenda might cause disappointment and pessimism which, it is hoped, would prove unjustified in the end.

In my opinion, the Soviet delegation in Helsinki has an advantage over the American. As is evident from John Finney's dispatch, the contradictions between the Disarmament Agency and Defense Department are still acute. A children's fairy tale about Dr. Doolittle describes an odd creature resembling a horse with two heads each facing the other way—push-and-pull. Any attempt to gallop away on this creature ends in a fiasco.

If the strivings of the Chiefs of Staff Committee and the Arms Control and Disarmament Agency run in diametrically opposite directions, the American delegation in Helsinki will have a hard time.

As for the Soviet side, its efforts are made easier by the fact that there are no two views in Moscow on the ending of the arms race and on disarmament. "Disarmament is the ideal of socialism"—these words by Lenin were and are at the root of Soviet foreign policy.

John Finney is right, to my mind, when he mentions the weak points of the Nixon Administration's main aim concerning the limitation, rather than reduction, of the arsenals of weapons. The restriction of strategic armaments may be viewed as an intermediate target, but the main and final goal still remains the consistent reduction of armaments and the destruction of their stockpiles.

"Third countries"—I use the term in the broadest sense—and those not meeting in Helsinki await from the great powers, not the freezing of their enormous war potentials, but some practical steps on disarmament

141

which would lead in the end to progress on this—mankind's number one problem.

VADIM ARDATOVSKY
Political Commentator
Novosti Press Agency
Moscow, Nov. 14, 1969

Threat of MIRV

To the Editor:

The United States plans June deployment of multiple independently targetable re-entry vehicles (MIRV's). If that happens, the strategic arms race will enter a new and unnecessarily dangerous era because with MIRV's a missile force of a given size may be able to destroy a larger number of adversary silo-based missiles.

Thus United States spokesmen argue that high yield Soviet MIRV's are ominous because with them the United States ICBM force could be destroyed. They argue that United States MIRV's, because of their much lower yield, would not be effective counterforce weapons, but will only enhance our retaliatory capability. Actually, the Soviet Union must assume that once United States MIRV's are deployed, normal improvement in accuracy will lead to a counterforce capability within a few years.

Adoption by the Russians of a launch-on-warning doctrine for their ICBM's is a likely and shuddering response. It would make mankind's survival dependent on Soviet radars and computers never giving a false signal of an American attack.

For several reasons the Russians are far more likely to adopt such a doctrine than would we if we perceived our ICBM's to be threatened. First, they are less likely to rely heavily on their missile launching submarine force for deterrence because of its smaller size, because there is less experience with it and less of a naval tradition, and because United States anti-submarine warfare capabilities are probably superior to those of the U.S.S.R.

Second, the Russians are less likely to rely heavily on their bombers because of historical precedent and the relatively small numbers.

Third, the United States can better afford to restructure its strategic forces as a response to increased vulnerability of ICBM's. A launch-on-warning doctrine is cheap and easily implemented, but superhardening,

142

active defense, mobile land-based systems, new bombers, or increased emphasis on sea-based systems—the responses, which are being considered by the U.S.—are very costly.

While United States MIRV test programs are well along, MIRV deployment can still be stopped. A United States decision to do so could be effectively monitored because it would be militarily unacceptable to deploy such systems without a continuing, easily observable test program. If the Soviets were to refrain from further multiple warhead tests, we could have acceptable confidence that they were exercising similar restraint.

MIRV's may be required some day to give us a deterrent capable of penetrating a heavy nationwide Soviet A.B.M. defense system with high confidence. Fortunately, however, the time required for such an A.B.M. deployment will be long. That required for a United States MIRV deployment will be relatively short. Thus, we can well wait until there is clear evidence of the former before proceeding with the latter.

Adoption by the Soviet Union of a launch-on-warning doctrine for its ICBM's is clearly not in the United States' interest. Neither is the needless expenditure of several billions of dollars. In the hope of preventing both, and also to enhance the prospects for SALT, United States MIRV program should be suspended.

GEORGE W. RATHJENS
HERBERT F. YORK
Cambridge, Mass., April 24, 1970

The writers, former Defense Department officials, are respectively professor of political science at M.I.T. and Dean of the Graduate School, U.C.L.A.

Nuclear Arms Race

To the Editor:

Defense Secretary Melvin Laird's assertion that the Soviet Union is strengthening its nuclear strike capability is a typical example of the way in which our Defense Department consistently overestimates the "Soviet threat" in order to convince us that billions of our tax dollars should be used for the development of more deadly and insane weapons systems. At present over 60 per cent of our Federal taxes, so desperately needed for health, education, welfare and other programs, are used for war.

It is indeed interesting that Secretary Laird's assertion about a Soviet missile build-up directly contradicts reports from senior Administration officials, which state that the Soviet Union has constructed no new sites since last August. But let's assume for a moment that Mr. Laird's assertions, though extremely vague, are correct. If this is the case, an important question to ask is why the Soviet Union is enlarging its nuclear arsenal.

In a recent book on United States military policy [*The Economy of Death,* Atheneum, 1969] Richard J. Barnet observes that the United States today has the largest conglomerate of military and economic power in the world. Therefore the military policy of our Government has a profound influence on other countries, including the Soviet Union. Since World War II, Soviet military build-ups have consistently followed those of the United States. The expansion of the Soviet missile force since 1963 followed our build-up of Minuteman and Polaris missiles in the early 1960's. For the past 25 years the United States has had considerable superiority over the Soviet Union in nuclear weapons, despite frequent assertions of "missile gaps" by Defense Department spokesmen.

Imagine how Soviet citizens feel about the fact that the United States increased its offensive nuclear strike capability by deploying ten Minuteman missiles armed with MIRV's carrying three nuclear warheads— each of which has ten times the power of the bomb dropped at Hiroshima. Imagine the further consternation and fear when they learn that the United States plans to place MIRV's on about 500 Minuteman missiles.

Our present deployment of MIRV could seriously obstruct the crucial Strategic Arms Limitation Talks currently being held in Vienna. These talks may represent the last real opportunity to end the insane escalation of the arms race.

Your news story indicated that the Soviet Union does not yet have a MIRV capability. Deployment by the United States will most certainly give their defense department an excuse to develop one. Though the further development of nuclear weapons means increased profits for the companies who receive the defense contracts, it will continue to decrease the security of the United States as well as the rest of the world.

DAVID H. CHISHOLM
Bloomington, Ind., July 13, 1970

V·Foreign Affairs

In reading the letters to the editor of *The Times* on foreign affairs one gets the feeling that the war in Vietnam has always been with us. It has been difficult during the last twelve years to open the paper on any day and not find a letter on the American presence in Indochina.

The war in Vietnam has accounted for more letters to *The Times* than any other single issue in the last ten years. These letters have explored the conduct of the war, its politics, its economics and its impact in this country and abroad. They have expressed the views of Congressmen, the Government, college faculty and students, servicemen in the field and ordinary citizens who have been asked to give their sons and support for an effort they really could not understand.

There is support for the war and the President's plans on the letters page of *The Times*. But a majority of the readership has strongly opposed our presence in Southeast Asia.

Other aspects of American foreign policy—foreign aid, relations with China, Greece, the Soviet Union, the President's war-making powers among them—have also attracted a large reader mail.

145

Comment on the Current Situation in Germany

To the Editor of *The New York Times*:

Would it not be in harmony with American traditions, and with the best aspects of the American character, to suspend our immigration quotas for a time, invite to America 100,000 of the Jews in Germany, and raise funds, by private and governmental subscription, to settle them upon a part of the lands that will be made fertile in Oregon and Washington by the Bonneville and Grand Coulee dams?

Perhaps the British Government can be persuaded to make a similar offer of lands in Southern Africa. If our Americanism is still vital, we shall stamp as treason any appeal to racial prejudice here; and if our Christian heritage still moves us, we shall restore the prestige of democracy and civilization by coming to the aid of a bitterly oppressed people.

WILL DURANT
Great Neck, N.Y., Nov. 12, 1938

Self-Defense Urged

To the Editor of *The New York Times*:

We are nearing the festive season when over six hundred millions of Christians in the world will celebrate the birth of Christ. Yet today a nation in Europe, supposed to be civilized, is savagely robbing and torturing the small remnant of His kinsfolk who are are unable to escape from these unspeakable horrors.

Has the Germany of von Goethe, Schiller and Walther von der Vogelweide repudiated Christian civilization and returned to the barbarism which prompted them to destroy ancient civilization and bring on the Dark Ages?

I am moved to write more in behalf of the six hundred millions of Gentiles who are disgraced and endangered by the terrible doings in Germany today, rather than for the Jewish victims. I am aghast at the indifference and neutrality of Christians of all nationalities. We must do something real to protect the Jews of Germany from slaughter and spoliation as a matter of self-defense. Our turn may come next.

HYACINTHE RINGROSE
New York, Nov. 13, 1938

146

War Crimes Trial

To the Editor of *The New York Times:*

I returned from Tokyo a few days ago and my attention was called to Pitman B. Potter's letter in your columns of June 2. Professor Potter has temperately expressed doubts and difficulties which troubled me when I first asked myself what was the legal basis of the Nuremberg and later the Tokyo trials.

I felt that the law of nations was a poor thing if it had no theory of how the practical problem should be solved of imposing penal sanctions according to law on the individuals, who led their nations into war and waged the war according to the vile methods adopted. Human beings' moral sense is deeply convinced that it is a crime for men to use political and executive power for wrongful self-interest and aggrandizement. The doubt often felt by conventional people is how to bridge the gap which sometimes exists between moral and legal ideas. But I believe, and so do others, that the gap has in this case been bridged.

I think that there exists an international criminal law as clear and positive in its terms, and as direct in its application to individuals who offend against it, as that which includes the laws of war, which refer to what are sometimes called war crimes in *stricto sensu* such as the murder of hostages or prisoners of war, outrages on the populations of occupied countries and the like.

No one, I imagine, at this time of day would dispute that such crimes are cognizable under international law by the appropriate tribunals or the military courts which international law has for centuries recognized to have jurisdiction to try such offenses. These are established by the Commander in Chief, who appoints the judges and has the executive power and executes the sentences. As instances I may refer to the trial of cases like those concerning concentration camps. I doubt if many international lawyers question the correctness of such procedure.

Military courts are courts different from national courts in the mode of creation and in their jurisdiction and in the law which they administer. The analogy to prize courts has always struck me.

The international military courts set up at Nuremberg and Tokyo are the same military courts adapted to the particular need of dealing with offenses which are the subject of their adjudication. The accused are political or military figures who are said to have created, determined and executed the aggressive purposes of the war and led their respective nations into it. To the extent that they have prescribed to their soldiers methods of terrorism and other breaches of the laws which are now authoritatively specified in The Hague and other Conventions they can be accused as guilty themselves as individuals for what the tools who obeyed their directives did and for the atrocities which their instruments have perpetrated. I cannot see any want of legal validity of such charges as established in fact.

Apart from and before the Pact of Paris of 1927 there might well be some doubt whether leading statesmen could be individually or collectively held criminally for initiating or waging an aggressive war, but the Pact of Paris was a solemn treaty to which practically all the nations of the world adhered. They agreed in precise terms that they renounced war as an instrument of policy. Treaties generally bind states, not individuals, but some treaties, such as the Pact of Paris and the various Conventions like The Hague and Geneva Conventions, have a further meaning because they evidence what international law is.

The Pact of Paris was not a scrap of paper. It was clearly agreed to between nations in order to settle the contentions raised by some lawyers that national sovereignty included an arbitrary power to initiate war, however unjust and evil. This theory appears to me to be not only diabolic but unsound in law. National sovereignty does not include a *liberum arbitrium* to perpetrate crimes outside the national body. The Pact, like The Hague and Geneva Conventions, did not generally use the word "crime," but if such a thing as waging unjust war is repudiated as being unlawful, no verbal definition of it in terms as being a crime is needed. By long practice of military courts such an unlawful act imports responsibility of the guilty individuals.

There is no need of a precise definition of a war of aggression as contrasted with a war of self–defense. It is a matter for the court to determine on the facts of each case whether the war is of the one sort or the other. I feel like the man who was asked to define an elephant. He replied he could not, nor was it worth his while to do so. He knew an elephant when he saw it. These grave questions are not concerned with border-line cases.

It may also be noted that statesmen and others who initiate and wage an unjust war, especially if treacherous and in breach of treaties are perpetrating through the soldiers and others who are their instruments an indefinite number of murders which they cannot justify as excusable under the laws of war. It is for them to justify these murders and if they cannot they stand open to indictment as murderers. The idea cannot be accepted that such persons are irresponsible and immune from any penal law. They are subject to punishment under international law.

Humanitarian treaties and Conventions like the Pact of Paris and The Hague and Geneva Conventions form part of the substance of international law which, like prize law, has its own source, its courts and its

148

executive authorities. It is not the same in character and substance as the law of any particular nation. There is no national law-giving authority. The law which has grown up exists in the form appropriate to it. It is not political; it is law in the strictest.sense of the word, with its own courts, its own precedents and its own machinery.

There is no question here of retrospective legislation. The charter of the two courts in stating their jurisdiction expressly does so on the footing that they are in accordance with international law. It is true that the judges belong to the winning side but that must be so in ordinary military law as in prize law, and the real question is whether the judges are men of judicial character and high attainments and do proceed impartially. The world will judge if the trials are fair, if the facts are duly elicited and proved and the law correctly applied.

I directly differ from your correspondent's pronouncement that the proceedings at Nuremberg and Tokyo do not represent international law. I think they do and that they are a demonstration of courts at their best rising to the height of the great responsibility laid on them.

WRIGHT
New York, June 20, 1946

The writer is a lawyer and a Lord of Appeal in Ordinary. He is chairman of the United Nations War Crimes Commission.

Formula for Europe

To the Editor of *The New York Times:*

Looking back over the diplomatic events since 1945 there appears to be a danger that the United States may exhaust its post-war efforts and authority in Europe in pursuit of secondary rather than primary objectives; that American policy may come to regard certain tactical operations as fundamental diplomatic strategy.

The primary objective in Europe might be defined as the successful negotiation with the U.S.S.R. of terms for the unification of Germany— and its long-run disarmament—compatible with the principles of political democracy, as those principles are understood in the United States and in Western Europe.

Since 1947 that primary objective would appear to have been largely subordinated to efforts to strengthen Western Europe as a military, political and economic entity. The reason for that subordination was the conviction that the U.S.S.R. was not prepared to consider the unification of Germany on terms compatible with Western political principles. And the Soviet position was judged, in turn, to stem from skepticism concerning the ability of Western European states to recover their economic and political health in the post-war.

There is no public evidence that the U.S.S.R. is now prepared to consider a German settlement based on such principles. There would appear, nevertheless, important reasons for the United States to reformulate its primary objectives in Europe; to state them publicly; and, more important, to explore by every diplomatic means the possibility of implementing them.

In the first place, western Germany emerges, by resources and by geography, as the keystone of the structure of Western Europe; and there is no reason to believe that western Germany's interests in the long run, or even in the reasonably short run, are likely to be any other than the reunification of Germany. That fact, if no other, would demand that the question of the reunification of Germany not be relegated to a secondary or perfunctory position in public thought or policy.

But there is another reason as well. The extraordinary importance attached to western Germany in a Western coalition, combined with the frustrations of past defeat and present separation from eastern Germany, imposes dangerous power and temptation on the German people. Given their recent history, the German people are ill-prepared to bear these strains over a long period with poise and restraint.

Aside from the instability of a policy and a structure based on the assumption of a continued split of Germany there is a fairly immediate danger. From the Western point of view the military problem of the European Continent is now usually defined as the countering of the potential groundforce superiority of the Soviet land armies.

If this appreciation is just it is self-evident that the ground-force defense of Western Europe could only be conducted with the participation of large American armies on the spot or by the mobilization of western Germany. There is, therefore, a powerful immediate logic in the view that a western German army be created or that western German ground forces be incorporated into the defense forces of Western Europe by other means. Until this happens, under present circumstances and dispositions the West must feel itself fundamentally without defense—so runs the argument.

If it does happen, however, the inherent fears of many Western European countries of western German strength will be increased; the relative influence of these countries will be diluted in favor of western Germany; and the political unity of the West placed under great strain. But

150

even more important, the danger of a parallel arming of the eastern Germans, or the movement on to German soil of strong fighting contingents of the Soviet armies, will become real. With this stage in the Cold War, the danger of war will also become real.

It is difficult to envisage a less stable situation than the arming of German nationals, on either side of an arbitrary line, by hostile political groups.

At the present time the United States still enjoys in Europe unique authority and powers of leadership. This authority and power to lead is likely to diminish, as time goes on. Indeed, it is a principal aim of American policy to achieve a position where the reduction of American support and concern will prove possible, without a crisis in Western affairs.

It would seem dangerous, however, given the peculiar structure of Western Europe, and especially the peculiar position within it of western Germany, for the United States to move from its present position, toward a stage of diminished authority, without most serious renewed efforts to achieve a German settlement. For, although direct American authority in Europe may diminish, the American stake and involvement in European security affairs is not likely to diminish. If Europe goes to war, we will go to war.

Whether or not such a settlement is possible will depend, of course, on the U.S.S.R., as well as the United States, Great Britain, and France. It may or may not be that a politically democratic, unified Germany, militarily neutralized, would have some appeal to the Soviet Government. At the minimum, however, it would appear to be the American as well as the world interest that this possibility be explored seriously; and that the American terms for such a settlement be, in their broad outlines, publicly known. It does not appear sufficient that the impossibility of such a settlement be assumed, while the United States continues to pursue secondary and defensive aims, as though they were fundamental objectives.

And should a settlement not now prove possible, it appears important that the United States be fully aware of the instability, strains and dangers of the present state of Western European affairs. A continuance of present, or even increased, tensions may have to be accepted. If so, they should not be accepted with complacence, or with a sense that American policy is achieving more than, in fact, it is.

As time goes by, in retrospect it is likely to appear that a major distinction of the American contribution to the Second World War was the manner in which the major aims were clearly defined, and then pursued stubbornly, against difficulty and temptation. It would be an unhappy irony if our post-war diplomacy should prove to have dissipated our authority in transitory tactical maneuvers.

W. W. ROSTOW
Cambridge, Eng., Dec. 10, 1949

The writer is Visiting Professor of American History at King's College, Cambridge.

Russia's Racial Policy

To the Editor of *The New York Times:*

In your issue of March 18 you print a letter and a typically excellent *Times* editorial on Soviet anti-Semitism. The appendix of my recent book *Conservatism Revisited* consists of a documented monograph on "National Bolshevism: The Soviet-Reichswehr Alliance and Russia's Anti-Semitic Drive of 1949." The documentation contains the most complete bibliography published so far on the current Soviet anti-Semitism, including names and dates of anti-Semitic or anti-cosmopolitan Soviet cartoons and articles. I mention this bibliography in case it may be of service to serious students of the problem.

The facts refute the Soviet denials of anti-Semitism made for foreign consumption in Stalinism's double game of intolerant nationalism at home and pious internationalism abroad. The facts likewise refute the more extreme American allegations, absurdly equating Nazi anti-Semitism with Soviet anti-Semitism. The latter has not even remotely approached Hitler's satanic gas chambers.

Soviet governmental anti-Semitism apparently emerged in the purge of Lenin's old Bolsheviks, the so-called "Trotskyite Fascist beasts." This purge whose "evidence" was exposed by the committee of the philosopher John Dewey, in part paved the way for Stalin's wooing of Hitler by eliminating Russia's leading anti-Nazi internationalists, including such old Bolsheviks of Jewish origin as Kamenev, Zinoviev, etc. During the 1939 pact Stalin turned over helpless Jewish refugees to the Gestapo in order to demonstrate his loyalty to Hitler. (cf. Mrs. Buber-Neumann's memoirs on this.)

In the 1949 Soviet press campaign the Slavic surnames of a number of Russian cosmopolitans were "unmasked" as originally having been Jewish. Meanwhile, the removal from high office of Russia's Jewish citizens has been frequently analyzed in Prof. Harry Schwartz's inter-

152

esting *Times* dispatches. Yet there are exceptions; there are the recent Stalin prizes to Jews; and the Soviet Constitution does at least pay its hypocritical lip-service to racial tolerance. All of which was not the case with Hitler, and shows the danger of sensational, unscholarly analogies.

The duty of all Americans who would conserve our free traditions is to oppose anti-Semitism as outspokenly and "tactlessly" as possible wherever it occurs, whether in Russia or—at home. Lacking either logic or integrity are those American chauvinists who only attack Soviet intolerance without attacking its home manifestations and those bewildered "Wallaceite" mentalities who only attack it at home (or say, in Spain) without also attacking the far graver Soviet anti-Semitism.

Since the readers of your editorial may assume this is a new development in Russian communism, it may interest and even astonish them to hear part of Stalin's little-known personal "Report on the London Congress," published in 1907 in the "Bakinskii Proletarii":

"Not less interesting is the composition of the Congress from the standpoint of nationalities. Statistics showed that the majority of the Menshevik faction consists of Jews. . . . On the other hand, the overwhelming majority of the Bolsheviks consists of Russians. . . . For this reason, one of the Bolsheviks observed in jest (it seems Comrade Aleksinsky) that the Mensheviks are a Jewish faction, the Bolsheviks a Russian faction, whence it wouldn't be a bad idea for us Bolsheviks to arrange a pogrom in the party."

PETER VIERECK
Associate Professor of Russian and European History
Mount Holyoke College
South Hadley, Mass., March 18, 1950

Events at Time of Yalta

To the Editor of *The New York Times:*

In your editorial of Sept. 17 "Soviet Grip on China" you say that new developments in the Far East "make it necessary to consider again events which are in part the consequence of a secret protocol which the United States approved at Yalta."

You continue: "That protocol gave Soviet Russia control of Manchuria, a fact which Nationalist China was compelled to confirm by treaty; it aided the Communist conquest of all China, and it brought

Russia back to the Yellow Sea. Now the latest news from Moscow confirms anew that Russia is there to stay and that not even a Communist China can dislodge the Soviets from this strategic position."

There was a "secret protocol," and it was embodied in the 1945 treaty, not because the United States forced the Nationalist Government to accept its terms but because Chiang Kai-shek was so eager to have an understanding with the Russians that he was willing to grant them more than the protocol contemplated.

The record shows that the Generalissimo was "generally satisfied" with the treaty, and Mme. Chiang Kai-shek, then visiting in this country, thanked President Truman for the help the United States Government had given the Chinese plenipotentiaries in working out the agreements.

Since *The New York Times* dragged in the Yalta protocol as having a direct bearing on Russian control of Manchuria, it should, as a matter of simple fairness, have pointed out that the protocol expressly declares that "China shall retain full sovereignty in Manchuria." If Stalin reneged on this, as he did on other things, surely his treachery should not, even by implication, be made part of what happened at Yalta.

But even if the United States had "compelled" Nationalist China to confirm the "secret protocol" by treaty, whatever the concessions and whatever their source, the fact remains that the treaty itself once had the glowing praise of *The New York Times*. For on Aug. 28, 1945, *The Times* called this pact "a victory for peace as great as any scored on the battlefield."

Having dwelt upon the benefits the Nationalists would derive from the treaty—notably that Russia's pledge "pulls the rug from under the Chinese Communists"—the editorial went on: "For all these benefits China had to pay a price, but under the circumstances that price is neither unreasonable nor contrary to the interests of other nations. . . .

"Driven by the same geographic factors that sent Czarist Russia on the search for warm-water ports, Soviet Russia has also arrived at the Pacific, and the means she used toward this end differ little from those of the so-called 'imperialism,' which puts Britain's retention of Hong Kong and any American acquisition of Pacific bases in a new light. But it is one of the virtues of the Russo-Chinese agreements that they are based on reality and mutual interest instead of abstract theory, and it is this element which makes them the great contribution toward peace that they so plainly are."

Every item of the "secret protocol" is contained in the pact which drew this approbation. The concessions which the United States "compelled" Nationalist China to make were, therefore, expressly approved by *The New York Times* in 1945. Why, then, does *The Times* call Yalta from the vast deep, unless its support of General Eisenhower has made it willing to rewrite history and belie itself?

FRANKLIN D. ROOSEVELT Jr.
Member of Congress
Washington, Oct. 1, 1952

Treaty-Making and Yalta

To the Editor of *The New York Times:*

In your editorial of Jan. 24 entitled "Senator Bricker's Backers" you accept the oft-repeated argument that it was Russia's failure to live up to the agreements made at Yalta rather than the Yalta agreements themselves which has caused some of the heartbreak and problems of postwar Europe.

The Atlantic Charter framed in 1941 by Roosevelt and Churchill stated in the second paragraph "a desire to see no territorial changes that do not accord with the friendly expressed wishes of the people concerned." The Second World War began by England abiding by her guarantee to Poland of the integrity of Poland's frontiers. The United States, when it entered the war in 1941, also promised the restoration of pre-war Poland. In violation of the second paragraph of the Atlantic Charter and the promises given by both England and the United States half of pre-war Poland was given to Russia at Yalta.

At Yalta it was agreed that reparations would not be just in the form of cash, but they should come from three sources—namely, Germany's natural wealth, current production and manpower and labor. The last item, the approval of slave labor as reparations, is a direct violation of the Geneva Convention concerning the treatment of prisoners of war. James Byrnes, who attended Yalta as an adviser, was ignorant of this agreement of the United States and said later in his book, "Had I known of it, I would have urged the President to oppose the inclusion in the protocol of any provision for the use of large groups of human beings as enforced slave laborers."

These are just two of the agreements made at Yalta and not because they were broken were the cause of some of the problems of postwar Europe.

You also stated in the editorial that the United States Senate would undoubtedly have ratified the Yalta pact because of the importance of

155

getting Russia into the war in the Far East. Giving the control of China's Manchuria to Russia was the purchase price to which the Senate would have had to agree. They would of course have had to consider the moral aspects of the problem, that there was no representative from China at Yalta, and in addition that in Cairo in 1943 Roosevelt had promised Chiang Kai-shek the restoration of Manchuria to China.

In addition the United States Senate would undoubtedly have consulted with the two executive departments most closely involved in such a matter, the State Department and the military services. This is something that President Roosevelt did not do. According to Edward Stettinius, Secretary of State at the time, the State Department was never consulted as to the political repercussions of Russia's demands. In fact they were never told of the demands James Byrnes substantiates in this report. Roosevelt told Stettinius at the time the question of Russia coming into the war in the Far East was purely a military matter and the political knowledge of the State Department was not needed.

However, General Marshall, Chief of Staff, stated before the Senate Committee investigating the dismissal of General MacArthur that he was never consulted nor even knew of Russia's demands. Furthermore, General MacArthur, chief military figure in the war against Japan, was never consulted as to the concessions made Russia. Stimson, Secretary of War at the time, has stated that he did not know of this agreement with Russia until some time after it had been executed, and Admiral Leahy, who was Roosevelt's chief military adviser, has stated that he was always against bringing Russia into the Pacific under any conditions.

Therefore, Roosevelt made the agreement with Russia with inadequate knowledge and without consulting any of the personages, either military or political, who would ordinarily have had the most complete knowledge of the problems involved. Harriman and Hopkins were his sole advisers on the question of whether Russia should be brought into the war and what post-war problems would be created by our concessions to her.

I believe the United States Senate, if this matter had been put up to them, would have done a more thorough job.

ROBERT F. KENNEDY
Washington, Jan. 26, 1954

The writer of the foregoing letter, former assistant counsel of the Senate Investigating Committee, is with the Hoover Commission on Reorganization.

Agreement at Yalta

To the Editor of *The New York Times:*

Robert F. Kennedy's letter, published Feb. 3, is such an astonishing mixture of distortion and error that it deserves comment. In attempting to rebuke *The Times* for arguing that the trouble at Yalta lay not with the agreements but with subsequent Soviet violations, Mr. Kennedy suggests that the Yalta Far Eastern agreement gave Manchuria to Soviet Russia. The fact is that the Soviet Union, under the Yalta agreement, pledged that "China shall retain full sovereignty in Manchuria" and further pledged that by China it meant "the National Government of China." Obviously, the Soviet Union, in order to achieve its purposes in the Far East, had thus to break the Yalta agreement. *The Times* was correct in making this point, and Mr. Kennedy is evidently wrong when he attempts to contend otherwise.

He is further wrong in suggesting that President Roosevelt undertook his negotiations with Stalin without appreciation of the military factors involved. To make this suggestion, Mr. Kennedy has to ignore the memoranda to the President from the Joint Chiefs of Staff of Jan. 22 and 23, 1945, calling for Russia's entry into the Far Eastern war "at as early a date as possible." The attitude of the military is additionally revealed by the statement of Secretary of State Stettinius, concerning a meeting with the military leaders on April 25, 1945, that "the United States military representatives pleaded for patience with the Soviet Union because they feared that a crack-down would endanger Russian entry into the Far Eastern war."

Mr. Kennedy must further ignore the fact that in July Secretary of War Stimson was informed by the Pentagon that an unassisted American invasion of Japan would cost "over a million casualties," and that, according to Stettinius, the military even after the first test of the atomic bomb, "insisted that the Soviet Union had to be brought into the Far Eastern war." He must also omit mention of General MacArthur's statement to Secretary of the Navy Forrestal that "we should secure the commitment of the Russians to active and vigorous prosecution of a campaign against the Japanese" or of MacArthur's complaint that the Russians were not asking for enough in the way of war materials.

These facts are easily ascertainable. How, then, can Mr. Kennedy imply with a straight face that the decision to secure Russian participation was taken without consultation with the military authorities?

Mr. Kennedy's larger point is apparently that the Bricker amendment would be a fine thing, because it would subject Executive actions like the Far Eastern agreement at Yalta to Congressional debate. His argument, on the contrary, brilliantly illustrates the futility of the Bricker amendment. Little seemed more important in the spring of 1945 than to conceal the date of the Soviet entry from the Japanese; that is why, of course, China could not be apprised of the Yalta agreement, because the notorious laxness of Chinese security insured that anything communicated to Chungking would soon be known in Tokyo.

Does Mr. Kennedy really think that so delicate a military matter should have been made the subject of an open debate in Congress? Does he really believe that in the future we should conduct our foreign or military policy by exposing our most secret and crucial plans to the enemy?

By his own illustration he thus convicts the Bricker amendment of absurdity and danger. Indeed, he shows quite convincingly how very little could be better designed than this amendment to render an alert and flexible American foreign policy practically impossible.

ARTHUR SCHLESINGER Jr.
Cambridge, Mass., Feb. 4, 1954

The writer of the foregoing letter is Professor of History at Harvard and a writer on political affairs.

Suggestions for Germany

To the Editor of *The New York Times:*

I wish to thank you for the interest which you showed in my remarks in the Senate on Feb. 12. In your editorial of Feb. 14 you expressed the view that I was wrong on several points and that the sooner I rectified them "the better for the West and for peace."

I may indeed be wrong, as I noted. It is also possible that you may have misunderstood the points to which you refer.

As for the need for talks between the two German authorities, I did not equate two authorities with two Germanys, a distinction which you passed over. Let me assure you, therefore, that I have no desire to formally recognize the German partition. My suggestion was meant to point out that the Germans themselves, who have already talked successfully on some matters, might also be successful in talking on others of greater importance. I do not believe this is the equivalent of formalizing the partition. Certainly it does not mean "forcing West Germany into a deal with Moscow."

The offer of the Western nations to include Germans of both East and West in the approaching great-power talks is a modification of what I had in mind. It would be consonant with my view on the essentiality of a heavy German contribution to solution of the problem of German unification.

Your second concern may be the result of a hasty reading of the speech. You say I regard "free elections as merely an unrealizable slogan." If you will re-read the text you will find that I said "free all-German elections." Certainly free elections are devoutly to be wished for; but I see no likelihood of free all-German elections. My thought was that it would be worth while exploring the possibilities of assuring free peaceful political expression in the Eastern zone of Germany and free elections in each zone separately, as a step in unification.

I made the point that without some such assurances "the search for peace can lead to the jeopardizing of freedom." If there are Trojan horses in this suggestion, as you fear, I believe that further thought may lead you to the conclusion that they can be those of freedom planted in the midst of totalitarian East Germany, rather than the reverse.

Finally, you express concern over my suggestions regarding Berlin. Again, I believe your concern derives from a misinterpretation. First you say that I propose "to take Berlin out of the context of the German problem." Certainly Berlin is a part of the total German problem. It is also the part which requires the most immediate attention. To deal with Berlin in that sense is not to take it "out of the context of the German problem." It is to deal with it on the basis of the priority which it clearly must have from our point of view.

Your greatest concern is that I "would reunite 'Greater Berlin' under an all-Berlin Government, withdraw the Western forces and replace them first with a United Nations police force and later with German militia under NATO guarantees." If you read the speech again, I believe you will find this interpretation is quite erroneous.

I did call for efforts to reunify Greater Berlin and its public services which, incidentally, are already partly unified. I did propose U.N. conciliation. Further, I suggested that if this conciliation were to produce unification of the city, then a U.N. interim emergency force would replace both Soviet and allied forces in the city, not just the latter, as you infer.

I did not propose that this U.N. police force would give way eventually to a Germanized militia as you stated. Quite the contrary, I introduced the concept of a German militia not as a sequel but as an alternative, if U.N. conciliation failed to unify the city.

I emphasized that if Berlin could not be unified, forces representing the concept of freedom "must remain in Berlin" whether or not the Russians left and that these forces had to be "Germanized" as rapidly as possible. In context, I believe it is clear that "Germanizing" meant replacing the Allied Forces in West Berlin with West Germans, backed by NATO guarantees.

With all due respect, I should point out that editorials in other papers did understand the proposal as I intended it to be understood (i.e., *Washington Star*, Feb. 14).

MIKE MANSFIELD
United States Senator from Montana
Washington, Feb. 16, 1959

Europe's Common Market

To the Editor of *The New York Times:*

When the European Economic Community, or Common Market, came into being it was greeted with warm acclaim in the United States. Economic and eventual political unification of the core of Europe could be expected to strengthen the Western front and to exert a stabilizing influence on the international situation in general.

More recently, however, public opinion in this country has been puzzled by failure of the six Common Market countries and their seven European neighbors to agree on the generally anticipated elimination of tariffs between them. Following a decade of harmonious European cooperation, there developed a split to which no ready answer has been found as yet.

In the United States this prompted a reappraisal of some of the other features of the Common Market, especially of its common tariff against nonmembers, now receiving a "second look" at the result of concern over the continuous deficit in the United States balance of payments.

In the light of the above it may be timely to recall several following facts. The end goal and indeed the *raison d'être* of the Common Market is the creation of a United States in Europe, not much different from the United States of America. Viewed from this goal, the Common Market represents merely an interim phase, a mechanism required to launch the final objective into orbit.

Nothing would be more unfortunate than if public opinion in the United States were to waver in support of this historic project under the

160

impact of current domestic issues (such as the United States balance of payments) which may well take care of themselves as a result of measures either taken or contemplated.

Sentiment in this country toward the Common Market could probably be materially strengthened if the six member nations were to make an unequivocal gesture designed to allay United States misgivings over the possibility of erection of a "tariff wall" against American exports. Actually, concern over such a tariff wall may well prove unfounded, because a prospering Europe will have to stimulate exports in order to pay for rising imports. This alone will give its trading partners a strong bargaining position.

Be that as it may, it would doubtless create a favorable reaction in this country and elsewhere if the Common Market countries were to issue a clear cut affirmation of a low tariff policy against the outside world. Such a statement should be feasible now because it has already become apparent that even high tariff countries such as France have nothing to fear from opening their doors to world competition.

Eventually cooperation between the "Sixes" and "Sevens" in Europe may be extended to embrace wider areas. Such a step would indeed symbolize the goal of progressive liberalization of world trade, even though inclusion of an industrial giant such as the United States would be bound to alter the scales considerably.

Some observers feel that at this early stage of the Common Market, any too close alignment with nonmembers may be premature and might even jeopardize European integration. An answer would also have to be found to the reasoning on the part of third countries that such an extended grouping would not be any less exclusive than a European community, the only difference being one of size.

During its brief span of life the Common Market has displayed a vigor which impressed even its sponsors. At the same time, formidable hurdles have come into view. It would be surprising if it had been otherwise. Existence of difficulties does not reflect on the validity of the final goal, a United States of Europe.

J. STRESEMANN
New York, Jan. 6, 1960

Munich Events Reviewed

To the Editor of *The New York Times*:

I have been reading C. L. Sulzberger's article on Berlin and Munich in your issue of Sept. 30. As Mr. Sulzberger taxes the French Government with "cowardice" (this Government was unanimously backed up by Parliament) and as I was a member of that Government as Foreign Affairs Minister, I would be grateful if you would bring to the notice of your readers the following comments:

Mr. Sulzberger contends that as a result of the Munich agreement "the chance of any potentially strong stand on Germany's eastern border was removed, France's alliance scheme dissolved and that in 1938 World War II would have come "earlier and under circumstances less favorable to Hitler."

I would draw your attention to the following facts:

In 1938 our military authorities stated that defeat was a certainty. "Within a fortnight there will be nothing left of the French Air Force," the chief of our air staff declared, while the artillery chief stated "there would be no modern guns available before a year."

Statements by our Allies were equally disappointing. Great Britain said: "For the first year of war, a hundred aircraft and two divisions without any modern equipment." "Not one man, not one cent" was Roosevelt's reply to our Ambassador's request for assistance.

The U.S.S.R. demanded free passage for their troops through Poland and Rumania, which both nations refused with fierce deliberation. Finally, the Czech military authorities informed us they were in no position to resist an attack by the German Army and that their own forces would have to seek refuge in the mountains. It was unanimously felt that the military and diplomatic situation was disastrous.

By 1939 our international relations had improved. Since Munich we had signed agreements with Rumania and Turkey. Also, Poland, which at the time of Munich was against Czechoslovakia, eventually fought on our side.

This lapse of time was on our side. Due to the progress achieved in the two years between 1938 and 1940 the Royal Air Force won the air battle over London, which proved a vital factor in bringing victory to the Allies. This fact had been recognized by United Kingdom experts as also on Nov. 19, 1946, by the Prime Minister, Clement Attlee.

Ian MacLeod, the new leader of the House of Commons and Chairman of the Conservative party, in the Oct. 15 issue of *The Sunday Times* of London confirmed this fact in the following words: "Some things seem completely clear to me. First neither Britain nor the Empire could have or would have gone to war in 1938. The gain of a year from Munich to September, 1939, was, on balance, of far more advantage to Britain than to the Axis Powers."

And Hitler stated before his death: "We should have gone to war in 1938."

GEORGES BONNET
Paris, Oct. 25, 1961

The writer, a member of the French National Assembly, was Minister of Foreign Affairs in the Daladier Cabinet, 1938–39.

Vietnam Policy Assessed

To the Editor:

Why are we in South Vietnam? The President has said, "We are very anxious to do what we can to help those people preserve their freedom." Events of the past few days do not alter the fact that we have no business in Southeast Asia.

Until we intervened in the civil war, South Vietnam did not appear to be threatened from without. Even now the only foreign army in South Vietnam is the American Army. We are defending the Saigon Government in a civil war. It is not clear that we are defending the people's freedom. The Government is a military dictatorship. No one claims that General Khanh was chosen by popular vote.

In 1963 President Kennedy said "the civil war" had gone on for ten years. On March 6 of this year, *The New York Times* said, "The war is largely a conflict of Southerners fought on Southern land." And General Khanh himself has said that on the Vietcong side "they are not all Communists." According to Walter Lippmann, "The truth, which is being obscured for the American people, is that the Saigon Government has the allegiance of probably no more than 30 per cent of the people and controls (even in daylight) not much more than a quarter of the territory."

The Saigon Government has done little to attract the allegiance of the people. It has herded peasants into "strategic hamlets" and kept them there except for daily work in the fields. Last June one "scorched-earth operation" destroyed a thousand tons of rice and a great quantity of livestock to deprive the Vietcong of supplies. An earlier Associated Press photograph showed a child burned by bombs dropped on a village believed to contain guerrillas.

Our Defense Department acknowledges that we furnish napalm bombs. Two thousand Vietnamese women sat in at Government outposts protesting the nighttime artillery bombardment of their villages, doubtless intended to kill Vietcong but killing peaceful villagers as well.

Our intervention cannot be justified on the ground that a bad minority is seeking to overthrow the government of a good majority. If it can be justified at all, it must be on the theory that if South Vietnam were "lost" the whole of Southeast Asia would follow and that this would be a disaster to the West. But no one knows if the whole of Southeast Asia would follow.

And even if a few thousand square miles and a few million people were added to the vast empire of Communist China, it would not critically change the power situation. When, if not before, Communist China has atomic weapons, it will no more tolerate American military action in Southeast Asia than we would tolerate Russian military action in Cuba. Our intervention in South Vietnam increases the danger of atomic war.

General Eisenhower and Secretary Dulles made the mistake of trying to stake out an American protectorate in Asia. The Kennedy Administration made this mistake of transforming military aid into military participation.

It is said that we are committed, and that the United States does not break its word.

Secretary McNamara says, "The road ahead will be long and hard," but "it is not in our tradition to back off when the going gets tough."

I believe our intervention continues chiefly because it is hard to admit we have been wrong. But dogged perseverance in a costly mistake is no virtue. Successive Administrations have said we shall stay in the war. But the Secretary of Defense, the Secretary of State, and even the President, have no authority under the Constitution to commit us to any policy for years or generations. Even Congress and the President together cannot bind their successors. All laws are subject to amendment and repeal. All policies may be reviewed.

As Senator Gruening has said, after "ten years of tragic futility . . . it is time to reassess our policies and that we quit . . ." Senator Morse, as a member of the Foreign Relations Committee, says "the military experts recognize that the war cannot be won with conventional weapons." He concludes: "We should never have gone in. We should never have stayed in. We should get out."

Simply getting out would be better than simply staying in. But we might well propose to both sides that free elections be held under United Nations auspices to establish a democratic government. We might also ask the United Nations to undertake conciliation.

164

The Secretary General has recommended reconvening the 1954 Geneva Conference regarding what had been French Indochina. We might seek an agreement among the great powers chiefly concerned that none will make or support any war in Southeast Asia.

A plan is not necessarily useless because General de Gaulle advocates it. If we did not achieve a political settlement, we should be no worse off than we are now.

HENRY W. EDGERTON
Monhegan Island, Me., Aug. 6, 1964

The writer is senior Circuit Judge of the United States Court of Appeals, District of Columbia Circuit.

U.S. in Vietnam

To the Editor:

Max Frankel's general story regarding Vietnam and James Reston's specific report that some members of the Administration are urging that our Government "provoke an incident" in the Gulf of Tonkin that would justify an attack on North Vietnam are extremely disturbing.

As the President has said, an expansion of the war would not be in the interests of the United States.

It appears that those within the Administration who urge a change in our policy and a larger involvement in Vietnam have mistaken the intent of Congress in approving a resolution supporting the President's response to provocation in the Gulf of Tonkin in early August. The Congressional resolution endorsed the President's specific action, but, it in no way approved in advance or gave Congressional endorsement to an expansion of the war.

This point has often been misunderstood since some, both in the Congress and in the press, have offered a different interpretation of the resolution.

In colloquy with the Chairman of the Senate Foreign Relations Committee, Senator J. William Fulbright, legislative history was laid down defining this precise point. Although, of course, the Congressional resolution does not limit the President's authority under the Constitution, neither does it offer Congressional endorsement and support for an expanded new course of action.

165

On Aug. 7, on the Senate floor I asked Senator Fulbright whether he could accept the following as an amendment to the resolution.

"The Congress also approves and supports the efforts of the President to bring the problem of peace in Southeast Asia to the Security Council of the United Nations, and the President's declaration that the United States, seeking no extension of the present military conflict, will respond to provocation in a manner that is 'limited and fitting.' Our continuing policy is to limit our role to the provision of aid, training assistance, and military advice, and it is the sense of Congress that, except when provoked to a greater response, we should continue to attempt to avoid a direct military involvement in the Southeast Asian conflict."

Senator Fulbright replied:

"It states fairly accurately what the President has said would be our policy, and what I stated my understanding was as to our policy; also what other Senators have stated."

Because he did not wish to delay approval of the resolution, however, Senator Fulbright could not accept the amendment. Nonetheless, he went on to state:

"I regret that I cannot do it, even though I do not at all disagree with the amendment as a general statement of policy."

When I suggested to him that others may not have the same understanding of the Congressional resolution, Senator Fulbright made it absolutely clear that the Senate Foreign Relations Committee in recommending the resolution viewed it in the same limited sense as the language of my amendment. Senator Fulbright stated:

"Most members of the committee, with one or two exceptions, interpret it the same way."

I would hope that those aides within the Administration who are urging that our Government "provoke an incident" that might expand the war in Vietnam would carefully review the legislative history which defines, limits and interprets the sense of Congress in approving the resolution.

For as I believe most Senators feel, our basic mission in Vietnam is one of providing material support and advice. It is not to substitute our armed forces for those of the South Vietnamese Government, nor to join with them in a land war, nor to fight the war for them.

GAYLORD NELSON
U.S. Senator from Wisconsin
Washington, Oct. 2, 1964

World Court Opinion on War

To the Editor:

President Johnson has taken the decision to renew the bombing of North Vietnam. We are informed that this fatal decision was arrived at after the President's careful consideration of the human, ethical, political and military factors involved.

It seems that legal considerations have not been taken into account. We know that the American people and their Government have always declared the paramountcy of the rule of law. The question should be asked: Does the bombing of North Vietnam conform to the obligations of the United States under the Charter of the United Nations?

Through the Security Council, on the initiative of President Johnson himself, this question could be referred to the International Court of Justice in The Hague in its advisory capacity.

The court's opinion might provide a new starting point for a peaceful settlement.

ROGER PINTO
Paris, Jan. 31, 1966

The writer is Professor of Law at the University of Paris. He was legal consultant to the French delegation at the U.N. from 1949 to 1956.

Russell Defends War Crimes Trial

To the Editor:

The New York Times reports from Saigon that the United States, "pleased with the effectiveness of chemical defoliation and crop destruction missions . . . is taking steps to triple the capability of those efforts." *The Times* further reports that in this year alone "1,324,430 gallons" have been sprayed.

Let me state first of all that I possess documentary evidence of the toxic character of these chemicals and of their extraordinary effects on human beings, which include paralysis, blindness, convulsions, hallucination and inability to achieve unconsciousness (to fall asleep).

You have published a letter criticizing our War Crimes Tribunal on the ground that the judges should not also be the accusers. This criticism rests on a basic misconception of the nature of the tribunal.

We are not establishing an adversary proceeding, because we cannot

167

compel Government witnesses to appear in their own defense, although President Johnson has been invited either to come or to appoint representatives. Rather, the tribunal functions as a commission of inquiry, formed by men who have *prima facie* evidence of crimes and, like a grand jury, have brought an indictment.

We are not stones without feeling, oblivious to the barrage of evidence concerning war crimes in Vietnam. We are people compelled by conscience to form a tribunal because we have witnessed the crimes against the people of Vietnam and wish to examine exhaustively their full meaning, with a view to assessing the responsibility of those who have perpetrated them.

Americans are familar with the bringing of indictments on the basis of *prima facie* evidence and also with the precedent of the Dewey Commission which, composed of eminent international figures, examined fairly the evidence concerning Stalin's purge trials in the late 1930's.

I suggest that those who raise procedural points in objecting to the International War Crimes Tribunal would be better occupied in assessing their own responsibility for the horrendous acts against the people of Vietnam, acts which our tribunal will examine relentlessly and exhaustively.

Justice Robert H. Jackson, Chief Counsel at Nuremberg, stated:

"If certain acts and violation of treaties are crimes, they are crimes whether the United States does them or whether Germany does them. We are not prepared to lay down a rule of criminal conduct against others which we would not be willing to have invoked against us."

BERTRAND RUSSELL
London, Sept. 16, 1966

Judicial Fallacy in Russell Tribunal

To the Editor:

In his Oct. 6 letter Bertrand Russell points out that criticism of his War Crimes Tribunal on the ground that judges should not also be accusers rests on a basic misconception of the nature of his tribunal. It will not function, he says, as a court in an "adversary proceeding" but rather "as a commission of inquiry, formed by men who have *prima facie* evidence of crimes and, like a grand jury, have brought an indictment."

168

He suggests that "those who raise procedural points in objecting to the International War Crimes Tribunal would be better occupied in assessing their own responsibility for the horrendous acts against the people of Vietnam. . . ."

Implicit in Lord Russell's argument is the assumption that the substantive truth regarding the alleged crimes can be ascertained without paying any attention to procedural safeguards. Here lies the fallacy of his position.

Even Bertrand Russell cannot equate the function of a grand jury with that of a judge. Nor can he find support by quoting Justice Jackson that we would be willing to have invoked against us a rule of criminal conduct which we ask to be applied against others. Justice Jackson had reference to a tribunal of independent judges, not to a commission masquerading as a court.

This is clear from a reading of the minutes of the International Conference on Military Trials which were published in 1949 after the Nuremberg trials were concluded. The United States and the Soviet Government had substantial differences of opinion as to the function of the International Tribunal to be established.

The Soviet position was that "there is no necessity in trials of this sort to accept the principle that the judge is a completely disinterested party with no previous knowledge of the case. The fact that the Nazi leaders are criminals has already been established by the Crimea and Moscow declarations. The task of the tribunal is only to determine the measure of guilt of each person and mete out the necessary punishment."

To this Justice Jackson replied that we could not accept the Soviet assumption that these declarations "already convict the parties and that the charges need not be tried before independent judges empowered to render an independent decision on guilt. These declarations are an accusation and not a conviction. That requires a judicial finding. We could not be parties to setting up a mere formal judicial body to ratify a political decision to convict."

Suppose the Nuremberg International Tribunal had been founded on the Soviet concept. Would it have merited the reputation for integrity and fairness which the Tribunal has, and would Bertrand Russell's self-appointed Commission of inquiry rush to appropriate for itself the label of International War Crimes Tribunal?

MORRIS AMCHAN
Former Deputy Chief Counsel
for War Crimes, Nuremberg
Arlington, Va., Oct. 7, 1966

Papandreou Sees Greek Democracy Imperiled

To the Editor:

In his Oct. 5 column C. L. Sulzberger casually suggests that the King "might suspend some of the Constitution should he consider it necessary."

Now, in a later column, he wonders how this "mild conjecture" could have touched off such a storm in Greece! Would he care to make this "mild conjecture" about the American Constitution?

If President Johnson, in the present emergency, were to suspend the November elections out of fear of a Republican victory and contemplate further suspension of some parts of the Constitution, I am sure there would be an uproar across the length and breadth of the United States. By what tortured logic and by what easy grace does Mr. Sulzberger condone in Greece what he surely would not accept for his own country?

The Greek people are determined to uphold the Constitution and fight any attempt to impose a dictatorship. A constitution is a precious document in a democracy, guaranteeing as it does the civil liberties of the people and their protection from the potential tyranny of the state. In Greece's case it also guarantee's the rights of the King. A tampering of it in any fashion can only succeed in undermining the very foundation of his throne.

Mr. Sulzberger has taken a fanatic pro-royal position, and in view of the recent letter by Frederick E. Nolting Jr. on the influence of *The New York Times* on the State Department, this has serious implications. Mr. Sulzberger's wife is Greek; her aunt is an intimate friend of the Queen Mother Frederika, and he maintains the closest personal relations with the King. Doesn't this raise some doubt about his impartiality as an objective analyst of the Greek political situation?

This affiliation may explain his slanderous attack on me. In the past year I have, without a doubt, been the most frequently and consistently maligned individual on your editorial page. He has pelted me with epithets ("arrogant," "loudest mouth," "unrestrainedly vain and ambitious," "hatchet man," etc.) as if calling names were the most effective form of argument.

This and other things raise the all-important question of Mr. Sulzberger's ethics as a journalist. When he said on Oct. 5 that I had "skipped off" to Sweden to contemplate the effect of the Aspida Report on my future, he knew full well that I had been honored many months before with an invitation to deliver the Wicksell Lectures on political economy.

He says the charges placed against me are "serious," but he neglects to say that the report was prepared by a one-man investigating committee (Lieut. Col. Loganis); 28 officers were kept in jail for more than a year without charges; and the chief witnesses to my "involvement" are two civilians placed in jail with the officers who "overheard" conversations: one the owner of the Lucky Bar and a convicted procurer of women, the other an irresponsible journalist who writes for the right-wing press.

But all of this beclouds deeper issues. The Aspida case will be tried in court, and we welcome it. What is of graver import is that King Constantine has become a partisan king, instead of king of all the people. In July of 1965 he literally threw out the one man, George Papandreou, who represented the majority of the people (an unprecedented 53 per cent of the popular vote of 1964).

He has come down, as we say, to the political arena. He can go back up by carrying out one of his highest duties, seeing that Parliament truly represents the will of the people. There is only one way to find out—elections.

ANDREAS G. PAPANDREOU
Deputy, Greek Parliament
Athens, Nov. 4, 1966

Kennedy's Role in Debate on War

To the Editor:

It strikes me that your Nov. 28 editorial entitled "Kennedy vs. Kennedy" might better have been entitled "*The Times* vs. *The Times*."

In commenting on Senator Robert F. Kennedy's television interview concerning the apparent change in the basis of United States involvement in Vietnam, you state that the questions of the validity of escalation were "hopelessly blurred by Senator Kennedy's distorted charge that the basic aims of American involvement have been changed from those that prevailed when John F. Kennedy was President."

But only last month, in your lead editorial of Oct. 15, commenting on Secretary Rusk's explanation of President Johnson's policy, you said, "The change of policy from Kennedy's 'their' war to Johnson's 'our' war—again no matter of detail—lies at the heart of the issue between the Administration and its critics."

When I look at this and at similar comment and analysis by Reston, Wicker, Finney and Brown, I wonder. I refuse to believe that the editors of *The Times* would change their position merely to attack Senator Kennedy. Could it be that they have failed to read their own editorials?

My own feeling is that this recent editorial blurs the debate just as badly as you allege that Senator Kennedy's statement did—and yours was presumably composed on a typewriter and reflected upon, while his statement was made under the pressure of questioning on TV.

You say that it always was one of the objectives of the United States in Vietnam to contain Communist expansionism in Asia. That is so. But it is one thing to contain the subtle expansionism of Communist-inspired revolutionary warfare by aiding native nationalism and quite another to attempt to contain it by making the struggle an American war. This is what *The Times* presumably meant when it spoke of the change from "their" war to "our" war.

And I also think this is what underlay what Senator Kennedy was saying. For when you make it "our" war, American prestige becomes involved in a new and fundamental way, and the aims themselves then begin to undergo a change.

ROGER HILSMAN
New York, Nov. 29, 1967

The writer was formerly Assistant Secretary of State for Far Eastern Affairs.

[*The Times* has consistently criticized an escalation of the Vietnam war under the Johnson Administration that has transferred the principal responsibility for fighting it from South Vietnamese to American troops—from "their" war to "our" war. This is quite different from suggesting, as Senator Kennedy did, that the basic purposes of the war as envisioned by President Kennedy—protection of the independence of South Vietnam and containment of Chinese expansionism—have been materially altered by President Johnson.—Editor, *The Times*.]

U.S. Police Role

To the Editor:

The fourteen signatories of the statement on "The United States and Eastern Asia" invite consideration of their major political themes. The challenge of their theses must be accepted by those concerned with the national interest—and the interests of humanity.

The authors of that document hold that "to avoid a major war in the Asia-Pacific region it is essential that the United States continue to deter, restrain and counterbalance Chinese power." Regarding Southeast Asia, they assume as an acknowledged fact that the Vietnam war had its origins in external Communist aggression and patently find our war against the Vietnamese to be politically fitting and just—one in which we must not accept defeat.

Thus they evidently support, with only inconsequential qualifications, the Administration's China policy, the concept of maintaining military presence in the rimlands of Asia, and Washington's strategy in the widening war in Southeast Asia.

But the United States is not in fact charged by law or political exigency with policing the world; instead, the function of maintaining world order has been delegated to the United Nations by virtue of the U.N. Charter.

The writers speak of "aggression" and "commitments." The valid legal commitments relative to Southeast Asia are embodied in the U.N. Charter and the SEATO pact. Had there been Chinese aggression, or aggression by North Vietnam against the South, SEATO as a body and the United Nations would both have been involved from the beginning. Such was not the case.

We do not charge Britain and France with failure to fulfill either their SEATO or U.N. obligations for the simple reason that the charge could not be substantiated. We are in Vietnam not in service of a legal obligation or of idealism but to serve unilateral "commitments" undertaken arbitrarily within the framework of our national policy respecting China and its presumed Communist accomplices.

The authors hold in effect that the war must go on to bring us victory. They propose, indeed, that there should be "innovation of a de-escalatory nature," but they as well as others can see that escalation is actually in course, with China envisaged as the actual ultimate foe. But this is a needless, fruitless war. China at present is "contained" by its own vast weaknesses, and Vietnam in any political complexion cannot conceivably threaten the American national security.

The war we wage upon the poor, misery-ridden Vietnamese belies our avowed good intentions in the international field and alienates us from world sympathy and world respect.

We should adjust our political objectives with respect to China and Southeast Asia, and seek, as proposed by Pope Paul, peace without victory.

O. EDMUND CLUBB
Former Director
Office of Chinese Affairs
Department of State
Lecturer in Government
Columbia University
New York, Dec. 23, 1967

173

Morale of Servicemen

To the Editor:

One aspect of the President's dramatic announcement is the question of morale he raises among those soldiers serving now, or about to be assigned to units in South Vietnam.

Is the Commander in Chief abandoning them in the first step toward admitted error? Is he "copping out" on the cause from a safely entrenched position 8,000 miles from the blood and mud of Asian foxholes?

On the contrary, the President is raising himself above the dogged persistence of those who choose to enforce their ideas to the bitterly prolonged and predictable end. He has stated what he believes to be this country's commitment, dedicated himself strongly to maintaining that commitment and is now, in effect, calling for new leaders and new solutions.

By doing so President Johnson has gained genuine respect from many servicemen who previously regarded him as just slightly less than obsessed.

(Pvt.) GERALD T. FITZGERALD
Assigned to 82nd Airborne
Fort Bragg, N.C., April 1, 1968

Bombing Pause

To the Editor:

It is a sad day for America when the President himself confirms what informed citizens have known all along: that American pilots have indeed been bombing and terrorizing populated areas; that American pilots have indeed been bombing and ruining food-producing areas.

However, saddest of all is the realization that it was always in the power of the President to stop these atrocities and to save thousands of lives. Yet he waited until the proper, propitious, political moment to do so.

SYLVIA R. FREEDLAND
Melrose Park, Pa., April 1, 1968

For Withdrawal Now

To the Editor:

Dean Acheson, in your Nov. 24 issue supporting President Nixon's Vietnam policy, concludes by saying:

"If there is a better plan than the President's let's hear it."

There is a much better plan. It is to accept Senator George Aiken's proposal made months ago for the United States to declare we have won the war; then we should pull out just as rapidly as we can. Senator Charles Goodell's bill to end the U.S. military presence by Dec. 1, 1970 would carry out that purpose. I know all of the arguments against a unilateral withdrawal, but the fact is that President Nixon's Nov. 3 plan will not only not end the war but will prolong it.

Our boys will continue to die in vain and the costly drain on our resources to the exclusion of most of our vital domestic programs will continue. There will be no peace by negotiation because our adversaries feel quite understandably that there is nothing to negotiate.

Sooner or later withdrawal without further ado will become inevitable. Why not now before we sacrifice needlessly more American lives, kill more South and North Vietnamese, destroy more of the land we are allegedly "saving," and foster ever deepening dissent at home?

ERNEST GRUENING
Former United States Senator from Alaska
Washington, Nov. 24, 1969

New Foreign Policy Needed

To the Editor:

Commenting on the Nixon doctrine of "partnership" and "negotiation" for peace, James Reston, in his Feb. 20 column, writes from London that our European friends agree that the United States is greatly over-extended in the world. But he finds little or no evidence that they will assume more military responsibility themselves, even if the United States brings home many of its troops now in Europe.

They think that "The American commitment to defend Europe against Soviet aggression is sufficient to deter the Soviets from attacking Western Europe," and, in any event, that several expensive divisions provided by them would not impresss Moscow.

Since "the large majority of the allied governments" reject the Nixon premise of more military sharing on their part, Nixon's reappraisal "relies primarily on the hope that he can also persuade the Soviet Union to reappraise its expansionist policies and join him in an era of Great Power withdrawal and negotiation."

The Soviets are apparently in a mood to end the cold war. But it does not follow that they will end their military control of East Europe soon. No people who had suffered three deep invasions of their territory since 1913, including the Western interventions of 1918–20, could give up secure control of the invasion corridor. This is a core interest of the deepest character.

Of less intensity but very real is our core interest in West Europe.

What is required now is mutual recognition that neither side intends to invade militarily the European sphere of interest of the other. Indeed this has been the case since 1945, in spite of the years of talk by Secretary of State Dulles about rolling back the Iron Curtain. On their part the Soviets were too intent on riveting it in place to want to go beyond it.

Vietnam has finally convinced our leaders that they need help in policing the world, to defend "the American way" in it. What is now required is a realization that this cannot be done, that peoples everywhere will insist on living in their own way, and that the saving of our natural environment from destruction is a far more desperate problem than the protection of American investments abroad.

D. F. FLEMING
Nashville, Tenn., Feb. 28, 1970

The writer is the author of "The Cold War and its Origins, 1917–1960".

The Meaning of Cambodia

To the Editor:

An appalling aspect of the President's dispatch of troops into Cambodia has been the inability of responsible elements of the press, including *The Times* to view the maneuver as a tactic of disengagement.

It is not only rudimentary military science but diplomatic as well, that a government sometimes must attack in order to withdraw with minimum loss. Even a nation as scornful of history as ours has editors whose personal memories surely encompass the British withdrawal at Dunkirk, when complete disaster was averted by continuing vigorous attacks against the Nazi army.

176

It may well be, as *The Times* said that the President's explanation has "a familiar and wholly unconvincing ring," "the same kind of reassuring rhetoric" etc., and that "time and bitter experience have exhausted credulity." But surely our mental processes are not exhausted.

Responsible men, aware of the soundness of the military and diplomatic tactic of striking at the enemy in a country which has appealed for help, should not allow their reason to be frozen and deny their government the benefit of any doubt.

I say all this as one who views our deep involvement in Southeast Asia as a blunder. But once committed, the blunder must be rectified with all the resources of reason at one's command. To effect disengagement in Southeast Asia we must employ the full reservoir of military and diplomatic tactics available. If this nation is not capable of seeing and doing this, it is in a bad way indeed.

SMITH SIMPSON
Annandale, Va., May 3, 1970

The writer of the above letter is a retired Foreign Service officer.

Congress and Cambodia

To the Editor:

Your editorial on "Congress and the War" goes right to the heart of the crisis facing the American Government.

We have found ourselves coasting toward deeper involvement in a land war in Indochina in the absence of any decision by the Congress on behalf of the American people. As you have noted, Congress has fallen into the habit of acquiescing in decisions made in the White House.

The invasion of Cambodia and the resumption of the bombing of North Vietnam represent a new phase of the conflict. They throw into sharper focus the need for Congress to fulfill its responsibilities.

For this reason, we and other Senators have submitted an amendment to be attached to the Defense Procurement Authorization Bill which would cut off funds for American military operations in Vietnam, Laos and Cambodia, allowing, of course, for the safe withdrawal of U.S. troops.

The withdrawal of U.S. forces from Vietnam would be completed by June 30, 1971, from Laos by Dec. 31, 1970 and from Cambodia within thirty days from enactment.

Adoption of the amendment is the most concrete and meaningful action that Congress can take to reassert its constitutional authority and to bring an end to the war in Indochina. Admittedly, the President as Commander in Chief has the power to determine how our forces are deployed, but Congress can decide whether they should be deployed.

We are pledged to bringing the amendment to a vote in the Senate. We shall press for a vote within thirty days. We appreciate the sentiments expressed in your editorial which underscore our own concerns about Congress's constitutional role. We hope that many Americans will speak out in support of this position in the next month.

GEORGE MCGOVERN, MARK O. HATFIELD
CHARLES E. GOODELL
ALAN CRANSTON
HAROLD E. HUGHES
Washington, May 6, 1970

Presidential Authority

To the Editor:

It is a highly dubious supposition that the incursion of American troops into Cambodia will speed an honorable peace or the safe return of our soldiers. One may legitimately challenge the President's judgment, but our emotional revulsion should not becloud the fact that his action was neither unauthorized nor illegal.

Under our Constitution the President is exclusively responsible for foreign affairs and is Commander in Chief of the armed forces. In the Tonkin Resolution Congress overwhelmingly authorized the President to take all necessary measures to repel attack and to prevent further aggression.

If a belligerent violates neutral territory of a state which fails to repel the invader, the other belligerent may lawfully enter the territory to prevent the violation from operating to his disadvantage.

Fifty-four years ago U.S. forces penetrated 68 miles into the sovereign state of Mexico, against the wishes of that Government, in pursuit of Pancho Villa. President Wilson justified the action "because there were no military forces in Mexico that would protect our border from hostile attack and our own people from violence."

Unfortunately no court exists today with authority to adjudicate the legality of the Vietnam war. The absence of a binding definition of ag-

178

gression encourages the U.S. to embrace its own view that where our purpose is only self-defense the invasion is legitimate.

National and international law must be improved before we can find permanent peace. Until then the democratic and probably most effective way to register discontent with the judgment of the duly elected Chief Executive is via the mail and ballot box.

BENJAMIN B. FERENCZ
Former Executive Counsel
Nuremberg War Crimes Trials
New York, May 11, 1970

Widening the Peace

To the Editor:

Now that some of the initial hysteria following our entrance into Cambodia has subsided, a few observations are in order.

Plainly, we have not become involved in a "Cambodian Quagmire" as you forecast nor has the country come apart at the seams. On the contrary, the rear areas of the enemy have been thrown into disarray along a three-or four-hundred mile line; his large stores of arms and rice have been captured; many of his men have been taken prisoner. To anyone but a professional "dove," the operation may well have shortened the war.

But of greater moment, the enemy has surely lost face. Not only has he suffered a humiliating defeat, but his "impertinent" pretense that he has had no men in Cambodia has been laid bare for everyone to see. He has been caught red-handed in a flagrant violation of neutrality. Worse still, he is even now trying to foment revolution in Cambodia, in order to set up a puppet government by force. This, in shameful disregard of the truth, long preached by Hanoi, that every country (except South Vietnam) must be allowed to settle its own affairs, in its own way.

I suggest that the constructive thing to do now is to widen the peace. We should demand that the shape of the Paris table be changed, once again, and that places be set for Cambodia, Laos and Thailand. They, with South Vietnam, would then face their common enemy, and have an opportunity to work out a comprehensive settlement. The Paris talks have shown so far that the thing cannot quickly be done piecemeal.

ROSCOE T. STEFFEN
San Francisco, May 29, 1970

For Truce in Indochina

To the Editor:

The Paris peace talks now bear the onus of two years of failure. It is now apparent that new initiatives are required to bring peace in Indochina. Since most wars end by negotiation or surrender, and since there will obviously be no surrender in Indochina, it is imperative that we begin real negotiations now, rather than thousands of casualties later.

In July I recommended on the floor of the Senate that the United States apply President Nixon's Middle East peace formula to the Indochina war by emphasizing truce and negotiation with United Nations' help. I suggested that the U.S. propose the appointment of a U.N. representative to meet with all parties to the Indochina war in an effort to arrange a 90-day truce and to reach an agreement on the form of an international peace conference.

I have no preconceived notions about the form a peace conference on Indochina should take, although an all-Asian conference or a reconvened Geneva Conference might be considered.

Two principal objections to my proposal can logically be made:

That the North Vietnamese have rejected peace initiatives emanating from the United Nations before, and would not be likely to be any more receptive now.

That a cease-fire is not practical.

To the first objection, I would again say, as I did on the Senate floor, that the initiative would not come from the United Nations, but from the United States. The U.N. would serve as an instrumentality assisting the belligerents in finding a formula for ending the conflict.

Moreover, should U.N. participation on any basis prove unacceptable to any of the parties, the proposal could be altered to provide for representatives of the International Control Commission—from India, Canada and Poland—to make the initial overtures toward arranging the truce and the form of an international conference.

And, finally, should the involvement of the I.C.C. constitute a basis for rejecting the proposal, private negotiations could be held among the four parties now meeting in Paris to determine an international format agreeable to them all.

With respect to a cease-fire, I would agree that it might prove unworkable if it took the form of a "standstill" truce. But if all parties were to agree to a regroupment of main forces into fixed base areas, the cease-fire could be adequately controlled and monitored. Isolated guerrilla violations could be clearly identified.

I strongly believe that a political settlement in Indochina is vastly preferable to a legislated, fixed-time withdrawal, because it would end the war, not just end American participation in the war.

I believe that this plan is just as feasible as the initial proposals made by Secretary Rogers regarding the Middle East, and I welcome further suggestions.

New ideas are needed if we are to end the tragic losses—human and economic—that this country and its allies have suffered in Indochina.

CHARLES H. PERCY
U.S. Senator from Illinois
Washington, Aug. 18, 1970

On Nixon's Plan to End War

To the Editor:

While any meaningful effort toward peace is noteworthy, the pre-election peace proposal by President Nixon introduced only one forceful new element to the Paris negotiations—domestic politics.

The idea of a cease-fire, however tempting it may be, is, to quote Ambassador Bruce's analogy, "old wine in new bottles." Presidents Eisenhower, Kennedy, and Johnson expounded the theme on several occasions. It has also been proposed by the North Vietnamese and Vietcong. The most recent suggestion was Mme. Binh's peace initiative on Sept. 17 which was rejected instantly by Ambassador Bruce—setting the precedent for instant rejection of President Nixon's proposal.

Further, President Nixon's introduction of an international Indochina conference would further complicate the profound issues of international politics that are so much a part of this war. In the 4,000 year history of the people of Vietnam, foreign invaders have almost constantly dominated their homeland. In the contemporary period, as soon as the French withdrew from their colonial intervention, America, contrary to its heritage, filled the vacuum with its troops and its war machinery. Does President Nixon not put the North Vietnamese in an untenable position in the struggle between the Chinese and the Russians?

Of course, President Nixon is entitled to a personal interpretation of the Sept. 17 proposal. But having read it carefully, I recall that the North asked only for the removal of Khiem, Ky and Thieu. Not all Americans feel that the present regime representing the South Vietnamese Government are sanctified in the qualities of good government.

181

Asking the North Vietnamese to accept the three major political personalities in the South Vietnamese Government is like asking the American people to accept corruption and repression as an inescapable way of life. If Thieu, Khiem and Ky were extraordinary patriots they would be well advised to recognize the peace-blocking divisiveness of their official presence and would withdraw from politics.

President Nixon, in his address, said our casualties since the completion of the Cambodian operations are at the lowest level for a comparable period in the last four and a half years. The fact is that more than 25,000 mortal men—Americans and Vietnamese—have been killed during the period the President refers to.

The American Government under its Presidential leadership is contributing to the stalemate by a confusing and apparently contradictory personal policy in dealing with elements of the Communist community.

No one single statement made in the President's address could not have been made months ago, or right after the Cambodian withdrawal.

WILLIAM R. ANDERSON, M.C.
Sixth District, Tennessee
Washington, Oct. 9, 1970

Laws of War

To the Editor:

The dilemma posed by the Mylai trials raises embarrassing questions that can best be met by a frank admission of past error.

Prof. Telford Taylor, former chief United States prosecutor at Nuremberg, is correct when he states that Gen. William C. Westmoreland, the Army Chief of Staff, "might be convicted as a war criminal" under the rule of the case of General Yamashita—assuming, indeed, that atrocities did occur at Mylai.

Professor Taylor's only error is in the use of "might be." Under the Yamashita rule as set down by the United States Supreme Court, Westmoreland would be convicted.

Likewise with the statement of the general counsel of the Army who is quoted as saying that the Yamashita precedent does not apply because the Army believed that Westmoreland had taken "reasonable precautions" to prevent the alleged atrocities. Under the rule of the Yamashita case this is irrelevant.

The fact that General Yamashita had no knowledge and indeed could

182

not have known of the atrocities in the Philippines was held to be immaterial, and the effectiveness of his precautionary advices was decreed to be foreign to the issue in his case.

The United States Supreme Court decided that the protection of civilians in a war zone rests on the rule that an armed force "must be commanded by a person responsible for his subordinates."

So simple and pointed was this finding of guilt based on the theory of "command responsibility" that the late Justice Frank Murphy wrote in his Yamashita dissent: "No one in a position of command in an Army from sergeant to general can escape those implications. Indeed, the fate of some future President of the United States and his Chiefs of Staff and military advisers may well have been sealed by this decision."

Shall we merely say "amen" to Justice Murphy's prophecy? Or shall we admit that we are horrified at the thought of trying General Westmoreland and former President Johnson for these capital crimes?

The concept of punishing a man, not for anything he has done but because of a position he has held, is abhorrent. It smacks of totalitarian tyranny rather than Anglo-Saxon law. The case of General Yamashita was a lone and disgraceful departure from this most important touchstone of human freedom.

The answer to the dilemma is not a cynical decree that we have one law for the vanquished and another for ourselves. Rather it is frankly to face the fact that the Yamashita case and also some other of the post-World War II war crimes trials were exercises in vengeance rather than law. The case of Yamashita was not only a grievous miscarriage of justice—it made bad law.

Inherent in the World War II convictions for "violation of the laws of war" is the assumption that there are good ways to kill and bad ways to kill; that it is criminal to shoot unarmed civilians at point-black range but legal to bomb them from the skies; indeed, that the slaughter of babies is acceptable if we are sufficiently revolted by the policies of the political leaders of the parents of those babies.

Even belated reversal of such hypocrisy would go far to solve our present dilemma. But more important, it would constitute a necessary step toward the understanding that we cannot progress in our long struggle to become civilized if we persist in attempting to legalize methods of conducting an essentially criminal pastime.

A. FRANK REEL
New York, Jan. 12, 1971

The writer was defense attorney for General Yamashita and is the author of "The Case of General Yamashita."

183

VI•Human Interest

There is little we can laugh at today—given the massive blunders of our national, state and local establishments. The foibles of our fellow man, however, make for some of the most interesting reading in *The Times'* letters columns.

One can read a wealth of weighty missives on the great issues, but never enough on those questions that get to the core of life in the city and suburb—the "gut" issues of a clean street, an efficient subway, a responsive City Hall, a helpful clerk and some plain, simple humanity.

Ideas to ameliorate the rigors of present–day living—some deceptively simple and hence attractive—flow freely from the fertile intelligence of the readership. There is little that gets by the reader that doesn't bring a new suggestion, an improvement on a foolproof idea, or total rejection, in a phrase, of a reader's carefully constructed proposals.

Together these short letters provide a clue to our character and personalities and articulate for many of us hopes for a better life.

A Protest Against Longer Skirts

To the Editor of *The New York Times:*

I am writing to your influential paper in the hope that you will publish this letter, to help bring to an end a frumpish fashion. I mean these horrible longer skirts and dresses that the dictatorial fashion experts have brought out. They are a definite offense to the gaze and an insult to a Maker who gave women legs to show, not conceal behind a screen of cloth.

I wouldn't walk two yards with a woman in a long skirt. Why can't women have character and individuality enough to wear what they desire, and not what fashion says? Prudery and narrow-mindedness are the sinister forces working behind the fashion designers.

American Women, I call on all of you to resist to the utmost a hideous fashion. Wear your skirts as short as you desire in the name of beauty and freedom of movement. How can you move with a horrible old sack of skirt flopping around? This is 1947 not 1847.

E. G. HALL
Northhampton, Mass., June 30, 1947

An Income Tax Anecdote

To the Editor of *The New York Times:*

As I was filling out my tax return I remembered the amusing story about the early years of Conan Doyle, before he had taken up writing "Sherlock Holmes," and when he was a very poor young doctor with almost no practice at all. One year he made so little money that he filled out a return to the British Treasury effectively proving that he was not liable to any income tax at all. The officials at the British Treasury thought he was trying to put something over on them and so they returned the tax form to Conan Doyle scrawling all over it "Very unsatisfactory."

Conan Doyle returned the form right back again to the British Treasury with the postscript, "I entirely agree."

LANGDON P. MARVIN
Washington, March 14, 1948

But Clean Streets Are Wanted

To the Editor of *The New York Times:*

The Sanitation Department's new slogan—"Just a Drop in the Basket Helps Keep New York Clean"—is still far inferior in style and courtesy to the one the Scots use in the city of Edinburgh: "The Amenity of Our Streets Is Commended to Your Care."

Robert Bierstedt
New York, Nov. 15, 1963

U.S. Embassy Geese

To the Editor:

Though I am compelled to speak from general knowledge, I must sharply question the New Delhi news dispatch of your J. Anthony Lukas under the date of June 5 in which he accuses one of the Canada geese, formerly of the Chancery fountain, of having bitten an old lady.

These geese are my friends; indeed, I installed them in the pool and we came to know each other well. They are proud and aristocratic, rather contemptuous in bearing even away from an embassy, and sometimes a trifle mean.

But they would never, never bite an old lady. One bit an automobile one day and broke his neck doing so. That is the kind of bird they are.

John Kenneth Galbraith
Cambridge, Mass., June 7, 1965

Street Lighting

To the Editor:

One of the simplest deterrents to crime in New York would be to light up our city streets. All of us know the different feeling experienced in strolling on a brightly lighted thoroughfare as compared with hurrying on a dimly lit street. The perpetrators of acts of violence, whether committed within a building or on the outside, show greater boldness when they can hide their faces in darkness.

187

The existing street lamp should perhaps be trebled in intensity and new poles erected where necessary. It would cost money, but surely it would not be prohibitive when compared with moneys spent in other ways processing crime after it has occurred. New York City's Police Department budget for this year is $365 million; perhaps the dollars spent on brighter lights could be well justified.

Brighter city streets could by no means be expected to abolish crime; but they would be a giant step in the right direction.

E. POND
New York, July 20, 1966

Advice for Bus Drivers

To the Editor:

Joseph Schack (letter Feb. 23) is fortunate to have seen buses traveling only in twos or threes; this is really only a mini-pack. The proper size for a bus pack is six or seven, as any self-respecting bus driver knows. There are many advantages in a pack this size. Infinite variations can be played on the theme of which bus is going to pass which other bus next, how many can be lined up abreast to chat companionably through the windows, thus preventing any other traffic from passing, etc, etc.

Sometimes, with good management, it is even possible to prevent passengers from getting on at all, by drawing up way past the bus stop, in front of the already crammed bus which did stop but which is now closing its doors on the fifteen or twenty people left standing in the snow or rain. And so another gay evening passes in Fun City.

The only reasonably pleasant and efficient way left to get around Manhattan now is to walk—always—provided you remember not to breathe in at the wrong moment, especially as one of those bus packs takes off in a cloud of fumes.

AILEEN MOWRY
A Homesick Londoner
New York, Feb. 23, 1967

Tow-Away Harassment

To the Editor:

I should like to raise one small voice in opposition to the chorus of acclaim being accorded the city's new auto tow-away policy.

In extending the ban beyond midtown, the police have reached into neighborhoods where residents are afforded the dubious benefits of alternate side of the street parking. The result has been that ten or fifteen minutes before the parking ban expires in such zones, tow trucks are now seen hauling away autos whose owners have already had to struggle through the unpleasantly competitive business of finding a place where the car will be secure until the next change in rules.

Such exhibitionism by the police serves no useful purpose (a ticket for such a violation would be more than ample punishment) when at the same time almost any avenue or street you may choose is choked with unticketed and untowed double-parked cars and trucks.

The tow-away practice, of which I heartily approve, was designed to clear such streets, not to serve as harassment to motorists in residential areas. Such abuses of the practice also can only serve to alienate the police from the community which they are supposed to be serving.

NED SCHNURMAN
New York, Jan. 20, 1967

In a Hough

To the Editor:

The appalling difficulties confronting anyone who tries to learn English are illustrated by a correspondence now going on in the columns of *The Daily Telegraph* of London about the pronunciation of words with "ough" in them.

One reader, Admiral Sir Geoffrey Miles, has cited the sentence "A rough-coated dough-faced ploughman thoughtfully strode coughing and hiccoughing through the streets of Scarborough," which accounts for eight, and the Rector of Upper Boddington, in Northants, the Rev. Conrad J. Ough, has reported that he has heard there is a ninth. (His own name, he explains, is pronounced "oh," and he recalls that when he was introduced as a shy young curate to his first parish, the vicar said: "You young ladies at the back must be careful not to say Ough (oh) dear in his presence.")

189

One reader says: "Surely Admiral Sir Geoffrey Miles must at some time have anchored a dreadnought in a lough?" Another says: "How about Brougham?" A third says: "I can add 'hough,' pronounced 'hoh,' meaning 'to a hamstring.' "

And a Mr. Hougham (pronounced huffam) remarks that while working recently in his company's Madrid office "you can perhaps imagine the Spaniards' comments on the English language when I was joined by another Englishman—Mr. Hough (how)."

It would be interesting to hear of any American variations.

ALEX H. FAULKNER
The Daily Telegraph and *Morning Post,* London
New York, Feb. 8, 1968

Oh Nough!

To the Editor:

Alex H. Faulkner's "rough-coated dough-faced ploughman" has three choices of "trough." According to my Webster Collegiate, he can lead his horse to water in England and America at a trawf or trawth. But he will find Yankee bakers mixing their dough in a tro and British bakers in a trou. Enough said.

MARGO MILLER
Boston, Feb. 17, 1968

City Perspective

To the Editor:

May the city be always in a state of demolition. It's getting to be that our only vistas are those temporary ones made possible by a razed building. The subsequent months—prior to the completion of a slab replacement—are to be cherished.

Though one may not favor muddy, wobbly boardwalks or fumes and noise from construction equipment, still a city dweller can't help but feel grateful for the view afforded by the ephemeral "open space."

190

What's the use of city planning if well-designed, esthetic structures can't be viewed in their environment—unless, perhaps, from a helicopter or by a pigeon? I'll continue to trip on wooden sidewalks if that is the only time I feel a sense of perspective.

JOAN TOWE
New York, March 25, 1968

Self-Indulgent Parades

To the Editor:

When are we New Yorkers going to grow up and admit that we can no longer afford the luxury of parades?

Weekday parades cause untold hardship to merchants and their would-be customers while weekend parades cause miles long honking horrors that restrict our mobility in Manhattan—cutting off Central Park, Lincoln Center and the theaters.

With our already tight city budget, it seems to me that we could find a more constructive use for our money than paying parade overtime to police and Park Department men.

What organization will be the first to put the welfare of the city ahead of its self-indulgence? Whichever it is, it will win the undying gratitude of its fellow New Yorkers.

PRISCILLA B. HOEFER
New York, May 29, 1969

Promoting Smoking

To the Editor:

From now on all U.S. Air Force medical facilities will prohibit patient smoking and cigarette machines.

Yet New York State uses our tax money to give cigarettes to boys and girls in reform schools and drug addicts and alcoholics in state hospitals.

MARVIN EWELL
North Troy, N.Y., Sept. 23, 1969

191

Source of Phrase

To the Editor:

Your excellent editorial on the arms race wrongly gives me credit for the phrase "scorpions in a bottle." The fault for your inadvertent error is mine. I had assumed that the phrase was now so much a part of the language that quotation marks and attribution would be unnecessary. Let me now report that the inventor of the metaphor, to the best of my knowledge, was Vannevar Bush, talking in a small group in Princeton in 1952.

The phrase and its surrounding argument were later given wide currency by Robert Oppenheimer in an important article in "Foreign Affairs" in 1953.

In their efforts to turn the arms race back, neither Dr. Bush nor Dr. Oppenheimer ever sought credit for such phrase-making, being vastly more concerned wtih the danger than with the choice of words to describe it. But when even *The Times* can be misled, the record should be set straight.

McGeorge Bundy
New York, Sept. 24, 1969

Our National Infinitive

To the Editor:

The trouble with our country is that the national infinitive is split by an adverb that tells us we ought to successfully act before we've been able to deeply understand what it is we want to really do.

Splitting infinitives is not just ungainly, it is a sign that action, if taken, will be qualified; but more probably contemplation of action will take the place of action, and that contemplation itself will be qualified.

In other words it is a good way to sound as if you mean well when you really mean nothing at all.

Cynthia Gooding
Princeton, N.J., Oct. 19, 1969

192

To Move Traffic

To the Editor:

Referring to the editorial of Nov. 28 "Moving Midtown Traffic," may I suggest to you, and the city, the system practiced in Mexico City.

There, they do not issue parking summonses; they merely remove the plates from the vehicle, which are turned into the precinct to which the officer is attached. To recover them, one must go to the precinct and pay the applicable fine.

Aware of the practice, the public does not dare to park illegally.

BERNARD F. FLYNN Jr.
Dover, N.J., Nov. 28, 1969

Decade's End

To the Editor:

The "end" of this decade brings attention to the fact that most of us, including writers for *The Times,* do not really know when this decade ends. Actually, if one would reflect, one would realize that the year 1 marks the beginning of our present calendar and the year 10 was the end of the first decade. If we pursue this simple fact, we would know that the decade of the 60's really ends on Dec. 31, 1970.

May I anticipate the heralding of the 21st century, which really begins on Jan. 1, 2001, and will, as I anticipate, be celebrated on the New Year's Eve of Dec. 31, 1999.

GEORGE KOROT
Jamaica, N.Y., Dec. 15, 1969

Discord in Carols

To the Editor:

The indiscriminate meddling with our traditional Christmas carols has gone about far enough.

I refer to the work of commercial arrangers who change rhythms, change harmonies, change melodies of the well-known carols in a way that is not only useless but destructive to the quality of the music.

193

And some of these carols are great compositions. Recall that "Joy to the World" is by Handel, "Hark, the Herald Angels Sing" is by Mendelssohn. What hack has the right to change these? Most of the other long-familiar ones are also good music. They should not be allowed to be defiled by the vulgar practitioners of the musical demimonde.

In the first place, the good Christmas carols, those that have been heard for decade after decade and even, in the case of some, for centuries, should be sung, not played by an orchestra.

If this is not practical from a commercial viewpoint, and I don't suppose it is, the law should at least require that these venerable pieces should have their integrity honored, just as the "Star-Spangled Banner" is honored, or a painting by Rembrandt or a national monument is honored.

I feel that those who fail reasonably to preserve the original elements of Christmas carols should be punished just as one would be punished if caught, say, painting the statue of Abraham Lincoln in pink and purple.

W. W. York
Professor of Music
Olivet College
Olivet, Mich., Dec. 15, 1969

Man, Ape and Centaur

To the Editor:

The news story by Harold M. Schmeck Jr. throws refreshing light on the relative proximity of the ape and the man, of man and the horse and of horse and donkey. Mankind has already had sufficient experience with the product of each of these pairs to suggest worthwhile conclusions today.

If civilized man may be said to approximate the product of the first of these pairs, its potential can be laid aside. As to the last of them, our experience has been indeed worthwhile as effecting a good end in itself—produced only on special order for man's sole benefit, tireless in work, stubbornly opposed to misuse, and offering no threat to the world by virtue of rampant reproduction. On but one of these counts can we ourselves match that time-tested combination.

How is it that we have overlooked antiquity's experience with the

194

centaur? Fleet of foot, strong of limb, beautiful to behold, adaptable to all the tasks of horse and man, and above all pre-eminent in education as demonstrated by the renowned centaur Chiron, who taught at Corinth, among other places. Here indeed is a proximity worth another test in modern times.

JULIAN H. WHITTLESEY
New York, Dec. 12, 1969

Non-Stick Stamps

To the Editor:

I have just finished two sheets of 100 stamps each. I have simultaneously finished two rolls of Scotch tape, which I had to use to keep the stamps from falling off the envelopes. Stamps still taste bad, but they won't stick. I claim that the Post Office should supply a roll of Scotch tape with every 100 stamps, but mine won't even sell me one. I'd like to go back where I came from: 1902.

OGDEN NASH
Baltimore, Dec. 19, 1969

Spelling Goes to Pot

To the Editor:

Graffiti seen on a city bus: "Sannta Klass smoks pott." Isn't it shocking that today's youngsters can't spell?

LEO J. MARGOLIN
New York, Dec. 15, 1969

Nickel Ferry Ride

To the Editor:

I question the wisdom of Mayor Lindsay's proposal to change the ferry fare. Legalisms aside, and the law appears to favor the present fare, the nickel ferry ride to Staten Island is a beautiful anachronism which deserves preservation—like some precious heirloom. No one challenges what the analysts and statisticians have found, but $3 million is a pittance in a budget of nearly $8 billion.

If I were one of the Mayor's advisers I could bring him $10 million worth of public relations for the $3 million. I would advertise the nickel fare far and wide, in every state and country.

Farmers receive subsidies, oil people get depletion allowances, the postal system operates at a deficit. Why pick on this minuscule item? Actually, if the ferry fare goes up to 25 cents, many of us will turn to car pools to get to work, causing parking problems and adding to the pollution, and the anticipated $3 million in savings will not be realized.

Let's keep the Staten Island ferry fare at five cents.

IRVING HAUPTMAN
Staten Island, N.Y., May 14, 1970

'Love It or Leave It'

To the Editor:

Every time I hear that patriotic slogan "America: Love It or Leave It" I am reminded of the more profound words of the greatest conservative of them all—Edmund Burke, who said: "To make us love our country, our country ought to be lovely."

JAMES A. MEANS
Charlottesville, Va., May 16, 1970

Park Avenue Flowers

To the Editor:

Why chrysanthemums in June? They're all along Park Avenue, masses of yellow and white horticultural anachronisms. Why not petunias or marigolds or any of the other flowers that are both in season and hardy enough to withstand even car exhaust?

The mums are just another unnatural touch to the Park Avenue scene, already overburdened with artificiality.

ROBERT S. MASON
New York, June 9, 1970

196

Prophetic Graffiti?

To the Editor:

At the West 86th Street subway station I saw this poster ad by the New York Transit Authority: "Have you noticed? Subway cars and stations are cleaner. Please help us keep them that way."

And among the tangle of rude and derisive scrawlings, I noticed this neatly printed comment:

"This is an attempt at a self-fulfilling prophecy. Since it would be nice if it came true, why are you so angry?"

PATRICK SIMONS
New York, July 11, 1970

Small Blessings

To the Editor:

In the midst of frustrations, one needs to give recognition to some good experiences that occur. For example, I recently enjoyed a comfortable, on-time, attractive ride on the Empire Service of the Penn Central to Syracuse; it would be a shame to lose this railroad.

Second, the print in the new telephone directory is clearer and thus easier to read.

The exact fare on the buses has worked very well and has resulted in faster service.

And finally we were courteously treated at the Internal Revenue Service with respect for us as individuals and not as potential criminals.

Small things, 'tis true, but worth mentioning.

JANE HENDERSON
New York, July 27, 1970

Add Small Blessings

To the Editor:

How refreshing to read Jane Henderson's Aug. 3 letter of small blessings in the midst of frustrations.

I saw a cab driver get out and help an elderly man from his cab; I saw a policeman smile benignly at two "hippies" walking and kissing in

197

Central Park; I read of Captain Watkins and Premier Castro's civilized behavior on the occasion of the recent 747 hijacking; I saw three lanes of traffic stop without complaint because of a dog loose on the East River Drive.

I, too, have some optimism about my fellow humans.

PAUL METZGER, M.D.
New York, Aug. 3, 1970

Conversation Crutch

To the Editor:

The comma has been replaced—almost. It has been dropped out of the conversations of thousands of people and replaced by "you know." Just listen to television interviews or the conversations of people whom you might expect to know better, and you will be distressed by the constant repetition of these two words. I am always tempted to say—"no, I don't know!" How about a reform movement to clean up the careless use of such conversational crutches.

CHARLES R. STIRES
Amagansett, L.I., July 29, 1970

Smoother Subway Ride

To the Editor:

Has the Metropolitan Transportation Authority ever considered the purchase of rubber-wheeled subway cars similar to those in use throughout the Paris metro?

Rubber wheels greatly reduce noise level (which presently requires conversing in an intensity above a low bellow) and increase the smoothness of the ride.

If the major drawback is the need for special type track, perhaps this track can be used on the new Second Avenue line.

ARNOLD S. KAFFEN
Flushing, N.Y., Aug. 24, 1970

Cleanup Proposals

To the Editor:

New York is among the dirtiest cities in the Western Hemisphere. However, since all we ever get from the Mayor and Sanitationmen's Union is doubletalk, here are two concrete suggestions which would help immeasurably in cleaning up the mess:

Employ able-bodied welfare recipients as cleaners. Arm them with brooms and shovels and put them to honest work.

Close the subways down for an hour each night, and then clean the stations thoroughly.

Both these solutions work in other countries. Unlike Mayor Lindsay, I would feel no pain to see welfare workers cleaning the streets. It is a highly pernicious idea that some work is degrading and others not. All work is honorable and has its place. We can't all be president of General Motors.

WILLIAM GUEST
New York, Aug. 26, 1970

Toll Plan

To the Editor:

I read with some interest about the Port Authority's new toll plan for the Hudson crossings. Although this plan has merit in that it will decrease congestion at these crossings, the Authority has fallen into a familiar trap—it is addressing itself to the problem of moving cars instead of moving people.

I submit that an alternate plan would substantially decrease traffic congestion and also diminish air pollution levels during the peak hours. This would be to charge a $1 toll for each empty seat in each vehicle between 6:30 and 10:30 A.M. Thus a standard sedan with driver alone would pay $5 to enter Manhattan during the rush hour. The same sedan, full, would pass for free. A motorcycle without passenger would pay $1, a Volkswagen with two occupants would pay $2.

The effect of this plan would be to discourage people from driving large cars into midtown and producing eight cylinders worth of pollution and ten feet worth of congestion in order to transport one person. It would encourage smaller cars which tend to pollute less and take up less space. It would greatly encourage car pools and use of mass transit. It would also generate revenue which should be earmarked for improvement of mass transit.

In order to be workable and equitable, the plan would have to be put into effect on all crossings into Manhattan—but buses and large trucks would be exempt so this should not prove a hardship. Also, the tolls need only be in effect during the morning (or evening) rush hour.

I have not made a formal survey, but the average car entering midtown during the morning rush hour appears to have about 1.3 occupants. If we could raise the average to even 2.5 we would cut the number of cars by half and make a significant dent in air pollution levels.

HUGH C. FERRY
Ossining, N.Y., Aug. 17, 1970

Subway Sound System

To the Editor:

Yet one more example of the remarkable insensitivity of the Metropolitan Transportation Authority is the shrill rasping sound systems that have been installed in many subway cars so that stations may be announced.

In addition to being virtually deafened by the screeching of subway trains as they turn corners and come to stops, we must also endure the screeching of announcements.

ROBERT W. WILSON
Brooklyn, N.Y., Sept. 1, 1970

City's Car-Towing Plan

To the Editor:

"Fun City" knows a good thing when it sees one and even improves on it. While some small towns have been accused of setting speed traps for unsuspecting out-of-town motorists, New York has its tow-away program.

Having parked the other day a little too close to a hydrant (ten feet, according to the summons), we had to bail out our car for $50. A casual examination of license plates of impounded cars at Piers 95 and 96 revealed an almost total absence of license plates from New York City. Out-of-towners and upstate New Yorkers were well represented.

There must be better attractions for visitors to Gotham than the "car jail" at the shores of the Hudson River. A $75 bloodletting for a minor parking infraction could hardly be considered part of a summer festival.

HAROLD LOEW
Princeton, N.J., Sept. 11, 1970

Credit Cards for Taxis

To the Editor:
The new requirement that strong-boxes be used in metered cabs has a drawback in that passengers must have approximately the correct fare.

If all metered cabs were permitted to accept major credit cards for fares under $5 or $10, this disadvantage would be greatly lessened. Such a move might also encourage more individuals who use credit cards often to ride taxis more often.

THOMAS P. ICATAR
New York, Sept. 13, 1970

Posters on City Property

To the Editor:
With the efforts being directed toward the improvement of the city's appearance, it is timely for Milton Musicus, Municipal Service Administrator, to inform all political candidates in no uncertain terms that defacement with campaign posters of lampposts and other city property will not be countenanced.

Further, all citizens should refuse to vote for any candidate who permits the use of such posters on this behalf.

EDWARD L. WEISS
New York, Sept. 22, 1970

201

Island of Refuse

To the Editor:

How about compressing the garbage into concrete coated blocks and dumping them into shallow water in the ocean or in Long Island Sound?

After some time, a man-made island would be formed. Its real estate value would probably more than cover all the expenses involved.

The immediate dividend would be the solution of the garbage disposal problem without air pollution.

ISAAC DABBY
Forest Hills, N.Y., Sept. 11, 1970

To Warn Migrating Birds

To the Editor:

Isn't there some way to stop the yearly murder of birds by the Empire State Building? Is it necessary for office lights to be on all night, except for the red one on top to warn low-flying pilots? Can't the bird lovers enlist some scientific friends to devise a plan, such as a circle of vibrations, during the bird migration season?

The area is not residential, and the noise, if any, would not be heard over the airplanes, car traffic and usual police and ambulance sirens and perhaps gun shots. We have too few birds and are cruelly killing too many.

MURDOCK PEMBERTON
New York, Sept. 30, 1970

Are Cities Fit Places for Humans?

To the Editor:

As Richard W. Wallach observes in his Sept. 29 letter about S. J. Perelman's flight to London, the relative merits of that city and of New York as places for the enjoyment of life are endlessly debatable. As a Londoner I await Mr. Perelman's verdict with some trepidation.

What I think is interesting in any discussion of whether cities are fit

202

places for humans is the argument of your Mayor, Mr. Lindsay, in his book, "The City," that Americans have a deep and abiding distrust of such places.

He points out that although by the 200th anniversary of the Republic 80 per cent of all Americans will be living in metropolitan areas, this sentiment still works against the interests of their inhabitants, who are regarded by state and Federal legislators as rather undesirable step-children, unworthy of help.

"In one sense," he says, "we can trace all the problems of the American city back to a single starting point: we Americans don't like our cities very much." He quotes Thomas Jefferson—"I view great cities as pestilential to the morale, the health, and the liberties of man"—and de Tocqueville—"I look upon the size of certain American cities, and especially on the nature of their population as a real danger which threatens the future security of the New World."

In other words, Americans have a Jean Jacques Rousseau complex, and while the vast majority now live in surroundings which their fore-fathers, fleeing the horrors of the European Industrial Revolution, loathed, most of them apparently hanker after the supposedly simple life of the farm, the woods and the mountains, and so have a built-in reluctance to improve their present habitat.

If some people find life in London a little more urbane than it is in New York or Chicago or Los Angeles, perhaps that is because Londoners got through this phase earlier, and faced up to the fact that they live where they do, and had better make the best of it.

ALEX FAULKNER
New York, Sept. 29, 1970

Administration's Faith

To the Editor:

The twin Op-Ed columns of Oct. 2 by Billy Graham and Dr. Arnold Hutschnecker, both identified as intimates of President Nixon, illustrate the axiom that a man can best be judged by his friends.

While Dr. Graham suggests that the precise date of The Second Coming cannot be identified with mathematical certainty, Dr. Hutschnecker assures us that he can identify delinquents because "there is no error in the testing since the test is mathematical."

203

It is this unerring faith in Providence—be it mathematical or meta-physical—that seems so characteristic of the Nixon Administration.

Indeed, one imagines Dr. Hutschnecker dreaming of the perfect examination which will neatly departmentalize six-year-olds into future murderers, armed robbers, and jaywalkers. At the same time, the Reverend Graham is scrutinizing Biblical texts and the statistical abstract for indicia of Christ's return. And borrowing from his two friends, Richard Nixon seems to be facing the foreign and domestic problems of this nation by grasping for a chimera while waiting for the Messiah.

M. H. WALD
Cambridge, Mass., Oct. 2, 1970

'Not a Working Number'

To the Editor:

"When I call no one answers," is the plaintive cry of Isaiah (50:2). He might well have been reflecting the exasperation and resignation of today's New Yorker, who dials a telephone number in the vain hope that his call might go through the first time.

Last night offered the ultimate in telephonic decay. I dialed 411 (Information) and after a short hum, heard a sympathetic recorded voice saying: "I'm sorry, the number you have reached is not a working number; please check the listing and . . ."

I wonder what Isaiah would have said to that?

(Rabbi) HASKEL HOOKSTEIN
New York, Nov. 9, 1970

Lining Up for Buses

To the Editor:

There is a lack of system in the order of waiting for buses. Why should the person who happens to be in front of the bus door when it stops get on first, before others who have been standing perhaps ten minutes or more?

This does not prevail at theater box offices, at ticket windows in railroad stations and intercity bus lines. There the latecomers are properly behind those who came earlier.

There could be a neat placard beneath the "Bus Stop" sign asking riders to form a line while awaiting the bus.

RUTH N. MARX
New York, Oct. 24, 1970

Words of African Origin

To the Editor:

I was much interested in David Dalby's Nov. 10 Op-Ed article on the West African origin of many American words. Mr. Dalby lists a score of words that he says "have an African or probable African origin."

Without further comment, I point out that The American Heritage Dictionary—generally strong on etymology—does not attribute a single word in that list to African origin.

JOSEPH N. ULMAN JR.
Bethany, Conn., Nov. 10, 1970

Derivation of 'O.K.'

To the Editor:

With regard to David Dalby's No. 10 Op-Ed article, "Jazz, Jitter and Jam," concerning the African impact on our American culture, I beg to disagree with one of his "historical facts."

The terminology O.K. was first introduced into the American vernacular by the eighth President of the United States, Martin Van Buren (1836–1840), who signed his correspondence with the initials O.K. (Old Kinderhook) in reference to his birthplace, Kinderhook, N.Y., which meant "Do it." What did O.K. mean in Mandingo?

THOMAS SPELIOS
Fort Lee, N.J., Nov. 10, 1970

More on 'O.K.'

To the Editor:

I was interested to read the Dec. 4 letter of Thomas Spelios concerning the derivation of the term "O.K."

I have always understood that the expression originated at the docks in New Orleans, where purchasers bargained for bales of cotton. Once the bargain was made the purchaser said *"Au Quai"* ("to the quay") and the bale was then carried on to the dock.

KATHARINE A. PARK
New York, Dec. 6, 1970

Cherokee for 'O.K.'

To the Editor:

I disagree with the explanation offered by Thomas Spelios (letter Dec. 4) concerning the origin of O.K.

The terminology O.K. preceded President Martin Van Buren with President Andrew Jackson (1829–37) who used the initials O.K. to denote "in agreement" from the Cherokee *Hoke*. Jackson, as is well known, was part Cherokee.

PAUL FLETCHER
New York, Dec. 7, 1970

Still More on 'O.K.'

To the Editor:

I distrust *"au quai"* as the origin of "O.K." as much as I distrust Allen Walker Read's solution to the problem, published in *The Saturday Review,* July 19, 1941 (the Old Kinderhook Club of 1840) which my unabridged Webster's has adopted as gospel truth.

Far more likely, it seems to me, is a derivation from the Spanish word *hoque* (pronounced okay), the shortened and more common form of *alboroque,* which my Vox dictionary defines as: "treat stood by buyer or seller after closing a deal." Words in Spanish beginning with "al" are Arabic in origin, which certainly makes this word antedate Old Kinder-hook by many centuries. Any objections? If so, I would be glad to hear them.

HERMA BRIFFAULT
New York, Dec. 17, 1970

Lovely in London?

To the Editor:

In appreciation of your glorious picture of London (The Talk of London Dec. 19), may I ask:

Have the Mods and Skinheads all been blitzed?
Is Carnaby Street sedately ritzed?
Does no one raise a Cockney howl
At the racist slurs of Mr. Powell?

C. P.
New York, Dec. 19, 1970

VII • National Affairs

Welfare, inflation, unemployment, a stuttering economy, the alienation of youth, resistance to the draft, increasing drug use, urban decay, hunger and declining health facilities—all problems facing a nation that in recent years has spent its major energies in a frustrating war in Indochina.

These and other problems can be seen pricking at the national conscience through the letters pages of *The New York Times*. Here, concerned citizens give voice to what they feel is hurting America. In their suggestions for change can be seen the constant theme that the nation's priorities need reshuffling.

The problems and issues perplexing Americans are as multi-faceted and disparate as the country itself. Sadly, most of them are not new, as a sampling of the letters makes clear. Equally depressing is the fact that we do not seem to be much further along the road to solutions than we were a decade or even a generation ago.

Limiting the Judiciary

To the Editor of *The New York Times:*

I quite agree with your editorial of Feb. 26 that Senate bill 2646 threatens a dispersal of judicial power that would lead to much confusion. At the same time the measure deals with a real problem which is recognized, for instance, by Judge Learned Hand in his Harvard lectures —that of keeping the Court out of legislative territory; and I might add, out of executive territory too.

There can be no doubt that on June 17 last the Court went on a virtual binge and thrust its nose into matters beyond its competence, with the result that (in my judgment at least) it should have aforesaid nose well tweaked.

Its holding in the *Watkins* case, in which it claims the right to recast Congressional resolutions authorizing committee investigations, is quite irresponsible and indefensible, interfering as it does with the great primal power, an inheritance of the Mother of Parliaments, as Inquest of Realm. For the transmission of this right to Congress via the early State Legislature, see the authoritative article by Dr. George B. Galloway, "Investigations, Governmental," in the *Encyclopedia of Social Sciences* (N.Y., 1932).

Equally irresponsible was the Court's holding in the *Yates* case on the same occasion. This practically repealed the Smith Act, although a year earlier the Court had held, in the *Nelson* case, that the act repealed all state anti-sedition acts, the total result being to leave the country exposed to unjustifiable propaganda urging the right of revolution.

What, then, is the remedy for this vicious nonsense? I would suggest a declaratory act of Congress assertive of the correct reading of the Constitution on the points involved in the above-mentioned cases. And I would add a reference to the Court's weird holding in *Cole* v. *Young* (July 2, 1956), in which the unique doctrine is arrived at that the Court may undertake to pit its judgment against that of an executive official as to the loyalty or reliability of a subordinate of the official.

The country needs protection against the aggressive tendency of the Court, no doubt. Unfortunately, Senate bill 2646 goes so far that its adoption would violate that ancient maxim of common sense, not to throw the baby out with the bath.

EDWARD S. CORWIN
Princeton, N.J., March 10, 1958

Mr. Corwin, an authority on constitutional law, is the author, among other books, of "Court Over Constitution."

Role of the Supreme Court

To the Editor of *The New York Times:*

Prof. Edward Corwin's letter published on March 16 on the "aggressive tendency" of the Supreme Court strides to its conclusions on the matched stilts of bare assertion and strong language.

The stilts would crumble of themselves were they not reinforced by the authority Professor Corwin's writings have earned him among the general public. As it is, it may be worth pointing out that, in characterizing the decisions he dislikes as "irresponsible," "indefensible" and a "virtual binge." Mr. Corwin has, to paraphrase him, fashioned an epistolary brick without straw.

The *Yates* case, far from practically repealing the Smith Act, rested on the proposition that, to be convicted of violating that act, you must be shown, in accordance with normal legal standards of construction and proof, actually to have violated it. Professor Corwin projects a deeper issue, for he cites the case as an incursion by the court into "legislative territory."

The First Amendment says that "Congress shall make no law . . . abridging the freedom of speech. . . ." Rather obviously, these words set bounds to the "legislative territory." It is not quite "indefensible" to hold that, in a country where judicial review is an established institution, it is the Court's business, when the issue comes up in a case within its jurisdiction, to mark the boundary.

If this is not true, let's stop preening ourselves before the world on constitutional protection for freedom of speech. A limitation on Congress which does not really limit Congress is a mere sham.

But all this is *obiter,* as far as the *Yates* case is concerned. The case did not reach a constitutional issue; it construed a statute and passed on evidence. On what possible theory can the performance of these distinctively judicial functions be condemned as a raid on "legislative territory"?

Does Professor Corwin think some people should go to the penitentiary without judicial inquiry into the evidence against them, and without judicial determination of the question whether their conduct is prohibited by the statute under which they are charged? Or does he just disagree, as a technical matter, with the court's rulings on these points of law?

Professor Corwin alone could explain what he means by saying that the *Watkins* opinion "claims the right to recast Congressional resolutions authorizing committee investigations. . . ." The *Watkins* case held only that if a man is to be convicted for refusing to answer a ques-

211

tion "pertinent" to an inquiry he must have been given some means of telling whether the question was "pertinent." Professor Corwin, however, sees the issues in a larger frame, and assails the decision as "interfering with the great primal power" of investigation, transplanted from Westminster.

Does he believe that a "great primal power" of limitless inquisition was somehow transmitted from Parliament to Congress without coming under subjection to those constitutional limitations which, in clearest contrast to the Birtish model, bind all our departments of government? Is it really "irresponsible" to hold that Congress is responsible to the Constitution, even when "investigating"? It would take more than an encyclopedia article to convince me of this.

Since Professor Corwin has introduced the term "vicious nonsense," I feel free to apply it to the doctrine that the committees of Congress, when exercising a function loosely ancillary to legislation, are magically exempt from the Bill of Rights, though Congress as a whole, when performing its central function of legislation, clearly is not.

In an article elsewhere in the same issue of *The Times,* reference is made to the insight of Charles Warren to the effect that bitter attacks on the Court are usually to be explained not on the basis of "dogmatic political theories" as to the proper relations among the components of our government, but rather on the basis of the critic's dislike of a particular trend of decision.

This is so clearly true that a sense of humor, in co-action with a sense of history, should prevent those who do not like the present court's civil-liberties trend from taking up this most hackneyed of positions.

CHARLES L. BLACK JR.
New Haven, Conn., March 17, 1958

The writer is the Henry R. Luce Professor of Jurisprudence in the Law School of Yale University.

Conflicts of Interest

To the Editor of *The New York Times:*

In reading the provocative editorial "Legislative Ethics" published in *The New York Times* on Dec. 2, I was reminded of the intelligent and well-developed practices on conflicts of interest that prevail in the British House of Commons. The experience of centuries has produced there a partial response to this perennial problem that might well be apposite in the case of the New York Legislature.

By custom, the House of Commons distinguishes between two types of conflicts of interest, prescribing a different formula for dealing with each. On the one hand are those situations where a Member may be personally affected financially by the disposition of pending legislation. In such cases of "direct pecuniary interest" the affected legislator is precluded not only from voting on the proposed law, but even from participating in the discussion and debate preliminary to the vote.

On the other hand are those instances where a Member's connection with the subject matter of a proposed bill, while not involving direct financial gain or loss to him, could be construed to color his judgment on the merits of the bill. Then tradition requires that the Member simply "declare his interest."

That is, though he may participate in parliamentary debate, and even vote, the Member must first announce publicly on the floor of the House the nature of his "interest" (whether a directorship in a corporation, previous employment in an affected industry, or even residence in a particular area), if it be one that reasonable men would consider an obstacle to impartiality.

While representing at best only one phase of a solution to the dilemma posed by legislative conflicts of interest, the genius of this approach is that it recognizes and touches the very heart of the problem: the need to insure continued public confidence in the integrity of democratic institutions and the officials who are the custodians of them.

So long as legislative officers are obliged to make known their bias, public pressure and the power of the ballot can assume their rightful roles in curbing and correcting abuse. Moreover, this approach properly places the onus of stepping forward on the legislator himself.

By explicitly obliging him to make his interest known, the practice of declaring an interest operates as a brake on the basically decent man who might be tempted by a less well defined policy to rationalize dishonesty.

HARRISON J. GOLDIN
Washington, Dec. 7, 1961

213

For Federal Welfare Programs

To the Editor of *The New York Times:*

The inhuman shipment of jobless Negroes and their helpless families North, like so many cattle, by Southern segregationists makes clear that we must have federally controlled welfare programs.

There is no other way to insure that these delinquent Southern states will assume their responsibilities and will do so in a fashion worthy of this great nation.

The people who are loudest in denouncing what they call the decline of states' rights are doing the most to make the extension of Federal control necessary.

ALAN MCILHENNY
Villanova, Pa., May 23, 1962

Building Supersonic Plane

To the Editor:

Your editorial of May 3 on the United States supersonic transport program indicates constructive progress in thinking about this next step in air transportation. Conditional support has replaced what appeared to be opposition, and your attention and that of your readers to the question how to proceed in the public interest are needed and appreciated.

The idea you have advanced for a joint venture is sound in principle and appealing as a policy. If two or more United States aircraft manufacturers initiate a consortium or joint venture to design and build a safe, comfortable and profitable civil supersonic transport, their proposal would be welcomed and considered with care.

Not only is there no bar to such proposal being entertained—there never has been during the past three years—I for one would urge the Department of Justice to interpose no objection on antitrust grounds in the light of the foreign competition and the clear national interest factors in the program. In fact, I would personally welcome two competing joint ventures in this early development phase, and have so advocated publicly and privately since 1960.

Furthermore, as far back as the spring of 1961 British aircraft interests were advised that our Government had no objection to their seeking a joint venture with one or more private United States companies. The French received, and likewise acted upon, this "open door" attitude by this Government, but nothing came of U.K. or French overtures to our air-frame firms.

All exhortations and explorations between U.S. manufacturers have failed to date. Why? Is this option still open? Yes, it is still open, but here are the reasons given by industry for considering the idea unrealistic.

"A camel is a horse designed by a committee"; i.e. unity of design is essential to success and two sets of engineers could only achieve a compromised design, especially when all U.S. designers are convinced that a titanium Mach 3.0 airplane is optimum and the U.K.-French concept is limited to aluminum Mach 2.0.

"There has to be a husband in every marriage"; i.e. the air-frame manufacturers, intensively competitive as they are, could not agree on who is to be boss of the job.

It would be difficult to allocate and share the financial risk among venturers.

It would be difficult to share the work and agree on subcontractors.

The Attorney General might consider a joint venture that resulted in only one United States source of the air transport of the seventies as an illegal monopoly. (This is a danger, it is agreed, even though the British-French consortium provides the competition and the United States Government participates in financing and controlling the project.)

The reality, therefore, is that the joint-venure idea has been considered, advocated and urged for at least three years, but none of the aircraft companies have adopted it.

If you approve the principle of the United States designing and building a safe, comfortable and profitable SST, then you should be willing to support a Government-air-frame-maker-engine-manufacturer partnership in which the risks are carefully calculated and fairly shared with subcontractors and airline customers (through advance payments). Then the taxpayers and stockholders would recover their investment from the travelers who enjoy the Supersonic Seventies.

N. E. HALABY
Administrator, Federal Aviation Agency
Washington, June 15, 1964

Decision on Redistricting

To the Editor:

The Supreme Court's decision on reapportionment, embodying the principal of one man, one vote, is an outstanding example of the occasional revolutionary exercises of power by this unique but "undemocratic" institution. And yet, paradoxically, its decision is a logical, evolutionary development of the theory that the Court ought not to meddle in the affairs of men.

From shortly after the Civil War to the middle of the New Deal period the Court set itself up as a guardian of a particular form of society and from time to time struck down efforts by legislatures, national and state, to effect changes in that society. This appropriation of power was roundly criticized for decades. But it was not until the stresses of the Great Depression that popular resentment became powerful enough to convince the Court to retreat.

At the same time that members of the Court debated the exercise of power in areas of general social and economic matters, the Court was building a record of enforcing the Bill of Rights, including by degrees the use of the 14th Amendment to impose, so to speak, many of the commands of the Bill of Rights on the several states.

Out of this philosophical debate among the members of the Court—and among scholars, too—there came a thesis, sometimes explicit, sometimes implicit, that the Court was justified in preserving and enforcing free political processes but not justified in substituting its judgment for the judgment of those who made the political decisions about social and economic matters. In effect, the Court said that if the channels of political decision are free, there is little that the Court need do to insure a democratic society.

But political processes in a democratic society are hardly free if an apportionment system in state after state freezes representation for decades—decades in which the social and economic problems of the society are ever changing. And so, having given up power over the substance of the acts of government and moved on to the more fundamental business of monitoring the political process, it is a relatively small judicial step to reach the ultimate requirement that free, democratic political processes produce a truly representative legislature. Thus, the reapportionment decisions were almost inevitable.

The foregoing, I hasten to add, is not the whole story of the philosophy of the Court's exercise of power. Problems of segregation and criminal justice differ, but only in degree. In essence, the Supreme Court

216

today limits its assertions of power to those few areas necessary to preserve and further a democratic society.

GEORGE D. BRADEN
New York, June 23, 1964

Tax Aid to Poor

To the Editor:

The adoption of a "negative income tax" as a strategy in the war on poverty has of late received increasing attention, which is much to be desired.

Full employment is indispensable to the elimination of poverty in the United States. However, for at least another generation it will not be enough. In our present and prospective economy the jobs the poor are likely to get will not provide enough income to achieve that level of family stability and parity with the rest of the community that lead children out of the cycle of inadequate preparation and inevitable failure.

In the current issue of *Daedalus,* the journal of the American Academy of Arts and Sciences, Prof. James Tobin describes in a most convincing manner how such an arrangement might work. The special object of his concern is the Negro family, which with half the income of whites must support a third more children. But any such system would, of course, apply to all persons.

For those to whom the negative income tax may appear a bizarre, even an absurd, idea, it may help to think of it as a version of the family or children's allowance. The United States is perhaps the only industrial democracy in the world that does not have such a system of automatic payments to families with minor children to help with the heavy expenses of that period.

Family allowances are, I believe, one of the few aspects of social policy to enjoy near-unanimous support in these countries. (Canada is a good instance.) They respond to a real need with a minimum of fuss.

It is of interest that while the idea is not yet a subject of general discussion in the United States, its supporters span a wide range of economic and social thought, from the most "conservative" to the most "liberal."

DANIEL P. MOYNIHAN
Middletown, Conn., Dec. 20, 1965

The writer was Assistant Secretary of Labor, 1963 to 1965.

217

Four-Year House Term

To the Editor:

Your Jan. 23 editorial (". . . and Weigh Four-Year Terms") was properly cautious about the adoption of a four-year term for members of the House of Representatives.

For almost 200 years our political system has operated according to a well-established rhythm, to which all parts of the system have made intricate and delicate adjustment. A halving of the frequency of national elections would have widespread and serious effects upon this system. Many of these effects have not even been identified nor seriously considered by those who have written on the subject.

For example, among the many ramifications that need to be explored would be the effect upon changes now under way in the South and in some of our big Northern cities. A reduction in the frequency of elections would frustrate, or at best delay, the growing participation and assertion of political power by formerly disfranchised Negroes. It also would decrease substantially the possibility of the development of a two-party system in areas long under one-party rule.

GEORGE E. AGREE
Executive Director
National Committee for an Effective Congress
New York, Jan. 25, 1966

For Federal System of Aid to Poor

To the Editor:

The conservation of human resources has now come to be recognized as a national problem. Poverty, wherever it exists, reduces human capacity. The poor of the rural South become the poor of the urban ghetto.

The time has come for a truly national system of public assistance, nationally financed and administered, with national standards adjusted to local conditions and requirements.

Such a national system of public assistance, while distinct in purpose and administration, would serve to undergird our national system of contributory social insurance ("social security"). To distort social insurance to alleviate residual poverty would be a serious error.

A national system of public assistance would relieve the rural South and the central cities of the North of mounting costs which should be borne by the nation as a whole. Lifted out of the restrictions of thousands of tax jurisdictions, a national system of public assistance could become a far more constructive and flexible instrument for the relief of poverty than any simplistic mechanism for distributing predetermined doles to a dependent class.

J. DOUGLAS BROWN
Princeton University
Princeton, N.J., Nov. 19, 1968

The writer, planner of the Social Security Act in 1934–35, was chairman of the first Advisory Council on Social Security in 1937–38.

For Electoral Reform

To the Editor:

President Nixon's proposals to modify the Electoral College system are a matter for deep concern. There is considerable public sentiment for eliminating the Electoral College, but Mr. Nixon favors retaining it and putting it on a proportional basis.

While there is merit to his suggestion that if no candidate gets 40 per cent of the vote there should be a popular runoff (this could apply to any system of Presidential election), proportional weighting of the Electoral College votes would—under the guise of reform—make a weak system worse.

The present system, which allows one electoral vote for each Senator and Representative, gives almost three times as much weight to a vote cast in a lightly populated state as it does to a vote cast in a heavily populated urban state. This 18th-century approach is at odds with a one-man, one-vote philosophy. But the balance is somewhat redressed by the fact that the universal usage of electing electors at large and without proportional representation allows the large states to send their electors as blocs for candidates sensitive to their problems.

The proportional system retains the weighting in favor of the non-urban and often anti-urban states while eliminating the redress of the large bloc. Its use in 1960 would have converted Mr. Nixon's popular minority into an Electoral College victory. While one can concede that this might seem attractive to Mr. Nixon, it hardly seems fair to the rest of the country.

219

Electoral reform should work to effect rather than thwart the popular will. The way to reform the Electoral College is to replace it with direct election.

HENDON CHUBB II
New York, Feb. 21, 1969

Inflationary Spending by Business

To the Editor:

In your recent editorial "Upsurge in Capital Spending" you join David Kennedy, Secretary of the Treasury, and certainly many others in seeing greater "peril of run-away inflation" in new indications of a considerable expansion in planned business capital spending. You then assert that these indications argue for extension of the 10 per cent income tax surcharge, which would cost income taxpayers an additional $12 or $13 billion in the next fiscal year.

But is there not a striking inconsistency in advocating higher taxes on all income taxpayers in order to counteract inflation stimulated by high business spending for plant and equipment? For we have an investment tax credit, whose avowed intent is to stimulate just such spending for equipment, along with highly liberalized depreciation allowances, which are presumed to encourage business spending for plant as well as equipment.

Your failure to mention the existing tax stimuli to investment, which are costing the Treasury billions of dollars of a magnitude not incomparable to the revenues being raised by the surcharge, may well have been inadvertent. Will it be reasonable, however, for the Administration to tax us all more heavily to combat inflation nourished by heavy business spending at the same time that business itself—and especially the biggest business spenders—is taxed more lightly precisely in order to encourage such spending?

This is just one large anomaly in proposals to continue the surcharge. The major one relates to the failure to come to grips with the war spending which is clearly the root cause of our current inflationary problems.

No increased taxes will curb inflation if they are matched by escalation in Vietnam or in the nuclear arms race. Conversely, a speedy end to our involvement in Vietnam and a reasonable curbing of arms ex-

220

penditures will be the one sure way to end our disturbing inflation—
without continuing the surcharge.

ROBERT EISNER
Professor of Economics
Northwestern University
Evanston, Ill., March 30, 1969

Spending Slowdown

To the Editor:

Your news story of Aug. 13 on the revision of money supply data by the Federal Reserve Board concludes: "It is possible that this group (identified in the preceding paragraph as 'some economists, known as the Chicago School and led by Prof. Milton Friedman') will use the new figures as an explanation, at least in part, for the failure so far of the inflation to moderate, despite a supposedly extremely restrictive monetary policy by the Federal Reserve."

As it happens, there is no "failure," as yet, requiring explanation on the part of those of us who have stressed the role of monetary policy in producing and stemming inflation. We have repeatedly emphasized that it takes a considerable time—about six to nine months on the average—before a slowdown in monetary growth is reflected in a slowdown in total spending and an even longer time before it is reflected in a slower rate of price rise.

We have all along predicted that the first half of 1969 would be highly inflationary in response to the rapid expansion in the quantity of money in the last half of 1968.

The growth in the quantity of money decelerated sharply at the end of 1968 according to both the old and the new figures. We are only just now getting to the point at which this can be expected to produce an appreciable slowdown in total spending, and there are many signs that such a slowdown is in process.

If the rate of price rise has not begun to abate by the fourth quarter of this year, it will be time to ask us for an explanation. As of the moment, everything is about on schedule.

The significance of the new figures is very different. On the surface, they appear to absolve the Fed from the criticism some of us have been making that, in recent months, the Fed has turned the monetary screw another notch, that it is again over-reacting as it has so often in the past.

In this detail—the pattern over the past few months—the new figures on money supply are inconsistent with other monetary aggregates.

The Fed has not yet released sufficient information about the statistical basis of its revised figures to enable outside students to reconcile these inconsistencies. Pending such information, I continue to believe that the evidence, taken as a whole, supports the view that the Fed has over-reacted sharply in the past few months.

MILTON FRIEDMAN
Professor of Economics
The University of Chicago
Chicago, Aug. 16, 1969

For Electoral Vote

To the Editor:

Election reforms are needed. But why are we so concerned about the Constitution and so naive about the conventions? It is not logical that we should undo a well-devised plan while we tolerate a dangerous custom.

We are not the first generation to think about the popular vote. Our fathers also considered the idea, but gave us instead the electoral system. They did not want some city to have greater strength than 44 of the states had in choosing the President. Also, the opponents of the electoral system fail to consider that we already have the popular vote within states.

It is almost certain that the intent of the constitutional provisions is the assignment of one vote to each district and two to each state. Had we followed this precisely in 1968, Nixon would have received 290 votes from 226 districts and 32 states. Humphrey would have had a total of 190 from 164 districts and 13 states.

Any one looking at the district votes across the country cannot fail to believe that the will of this nation was achieved in 1968. But if the only measure had been the popular vote, there would always have been many unresolved doubts.

There are many reasons why the district vote should be restored. Confidence in the whole election process would be greatly improved. Much of the incentive for vote fraud would be eliminated. Closeness of the

222

1960 and 1968 elections should have taught us of the hazards of a popular vote method.

Clyde E. Miller
Santa Ana, Calif., Sept. 30, 1969

Federal Food Plans

To the Editor:

In your editorial of Sept. 21, entitled "Making Food Programs Work," you urged the transfer of Federal food programs from the Department of Agriculture to the Department of Health, Education and Welfare. I agree that such a transfer may be desirable.

However, it will make no real difference which agency runs these programs unless some unit of Government is given the ultimate responsibility and authority for finding and feeding the poor. No such responsibility and authority exists under present legislation.

The results of this legislative gap are shocking. As of June, 1969, 413 counties provided no Federal food assistance and seven states had no food stamp program.

Even more disturbing is the fact that most counties are administering token programs.

In 701 of the 1,139 counties with a food stamp program, less than 20 percent of the poor participate in the program.

There are only 20 food stamp counties in which participation by the poor is more than 60 per cent.

The food stamp bill passed on Sept. 24 by the Senate offers the first real hope for remedying this tragic situation. That bill directs the Secretary of Agriculture to administer a food stamp program, either directly or indirectly, in any county which refuses to implement the program where there is need or where a program is not in existence as of Jan. 1, 1971. It also requires the Secretary to assume responsibility for administering food stamps in any county where participation by the poor is low.

By explicitly making the Federal Government ultimately responsible for assuring that food stamps will be available to those in need of assistance, the bill will make it difficult for Government officials to continue playing musical chairs with the problem of hunger and malnutrition. The Department of Agriculture will no longer have the excuse

223

that it lacks sufficient authority to override recalcitrant local

If the bill is enacted, and if the Secretary of Agriculture fail sume his responsibilities, then I think we should look to another agency to administer these programs.

WALTER F. MON
U.S. Senator from Minn
Washington, Sept. 30, 1

Agnew—Voice of Silent Majority

To the Editor:

Your criticism of Vice President Agnew in your editorial "Exercise in Folly" (Nov. 23) was unfair in many respects.

The very fact that you admit that he "touched on certain points that have long been of concern to thoughtful newspapermen" and that "the question of monopoly control can be serious" shows that his remarks had some very useful purpose. More than that, they had definitely cleared the political air of this country in other very important ways.

It has become clear now that the President has a very sizable majority to back him in his Vietnam policy. The vocal minority now knows that it is a minority. It apparently did not know it before.

The Senate Foreign Affairs Committee and many members of Congress are beginning to realize that they have not been expressing the will and intent of the now not-so-silent majority. This, in itself, is a factor leading toward the unification of the country.

The high point of the protest movement has been reached and passed. Part of the minority is being discouraged by the very vigorous stance of the majority opinion; another part is soberly reassessing its position and perhaps grudgingly admitting that the President's policy may after all succeed.

Thus, far from "exacerbating the divisions in this country," the Vice President's speeches have, in effect, tended to unify it in the direction of the majority. Its voice is now clearly being heard across the land.

The bandwagon effect works also the other way. The minority may still protest, but in a democratic country it is the will of the majority that should prevail.

WALTER BERNARD
Brookville, L.I., Nov. 30, 1969

Choices for Court

To the Editor:

President Nixon's petulant remarks about the failure of the Senate to confirm Judge Carswell are misguided in their thrust and alarming in their implications.

First, the Senate vote on Judge Carswell revealed a sectional pattern only in the affirmative vote: every Democratic vote for Carswell but one (Bible of Nevada) came from the South, while votes against confirmation came from every section of the country. Second, the President's reference to the Senate as "constituted the way it is today" is at best ambiguous, at worst dangerous. The Senate is constituted precisely as the Constitution originally provided; two Senators from each state. Under this arrangement the South is fully represented by any criteria.

Third, and most important, the President made clear his intention to limit appointments to the Supreme Court to present members of the Federal and state benches. Such a limitation would be most regrettable.

Few of the great judges of the Supreme Court had any previous judicial experience. Chief Justice Jay did not, nor Marshall, nor Taney, nor Chase, Waite, Fuller, Hughes, Stone or Warren—the majority of our Chief Justices. Other distinguished justices have been drawn from politics or from law schools—the great Justice Story, for example, Justice McLean, Justice Curtis or, in more recent times, Black, Frankfurter and Douglas.

Finally, the framers of the Constitution clearly did not expect or imagine any such limitation as the President proposes, for the Constitution did not create any inferior Federal courts but left this entirely to the discretion of the Congress.

HENRY STEELE COMMAGER
Amherst, Mass., April 10, 1970

Constructionism

To the Editor:

How reassuring it is that strict constructionists will be appointed to the Supreme Court at a time when a loose constructionist President, with alarmingly expansive notions of the war-power clause of the Constitution, occupies the White House.

JEROLD S. AUERBACH
Cambridge, Mass., May 17, 1970

Guidelines for Draft

To the Editor:

The Times editorial of June 17 rightly argees with the recent Supreme Court ruling that conscientious objection must not be tied to religion. The editorial did not, however, see the equal absurdity and injustice to a democratic state ruling on "individual sincerity" in ethics and morals.

The guidelines given by Dr. Curtis Tarr require a ruling not only on sincerity, but on whether or not training of some sort or other is "rigorous" and whether the beliefs are part of a system held also by "other wise men." It is the very basis of our system that the Government shall never rule on what is in our minds and hearts. There, at least, we are to be left alone.

Nowhere else in American law or administration is a state official asked to rule on the inner thoughts and attitudes of a citizen. In the courts, it is at least an act, not a thought, that is judged.

A Selective Service official recently remarked he needed "the wisdom of Solomon" to decide on sincerity. "Rigorous training" as an alliterative but ambiguous replacement for religious training will call for even more wisdom. It was the firm belief of our forefathers that they had fashioned a state where a Jesus, a Martin Luther or a Socrates could never be tried in the first place. Yet every one of those men held beliefs at odds with the rigorous training and belief systems of their youth. Every one of them might have been judged guilty of "insincerity" under Dr. Tarr's guidelines.

Your suggestion that "a partial answer" may be "opening up substitute options of service unrelated to violence and killing" is confusing. If you mean alternative service, that is now available (and often rejected by youth as too much participation in an evil system).

You may be suggesting "national service," extending the draft to all young men (and young women perhaps), sending some to military service and others to civilian but "useful" activities. If that is what you mean, you are advocating an extension of the control over youth by the state at a time when youth are demanding their freedom and standing by their consciences in doing so at the risk of prison and mass emigration.

The real solution is to return to the American tradition of allowing the individual to choose for himself. The Welsh decision points up the logical absurdity of having a compulsory military draft and trying to be fair in allowing conscientious objection.

If all men (regardless of their education or articulateness) are given the true choice of conscience, the draft becomes impossible. The state has no right to rule over conscience, and it cannot do so. The answer is simple: End the draft.

THOMAS C. REEVES
National Director
National Council to Repeal the Draft
Washington, June 18, 1970

Senators Back National Health Plan

To the Editor:

Your July 9 editorial adopts a timid approach to national health insurance and is based on an unfortunate philosophy of the role of such insurance in improving the quality of health care in America. As members of the Committee of 100 for National Health Insurance and as Senate sponsors of the bill soon to be introduced in Congress, we believe that the program offers the best hope of achieving the broad reforms so urgently needed in each of the three basic aspects of our health care system—organization, delivery and financing.

At the bottom, the failures you cite in Medicare and Medicaid were the result of their inadequate scope. In spite of the important successes of those programs, we know now that health insurance cannot simply be a financing mechanism. We know that health insurance alone cannot be translated instantaneously into more doctors, more nurses, more health facilities, or better organization of the delivery system.

Instead, as the Committee for National Health Insurance proposed, the insurance program must be used as a catalyst to improve the health system. Thomas Paine declared at the founding of the American Republic: "Give me a lever and we shall move the world." We say, give us the lever of national health insurance and we shall move the medical world and achieve the comprehensive reforms that are so desperately needed.

To those who say that national health insurance won't work unless we first have an enormous increase in health manpower and health facilities and a revolution in the delivery of health care, we reply that until we begin implementing a program of national health insurance, neither Congress nor the medical profession will ever take the basic steps that are necessary to improve the system. Without national health insurance to

227

galvanize us into action, we shall simply continue to patch the present system beyond any reasonable hope of improvement.

EDWARD M. KENNEDY
U.S. Senator from Massachusetts
RALPH YARBOROUGH
U.S. Senator from Texas
Washington, July 10, 1970

For a Volunteer Army

To the Editor:

Your Aug. 28 editorial "No American Mercenaries" implies by its title that our armed forces would become a group of mercenaries, men who sell their combat services to other countries, under an all-volunteer system. This clearly was not the case in our over 170 years experience with an all-volunteer military nor has it been with our less than 35 years experience with a conscripted force.

The legislation, which had the support of 37 Senators, would have raised basic pay of enlistees and first-term officers. Today, when a man is coerced into the armed forces and subsidizes almost 50 per cent of his service, including pay, food, lodging, and medical benefits—when over 20,000 servicemen are on welfare—it is a disgrace to our society that those who bear the responsibility of our country's defense do not receive equitable pay.

To claim that by raising military pay to an equitable level would greatly induce the poor and the black to join the military is factually incorrect. The pay level within the military is already generally above the poverty level, so the financial inducement to the poor is presently existent.

Although there would be a slight increase in the ratio of non-whites to whites in an all-volunteer military, as projected by the President's Commission on an All-Volunteer Armed Force, their proportion in the armed forces would be roughly the same as their ratio to the overall population.

Asserting that a volunteer armed force would be static, insolated and contrary to "the concept of the militia" is also a contradiction of facts. In an all-volunteer force of 2.5 million men (projected force strength within the next three years) there would be an annual turnover of 325,000 men.

228

Military isolationism is determined by civilian controls applied by the President and Congress, economic influences and the state of international relations. There is no positive correlation between the manner of recruitment and the frequency of *coup d'état*. Our country has had conscription only three times in its history, the past 20 years being the first time we have had a peacetime draft.

The alternative to voluntarism that is offered by *The Times* is national compulsory service which is diametrically opposed to the cornerstone of our country's foundation, the value of individual liberty.

Universal conscription, particularly during peacetime, is anathema to our Republic and individual rights. In monetary terms, it would cost a minimum of an additional annual $16 billion and perhaps as much as $40 billion. We would become in the process the essence of the totalitarianism against which we have so valiantly fought since our founding and negate the very rationale of our creation.

MARK O. HATFIELD
U.S. Senator from Oregon
Washington, Aug. 31, 1970

To Prevent Deadlock in Presidential Election

To the Editor:

It now appears unlikely that the proposed constitutional amendment providing for direct popular election of the President will receive the necessary two-thirds vote in the Senate this session. This ought not to mean, however, that reform in the method of choosing our Presidents must again be postponed.

The truly serious dangers in the present system could be avoided through a more limited amendment that would in all likelihood be favored by both the supporters and the opponents of direct popular vote. If the present proposal fails, such a substitute should immediately be considered.

The existing method has been objected to on three grounds:

Individual Presidential electors have occasionally cast their votes contrary to the mandate of the voters who had chosen them. In a close election, such defections could be decisive. There is therefore always a possibility of a stolen or disputed election.

If no candidate obtains a majority of electoral votes, the election is referred to the House of Representatives, where each state casts one vote. A state whose delegation is divided casts no vote at all, and yet a majority of all of the states is necessary to elect a new President. Where the major parties are closely balanced, there is a distinct possibility of neither leading candidate securing the backing of a majority of the states. Wallace forces might then attempt to make a "deal" with one of them, or there might be a protracted deadlock, with no President chosen by Jan. 20.

The candidate with the most popular votes may nevertheless lose in electoral votes.

Opposition to direct popular vote has centered almost entirely on the third of these points. The shift from electoral votes to popular votes as the criterion of victory might cause changes in the political balance of power, and those who believe their interests would be hurt by the change are understandably apprehensive. Fear has also been expressed that the two-party system would be jeopardized.

But nobody to my knowledge has expressed opposition to the amendment on either the ground that it would destroy the chance for an elector to break faith with those who had chosen him, or because it would remove the possibility of deadlock in the House of Representatives.

With the possible exception of George Wallace, there are few people in our political life who would welcome the chaos that would follow either a stolen or a stalemated election. An amendment narrowly drawn to avoid these dangers ought to receive widespread support.

Thus, if we have to postpone a decision on direct popular vote we ought not delay in coping with the truly frightening pitfalls in the present system of electing Presidents. The two serious risks—that of the faithless elector, and the chance of stalemate in the House of Representatives —are the real dangers that should urgently be dealt with. We can live with a President who comes in second in popular votes, but we may not be able to survive a stolen or deadlocked election.

A constitutional amendment to meet the problem would be quite simple. The defecting elector could be taken care of merely by eliminating the office of elector, and counting the electoral votes automatically. Deadlock could be avoided by referring the election to a joint session of the Senate and the House, with each member (instead of each state) casting one vote, only the two (instead of three) leading candidates in contention, and a majority of a quorum sufficient for election.

We should not wait to act until a crisis is upon us.

ALBERT J. ROSENTHAL
Professor of Law, Columbia University
New York, Sept. 22, 1970

230

Family Assistance Plan Backed

To the Editor:

The Times is to be commended for supporting President Nixon's welfare reform bill, the Family Assistance Plan. While the Plan does contain imperfections, Senator Ribicoff's proposal to conduct an experiment in selected welfare districts for a year prior to implementation would give the Congress an opportunity to appraise its feasibility.

However, is it necessary to wait in the case of the aged, the blind and the permanently and totally disabled who are now receiving public assistance. Unlike others on welfare, the life circumstances of these adult recipients seldom change in terms of their continuing eligibility for financial aid.

The Family Assistance Plan would eliminate the present assistance programs for the aged, blind and disabled and would establish instead a new combined Federal-state program to cover them. The Federal Government would administer this new program, if agreed to by the States, and would assume 100 per cent of the administrative costs.

These three adult categories, know as Old Age Assistance, Assistance to the Blind and Aid to the Permanently and Totally Disabled, constitute 59 per cent of the total public assistance caseload for the nation. In the year 1969 the cost of administering these three categories, apart from the cost of their financial grants, was $357,077,000. The share of the states and the local welfare districts was $148,885,000.

Consequently, if we federalized the administration of public assistance to the aged, blind and disabled we would not only bring them the benefits of welfare reform, we would also relieve the States and the localities of the cost of administration. For New York State that would be $19 million of State and local money annually, of which more than $7 million would be saved by New York City.

This assumption of administrative costs by the Federal Government would not be an intolerable financial burden since it reimburses the states and local welfare districts approximately 58 per cent of what they now spend for administration.

Also, approval of that part of the Family Assistance Plan which provides for the aged, blind and disabled would separate out 59 per cent of the public assistance caseload. The remaining 41 per cent, which includes the most sensitive cases involving such problems as desertion, dependency of children, unemployment, and work incentive, could then be dealt with more effectively under Senator Ribicoff's proposal for a year-long appraisal.

Executive Vice President
Federation of Protestant Welfare Agencies

New York, Sept. 28, 1970

The writer was formerly First Deputy Commissioner of the New York City Department of Social Services.

Findings on Obscenity and Pornography

To the Editor:

The excerpts from the majority report of the Commission on Obscenity and Pornography reveal a number of dubious premises, allegations and conclusions. For example, the commission states that there is no empirical evidence that exposure to pornography leads to sexually harmful or deviant practices. While this may be true, a more accurate statement would have been: "The causes of sexual aggression and deviancy are currently uncertain." Any number of responsible scientists would support this assertion.

The commission gives us a reassuring comment on the nonharmful relationship between pornography and "the moral climate of America as a whole." It is quite ludicrous for the commission to leave the impression that it has given us a scientific judgment concerning the comparative moral quality of our society today compared to that of an earlier period when moral patterns differed and pornography was far less widespread. Or to contend that it can scientifically ascertain what factors are or are not responsible for those differences. The only honest answer is, "Science cannot tell us."

The commission apparently chose to disregard the conclusions of respected social scientists like J. D. Unwin and Pitirim Sorokin that societies which experience a relaxation of sexual standards eventually suffer a decline in creativity and the rate of cultural advance. True, these conclusions are not scientifically disproved. They do, however, correspond to the intuitions of a majority of Americans who are fearful of the long-range effects of sexual permissiveness—a permissiveness which is unquestionably encouraged by the pornography industry and the en-

232

tertainment industry in general. Since no one can prove that these fears are ill-founded, they deserve to be treated with respect.

As for the commission's claim that the majority of Americans want total freedom for adults to see and read explicit sexual materials if they wish, this may appear to say more than it really says. I am convinced that if Gallup asks the American people if they think stage and screen should be completely free commercially to exhibit scenes of sexual intercourse and sexual perversion to adults, an overwhelming majority of Americans would dissent. That dissent would not represent an ominously repressive attitude but a healthy reaction of shock and indignation over entrepreneurs who acknowledge no bounds of decency in their rush for the dollar.

Of course it is chic for intellectuals to treat this phenomenon with levity or to look upon it as one more step toward freedom, but it reflects no credit upon the intellectual community that it refuses to examine these abuses with the sobriety they deserve. We are seeing only the beginning of "anything goes" in entertainment; when we have seen its culmination some years hence, there may be a re-examination of the premise that freedom of entertainment knows no limits and that balance and proportion have nothing to contribute when the latest interpretation of freedom knocks on the door.

This is the Age of Excess. It was too much to hope, therefore, that the current explosion of sexual permissiveness (an interesting byproduct of war) would not go to the opposite extreme of the Victorian period. The moral fallout will not be fully evident for years, no doubt, but when it comes it should prove enlightening to those who over-rate man's capacity to cope with an uninhibited sexual environment.

Meanwhile, the intellectual community has largely abandoned its responsibility to cast a critical eye on the moral implications of what goes on in the entertainment world. Its dereliction is a serious one.

REO M. CHRISTENSON
Professor of Political Science
Miami University
Oxford, Ohio, Oct. 9, 1970

233

Packing the Congress

To the Editor:

Those old enough will remember the uproar when Franklin Roosevelt attempted to pack the Supreme Court with Justices who would "cooperate" with the Executive by making decisions upholding his Administration's policies. The judicial branch of the Government was to become subservient to the Executive and the very integrity of our form of government with its checks and balances was threatened.

Today an attempt to make the legislative branch of the Government subservient to the Executive is being undertaken by the Nixon-Agnew Administration. In this endeavor the Executive is being aided and abetted by the American Security Council and similar organizations.

Agnew is stumping the nation to persuade the voters to purge certain Representatives whom they have sent to Congress and elect others who will "cooperate" with the Executive.

To "cooperate" means to vote for legislation recommended by the Executive, to raise taxes recommended by the Executive and to make appropriations for such purposes as may be recommended by the Executive, including the support of armies in undeclared wars.

In substance the people of the United States are being requested to replace an independent legislative branch of the Government with representatives who will "cooperate" with the Executive. It is time for the citizens of the nation to stop, look and listen. Unless they do so, the road to eventual dictatorship is wide open.

JEREMIAH M. EVARTS
New York, Oct. 10, 1970

For the Quota Bill and Why

To the Editor:

I was among the few economists who chose not to subscribe to the "Appeal for Freer Trade" asking Congress to reject and the President to veto if necessary the import-limiting trade bill.

We are doubtless few compared to the 4,390 economists who signed the "appeal" circulated to the profession by prominent economists. We nonsubscribers felt concern about the rising tide of importation which has injured a series of industries and wiped out our traditional commodity trade surplus.

234

If this tidal wave followed lines of comparative advantage, we would not object. But the tidal wave rather grows out of the dollar exchange rates shaped up mainly in the late forties and fifties to promote the economic and industrial recovery, or intensified economic development of our present industrial competitors, many of them badly hurt in World War II.

These exchange rates, in conjunction with foreign currency wage levels, result in very low labor costs of production abroad which, together with the pickup of foreign labor productivity which has offset foreign wage inflation, has played havoc with our more vulnerable industries.

Many economists who signed the appeal would agree that present exchange rates significantly overvalue the dollar, especially when allowance is made for American capital outflow and governmental transfers. To repress the effects of this overvalued dollar must we subsidize farm exports, restrict direct investment abroad, tax domestic purchases of foreign bond issues, attempt to restrict American tourist outflows, and finally undermine our own prosperity and slow down our economic growth to prevent an undue growth of our payment deficit?

The proper remedy for an overvalued exchange rate is exchange-rate adjustment ("devaluation") and not important restrictions, especially giving selective relief to particular industries. Unfortunately, exchange-rate relief by unilateral devaluation is precluded by the transformation of our domestic money into an international standard of value. Under present institutional arrangements, our exchange rates can only be changed by decisions of our trading competitors to choose to "revalue" ("appreciate") their currencies or to let their currencies "float."

I cannot watch the gradual liquidation of American industrial potential on the vain hope that foreign monetary authorities will be sensitive to our needs and capacities and will establish exchange rates that would permit us competitive terms of trade at full employment. Nor am I willing to wait until we change the institutional arrangements around which powerful vested interests are clustered.

Rather than that, I go for the "quota" bill with all of its imperfections.

MANUEL GOTTLIEB
Professor of Economics
University of Wisconsin
Milwaukee, Oct. 8, 1970

Disaster Areas: Cities and States

To the Editor:

For a people increasingly caught up in the rhetoric of "quality of life," we are surely a nation of ostriches. We refuse to see that we are experiencing a new kind of Malthusianism: state and local revenues increase arithmetically; state and local needs and costs explode geometrically.

The consequences of the differing slopes of these two curves are becoming clearer every day. Essential services are being eroded. Streets remain unrepaired. Schools cut back on essential programs and fail to undertake crucial innovations. Offal becomes awfuller. Housing becomes dilapidated and finally derelict. Industry moves to Bucolia—reducing state and local urban revenues still further. Crime and delinquency mount. Environmental clean-ups are indefinitely postponed. Health and welfare services crumble into sullen perfunctoriness. Traffic congestion takes the joy out of any form of mobility—pedestrian or vehicular. Race relations become angrier.

For all this there are reasons and they are many and complex.

There may be euphemisms for the cure, but the essential and painful medicine is a massive increase in Federal aid. Money is not the total solution, but it is clearly far ahead of whatever is in second place; urbanized states and localities need massive infusions of Federal tax money tied to evidences of equalized state and local tax effort, and to indexes of local need.

Why cannot the states and localities do it by themselves? The fact is that in a governmental world of disparate, competitive and unequal state and local jurisdictions, and in an economic world of private decision making, there is no conceivable way in which any single state or locality can lick its own fiscal problems.

If, for example, state and local authorities try to be responsible—e.g. raising local taxes to meet rapidly escalating needs and costs—private citizens and corporations still have the right to seek low-tax, low-service areas for relocation or for new plant. At the same time, as these key elements in the tax base withdraw, the needy flock to the public jurisdictions whose very humaneness drives up tax rates.

Only the Federal Government can provide a meaningful escape from this impossible trap. Only the Federal Government has the revenue powers and the redistributive powers that can save our most heavily burdened state and local governments. Only the Federal Government has the "clout" to promote an equalized tax effort among state and local jurisdictions in this nation, and to require the kinds of delivery-service managerial improvements that must accompany increased funds if citizen-beneficiaries are in truth to benefit from additional appropriations.

What will it take to move our national leaders to understand what is happening and what they must do? Presidential leadership is essential but insufficient. The crux of the matter is in the Congress.

Senators and Representatives in both parties from hard-pressed urban areas must find a way of overcoming their reluctance to take on the rural-suburban gentility that has dominated the Congress and has distorted this nation's conscience for more than a generation.

The time has come to end what Representative Daddario used to call the "one-way log-roll" ("you scratch ma back, and mebbe ah'll speak to you in the corridah one day"). The time has come for urban-oriented Senators and Representatives to take off their gloves and to fight for their constituents. The time has come for metropolitan constituents to explain to their urban Senators and Representatives what will happen if they do not.

STEPHEN K. BAILEY
Chairman, Policy Institute
Syracuse University Research Corp.
Regent of the State of New York
Syracuse, N.Y., Nov. 23, 1970

High Priority for Revenue Sharing

To the Editor:

I would like to comment on your Nov. 30 editorial entitled "Will Federalism Collapse?"

In that message you argue very strongly and cogently for implementing a program of sharing Federal revenues with our state and local governments. We believe that the need for revenue sharing is both clear and pressing, and I am pleased to note your concurrence in that view.

As you know, President Nixon last year submitted to the Congress a comprehensive revenue-sharing proposal designed to bring fiscal relief to every state, city and county in America. This marked the first time that revenue sharing has ever received Presidential support, and reflects this Administration's strong desire to address the problems of federalism in a direct and straightforward manner.

The President himself has taken great pains to establish the importance of the effort to share a portion of Federal revenues with state and local

237

governments. In a recent message to Congress on needed legislation, President Nixon described revenue sharing in the following terms: ". . . It would be difficult to identify another proposal that has received such widespread endorsement. It is elemental economics, elemental good sense, elemental good government."

The President went on to state: "Both parties endorsed revenue sharing in their 1968 platforms and it has widespread support. Yet neither the House nor the Senate has held hearings on the Administration's bill."

Revenue sharing has an impressive record of bipartisan support at all levels of government. Others, such as Walter W. Heller, have put forward similar proposals. Quite frankly, we have attempted to construct a revenue-sharing plan incorporating the best features of the various suggested plans. Thus, unlike Dr. Heller's proposal, we have specifically included our hard-pressed cities, counties and towns in the revenue-sharing distribution.

Despite the strong demonstration of need and the impressive breadth of support behind revenue sharing, we have yet to see any positive action from the Congress. I was astonished that your editorial made no mention whatsoever of this unfortunate lack of progress by the legislative branch. Certainly revenue sharing deserves a prompt and thorough hearing.

Recurring accounts of serious fiscal distress in our local governments only serve to underscore the high priority which revenue sharing has assumed. This is one instance where Presidential leadership needs to be joined by Congressional responsibility.

DAVID M. KENNEDY
Secretary of the Treasury
Washington, Dec. 4, 1970

What's Wrong With the Welfare Plan

To the Editor:

Why does *The Times* so enthusiastically support the Family Assistance Plan? The package, hailed as "welfare reform," changes so frequently that it is even difficult to know what is being proposed. However, some things are reasonably clear.

The plan will do little to raise the living standards of the majority of families on welfare except to provide for some additional food stamps. The Federal minimum exceeds the relief standards of only eight states and Puerto Rico. Ninety per cent of present recipients, if they are to be as well (or as badly) off as before, must rely on the supplementation which the states are required to provide, and unless their states delegate administration to the Federal Government they will suffer the inconvenience of dealing with two agencies.

Incidentally, state supplementation will perpetuate the wide variation in payments which is alleged to encourage the poor to migrate to the more liberal states. Instead of correcting the present shocking shortchanging of families with children, the plan intensifies it by setting a minimum annual income for the adult needy categories (aged, blind and disabled) of $2,400 for a man and wife but only $1,600 for a family with two children.

Nationwide payment of assistance to the working poor, hailed as a novel reform though long the policy in New York and one or two other states, will indeed make assistance available to additional millions. But unless the states are required to supplement earnings (which they were not in the latest printed version of the plan) this benefit will be confined to families whose earnings and assistance payments fall below $3,920, the Federal cutoff point.

Nor will the plan do much to substitute "workfare" for "welfare," even if nationwide unemployment declines. Disregarding part of welfare recipients' earnings may encourage some to earn, though it is noteworthy that the level of the disregard is lower for the supplemental than for the Federal part of the program. But the bill does nothing about a major disincentive to earn—namely, that a family's earnings plus its F.A.P. may render it ineligible for food stamps, subsidized housing and Medicaid.

The main group affected by the requirement that adult recipients must register for and accept available work or training will be husbandless A.F.D.C. (Aid to Families With Dependent Children) mothers of children over six for whom appropriate substitute care can be provided, because all other mothers are exempted, while three and a half million of the over twelve million welfare recipients are aged, blind or disabled and 6,000,000 are children. In any case, far too little attention has been paid to the danger that requiring recipients to take jobs paying only 75 per cent of the Federal minimum wage, plus subsidizing low-wage employment by payments to the working poor, will tend to depress wages.

Financially, the Federal reimbursement provisions will be of little help to states such as New York, with unusually heavy concentrations of welfare recipients.

Finally, those who favor welfare reform because they are unhappy about mounting relief rolls will be in for a shock. For disregarding a sizable fraction of earnings and including the working poor will vastly increase the welfare population—to between 19.2 and 23.8 million in the first year, according to Administration estimates.

Nothing will be lost by nonaction this year. Delay would give the Congress and the Administration time to develop an effective program of welfare reform. Such a reform would look not merely to the welfare system itself and its perpetual enlargement but would rather seek to keep as many people as possible off welfare by the adoption and expansion of other and more appropriate income security measures such as social insurance, children's allowances and the public provision of jobs at decent pay.

EVELINE M. BURNS
New York, Dec. 12, 1970

The writer, Professor Emeritus of Social Work at Columbia University, is the author of, among other works, "Social Security and Public Policy."

Prayer in the Pentagon

To the Editor:

Are American citizens supposed to be reassured by the Dec. 16 news story to the effect that a special room has now been dedicated by Defense Secretary Melvin R. Laird "for meditation and prayer"? Some of us had assumed that every room in the Pentagon is used for meditation and possibly for prayer as well, considering the decisions that have been made there.

LETTIE GAY CARSON
Millerton, N.Y., Dec. 17, 1970

Galbraith Defending Nixon

To the Editor:

Perhaps it is the Christmas season, perhaps it is absence working its classic wonder on my mellowing heart, but I find myself wanting to defend President Nixon.

As many have said, his appointment of Gov. John B. Connally Jr. as Secretary of the Treasury is a bipartisan gesture of a rather limited sort.

240

The Governor is a stalwart conservative. For the party as a whole it is a reward comparable with making Senator Stennis Secretary of State, although unquestionably better than making Governor Maddox Secretary of Health, Education and Welfare. But the President won the last election. Surely that accords him the privilege of appointing people of whom he approves and whose approval he enjoys.

And what is wrong with having conservatives with the Republicans rather than with the Democrats? How else, indeed, can we have a choice? In accepting his new post, Governor Connally is helping to clear up one of the prime ambiguities of our party system and he also deserves our thanks.

I see it suggested, further, that Governor Connally has no visible qualification for dealing with the distressing combination of inflation and recession that now besets us. This may well be so. But can the President be blamed for reflecting on how his professionals managed to contrive this misfortune and then concluding that an amateur, however rank, could not be worse?

JOHN KENNETH GALBRAITH
Cambridge, England, Dec. 17, 1970

Useful Function of the Filibuster

To the Editor:

Your Jan. 27 editorial concerning the current debate on Senate Rule 22 (filibuster rule) misrepresents the nature of Vice President Agnew's decision not to rule on the constitutionality of the Senate's rules and belittles one of the most significant debates in which the Senate is likely to be engaged in this year.

On Jan. 26, in reply to a parliamentary inquiry, the Vice President in his capacity as President of the Senate said: "in response to any point of order as to the constitutionality of the procedure or as to whether or not the Senate is a continuing body which involves a constitutional question, the Chair, under the uniform precedents of the Senate, will submit the same to the Senate for decision."

You called this "a significant departure from the decisions of his recent predecessors." Nothing could be further from the truth. While several Vice Presidents have issued "advisory opinions" concerning the relationship of Rule 22 to attempts to change that rule, only once has a

Vice President attempted to usurp the Senate's constitutional power to determine the constitutionality of its procedures. That was in January, 1969, and Vice President Humphrey was promptly overruled by the Senate. The precedent is perfectly clear—as to the constitutionality of its rules, only the Senate itself has the power to decide.

More alarming than this careless error of fact was your description of the current Senate debate on Rule 22 as a "pointless filibuster." *The Times* obviously assumes that there is only one side to this issue and that there are no contrary arguments which deserve consideration. This attitude illustrates perfectly the danger that Rule 22 is designed to prevent. Unbridled majority rule inevitably becomes arrogant in the certainty of its own wisdom and disdainful of any other viewpoint.

Your apparent willingness to confer upon any majority sole title to universal truth and wisdom is particularly surprising to me. The unparalleled caution which characterized the Senate's consideration of President Nixon's Supreme Court nominations, the "extended debate" over our country's policies in Southeast Asia and the refusal of certain Senators to acquiesce in the conference report on SST appropriations are only a few instances in which the cause you supported depended upon the threat of "extended debate" under Rule 22. Even a cursory examination of the history of the last Congress demonstrates the dangers of undiluted majoritarianism and the value of careful deliberation in the legislative process. Certainly this history requires at the least that the present Senate give more than a passing glance to a proposal which would threaten its deliberative character.

I am confident that what your editorial describes as a "pointless filibuster" will point out the wisdom of preserving the Senate's great tradition of free speech. Furthermore, I am also confident that the Senate, unlike *The Times*, will exercise great thoughtfulness and care as it resolves the important issues raised in this debate.

SAM J. ERVIN Jr.
Chairman, Senate Subcommittee
on Constitutional Rights
Washington, Jan. 28, 1971

242

Rule 22: Why Not Senate Vote?

To the Editor:

The complicated—and to the nonspecialist, confusing—parliamentary procedure for amending the Senate's filibuster rule—Rule 22 which calls for a two-thirds vote to end a filibuster—was the subject of a letter from Senator Sam Ervin which you published on Feb. 8.

The Senator is correct that former Vice President Humphrey is the only presiding officer of the Senate actually to have ruled that a filibuster on a resolution amending the rule can be ended by a majority vote because of its special status under the Constitution. In 1969 now-Senator Humphrey ruled that closure had been invoked by the vote of a majority, and anticipating an appeal from this ruling, he also held that any such appeal was nondebatable. On appeal, his ruling was reversed by the Senate.

But the significant precedent gleaned from the whole procedure was not what the Senate in fact decided, but that we were able to decide anything at all. For, until this Humphrey ruling, in all the years of Senate debate on amending Rule 22, we had been unable to reach any decision on the merits because the Rule we sought to amend was invoked against us and our efforts were frustrated by the very filibuster we could not get at. Only the Humphrey ruling, by holding that the appeal from his ruling was nondebatable, enabled us to vote at all.

Although opponents of Rule 22 were unsuccessful in upholding Humphrey's ruling, we still believe we have a good case. More importantly however, we believe strongly that we have a right to put this question to the Senate, urging our colleagues to reverse the 1969 position.

We feel the need for amending Rule 22 to be more persuasive than ever. The issues of peace and war, welfare reform, inflation, unemployment, the cities and racial relations are so momentous that we cannot give a veto power over their resolution to a minority of the Senate—be that minority conservative or liberal. Indeed, liberals have begun to use the filibuster too, as they are certainly entitled to do as long as it is in the rules. But they would gladly give it up in pursuit of the greater objective of the Senate's being able to act and not being legislatively paralyzed.

The pitfall in Vice President Agnew's stated position is that without a ruling from the presiding officer that because of the constitutional question at issue in amending Rule 22 the issue is no longer debatable, any referral to the Senate for decision is tantamount to acquiscence in a continued filibuster. The failure to make such a ruling is itself a decision to kill the motion.

243

We do not question the Vice President's decision to let the Senate itself decide these questions—which, after all, was the ultimate result of the Humphrey ruling. However, because we know from long experience the fate of any such question which is itself subject to unlimited debate, we are urging the Vice President to use the procedure invoked by Senator Humphrey as Vice President in 1969.

For, we believe that on so critical an issue as the effort to amend Rule 22, we ought at least to have had—what we believe to be our constitutional right—the opportunity to vote on it.

JACOB K. JAVITS
U.S. Senator from New York
Washington, Feb. 10, 1971

Power of Money in Politics

To the Editor:

In a Feb. 3 editorial you ask whether "the power of money in politics is to be brought under democratic constraint" and suggest that "the big givers" have an undue influence on the elective process.

Legislation is now being drafted to repeal the provisions of the Corrupt Practices Act of 1925 that placed a ceiling of $5,000 on the amount an individual could give to any candidate or committee in a Federal election, and there are several good reasons for such repeal: The limit is not enforceable, as a limitation of freedom of expression it is probably in violation of the First Amendment; and corrupt practices in the election process can be eliminated more effectively by requiring full and prompt disclosure of the sources and disposition of all funds.

You too are in favor of more complete disclosure procedures, but you would also impose "democratic constraint" on the amount any individual can give. This raises a question: Should there be democratic constraints on other campaign resources, e.g., the number of volunteers in a campaign, the intelligence of the staff workers and the amount of volunteered time?

Democratization of campaign financing can much better be achieved by instituting the following procedures:

(1) Set a ceiling, calculated on the number of eligible voters in a district, on the amount a candidate for any Federal office may spend;
(2) Equalize the amount of media time and space available to each

244

candidate; (3) Provide a modest Federal subsidy for the start-up costs of Federal campaigns; (4) Permit a tax credit of up to $10 for political donations; (5) Require full disclosure of all revenues as well as all expenses, with invalidation of an election the penalty for noncompliance and heavy fines for incomplete or fraudulent disclosure, and (6) Require that individuals giving or lending $5,000 or more in aggregate report such contributions to a Federal elections commission for publication prior to an election.

Under such rules, major donations from individuals would still be permitted but the need for large gifts would be reduced. Still another provision could deter major gifts, namely that if fund-raising efforts for a candidate exceeded his particular fund ceiling, the excess would go to the Treasury.

As a major donor to political campaigns myself, I fully endorse your intent to assist in reforming campaign financing. For each of the last three years I have compiled a memorandum listing my donations to Federal campaigns and sent it to the candidates and to the Citizens Research Foundation. And I would gladly report it to the Federal Government and the press if this were required.

STEWART R. MOTT
New York, Feb. 18, 1971

VIII•The Middle East

Next to the war in Southeast Asia, the issue that brought the greatest volume of mail to the letters pages of *The Times* in the last decade was the crisis in the the Middle East. Even before the establishment of the State of Israel in 1948, the subject stirred Moslem, Christian and Jew to emotional debate in the columns of the newspaper.

The birth of the new state and the war that followed, the Suez crisis of 1956, the Six-Day War of 1967, the growing Soviet presence in the Mideast, the Palestine guerrilla movement and the efforts for peace in 1970 were all discussed with uncommon passion.

Every statement, every claim, every charge brought an immediate counter-statement, claim and charge. On no other issue were there such sensitive antennae at work, such a willingness and readiness to debate and such conviction that the truth, indeed, was with each letter writer alone.

Arabs as Defenders

To the Editor of *The New York Times:*

James G. McDonald, in his letter published on Feb. 13, has sought to place the unique responsibility for the present situation in Palestine on the Arabs. "The Arabs alone are the aggressors," he declares. Mr. McDonald, like many of his Zionist friends, is trying to convince the American public that the history of Palestine began on Nov. 29 and that what happened before has no relevance.

In seeking to determine who are the aggressors and who the victims, it is surely relevant to inquire to whom the land belongs and who are the newcomers therein. If to defend one's country against invasion; if to oppose the erection of a foreign state on the soil you have occupied for many centuries; if to refuse the splitting up of your country into three areas all under different regimes—if all this is aggression—then indeed the Arabs are the aggressors. They are the same sort of aggressors as were the Poles and Czechs in 1939.

I do not believe the American public can any longer be deceived by the sort of argument Mr. McDonald is using. Nor will his argument that the United Nations decision to partition Palestine was a compromise bear inspection. The Jewish Agency, Mr. McDonald naively remarks, "made large sacrifices to Jewish claims and of Jewish traditional aspirations," by agreeing to the noninclusion in their state of areas which are almost entirely Arab. Where is the sacrifice involved in giving up half of what you do not possess? If your claims to the whole are not valid, how can you pretend that your reduction of those claims by any amount represents a concession? If your claim to the whole is valid, then you should not give up half; and if it is invalid, then you have no right to anything at all.

The Jewish Agency in accepting partition merely proceeded on the basis that half a cake is better than no cake at all. The Arabs, to whom the cake belongs and to whom it is vital for their nourishment, are not being uncompromising by refusing to surrender half; they are only acting in self-defense.

A determined attempt is being made—and Mr. McDonald's letter is part of that attempt—to present to the public a picture in which the Arabs are defying the United Nations and therefore the decision and the conscience of the world. But decisions, taken by no matter whom, need moral authority, as well as a technical majority, in order to be respected.

I do not wish to go into the question of how the partition recommendation was lobbied throughout the United Nations, nor to inquire into the legality of this recommendation, which, it can be held, violated the Charter in at least two respects; but this much is clear to the Arabs, and the American public is beginning to realize it also, that the United Nations has put itself on weak grounds in recommending the division of a country against the wishes and the interests of the majority of that country's population. For it is not only the entire Arab population of Palestine which rejects partition; it is also a fact that a considerable section of the Jewish population also rejects it and would welcome another and saner solution.

The United Nations will not be discredited and will not be destroyed if it now has the courage to recognize that it acted hastily and on false assumptions. Many of the delegations to the United Nations supported partition in the belief that it would bring peace to Palestine. The opposite has been the result, and therefore the fundamental assumption of the whole partition plan has proved to have been mistaken. By staking the future of the United Nations on one hasty and ill-understood decision, it is the Zionists and their friends who are gambling with the future of the world organization on whose existence and success the Arabs, as well as all the Moslem peoples of Asia, had put such hopes.

CECIL HOURANI
The Arab Office
Washington, Feb. 14, 1948

For Middle East Stability

To the Editor of *The New York Times:*

It is to be regretted that *The New York Times* in an otherwise opportune editorial on Middle East tensions should lend its authority to a wildly inflated estimate of the number of Arab refugees from Palestine. The problem is serious enough. It is not, however, as your editorial suggested, the crucial problem affecting American relations with the Middle East.

The existence of Israel is a convenient scapegoat for all the calamities that have befallen Western Asia in recent years. It obscures a continuing unprincipled struggle in that region between the Great Powers, harsh tribal feuds and bitter dynastic rivalries between the Hashimites and the royal houses of Egypt and Saudi Arabia, and an unresolved social conflict between palace and street, pasha and effendi throughout the Arab world.

249

American initiative in the Middle East is to be welcomed. It will have greater chance of success if it is based on an accurate appraisal of the difficulties and needs of the area. The facts concerning the Arab refugees are simply these:

At no time under the British mandate did the Arab population of Palestine exceed 1,000,000. Of this number a considerable proportion was nomadic, shifting seasonally across the lightly patrolled frontiers of Transjordan and Syria. Since the conclusion of active hostilities in Palestine the Arab population of Israel has grown to 150,000. Some 500,000 Arabs have been annexed, but not absorbed, as the assassination of King Abdullah indicates, by the newly created Hashimite Kingdom of Jordan, a forced union of Transjordan and eastern Palestine, for which no historical or traditional precedent, and certainly no political or economic raison d'être, can be maintained.

The majority of these Palestinian Arabs, now incorporated in Jordan by decree rather than choice, are no refugees, but indigenous residents of Samaria and southern Judea.

At the most there are some 350,000 Palestinian Arabs who can be legitimately termed refugees. Over 100,000 of these are in the Gaza strip of southern Palestine forcibly annexed by Egypt and administered virtually as a concentration camp. No attempt of any kind has been made to absorb them into the Egyptian economy. Like their brethren in Lebanon, Syria and Iraq, they miserably subsist on international charity, which, when administered by Arab Governments, is too frequently the object of misuse, diversion and outright peculation.

The problem of these unhappy victims of the Arab adventure and catastrophe of 1948 will continue to beset the Middle East as long as the Arab states make no serious effort to rehabilitate them and give them the chance to start a new life. Refugee despair will provide a motive force for political fanaticism and assassination and eventually encourage another Arab adventure against Israel.

At a time when the United States is beginning to recognize the crucial strategic and economic importance of the Middle East to the free world, it could do no better service to the Arab peoples themselves than to deploy all its force of moral suasion toward a lasting peaceful settlement with Israel, which would speedily create the conditions for economic and social betterment throughout the Middle East.

JACK WINOCOUR
Bedford Village, N.Y., July 28, 1951

250

Toward Middle East Peace

To the Editor of *The New York Times:*

One of the most formidable, and certainly the most concrete, obstacles to peace in the Middle East continues to be the tragic plight of the hundreds of thousands of Arab refugees. Until a beginning at least is made toward the solution of this vast problem there can be no hope for peace.

Hence I make no apology for suggesting the following new program, particularly since it follows in broad lines a proposal put forth by our distinguished senior statesman, Herbert Hoover, more than a decade ago.

Sensing the dangerous rising tension in the Holy Land, Mr. Hoover in 1945—three years before the clash of Arab-Jewish interests there degenerated into bitter warfare—suggested that the resettlement of large numbers of Palestine Arabs in Iraq would benefit all the peoples concerned.

Pointing to the fact that "in ancient times the irrigation of the Tigris and Euphrates valleys supported probably ten millions of people," he argued that this transfer—internationally organized and financed—would benefit not only Iraq, which acutely needs additional agricultural population, but also the whole Middle East.

Mr. Hoover concluded: "It would be a solution by engineering instead of by conflict. . . . The plan offers a challenge both to the statesmanship of the great powers and to the goodwill of all parties concerned. . . . It offers a method of settlement with both honor and wisdom."

In the course of the Arab-Israel conflict the bulk of the Palestine Arabs became refugees in nearby Arab lands. Herded in wretched camps, they have been kept alive by international charity (mostly American dollars) administered by the United Nations.

There has been no lack of schemes put forth in the United Nations and from other sources to solve the refugee problem. But only one of these has been realistic. Most of these plans—with the notable exception of the American Government-sponsored Eric Johnston plan for the division of the waters of the Jordan between Israel and the bordering Arab states—have had one fatal weakness. They have ignored the psychology of the Arab people and the pride which they take in their newly won sovereignty and dignities.

Why then not try an approach which would make the settlement of Arab refugees primarily an Arab-managed project and one which would obviously bring great economic and financial benefits to all the Arab countries involved?

In addition to Iraq, which Mr. Hoover had in mind as the country of resettlement of Palestinian Arabs, Jordan and Syria have sufficient and

251

uncultivated land—some of which would require irrigation—to absorb comfortably all the refugees and make of them productive citizens.

But these cardinal questions remain: Would enough capital be available? Would the auspices under which the project would be managed be acceptable to the Arabs? Would the terms of capitalization provide an inducement for the Arabs to back wholeheartedly this solution?

The necessary capital, even though it might require many hundreds of millions of dollars, could, I believe, be found, because this resettlement program would advance, perhaps decisively, the cause of peace in the Middle East. Here are some realistic sources of capital funds:

Compensation paid by the State of Israel for the land and properties of the Arab refugees;

Allocations from the United Nations;

Grants and loans from the United States and Great Britain;

Grants from foundations and welfare agencies.

Together these might total over a billion dollars. Such a huge capitalization figure is not fantastic. Compensation from Israel would reach a very large amount.

Mr. Dulles and Sir Anthony Eden have officially announced that both countries would be willing to participate financially through grants and loans in a basic settlement. And the United Nations would doubtless prefer to make a one-time sizable investment in a final solution, rather than annually spend many millions of dollars on relief without bringing peace a step nearer.

But what about Arab sensibilities and nationalistic hostility toward Israel and to any move that would indicate Arab acceptance of Israel as a permanent neighbor? Certainly the Arabs would mistrust any wholly foreign auspices for a resettlement program. But might they not accept if it were controlled by themselves?

An Arab colonization corporation could be formed to take charge of the entire operation. The controlling stock of this corporation could be made available primarily to Arabs. Liberal provisions could facilitate the purchase of these securities by nationals of the interested Arab countries.

The resettlement of hundreds of thousands of refugees would enormously increase economic values in those Arab countries that absorbed the newcomers. And as the program of the corporation became operative, the value of its shares—by that time listed on the world's largest stock exchanges—might be expected to have appreciated and to have brought considerable gains to the original stockholders.

Today a great foundation makes full use of the stock exchanges to finance its enterprises. A similar method could be applied to the resettlement of Arab refugees. There is no Ford empire to serve as a basis for these operations, but a large-scale and adequately financed colonization could produce industrial and agricultural assets of great value, and sufficient to provide a substantial coverage for the corporation stock.

Years of Arab-Israel recriminations have left the Arab refugees unrelieved, and have served only to increase the chances of war. A comprehensive resettlement program sponsored by the United Nations and organized and administered under Arab auspices could settle the refugees and save the peace.

This would be a costly operation. It might absorb more than a billion dollars. But whatever the amount, it would be but a fraction of the cost of war in the Middle East.

JAMES G. McDONALD
New York, Feb. 27, 1956

The writer is the former United States Ambassador to Israel.

Nationalizing Suez

To the Editor of *The New York Times:*

The understandable bitterness of the reaction against Egypt's nationalization of the Suez Canal Company has tended to obscure the distinction between the political and legal aspects of the situation.

Political apprehensions on the part of the Western powers are fully justified: by the abruptness of an action which it would have been in the interest of everybody to prepare gradually; doubt in leaving the control of the canal to a highly nationalist country controlled by an ambitious and emotional ruler; the lack of technical experience, financial resources and many other factors.

Legally, however, Egypt's action is not as clearly objectionable as it is politically, and it is particularly important that justified indignation should not lead the Western powers into a position where they have not international law clearly on their side.

Under the Convention of 1888, Egypt—which has succeeded to the obligations of Turkey—is under an obligation to keep the Suez Canal open for free use by the ships of all nations. But apart from the long-standing violation of this obligation in regard to Israel, Egypt has so far reaffirmed it.

The status of the Suez Canal Company is not in any direct way linked

253

with the Convention of 1888. Although the majority of the shares are held by French citizens and the British Government, the company has always been operated as a commercial enterprise. It obtained its status from two concessions given by the (Turkish) Viceroy of Egypt in 1854 and 1856. It has its domicile at Alexandria and its administrative seat at Paris.

Egypt claims that the Suez Canal is a purely Egyptian company. This is very doubtful. The company has always been regarded as having a special status, as is apparent from the Convention of 1949 between the company and the Egyptian Government.

Apart from reaffirming the concession of the company until at least 1968, this agreement accorded to the company several special privileges, such as a number of Egyptian members of the board smaller than that required for an ordinary Egyptian company. In turn, the company undertook certain obligations in regard to the gradual Egyptianization of the company, the share of the Egyptian Government in the revenues, the development of technical and navigational facilities, etc.

According to the chairman of the Suez Canal Company, the Egyptian Government less than two months ago concluded another agreement with the company providing for further investments, in full awareness by both sides that the concession would expire in 1968. The assertion by an official Egyptian spokesman that the company would never voluntarily have surrendered its concession is without foundation.

These agreements are neither purely Egyptian transactions, as Egypt contends, nor international treaties. Foreign governments are not directly involved. The fact that the British Government holds 46 per cent of the shares symbolizes the British stake but does not make the British Government a party. On the other hand, this is not a matter of "domestic jurisdiction," but clearly one of international political and legal concern, including the use of force.

There is no doubt that any state can nationalize any enterprise on its soil, subject to fair compensation—which Egypt has offered—in contrast to the Iranian Government when it expropriated the Anglo-Iranian Oil Company. It is, however, very doubtful whether the Suez Canal Company can be regarded as a purely national enterprise. No direct violation of an international treaty on the part of Egypt has so far occurred, except that any prolonged forced detention of foreign personnel would be an international wrong against which the powers concerned could take legal action.

There is, therefore, every reason for the strongest apprehension on the part of the Western powers not only about the timing of Egypt's action but about her ability to live up to her professed commitments. Thus fair compensation for the expropriated shares would absorb several years of net revenue. On the other hand, it is doubtful whether the Western powers would be justified in taking military reprisals at this stage, quite apart from the restraint which the United States Charter puts on them.

There is everything to be said for using strong concerted political and diplomatic pressure to bring about a public international regime, possibly an international supervisory board; and if necessary economic reprisals on the part of the states immediately affected and proportionate to the injury done, especially to British and French interests.

But military reprisals at this stage would prejudice the strong moral position of the West. Nor is it advisable to use force until at least an attempt has been made to use the services of the United Nations.

The attempt to bypass the United Nations through the London Conference already seems doomed to failure. Of the nations which have so far accepted the British invitation, nearly one-third, led by the Soviet Union, are likely to support the Egyptian stand more or less unconditionally.

Although neither the Security Council nor the General Assembly is likely to do more than reflect the existing split, the mediatory services of the Secretary General may well prove once again at least the prelude to a peaceful settlement.

W. FRIEDMANN
New York, Aug. 9, 1956

The writer is Professor of Law and Director of International Legal Research at the School of Law, Columbia University. He is the editor of the recently published "Anti-Trust Laws: A Comparative Symposium."

Seizure of Suez Examined

To the Editor of *The New York Times:*

The Suez Canal crisis raises a number of international legal issues which it may be useful to analyze dispassionately and objectively.

First we face the question of the proper exercise of the power of a government to seize property under its jurisdiction. If we concede with Prof. W. Friedmann in his very informative and interesting letter published in your issue of Aug. 12 that "there is no doubt that any state can nationalize any enterprise on its soil subject to fair compensation," we would inflict a death blow to international financing.

It is simply not true that by virtue of its rights of sovereignty a government may take over private property within its boundaries owned by its citizens or by foreigners, at any time, for any reason, and for any purpose. The right to nationalize should be used—if at all—very sparingly under most exceptional circumstances for the public welfare, and only provided the owner receives prompt, adequate and effective compensation and the seizure is subject to review by a competent and independent court.

The very special character of the Universal Suez Canal Company raises the gravest doubts as to the authority of the Egyptian Government to expropriate its assets even though Egypt offered to pay fair compensation to the stockholders. In his statement published in your issue of Aug. 13 rejecting the invitation to attend the London Conference Nasser attempts to argue at length that the Canal Company is simply "an Egyptian limited company subject to the country's laws and customs."

But in his reasoning the President looks to the form rather than the substance and character of the corporation. Aside from public agencies, a company cannot exist in this form except in accordance with a specific system of laws. There is no international charter or corporation law for the formation of legal entities.

Undeniably the Canal Company was technically organized in Egypt. But it is also true that the company enjoys certain important privileges not granted to any other company in Egypt, that its administration and principal place of business is outside the territory of the country of its birth and, most important, that it is controlled from abroad. Its majority stock is owned by the British Government and by French nationals; its shares are carried on the Paris Exchange and its operational and managerial functions are vested in an international board under the chairmanship of a French citizen. Therefore its legal status is unique. It is a company *sui generis* which does not follow any known national pattern and may rightly claim to be international.

The unilateral action by Egypt is a violation of its treaty obligations concerning the Suez Canal. As recently as Oct. 19, 1954, Gamal Abdel Nasser together with one of his ministers personally signed an agreement with Great Britain in Cairo. In its Article 8 he recognized "that the Suez Maritime Canal, which is an internal part of Egypt, is a waterway, economically, commercially and strategically of international importance" and expressed "the determination to uphold the convention guaranteeing the freedom of navigation of the canal signed at Constantinople on the 29th of October, 1888." The recent conduct of Egypt is unquestionably contrary to the special international regime of Suez assuring to all nations passage through the canal without hindrance and on a basis of equality.

Had the operation of the canal not been entrusted to an international company, the Treaty of Constantinople undoubtedly would have created an international body to insure that the canal would be and remain open to vessels of all nations and on a nondiscriminatory basis and would be operated safely, economically and effectively.

The Canal Company was the foundation on which the convention rested. This cannot be abruptly replaced by an Egyptian company assuming the functions of the Canal Company as President Nasser has implied.

There is an even more fundamental and important issue involved. The canal is not comparable to a "toll highway on United States territory," as the Ambassador of Syria contended in his letter published in your column on Aug. 2. Even though its banks are on the territory of Egypt, the canal is not, and never was built to be, a national waterway.

Regardless of the legal implications, about which Egypt and its supporters may not agree with the Western powers, the Suez crisis is of such gravity that all available diplomatic and political means should be used, and the Secretary General with his high prestige should be called upon to exercise his influence.

Assuming that in the interest of preserving peace in the Middle East this country and her allies should accept nationalization of the Canal Company, Egypt should be willing to agree to an effective substitute for the administration, operation, safety, economy and maintenance of the high technical requirements of the canal. Nothing short of a truly international body would suffice.

Since the freedom of the canal is of immediate or potential concern to all nations without distinction it may not be out of place to provide that the Secretary General of the United Nations be the ex-officio chairman of the board or commission of the Suez Canal. In addition, Egypt should submit to the jurisdiction of the Permanent Court of International Justice for all future disputes and complaints by the non-Egyptian users of Suez, including those who are denied passage through the canal.

Fritz E. Oppenheimer
New York, Aug. 16, 1956

The writer, an international lawyer, was assistant to the Legal Adviser in the State Department for several years. In this capacity he attended the Foreign Ministers' Conferences at Moscow, London and Paris.

257

Against Execution of Eichmann

To the Editor of *The New York Times:*

The case of Adolf Eichmann presents more than legal questions of national jurisdiction and venue. Transcending these, it presents a historic opportunity to the Government and people of Israel. They can make themselves a moral example to the civilized world if, in this instance of extreme and heinous guilt, they abstain from imposing capital punishment.

Clearly it will not be easy for the Israelis to reach such a height, knowing as they do that Eichmann participated in exterminating millions of their kin. Nor can Americans afford to strike a self-righteous pose, living as we do under the shame of our own laws of capital punishment which apply to various other crimes as well as murder. In this respect Israeli law is much superior to that of most American states; it does not authorize the death penalty even for murder in the usual sense of the word.

If Eichmann should be convicted and put to death, we could only say that the Israelis had conducted themselves "like the nations." On the other hand, if the prosecutor should recommend or the court should impose a sentence of life imprisonment, the whole world would respond with gratitude, renewed faith and admiration.

EDMOND CAHN
Professor of Law, New York University
New York, June 6, 1960

Warning on U.A.R. Role

To the Editor of *The New York Times:*

On Dec. 9 the U.N. General Assembly awarded the United Arab Republic a seat on the Security Council—a position of great honor and power. As far as anyone knows or can find out, the United States went along with this action. Certainly in the months that preceded the vote the State Department was an apologist, if not an open adovocate, for giving the U.A.R. this seat on the central peace and law enforcement body of the United Nations.

When in a letter to *The Times* early in October I protested against the possibility of the election of the U.A.R. to the Council, representatives of our State Department hastily tried to explain and justify the proposed selection. I found the explanation most unsatisfactory.

258

My original protest was doubly based on the dubious wisdom of seating on the Council a nation which persisted in violating and defying the Council's own resolutions on the Suez Canal, and was the most constant mischief-maker in the Middle East; and on the even greater error of failing to award this seat to one of the black African nations which, at that point, had no representation whatever on the Security Council. Instead of taking a course of constructive leadership in this situation, the United States went blindly along in the same old rut of appeasing Nasser, supinely accepting the mistaken notion that the seat in question "belonged" to the Arab League.

Now America and the rest of the free world are reaping the dubious dividends of this latest cultivation of the goodwill of Nasser.

At the beginning of this month there was held in Casablanca a conference of five neutralist nations: Ghana, Guinea, Morocco, Mali and the U.A.R.—all black African, except for the U.A.R. From this conference Nasser's voice and views emerged as the most potent, thanks in part at least to Egypt's recent elevation to membership on the Security Council.

At this Casablanca conference an African organization, modeled along the lines of NATO, was projected. Nasser, of course, expects to dominate this organization which he hopes to utilize for the advancement of his own designs—his dream of the creation of a great Afro-Asian empire, with himself at the head of it. This has always been his vision.

The first steps on the road could be to use this new African organization to wage political and military war, first against Israel, and then against others who have resisted or thwarted him—Jordan, Ethiopia, Iran, Iraq and Turkey.

Already at the Casablanca conference Nasser showed what was on his mind by forcing through an unscheduled resolution denouncing the acceptance from Israel of technological assistance or advice. Several African nations, including Ghana, have long been profiting from such assistance and cooperation.

What has been our recent reward from Nasser in return for our indulgence of him?

We are being attacked and vilified almost daily in the Egyptian press and over the official Cairo radio. While almost the entire rest of the world is hailing the inauguration of a new United States President, shrill and discordant notes arise along the Nile, with violent assaults against President-elect Kennedy and denunciations of his views and proposals.

What does this mean for the problems and challenges which confront the United States in this area? First of all, there must be a careful and incisive review of the substantial implications of the new African organiza-

259

tion and its possible or potential impact on the world power structure and on the diplomatic alignments in the Afro-Asian area. It may well be that forces have been set in motion which are beyond reversal and must be met at the next intersection rather than at the one already passed.

Where the point of next impact of these forces might be, or where the point of equilibrium might be, is beyond seeing at the moment. But we dare not avert our eyes from this situation, or from the real consequences of our past policies.

HERBERT H. LEHMAN
New York, Jan. 19, 1961

For Mideast Peace

To the Editor:

While the Security Council's cease fire has been accepted, it is clear the capability of the United Nations to preserve the peace as well as the Western concept of reliance on international guarantees to prevent aggression has been tested and—to date—found wanting.

In 1957, after the Sinai campaign, Israel believed her withdrawal of forces was based on the acceptance of four major assumptions reinforced by recognized principles of international law:

The Suez Canal would remain open to Israeli ships and cargoes:

The Strait of Tiran and the Gulf of Aqaba would comprehend international waters with rights of free and innocent passage guaranteed to all nations;

The Gaza Strip would not be under U.A.R.—but U.N.E.F.—administration, pending a peace settlement; and

Efforts would be made to move toward relationships of detente and peace.

The last 10 years have seen these concepts violated and the right of belligerency proclaimed and implemented.

The simple fact is that Israel—in light of the painful lessons of recent history—cannot be expected to go back to a *status quo ante*—where there was no peace—and where the stated design of some of her neighbors was "to destroy" her statehood. The mistakes and failures of implementation, of and since 1957, must not be repeated. No withdrawal should occur without completely new conditions of peace and stability obtaining.

260

I believe many in Israel who fought in the war of independence, in Sinai in 1956, and during the past few days, prayerfully hope now that there can be a withdrawal to peace—and not to an armistice.

For the future, Israel has the right to expect from the community of nations a new era—an era which, as Israeli Foreign Minister Abba Eban has stated, should embody acceptance of Israel's statehood and rejection of the fiction of nonexistence; direct contact between the parties as part of a pacific settlement; and recognition by external powers of broad principles such as peaceful commerce as opposed to belligerency.

These are basic starting points. The specifics must certainly include and guarantee free and innocent passage into the Gulf of Aqaba; and adherence to the unanimous Security Council resolution of Oct. 13, 1956, that "the operation of the (Suez) Canal should be insulated from the politics of any country," with the U.A.R. no longer claiming belligerent rights against Israeli ships and cargoes.

The status of the Old City of Jerusalem—to which Israel has returned "never to part from it again" in the words of Defense Minister Moshe Dayan—is probably not negotiable, except as the international guarantees for the holy places, and the west bank of the Jordan River will be central to Israel's position and future in any negotiations.

Further, any meaningful progress to a durable peace settlement must comprehend the some 900,000 refugees, equitable utilization of the Jordan River waters, multinational development opportunities—perhaps through a Middle Eastern development bank—and arms limitations.

The latter may be a starting point for serious and high-level talks with the Soviets, whose cooperation—to some degree—*is essential* to either detente or peace.

Certainly the Soviets must recognize that their $3-billion of arms aid to certain Arab states has hardly been the best investment, and its repetition would not offer the most likely means to stabilize Soviet influence in the Middle East. Further, renewal of the Middle East arms race would be inconsistent with the efforts the United States and the Soviets are making toward a nonproliferation agreement.

The current draft United States resolution before the Security Council recognizes the merits of direct talks among the countries in the area—utilizing the United Nations and third parties. Foreign Minister Eban has called for "face-to-face" discussions. The United Nations Charter clearly calls on the members themselves to settle international disputes.

This is not a bad place to begin.

OGDEN REID
Washington, June 9, 1967

The writer, member of Congress from the 26th District, New York, was Ambassador to Israel 1959–61.

Withdrawal of U.N.E.F.

To the Editor:

In his June 4 editorial page column entitled "Cairo: Quiet Flows the Nile" James Reston states that the Egyptians he has been talking to "even deny that they planned to get rid of the United Nations troops at the mouth of the Gulf of Aqaba. This, they say, was proposed by the Secretary General of the United Nations on the ground that if the U.N. couldn't keep its troops in one part of the crisis area, it wouldn't keep them in another part." This statement is repeated in Mr. Reston's news article in your issue of June 5, in which it is described as "the argument from the official side of Cairo."

If only for the sake of historical accuracy, I wish to make the following observations:

Whatever may have been said to Mr. Reston in Cairo, or by whom, I can assure you that there has not been the slightest hint of such a position here, and with good reason, for there is not a shred of truth to it. In critical times such as these, of course, it is common in official and unofficial circles alike to seek scapegoats (to a shameful degree at present in the United States) and to indulge in what may be called deception, if one wishes to be polite about it.

The letter received by the Commander of U.N.E.F. from the Chief of Staff of the U.A.R. Army on the night of May 16 demanded the withdrawal of "all United Nations troops which installed O.P.s along our borders." This unquestionably included Sharm el Sheikh which was, in fact, a United Nations Observation Post.

As reported by the Secretary General on May 18 to the General Assembly, this message to General Rikhye was quickly followed by a movement of U.A.R. troops up to the line in Sinai, and by a demand from the Chief of Staff of the U.A.R. Army at midday local time on May 17 for withdrawal within 24 hours of all U.N.E.F. detachments in Sinai, spe-

262

cifically including Sharm el Sheikh. In fact, U.A.R. troops arrived to take over the United Nations camp and positions at Sharm el Sheikh and Ras Nasrani at 1210 hours G.M.T. on May 18, demanding a response from the U.N.E.F. troops there within 15 minutes. They did not get it, and the U.N.E.F. troops remained there for six more days, although they were unable to function.

The official request for the withdrawal of U.N.E.F. was received by the Secretary General at 12 noon New York time on May 18, i.e. some four hours after the actual arrival of U.A.R. troops at Sharm el Sheikh.

The reason for the Secretary General's position that U.N.E.F. could not accept an order to withdraw from one part of the line and remain on another part was that to do this would in fact make U.N.E.F. a party to the resumption of war by opening the door to a direct military confrontation between Israel and the U.A.R. Once the U.A.R. decided to move its troops to any part of the line, which they could have done at any time during the past 10 years, U.N.E.F.'s presence ceased to have any useful function.

The line that had to be covered by U.N.E.F., incidentally, was 295 miles long while the total strength of the Force was 3,400 (1,800 on the line), with personal arms for self-defence only. At Sharm el Sheikh 32 men were stationed.

RALPH J. BUNCHE
Under Secretary
United Nations
United Nations, N.Y., June 9, 1967

Israel's Future Boundaries

To the Editor:

Stephen Green's letter on "Mideast Boundaries" (June 16) is based on a fallacy. He says that the "nations poised on both sides of the Israeli border" have been "calling for each other's destruction." This has been the clearly expressed intention of the Arab states for more than 20 years, and even now, in his moment of total defeat, Nasser has called for a fourth war in which the Arabs can be avenged.

The destruction of any of the Arab states has never been an Israeli policy, even if such a thing were possible. Its purpose has been self-defense. It is this purpose which will guide the Israeli decisions concerning the territories that they now occupy.

The Jordan River is a lifeline for Israel, so that Syria and Jordan must no longer be allowed to threaten to cut off this essential source of water as they have done in the past. The economic destruction of Israel by the closure of the Suez Canal and the Gulf of Aqaba must no longer be permitted.

The danger to the internal peace of Israel by a violently hostile minority in the Gaza Strip is the most difficult problem. In the past these refugees have been used as a political pawn. Nothing has been done to resettle them, as happened in 1923 when the war between Greece and Turkey in Asia Minor ended with the disastrous defeat of Greece. With the active help of the League of Nations, 1,400,000 refugees were transferred to Greece.

Whatever the final decision concerning the Gaza refugees may be, it is, however, essential that immediate aid should be given to them. Since 1950 little has been done: the United States has contributed nothing.

Mr. Green argues that, in face of all these dangers, Israel should be content with "our repeated guarantee of the territorial integrity of all nations in the Middle East." Israel will also have to provide "some form of compensation and repatriation for those displaced, along the lines of the United Nations Resolution of December 1948." It is obvious that these suggestions have been put forward for propaganda purposes, because no reasonable man can believe that they will be accepted by the Israeli Government.

Mr. Green's argument would also lead to the return of the Old City of Jerusalem to Jordanian control. He seems to forget that in recent years the Jews have been barred from entering it, even though their most sacred sites have been there for more than 2,000 years. There is no danger that any such exclusion will be exercised by Israel against the members of any other religion.

It is noteworthy that the most scrupulous care was taken by the Israeli Army to see that no harm should be done to the Christian churches or to the Great Mosque even during the height of battle. The novel idea of internationalization may seem to be attractive as a gesture, but in practice it has always proved a failure and the source of further disputes. We need only think of the example of Berlin.

ARTHUR L. GOODHART
New York, June 16, 1967

The writer was former Master of University College, Oxford.

Danger of Nuclear Proliferation

To the Editor:

I fear that unless a permanent solution to the Middle East problem is found, Israel will feel compelled to seek the illusory security of a nuclear deterrent. This then could lead to the world's first nuclear war. Suppose nuclear weapons had been available in the present situation—would Nasser have accepted defeat so easily if he had had the power to wipe out all of Israel?

I fear that next time both Israel and some Arab nations will have nuclear weapons unless a way is found to guarantee the security of Israel other than by means of nuclear deterrent. A first and essential step is for the major powers to cease selling and giving weapons to nations of the Middle East. Not only did the United States supply weapons to Israel, but to Jordan and Iran as well. Let us hope the State Department has learned its lesson and will now reverse its policy of being arms merchant to much of the world.

But even if the major powers would agree to stop supplying arms to other nations and in addition sign the nuclear non-proliferation treaty, such action might only postpone rather than prevent the next "holy war" in the Middle East.

Perhaps the only long-range solution is to build the United Nations into a stronger and more meaningful organization with a security force which can not only police the boundaries of Israel but provide swift and certain retaliation to whichever side would violate those boundaries. Such a strengthened United Nations not only could have prevented the present conflict but it also could have prevented the present Vietnam war.

. JAY OREAR
Chairman, Federation of American Scientists
Washington, June 20, 1967

Jordan's West Bank

To the Editor:

Among the issues to be settled after the recent Arab-Israeli war I should like to discuss only one, which is of crucial importance: the fate of the west bank of Jordan. There are decisive reasons why this region ought to be restored intact to Jordan.

265

The historic reasons need not be gone over again. This land is Arab and always has been.

Regardless of what we may think of the origins of the war, it is clear that Jordan was drawn reluctantly into a conflict of more powerful neighbors. Yet her people have suffered the heaviest and most menacing losses of all the combatants.

We have heard much about the security requirements of Israel. Nothing has been said yet about those of the defeated countries, but they exist and should be supported by the West. It must be obvious that the security problems of Jordan are now far more serious than those of "tiny Israel." The world should not recognize a frontier based on a selection of strong points by Israel, as it so shamefully recognized the strategic crippling of Czechoslovakia by Nazi Germany in 1938.

A million people live in western Jordan, cultivating the hill country or engaged in urban occupations. Without their lands and labor, and especially without the tourist trade of Arab Jerusalem, the economy of Jordan is not viable.

The Arabs of the west bank are people. By every standard of humanity and justice they must neither be evicted to become refugees nor ruled by alien conquerors, but remain free under their own Government. The tragedy of Palestine must not be enlarged.

The United States has formally and repeatedly proclaimed support for the territorial integrity of all nations in the area. During the recent events it appeared highly probable that this country would have acted to prevent any infringement on the territory of Israel.

Jordan has at least as strong a claim to the same protection, especially in the light of King Hussein's very courageous association with the United States and Britain in the past. Together with the Soviet Union, which is willing on this occasion, the United States is unquestionably able to compel Israel to restore the occupied lands, now as in 1956. Many eastern nations will again be watching her action as a test of honor.

GEORGE F. HOURANI
Ann Arbor, Mich., June 13, 1967

The writer is Professor of Islamic History and Philosophy at the University of Michigan.

266

Access to Holy Sites

To the Editor:

In your repeated editorials on Jerusalem you call for the "international control" or "at least symbolic international control" of the Old City of Jerusalem. (July 14.)

I am not sure how you expect this to be implemented pragmatically as I consider it impractical. Israel controls the New City, the Old City and all the access routes to Jerusalem, which I am sure she will not give up. She intends to internationalize the holy places, Christian, Moslem and Jewish, which, in effect, is some "international control."

Unless there is some kind of a peace treaty between Israel and the Arab states, your concept of "international control" won't have any meaning (to the access to Moslem holy places), as the Arabs from the neighboring countries would not be able to reach the Old City anyhow. It is well-known that the Catholics from the allied countries could not reach the Vatican during World War II, and the Israelis could not reach the Old City and the holy places in Arabia.

The solution, then, implies a peace treaty between Israel and the Arab states as the only means to a free access to the Old City.

DAVID H. ODEN
Department of History
Temple University
Philadelphia, July 17, 1967

Mideast Solution

To the Editor:

In two recent editorials (Oct. 16 and Nov. 1) you have defined with admirable clarity the terms of a solution for the crisis in the Middle East as well as a strategy for achieving it. That solution can only be a United Nations one, and the role of the proposed mediator not that of a messenger boy or a telephone booth, but that of a high-powered emissary of the United Nations, armed with instructions based not only upon the broad principles of the Charter but also upon resolutions and recommendations adopted by different organs of the international organization since November 1947.

The only point in your editorial of Nov. 1 which needs clarification is the reason for which the Arabs at this point reject direct negotiation as an alternative to a settlement based upon substantive decisions of the U.N. relative to the creation of a Jewish state in Palestine.

The Arabs do not refuse to enter into direct negotiations with the Israelis because, as you suggest, they cannot control their emotions, or because they refuse to look facts in the face; after all, they have been sitting and arguing with the Israelis for nearly 20 years across the same hypothetical table at the U.N. and in the Armistice Commissions. Their refusal of direct negotiations springs not from passion or pride but from a realistic appraisal of the possibilities of reaching an agreement.

To sit down with the Israelis to discuss the implementation of United Nations resolutions about frontiers, refugees, respect for territorial integrity, etc. would be one thing: to sit down with them without any framework or reference, any juridical or historic or internationally approved basis for discussion would be at the best fruitless, and at the worst a *Diktat*.

If the United Nations, or the United States, or the Israelis themselves want the Arabs to negotiate directly with Israel, the Arabs must know what Israel is: where does it begin and where does it end? what are its frontiers? who are its legitimate population? All these questions have remained unanswered for 20 years.

There are only two ways of answering them: the one is the way of force—to determine frontiers by armed conflict, and to bring in and drive out civilian populations behind guns and tanks; the other is for the United Nations to complete the responsibility which it took upon itself in 1947 when it created a Jewish state in Palestine, and to provide the juridical and territorial framework within which a *modus vivendi* between Arabs and Jews may eventually be found.

The alternatives which now present themselves are not a United Nations solution or direct negotiations: to present the matter in this way is simply to justify in advance the retention of territories seized by force. The real alternatives are a United Nations solution or an indefinite prolongation of war and instability.

But a United Nations solution implies more than sending a mediator to conduct an indirect negotiation: it implies arming him with precise instructions, and it means that the United Nations is not willing to abdicate its role as the parent of Israel, responsible for its existence and its behavior. And in a more general way it means that the United Nations has not abandoned its own principles and Charter, and still gives a meaning to territorial integrity.

The Arabs now accept a solution of the problem of Palestine within a

United Nations context. If the Israelis and their supporters do the same, the way to peace will be open.

CECIL HOURANI
New York, Nov. 1, 1967

The writer is a free-lance Anglo-Lebanese journalist who has served as a consultant and adviser to Arab Governments.

United Nations Mideast Role

To the Editor:

The proposal of Cecil Hourani, in his Nov. 5 letter for a United Nations solution of the Middle East crisis as the only real alternative to direct negotiations between the Israelis and the Arabs, is premised on a juridical fallacy regarding the relationship of the U.N. to a sovereign state of the international community.

"A U.N. solution," he states, "implies more than sending a mediator to conduct an indirect negotiation; it implies arming him with precise instructions, and it means that the United Nations is not willing to abdicate its role as the parent of Israel, responsible for its existence and its behavior."

Even if we would assume—which at best would be most difficult—that the United Nations is responsible for the existence of Israel, can international law accept as a principle that a new state is to be considered having limited sovereignty; that its exercise is subject to direction or control of its "parent," the United Nations, who acquires a status in the international community of a "juridical parent" and is responsible for the behavior of that state.

A moment's reflection should suffice to indicate that any such principle of international law would destroy the juridical basis of the equality of each state, and suggests all sorts of second- and third-class citizenship status for different states in the international community. It also suggests an authority for the United Nations which it neither has and which it specifically disclaimed when it withdrew its troops at Nasser's unilateral insistence.

Somehow the Middle East crisis will have to be solved within the framework of the existing juridical order. A paternalistic legalism which

269

is embodied in Mr. Hourani's proposal as well as that of other Arab advisers, is patently unsound and unrealistic.

MORRIS AMCHAN
Former Deputy Chief Counsel
For War Crimes, Nuremberg
Arlington, Va., Nov. 6, 1967

Threat to Israel in Restoring Frontiers

To the Editor:

In your April 23 news dispatch from Amman, Arab diplomats are quoted as saying that Israel will not withdraw from territories occupied during the war last June "until the United States exerts diplomatic and economic pressure on the Israeli Government."

Before such pressure is exerted it may be useful to consider what would be the effect on Israel if the *status quo*, as it existed in 1967 before the June war began, were restored. The 800 Russian tanks which were destroyed have been replaced; they could be concentrated again on the Negev frontier less than 35 miles from Tel Aviv, but this time they would be manned in part by some of the 3,000 "technicians" who have been advertised as coming from the Soviet Union.

The Gaza Strip, under Egyptian control, could again house the Palestine Liberation Army pledged to kill every Israeli man and woman across the border, and Russian guns would be back on the Golan Heights ready to devastate northern Galilee.

Perhaps the most serious of all is the Jordanian West Bank Territory which projects deeply into Israel, dividing the country nearly in half. Its hostile Arab Legion is now reinforced by 15,000 Iraqi soldiers and an unnumbered body of Syrian guerrillas. Is it surprising that Israel is not prepared to return to a *status quo* which today would be an even greater danger than the one which threatened its destruction in 1967?

It has been said that Israel must be prepared to accept some form of international guarantee, but three fundamental changes that have recently taken place would make such international protection illusory:

Before the June war began it was generally believed that the United States, Great Britain and France had guaranteed the Middle Eastern frontiers, but France immediately repudiated all responsibility. Today Great Britain, with its diminished forces, would no longer be able to commit itself to take any action if such a guarantee were revived. It would be intolerable to ask the United States to act as sole guarantor.

Until U Thant withdrew the United Nations peace-keeping force from Sinai on President Nasser's demand, there was a general belief that whenever a crisis arose the United Nations might be able to intervene to prevent war. That hope has probably been extinguished.

There is no evidence that the Russians took any active part in the June war. Such a step would have involved them in unacceptable risks. Today the situation is a completely different one, because the Soviet Union now seems to be prepared to play a dominant role. It is far more likely, therefore, that the Soviet Union would actively assist Egypt if it were probable that the Arabs would win a fourth war against an Israel whose frontiers could not be adequately defended.

The idea of an effective international guarantee is therefore a chimera.

In these circumstances can it be in the interest of the United States to bring pressure on Israel to withdraw unconditionally from the territories which are essential for its defense? It may be noted that this is a course which has been strongly recommended by Mr. Kosygin, but he can hardly be suspected of having the welfare of the United States at heart.

ARTHUR L. GOODHART
New York, April 23, 1968

The writer is Professor Emeritus at Oxford University.

Israeli Action

To the Editor:

For the humaneness of its conception and the meticulousness of its execution, the Israel action at the Beirut airport should be praised as a paradigmatic commando raid. Thirteen Lebanese airplanes were expeditiously demolished with no damage whatsoever to any foreign airplane and, more remarkable, with no physical injury to any person. We do not even hear of the bloodied heads, a la Columbia or Chicago, which our police spokesmen insist are concomitant to any massive clearing operation.

The Israel commando action can be unconditionally condemned only by a society that is so mesmerized by its idolatry for machines that it cannot see the ethical distinction between human beings and property.

Yet what is frightening is the dominion of the idolatry: we understand

and tolerate the body counts from Vietnam and the starvation statistics from Biafra, not to speak of the indiscriminate detonation of bombs in crowded centers of Tel Aviv and Jerusalem, but we are profoundly grieved by the demolition of 13 (replaceable and partially insured) machines. Accordingly, any distinction between an attack on a plane full of passengers and one on empty planes is considered scholastic.

We have solemnly condemned the Israelis for blowing up our gods; but the true abomination is not their deicide but our idolatry.

WARREN Z. HARVEY
Harrison, N.Y., Jan. 1, 1969

Inexcusable Act

To the Editor:

It was a shocking thing that Arab saboteurs did at the Athens airport. What Sirhan Sirhan did in Los Angeles in murdering a Presidential candidate was even more shocking.

The United States Government, however, did not retaliate with some violent act against an Arab country. But Israel unashamedly has shockingly retaliated in an inexcusable act of revenge at Beirut airport.

Violent revenge and retaliation ill become any nation with high moral principles. There is, in Israel's tradition, recorded in the best of her prophets, noble sentiment for mercy and loving-kindness. Or is that merely for personal, rather than national, behavior?

A desperate spirit of violence is abroad in the modern world. But it is sad to see its evidence in a state that has supposedly in its foundations an Isaiah or a Jeremiah. The costly, premeditated destruction at Beirut does not increase our respect for Israel, nor does it foster hopes for peace in our troubled world. I have never heard of peace by retaliation.

(Rev.) DAVID K. BARNWELL
Millington, N.J., Dec. 30, 1968

Rogers' Plan Backed

To the Editor:

Men and women of goodwill should feel somewhat heartened by the declaration of policy in the Middle East lately made by American Secretary of State Rogers.

This is not because he has rendered full justice to the Arabs of Palestine, but because he has made a move in the direction of impartiality without which no peace could be achieved.

Secretary of State Rogers is right in assuming that America has friends in the Arab world. America also has her cultural, commercial and oil connections in the area. For America's own interest as well as for world peace she should not act in a partial or biased way in the Middle East.

As a great power with a great humanitarian tradition, the United States is expected to defend the United Nations Charter and the principles of human rights for all mankind, including the Palestine Arabs.

The Israelis should clearly and unequivocally understand that there can be no peace in the Middle East until Jews, Christians and Moslems learn to live together on an equal footing in Palestine, which is equally holy and equally loved by all its legitimate inhabitants.

No party has the right to uproot and exclude another and still clamor for peace. Genuine peace cannot be achieved by war, occupation, destruction or repression.

Let us hope that an American policy of impartiality in the Middle East will contribute to the realization of a lasting peace in this vital area.

MOHAMMED FADHEL JAMALI
Former Prime Minister of Iraq
Tunis, Jan. 1, 1970

Mideast Equation

To the Editor:

Secretary of State William Rogers' desire to achieve equality of concession as between Israel and the Arab countries is commendable, but his equation is faulty.

He asks the Arab states to "accept a permanent peace" with Israel in exchange for her withdrawal from the occupied territories. A proper

273

equation would be for the Arabs to promise not to attempt to destroy Israel's Government in exchange for a pledge from Israel not to attempt to overthrow any of the Arab Governments.

Put this way, one sees that the Arabs are being asked to give what should not need to be asked and the Israelis what has not been withheld. So where is the equality?

Secretary Rogers' fault lies in assuming that for a nation to live in peace is a gift from its neighbors rather than a right. So he feels free to bargain with Israel's right to exist. No wonder the Israelis are disappointed and appalled.

Perhaps it is not stressed very often in the State Department these days, but it is a central principle of international morality that to refrain from war in a civilized world community is not a concession, but an obligation. Imagine the Mexican Government arguing: we'll refrain from attacking across the border if the United States will cede Texas back to us. Or more dramatically, imagine a burglar saying to his intended victim: I cede to you the right to breathe; what will you do for me in exchange?

If Secretary Rogers were to call upon the Arabs to exert themselves in a somewhat more constructive way than their present ways, e.g. in behalf of the refugees, both Arab and Jewish, who are the byproducts of their 20 years of belligerency, he could make a more genuine claim to "impartiality."

HARRY RUJA
Professor of Philosophy
San Diego State College
San Diego, Calif., Dec. 25, 1969

No Binationalism Now

To the Editor:

Many Arabs, from Yassir Arafat to Gamal Abdel Nasser, have been talking with a false show of reasonableness of a multinational state, Arab and Jew living together in harmony after the destruction of the state of Israel.

Coming from Arab mouths, this mocks the shattered dreams of a great man and notable scholar, Dr. Judah Magnes, late president of Hebrew University. Between 1930 and 1935 Dr. Magnes conceived the idea of a binational state in Palestine under the rallying cry of "Araba, Araba, Jafrim Jehuda." ("Arab, Arab, you are the brother of the Jew.")

The Arab reply was the bloody rioting of 1936–37, which in turn led to the formation of Wingate's night squads, the Haganah and Palmach, and the strengthening of Israeli nationalism and an end to the impractical idea of binationalism.

The Arabs killed the dream of Judah Magnes. They are in bad grace in reviving that dream 33 years later.

HOWARD L. MORRIS
New York, Feb. 19 ,1970

Sovietizing Middle East

To the Editor:

The United States is concerned about the Russian presence in the Middle East, and, therefore supports Israel. Russia is concerned about the American presence in the Middle East, and, by using the Arabs' need for defense, offers some support to the Arabs. The Arabs, who became refugees in several states, see enough threat to accept any support.

The Americans then attempt to balance the unbalanceable situation. Hence, with action and counteraction, the vicious circle goes on and on to serve the Big Powers' desire for domination—a desire, most unfortunately, at the expense of peace for all the inhabitants of the Middle East.

To Western analysts, the Russians are not interested in an immediate solution, for they want to use the conflict to foster their long-term goals. And the Israelis seem to be able to exploit the role of the Russians. Furthermore, the West is interested in settling the problem only on the terms of Western governments. And, finally, the Egyptians will soon be faced with the choice (as they perceive it) of being Communist and secure or continuation and possible expansion of the Israeli occupation.

Irrespective of the parties involved, the average layman would tend to agree that foreign influence is less painful to take than foreign occupation. Should the Western policies that confuse cause and effect continue, the Arabs might see enough reason to accept Communism.

It should not be forgotten, however, that the Israelis are reinforcing the emotional indoctrination that precedes Communism by their daily bombardment. To this end, it seems to me that Western foreign policy has failed, for it ignores the causes of the disease. Should the West con-

275

tinue that type of policy, and should the Arabs as a result become Communist, then I charge the West with the responsibility.

The West has a chance to seek just (really just) and mutual peace, and thus make the Arabs stop short of raising colorful red flags.

A. RASHAD ABDEL-KHALIK
Champaign, Ill., July 10, 1970

Genocide Against Jews Feared

To the Editor:

The liquidation of Israel is still a possibility and an Arab, if not an Egyptian objective, even when the probability of a Soviet-American "collision" in the Middle East has greatly increased in recent times.

When I refer to the liquidation of Israel, I do not mean the elimination of Israel as an independent country like Hungary and Czechoslovakia, odious enough as that objective must always be.

It is, therefore, relevant to record and analyze the recent utterances of the Palestinian Liberation Organization, the best-known leaders of which are George Habash and Yassir Arafat, and of its top institution, the Palestinian National Council.

The most recent and important utterance of this body is the revised National Covenant of the Palestine Liberation Organization, adopted by its fourth Congress in Cairo (July 10–17, 1968) and by the Popular Front for the Liberation of Palestine.

The National Covenant is the basic political document of the P.L.O. and agreement with its contents is a condition for joining the "Command of Armed Struggle" which now makes joint announcements for most of the terrorist organizations. Article 6 of the Covenant is important in the context of intended Jewish genocide:

"Jews who were customarily living in Palestine until the beginning of the Zionist invasion will be considered Palestinians."

The original version of the National Covenant, issued in 1964, could be said to imply that Jews living in Palestine in 1947 would be recognized as Palestinians and would, therefore, be allowed to continue living there. In the revised 1968 version, however, it is explicitly stated that only Jews who lived in Palestine "until the beginning of the Zionist invasion," i.e., until the Balfour Declaration in 1917, would be considered as Palestinians.

The rest would be aliens and, being so numerous, would, presumably, have to leave, if alive. Where would they go and how many would there be?

Not many Jews contrived to escape to the free countries of the West during Hitler's final solution. But how many will there be this time? The number of Jews now in Israel, 1970, is about 2,520,000; so even if the descendants of the original inhabitants are allowed to stay—which is, in fact, not allowed by Article 6 of the revised National Covenant—these would not come to more than one or two hundred thousand.

So there are some 2,400,000 Jews to be got rid of. This should not be too difficult.

On Feb. 28 Prof. Yusif A. Sayigh, Director of the Planning Centre of the Palestine Liberation Organization, wrote to *The London Times* saying that arguments or inferences similar to those above were wrong and deliberately misleading, particularly in regard to the date, 1917, of the Zionist invasion. He correctly pointed out that this date was not mentioned in Article 6 of the revised National Covenant; but no doubt unintentionally, he omitted to mention the specification of the date of the Zionist invasion, given in the resolutions of the fourth P.L.O. Congress which endorsed the revised National Covenant. This is the specification:

"Likewise, the National Council affirms that the aggression against the Arab nation and its land began with the Zionist invasion of Palestine in 1917."

Contrary to what Professor Sayigh said in his letter, there has been no revision of Article 6, nor of the resolution quoted immediately above.

There may or may not be a confrontation between America and Russia in the Middle East; but the fate of nearly two and a half million people must, in these circumstances, be in the balance. Genocide may be more difficult this time. Israel will not let itself be led like a lamb to the slaughter (or deportation—where?), but it is as well to be clear about what Professor Sayigh and his friends have in mind.

No Arab state or organization has as yet formally disavowed this new and equally horrible plan. As for cost-effectiveness, it is as well to remember that it can be applied to battle as well as to genocide.

ROTHSCHILD
London, Aug. 20, 1970

277

IX•Civil Liberties

Man's struggle for the liberties he is taught are assuredly his in the Constitution has often been one of his toughest. Twenty years ago that struggle involved loyalty oaths, subversion controls, McCarthyism and irrational fears about communism. More recently the issues have been preventive detention, no-knock raids and the Government's assault on violence with violence. At present our freedoms are jeopardized by the creation of computerized data banks.

Times readers have tracked every attempted erosion of their civil liberties assiduously. The Government and its supporters have defended their positions. It has been a lively debate and it promises to continue with recent revelations of Army spying on public and private citizens.

Subversion Controls Upheld

To the Editor of *The New York Times:*

Your editorial of April 22 disparaging the decision of the Subversive Activities Control Board in the case of the Communist party and belittling the resultant controls gives further circulation to misconceptions unfortunately already too widely current as to the work of the board and the provisions of the Internal Security Act under which it operates.

You complain that the legal process attendant upon the imposition of controls is too lengthy; when controls finally are applied you forsee the Communist party already driven underground and beyond reach of the controls. You go on to conjure up the specter of controls being extended to non-Communist groups, then, implicitly admitting that communism requires some kind of control, you propose, in substitute, a declaration of illegality.

Such arguments misconstrue the nature of the controls in that they fail to take account of the precision of the definitions marking off the field of control. Upon analysis, the arguments you muster against controls either refute one another or are refuted by the terms of the act.

Granting that, with more than a year already consumed by the board in reaching the finding that the party is a Soviet puppet, and granting also that another year or more may pass before the Supreme Court rules on the act's constitutionality, it does not follow that the party can elude the controls when they are applied. The underground does not provide it an escape hatch.

Annual public registration is mandatory upon all Communists, and the Registration, besides baring to the public the party membership of 24,796 which the F.B.I. has tabulated, will permit prosecution of those going underground. The annual financial accounting to be exacted by the party will open a window upon party finance and subsidization, an area now closed to the F.B.I. The controls applying to propaganda will affect not only such of the party's open publications as *The Daily Worker* and *Political Affairs,* will but reach into and control the clandestine radio and hidden printing press, for whose use the hearing showed the party to be prepared. In short, then, should the party have gone underground when the controls become applicable, their effect will be to bring it back above ground and keep it there.

More pernicious than your argument that controls will be ineffective is the one in which you contend that while communism may go uncontrolled, other, non-Communist, movements may be controlled. The act says in so many words that controls shall apply only to Communist-action and Communist-front organizations, and their extention to other organizations is precluded by criteria in which controllable organizations are defined. As Senator Ferguson remarked in a detailed analysis of the criteria recently published (cf. *Congressional Record*, April 20, p. 3515), the Department of Justice, were it to proceed against a non-Communist organization in the face of those criteria, would make itself a laughing stock.

Your proposal that the Communist conspiracy be suppressed by a declaration of illegality is so vague as to make intelligent comment difficult. But if you mean the declaration to apply to conspiratorial actions, the Smith Act already illegalizes them, while outlawry of the party, if that is what you have in mind, could in all likelihood be accomplished only by the slow and cumbrous process of amending the Constitution, considering the ban therein on bills of attainder.

KARL E. MUNDT
U.S. Senator from South Dakota
Washington, April 30, 1953

Attacks on McCarthyism

To the Editor of *The New York Times:*

Those who vehemently denounced what they chose to call the hysteria of witch-hunting, smears and unfair hounding of persons accused of Communistic leanings are now exhibiting a fantastic form of hysteria by their undiscriminating attacks on "McCarthyism."

They seem more concerned to defend academic opinions about an ill-defined freedom of speech and conduct than in rooting out Communists and bad security risks from Government, schools, colleges and other strategic positions of influence.

We are witnessing a display of the gullibility of many Americans in their readiness to accept insincere appeals to their idealism and generosity of heart. They are easy victims of the tactics of Communists to draw a red herring across the trail of Congressional investigations of subversive activities.

Many high-minded and patriotic citizens, notably in academic, church and press circles, are falling innocently for this stale device, as they have fallen for the Moscow "peace offensive," and formerly for the political device of the "Popular Democratic Front," so effectively used to delude liberally minded Americans during the late civil war in Spain.

If there really was hysteria in recent investigations of communism—

something I very much doubt—the hysteria of those who apparently are not wholeheartedly enlisted in the war against Communists, at home as well as abroad, is infinitely more reprehensible and more inimical to freedom and national security.

I do not attempt to extenuate any mistakes and defects in the methods employed by Senator McCarthy in his successful exposé of subversive activities by Communists and their fellow-travelers, but I can understand why he is regarded as their strongest foe. The cry of McCarthyism is serving effectively to divert attention from their sinister conspiracy to win the support of the friends of freedom.

Is this not an incredibly grotesque situation? Are Americans so unrealistic and naive as to further the cause of those seeking to destroy freedom? Do they really think, after the harrowing ordeal of Judge Medina in his patient handling of the disgraceful scenes during the trial of Communist leaders, that our courts are remiss in safeguarding freedom? Do they actually believe that we Americans are in danger of fascism and totalitarianism? If they have so low an opinion of American intelligence and character they are guilty of a hysteria that is most regrettable and alarming.

PHILIP MARSHALL BROWN
Charleston, S.C., May 23, 1953

America vs. McCarthy

To the Editor of *The New York Times:*

James Reston's expert analysis of March 7 in *The Times* of McCarthy's influence in Congress underlines the fact that once a man has attained political power he can be deprived of that power only by political means. Indignation must be not only felt, it must be expressed in democratic action because, as Elihu Root once said, a member of Congress feels that an organized minority will punish where an unorganized majority will not protect.

Mr. Reston might have quoted also from Woodrow Wilson's Kansas City address of May 6, 1911: "The man with power but without conscience, could, with an eloquent tongue, if he cared for nothing but his own power, put this whole country into flame, because this whole country believes that something is wrong, and is eager to follow those who profess to be able to lead it away from its difficulties."

282

The majority of Americans share President Eisenhower's obvious distaste for McCarthy to which your editorial of March 7 refers. Most of them would say that "distaste" is far too mild a word to express their reaction to a man who is perilously close to riding high on the ruins of America.

Whether or not the President comes out and speaks for the majority of American citizens, each voter has a chance to use the power of his ballot in the primaries which are close upon us. The voters of Maine have an obvious chance in the effort of a McCarthy man to bring that foreign influence into Maine to defeat Senator Margaret Chase Smith. But all through the country candidates can be asked to declare themselves: "Are you for McCarthy or are you for America?"

This is a national, not a partisan, issue—it arises inside parties, in the primaries, as well as ultimately in elections, between candidates of both parties. As your editorial says, the people of this country respect moral courage. They can display it themselves by making Americanism vs. McCarthyism the issue.

PHILIP C. JESSUP
New York, March 7, 1954

The writer is Hamilton Fish Professor of International Law and Diplomacy at Columbia University.

To Eliminate Subversives

To the Editor of *The New York Times:*

The case of Robert Oppenheimer exposes in a dramatic way the weakness of the procedures which the Eisenhower Administration has adopted to eliminate subversives from the Government service. Those procedures were prescribed in a series of Executive Orders signed by the President more than a year ago. In essence they call for a review of the files of all persons employed by the Government in sensitive positions.

If upon such a review "derogatory information" of significance appears notice of such information is given to the employe concerned and he is afforded an opportunity to explain. If his explanation is not deemed satisfactory a private hearing is afforded him with the privilege of representation by counsel. From an adverse determination he may appeal to a board of review and thence to higher authority. In the meantime he is denied access to classified information and may be suspended from his employment.

283

Superficially the system seems reasonable, but I submit that it has two basic defects. First, and most important, no provision is made for the exercise of responsible discretion in determining whether to initiate such a proceeding. Dr. Oppenheimer's case illustrates this perfectly. Here is a man who is well, and even intimately known to many important officials in this Administration. Admiral Lewis Strauss, chairman of the Atomic Energy Commission, and Gen. Robert Cutler, President Eisenhower's representative on the Security Council, have both been associated with Dr. Oppenheimer for many years and cannot fail to realize the intensity of his devotion to his country. President Eisenhower himself is well aware that few individuals have contributed as much as Robert Oppenheimer to the security of the United States during the past ten years.

These gentlemen now find themselves in a role which they can hardly relish—one that in its abdication of responsibility is uncomfortably like that of another much-harassed administrator who was called upon to deal with the most celebrated case of subversion in the history of the Western World. Yet, as Arthur Krock has pointed out, the established procedures require just such a washing of hands on the part of those officials to whom the public looks for leadership in matters of this sort. There is an essential lack of integrity about such a proceeding which cannot be denied.

A second defect lies in the extreme ambiguity of the word "derogatory." If we may judge by General Nichols' letter to Dr. Oppenheimer, it is "derogatory information" that a scientist opposed the development of the hydrogen bomb, although such opposition was clearly not inconsistent with unqualified loyalty. I have personal knowledge of a case where a distinguished scientist and public administrator was required before obtaining clearance to explain his opposition (along with that of many wise and responsible citizens) to so-called "anti-subversive" legislation against which more than one-fourth of the electorate of his community cast their ballots.

Sponsorship of meetings along with men such as General Eisenhower, General Marshall and Secretary Dulles has been classified as "derogatory information" because of the participation of others who have since been identified as subversive. Attendance at meetings with Russian scientists at the specific request of the Government of the United States has been similarly characterized.

The list might be extended by other equally fantastic examples familiar to those who have had the opportunity to observe the administration of the clearance procedures now in effect.

What a spectacle this makes of the United States before the rest of the world, and what a record we are writing before the bar of history!

284

Is it not time that the officials of our Government accepted the responsibility of exercising judgment in these matters by refusing to initiate proceedings where after full investigation of the facts they are themselves in no doubt as to the loyalty of the individuals involved, and by excluding inquiry into activities which are compatible with complete loyalty?

No doubt those who take such a position must run the risk of criticism and, where, as in the case of Harry Dexter White, their judgment proves to be faulty, of public condemnation, but is this not one of the legitimate risks of accepting public office?

WILLIAM L. MARBURY
Baltimore, April 19, 1954

The writer, together with former Under Secretary Royall, drafted the War Department legislation for control of atomic energy.

Government Security Risks

To the Editor of *The New York Times:*

The recent announcement by the Administration that 6,926 federal employes had been dismissed as security risks between May 28, 1953, and June 30, 1954, with 1,743 of the total involving subversive associations or activities, presents a misleading picture which needs more clarification than it is presently being afforded by both parties.

Under Executive Order 10241, which was signed by President Truman on April 28, 1951, the following standard was provided with reference to the dismissal of federal employes:

". . . the standard for the refusal of employment or the removal from employment in an executive department or agency on grounds relating to loyalty should be that, on all the evidence, there is reasonable doubt as to the loyalty of the person involved to the Government of the United States."

Although the loyalty criterion was not the suitable standard for all situations, it did provide reasonable protection for an employe whose past associations might have been unwise.

However, Executive Order 10450, which was signed by President Eisenhower on April 27, 1953, contained a significant change in standard. Henceforth federal employes about whom any information had been developed or received which would indicate that their retention "may not be clearly consistent with the interests of the national security" could be dropped from the rolls of nonsensitive as well as sensitive executive agencies.

Naturally, under such a broad standard it is possible for agency heads to dismiss employes because they do not believe that the latter are good security risks. It is no longer a question of loyalty, but of some executive officer's opinion as to the advisability of retaining a loyal employe who might have attended a Communist party meeting in, say, 1938, or who was a member of a labor union which for a time was Communist dominated. No longer is it necessary for the Government to assemble and present credible evidence to indicate disloyalty on the employe's part; it is enough to show that he associated as a youth with a person who subsequently became a subversive.

Under the subjective and centralized standard presently in effect it is not difficult to array an imposing set of figures to indicate that the present Administration is most energetic in policing its employes. Indeed, it is one that, coupled with a little party prodding, might induce executive heads to furnish a "quota" to justify the rash statements of its spokesmen. What is overlooked in the process is that the careers of loyal and superior public servants are smashed, the Government loses the services of valued personnel and the ability to attract suitable replacements, and the people gain an uneasy feeling that their Government is permeated by hordes of Russian espionage agents.

WILLIAM M. KUNSTLER
New York, Oct. 12, 1954

Educators' Stand Criticized

To the Editor of *The New York Times:*

The current concern of professional educators over the loyalty oath that will be required of scholarship recipients under the National Defense Education Act of 1958 prompts the observation that this may be unfair to the students, but is hardly more than the educators deserve.

The act provides diverse forms of Federal aid to foster the teaching of science, mathematics and languages. It was put forth as the nation's response to the challenge of sputnik. Written largely by the educators themselves, it gave official status to the preposterous notion that our failure to keep ahead of the Russians in rocket development was somehow a technological failure for which our education system was to blame.

In their eagerness to obtain Federal aid to education, our educators willingly subscribed to this dangerous nonsense. The essentials of rocket technology were developed by the Chinese in the 13th century: going on from there was a matter of effort, not genius.

America fell behind the Russians simply because our leaders were unwilling to pay the cost of keeping ahead of them. The sputnik failure was entirely a political failure. The Republican Executive and the Democratic Legislature failed to allocate sufficient resources to provide for the national defense.

No number of science teachers will help us avoid that kind of failure in the future. Our educators will have done no service in helping distract attention from the true nature of the problem. If they now find the same politicians who delight in slashing defense appropriations take equal pleasure in extracting loyalty oaths from schoolboys, it is late in their game to protest.

DANIEL P. MOYNIHAN
New York State Government Research Project
Maxwell Graduate School of Citizenship and
Public Affairs, Syracuse University
Syracuse, N.Y., March 3, 1959

Party Threat to Freedom

To the Editor of *The New York Times:*

I must take exception to your editorial of June 7 concerning the recent Supreme Court decisions on the Smith and Internal Security Acts, in which you stated "It is important to remember, as Justice Douglas pointed out . . . that only speech is involved in Smith Act prosecutions."

The one indisputable fact on this question is that, in the overwhelming majority of Smith Act prosecutions to date (about 150), it has been primarily conspiracy which has been prosecuted and, as the late Justice Jackson pointed out:

"The conspiracy principle has traditionally been employed to protect society against all 'ganging up' or concerted action in violation of its laws. No term passes that this court does not sustain convictions based on that doctrine for violations of the antitrust laws or other statutes. . . ." (Concurring Opinion, *C.I.O.* v. *Douds.*)

Your claim and the claim of Justice Douglas is tantamount to asserting that "only speech" is involved when persons are prosecuted for conspiring to fix prices, commit murder, kidnap, commit fraud, etc. Such claims are ridiculous.

Moreover, the specific point at issue in the recent Supreme Court decision on the Smith Act involved its membership clause. It was not speech on the part of Junius Scales that led to his trial and conviction. It was his cold, calculated act of joining the Communist party, remaining a member of it for many years and holding in it official posts which gave him an active role in the direction of an organization which, you tacitly admit in your editorial, is characterized by its "secret, conspiratorial nature and domination from abroad." And he did all this, he performed all these acts, the jury and courts have found, while knowing full well the nature of the Communist party and its aim of violent overthrow of this Government.

In the same editorial, you referred to the Internal Security Act of 1950 as a "noxious piece of legislation." This act does no more than try to compel the Communist party and its affiliated agencies to be at least partly honest. It is a constitutional (the Supreme Court finds), carefully considered attempt on the part of the Congress of this country to protect the American people from the type of fraud and deceit that characterize nearly all Communist activity.

Inasmuch as you have denounced this act as "noxious," I presume that you will now take the logical step of also denouncing as "noxious" all regulations of the Securities and Exchange Commission, our Pure Food and Drug laws, etc., which are designed to protect the American people from fraud and deceit on the part of the sellers of securities and foods and drugs. After all, fraud and deceit in these fields can rob the American people only of money and health (though it may also kill some of them).

Communist fraud and deceit, however, if permitted to go unchecked, can rob them of their freedom, which is far more precious, and cause the death of millions—as it has in many other countries. Behind the Iron and Bamboo Curtains, there are millions of graves, thousands of concentration camps and hundreds of varied forms of political, economic and religious repression which attest to this truth.

FRANCIS E. WALTER
Chairman, House Committee on Un-American Activities
Washington, June 8, 1961

288

What Smith Act Penalizes

To the Editor of *The New York Times:*

In the light of experience as a non-Communist expert witness in several of the Smith Act trials may I comment on the letter of Congressman Francis A. Walter in your issue of June 14. He challenges the statement in your informed and excellent editorial of June 7 that "only speech is involved in Smith Act prosecutions."

Your statement is an accurate and important one, the implications of which, unfortunately, are not comprehended by the general public. The exact character of prevalent misunderstanding is shown by the Congressman's counter-statement that "it has been primarily conspiracy which has been prosecuted." He thinks this means the trials were not speech prosecutions; but they were.

The reason is unusual but clear: the conspiracies that were charged were conspiracies to preach and teach a certain doctrine (forcible overthrow of government).

In other words, the Smith Act severely penalizes a certain kind of speech or teaching. What the conspiracy indictments did was to charge Communists with conspiring to engage in that kind of speech and teaching.

They were not charged with conspiring to overthow the Government. Technically, they were not even charged with actual speech or actual teaching that the Government should be overthrown. They were charged with conspiring (preparing to act in concert) to engage in such speech and teaching.

This is three jumps away from any overt action charge: first jump, conspiring to teach overthrow; second jump, teaching overthrow; third jump, conspiring to overthrow; fourth jump, attempting to overthrow.

Congressman Walter, like many others, apparently thought that the "conspiracy" aspect brought the cases out of the speech area, and closer to the action area, whereas the reverse is true. A conspiracy to say something is obviously further removed from doing it than actually saying it would be.

Here again one finds a root confusion that has had widespread and disastrous impact on the American tradition. The general impression among us seems to be that the Communist doctrine of revolution teaches forcible overthrow of capitalist governments at any time, any place, under any conditions. This impression, by a sort of reverse action, suggests and promotes the notion that the American tradition can never sanction forcible overthrow of established government any time, any place, under any conditions.

289

Both these impressions are profoundly mistaken, for Communist doctrine does not teach unconditional advocacy of forcible revolution, any more than American traditional doctrine teaches unconditional rejection of forcible revolution.

When one examines in detail the doctrines of both traditions in respect to the justification of revolutionary force, as I tried to do in my book on the Smith Act cases, one finds that the conditions explicitly laid down on either side are basically the same.

That is, forcible revolution is justified only when the government in question is a tyranny which is unwilling to carry out peacefully the will of the majority, and the masses (majority) support revolutionary measures.

This is the position taken in Communist doctrine, as it is the position taken in the Declaration of 1776 justifying the forcible revolution which established our sovereignty as a nation. If it is teaching about revolution that is to be penalized, there is no consistent way to punish Communist teaching that would not equally punish Jeffersonian teaching. I do not think we wish to do that. The Supreme Court majority which can be found to let such a law stand has now dwindled to the 5–4 margin.

JOHN SOMERVILLE
New York, June 15, 1961

Rights of Suspects

To the Editor:

Your editorial of Dec. 11 entitled "Those Troublesome Confessions" refers to "the proposed Model Code of the American Law Institute on pre-arraignment procedures." To date, the American Law Institute has not approved any such code. You must have had in mind the proposals of the reporters for the American Law Institute.

The editorial says the proposed code "approves, by implication at least, continuance of existing police practices"; which means that the police need not warn suspects of their constitutional rights prior to interrogation.

It also seems to imply that I think the rights of suspects will be adequately protected if the police so warn them. Neither attribution is correct.

As I understand it, the code proposed by the reporters of the American Law Institute would require a warning by the police but would not provide for an appointed lawyer for those financially unable to retain one. My view is that we cannot expect the police to advise a suspect effectively and disinterestedly of his right to remain silent at the same time as they are trying to elicit a confession from him.

The reporters' suggestion that elaborate recordings and monitoring devices be required to assure that the warning is effectively given, would also seem to reflect some discomfort with entrusting this function to police. How much simpler (and fairer) it would be to provide a lawyer to those unable to afford one at this critical stage.

As Mr. Justice Black has so wisely said, "The Constitution does not contemplate that prisoners shall be dependent upon Government agents for legal counsel and aid, however conscientious and able those agents may be. Undivided allegiance and faithful, devoted service to a client are the prized traditions of the American lawyer."

The reporters' refusal to provide lawyers for those unable to afford them would seem to imply that our society cannot "live with" the privilege against self-incrimination unless enough of its members are kept sufficiently ignorant of it so that it does not significantly hamper the quest for confessions.

This philosophy of institutionalizing ignorance of existing rights is a disturbing and dangerous one which I hope will not be adopted by so respected a body as the American Law Institute.

DAVID L. BAZELON
Washington, Dec. 13, 1965

The writer is Chief Judge, United States Court of Appeals for the District of Columbia.

John Mitchell Disputed on Civil Rights

To the Editor:

Our new Attorney General, John Mitchell, seems off to a bad start. In his initial news conference, as reported in *The Times* of Jan. 22, he urged two courses of conduct which are not merely repressive but unconstitutional.

I am not quarreling with his general "get tough" attitude, however misguided. I accept the proposition that President Nixon and Mr. Mitchell may have a popular mandate to lead the nation through the .

wilderness of such sterile and self-defeating posturing for four years, until we learn that violence is not curbed by counter-violence. I object, however, to ignoring plain constitutional mandates in the process.

First, the Constitution forbids denying anyone a parade permit on the grounds of previous riotous conduct, let alone "activism." Parade permits may be denied for reasons of proper traffic control. To forbid them to particular persons thought to be riotous or "activist" is a prior restraint upon free speech, forbidden by the First Amendment.

Second, the Constitution forbids the denial of bail to a criminal accused on the grounds that he is likely to commit "more crimes." The only allowable purpose for requiring bail as a condition of pretrial release under the Eighth Amendment is to assure the accused's presence for trial. Since he has not yet been convicted of a crime, the Attorney General's reference to "more" crimes involves a logic that collides with the presumption of innocence.

These two postulates of constitutional law are firmly settled and not dubious. They are among the most priceless safeguards of liberty won and cherished by this nation. When the Attorney General is heedless of them, he does more violence to the nation than the courses of conduct which he urges could possibly hope to prevent.

ANTHONY G. AMSTERDAM
Professor of Law
University of Pennsylvania
Philadelphia, Jan. 22, 1969

Justice Department Stand on Pretrial Detention

To the Editor:

I would appreciate the opportunity to present a summary of the Justice Department's position on pretrial detention, in response to your Nov. 26 editorial "Guilty . . . Until Innocent."

The legislation we have proposed has two objectives. It seeks to reduce violent crime, a significant percentage of which is committed by persons released on bail; and its attempts to eliminate the hypocrisy in the bail system of detaining some defendants in custody, without fixed standards or procedures, by requiring a bond which they cannot meet.

Our proposal would authorize the detention of certain dangerous de-

292

fendants only after a court hearing in which the Government demonstrates that "no combination of conditions of release" will reasonably assure the safety of the community. The Government must also show by a "substantial probability" that the defendant has committed a violent crime. If this burden is not met, a defendant will not be detained.

The presumption of innocence to which you refer is a time-honored canon of our law. It allocates the burden of proof at trial in a criminal case and requires the prosecution to satisfy a jury beyond a reasonable doubt that the accused has committed the crime with which he is charged. Nothing in our legislation would affect this presumption. The legislation deals only with potential custody prior to trial.

In your reference to the presumption of innocence is to suggest that our system of justice offers no precedent for pretrial detention, the suggestion is unwarranted. As you concede, there are "unquestionably . . . specific situations in which public safety requires than an arrested person be kept in custody. . . . " Instances of homicide and sexual psychopathy are clear examples. But the fact is, Federal and most state courts have been authorized to deny bail in capital cases from Colonial times when most serious crimes were punished by death. Historical analysis supports the conclusion that pretrial detention for serious offenses is consistent with our legal traditions.

Pretrial detention procedures must satisfy the requirements of due process. But the Constitution does not impose a ban on all restraint of persons prior to conviction. The test is one of reasonableness, which involved a weighing of the individual's interest in freedom against society's claims for protection against dangerous defendants. The detention we would authorize is limited to 60 days, the minimum period of time within which it is generally feasible to bring serious offenses to trial; and it would only follow an adversary hearing in which the defendant's counsel could introduce evidence. This is a vast improvement on present procedure.

You suggest that "speeding up the trial process" is the answer to the violent crimes committed on bail. For defendants affected by our proposal, the trial process would in fact be greatly accelerated. But it is almost impossible to improve on a gap of nearly 60 days between arrest and trial. Without detention during that time, dangerous defendants will be free to rob, rape, and otherwise jeopardize the safety of the community. In any event, a speedy trial is not the cure for improper detentions through the bail system.

I believe the great majority of American citizens, carefully weighing the necessity of fairness to the accused defendant against the necessity for improving protection afforded to innocent victims of crime, will conclude that the proposed legislation is reasonable, sound, and needed.

RICHARD G. KLEINDIENST
Deputy Attorney General
Washington, Dec. 11, 1969

Threats to Liberties

To the Editor:

A news article in *The Times* of April 12 reports that the Nixon Administration plans to embark on an enlarged program of wire-tapping and other means of surveillance of potentially violent radicals. While reading the article I could distinctly hear in the back of my mind another nail being hammered into the coffin of civil liberties.

This proposed witch hunt, added to Mr. Agnew's mindless attacks on freedom of the press, Mr. Nixon's insistence on appointing an opponent of civil liberties to the Supreme Court vacancy, his policy of doing as little as he possibly can to promote school integration, and Mr. Moynihan's recent advice on the Negroes add up to a disgraceful picture.

THOMAS A. LIESE
New York, April 13, 1970

Secret Service Files

To the Editor:

It has been reported that Secret Service computers file the names of persons who participate in "anti-U.S. Government demonstrations," who make statements about officials which are "irrational" or "embarrassing" —all of these categories defined by the Secret Service itself.

Such tactics are not simply "alien" to our form of government, as Senator Sam Ervin Jr. suggests (news story, June 28): they are surely destructive of the spirit upon which our form of government rests.

The "collective mind" of the Secret Service is understandably compulsive about security and efficiency. But it is precisely for this reason that it should not be allowed to pursue its own priorities and momentum to their logical extreme. In failing to understand the elementary psychological insight that the security of this Government rests as much on freedom from fear of spirited debate as it does upon efficiency and physical control of suspected people's movements, the security groups have warped the complex and fragile fabric of emotions which nurtures citizen trust and courage, and thereby strengthens democratic debate.

In behooves public figures of authority—and those who are not afraid of being listed in the growing security files—to reassert their control over that one-dimensional misunderstanding of security which is the Secret Service and similar agencies. We ought to support Senator Ervin and pressure our own representatives to continue to disclose and criticize the new security measures.

JAMES A. SLEEPER
Longmeadow, Mass., June 29, 1970

Release of 'Security' List

To the Editor:

The recent action of the House Internal Security Committee in defying a court order by releasing the names of a very mixed bag of "radicals" who have been speaking at campuses indicates that there is no generation gap between the House Internal Security Committee and the Committee on Un-American Activities, from which it sprang. This committee, by whatever name, has characteristically endeavored to explain complex and disturbing events as the work of "agitators." Once it was sit-down strikes; now it is campus disturbances.

During its more than 30 years of existence, the committee's main legislative accomplishment has been the passage of a law that was ruled unconstitutional. Its real business, since its beginnings under Martin Dies, has been the trade in names—"exposure purely for the sake of exposure" as Justice Black correctly described the process years ago.

Its monuments have been blacklists. As in the most recent adventure, the persons selected for exposure, though all distasteful to the committee, have covered a range of political opinion and activism and the affiliations attached to them have not always been accurate.

An injunction issued by a Federal Court judge to halt circulation of the latest list as an infringement of the rights of the persons named and as without legislative purpose came too late to do the victims much

295

good. But, then, the committee has never shown great regard for the law or for order.

Customarily directed by Congressmen of the third caliber and staffed by vigilante mentalities, this is not the first time that it has flouted the law. And it long ago achieved notoriety for the disorderly manner in which it carried out its campaigns.

Operating in the lower regions of the body politic, the Internal Security Committee may be thought of as a thermometer registering our national distemper. The latest show of activity, coming just before the election, suggests that its present movers see an opportunity to revive its past grandeur. Perhaps it is not too much to hope that even in these distracted times, the citizenry will recognize an example of political indecency and simplemindedness for what it is. That much, at least, three decades of the Un-American Activities Committee should have taught us.

WALTER GOODMAN
New York, Oct. 28, 1970

The writer is the author of "The Committee," a history of the House Un-American Activities Committee.

X • Ecology

The fight to preserve the nation's natural resources and to maintain a viable ecological balance is an old one. Conservationists have waged the battle for preservation doggedly against great odds. Today their ranks have been swelled by a new breed of young ecological activist. However, he may have arrived a bit too late.

Alerted by Rachel Carson's *Silent Spring,* Americans began looking at the water they drank, the air they breathed and the earth they walked on. They found them all dirtier. Nature's delicate balance, which gives earth and man the ability to renew themselves, is going awry as pesticides, man and his wastes cover the world eliminating some problems, but creating others.

Americans of all ages and interests have recently joined in a common cause and turned much of their energy to cleaning up our environment and to alerting the rest of us to the dangers of a dirty, shrinking world.

A subject of continuing interest to readers of *The Times,* conservation and ecology have increasingly become major topics of discussion in the newspaper's mailbag.

To Prevent Destruction by Lumber Interests

To the Editor of *The New York Times:*

The readers of your paper should be alerted to the danger that will threaten the Olympic Park, one of the finest of our national parks, as soon as Congress convenes again.

This park was established through the efforts of President Roosevelt, who took such interest in it that he made a trip personally to inspect the region and decide on the park's limits. He clearly saw that contrary to the common belief that Olympic Mountains, though very impressive from their snow fields and because they arise right from sea level, are not the park's most important feature. Those mountains are too vast to be ever in any danger of destruction, whether in a park or not. Its really unique and priceless feature is one easy to destroy, and if once gone impossible to replace for many centuries, if ever.

The President found that the region contained a few remnants of the wonderful rain forest that formerly covered large areas in the Northwest but has been destroyed to the very last tree everywhere else. Many of the trees of that remarkable forest, some of them nearly or quite 300 feet tall, are many centuries old, and were already there when Columbus discovered America.

To the indignation of the lumber-men and allied commercial interests, the President insisted that the small surviving tracts of this wonderful forest should be included in the park for the enjoyment of future generations of Americans. The local lumber-men, who had already made a squeezed lemon as far as forest is concerned out of all the rest of the Olympic Peninsula, never consented to any such thing, and have been boasting ever since that they would get those trees excluded from the park and made available for logging.

Now everybody, regardless of personal political opinions, must admit that the Democrats under Presidents Roosevelt and Truman made a splendid record in protecting the national parks. Not an acre of them did we lose in spite of the difficulties of the war period. But now the Democrats are out and the enemies of the parks think that their chance has come.

For over a year they have been attacking the park with propaganda, most of it entirely mendacious, to prepare the way for coming legislation to trim the park and exclude the forest they wish to destroy. Most of this propaganda could be wholly disproved if the Interior Department would tell the truth about the Olympic Park and its forests. But that department has been maintaining silence. Thus it gives valuable aid to the park's enemies and allows the public and, what is worse, many Congress-

298

men to believe or pretend to believe the false statements about the park.

Another disquieting fact is that Governor Langlie of Washington State has joined in the warfare on Olympic Park by appointing a committee to try to induce Congress to deprive the 150 million Americans, the owners of the park, of the best part of it without any compensation, and turn the forest over to be destroyed for the benefit of the citizens of three or four counties in his own state.

The public must be on its guard against the old idea that the lands and forests of the national parks are exploitable political resources.

WILLARD G. VAN NAME

New York, Dec. 16, 1953

The writer was formerly an associate curator of the American Museum of Natural History.

Spraying Vegetation

To the Editor of *The New York Times:*

"Climbing Color" on the editorial page and "Nature at Work" on the garden page of Sept. 18 extol the beauty of our country roadsides in the fall. I wonder how many *Times* readers realize how extensively our roadsides were devastated this summer by chemical sprays.

In travels as far north as Maine and west to Illinois I saw mile after mile of roadsides and railroad rights of way on which all plants but grass had been seared by poison and were apparently dead. The fence row thickets of sumac were dead; the Virginia creeper on the stone walls was dead; the butterfly weed that should have been a blaze of orange in mid-summer was gone; the tall New England asters that would have been a blaze of purple in the fall were dead.

It is claimed, I believe, that this spraying is done in the interests of efficiency and lower maintenance costs. Botanists, however, tell me that blanket spraying of all roadside vegetation which kills virtually every plant but grass, is not always the cheapest way to use this new vegetation management tool. Its wise use requires first a willingness to rate the maintenance of roadside beauty a bit higher than the achievement of the lowest possible costs and a willingness to consult botanists and ecologists who are experts on vegetation management.

Country driving is not always done solely to get somewhere. Many a city dweller drives into the country on a weekend simply to enjoy the scenery. Must he in the future travel solely between two monotonous strips of grass unbroken by any wildflowers or shrubs? Unless the present

299

trend toward blanket spraying is stopped it seems likely that this will be his fate.

RICHARD H. POUGH
New York, Sept. 21, 1955

The writer is chairman of the Department of Conservation and General Ecology at the American Museum of Natural History.

Resources for the Future

To the Editor of *The New York Times:*

It is good that *The New York Times* expressed editorial caution (April 8) about the optimism of technologists and economists on the future availability of resources to sustain increasing populations and increasing levels of living in the years ahead.

The Times' caution was mild enough. Indeed, this is one of the more crucial problems of this day. The report of the experts, issued by Resources for the Future, contains three very big "ifs." There will be enough and to spare only if technological advances can replace depleted natural supplies; if foreign raw materials can be imported in increasing amounts at reasonable prices; and if current practices of misuse and waste of remaining resources can be curtailed.

It is highly unlikely that sufficient raw materials will continue to be available from abroad if we are successful in helping underdeveloped nations industralize and use their own resources, to the full. It is not likely that our own people will be willing or able to pay the cost of reducing increased pollution of rivers, oceans and air if they will not abate pollution today.

Moreover, even if technology and economy can triumph over nature, it will be far less pleasant to live in a world of congestion and ugliness, in which we breathe ever more polluted air, and eat the products of algae, synthetics and sludge.

An almost superhuman effort will be required if our citizens and our governments are to value natural beauty and a better quality of life above these technological and economic promises.

SAMUEL H. ORDWAY Jr.
President, The Conservation Foundation
New York, April 8, 1963

300

Power Plants on the Hudson

To the Editor of *The New York Times:*

The subject of your May 29 editorial "Defacing the Hudson" is naturally of great concern to the Palisades Interstate Park Commission, and we would like to call your attention to various facts that we feel you have overlooked.

The Commission regrets that Consolidated Edison has found it necessary to build a power plant at Storm King and that Central Hudson is now proposing a plant at Breakneck Ridge. But we also have recognized that additional facility developments of this type must be made available to meet the requirements of a growing population.

First of all, we would like to make it quite clear that the history of the Palisades Interstate Park Commission shows that since its establishment in 1900 it has been a strong protector of the natural beauty of the Hudson, and that it has been alert to place these incomparable assets in public ownership by gift, purchase and eminent domain, and to protect them by zoning and other devices for the enjoyment of the present population and posterity. As a result not only the face of the Palisades but over 55,000 acres in New York and New Jersey, constituting the greatest suburban park system in any metropolis in the world, have been preserved in perpetuity.

For some time now the commission, as well as other civic organizations interested in the preservation of the Hudson River Valley, have been working with Consolidated Edison to make sure that the greatest consideration possible is given to scenic and other values in the construction of this power plant.

For instance, electricity now is to be transmitted across the Hudson by underwater cables. The company elected to do this on its own so that the unspoiled character of the area would be maintained. It is estimated that this underground transmission line has added $6,000,000 to the cost of the project.

Other facts that I think are important are as follows:

The Consolidated Edison plant will be at the river level, facing north. Most of the plant will be below the ground level and it has been designed to blend into the hillside and will be landscaped by an outstanding landscape architect.

Water will flow from the reservoir to the plant through a 40-foot-diameter, two-mile-long tunnel deep underground.

The reservoir will be two miles east of the river, at 1,100 feet, which is about the top of the mountain. A native broken-rock-faced dam will be

301

visible from the new Storm King Highway, but this will be landscaped with bushes and trees.

The site where the pump-generating facilities are to be built at the river level is not forest primeval. For the most part, the site is now occupied by houses in varying conditions of repair and an old hotel. Nearby, also at the river level, are an abandoned wood-working plant, a sunken barge and the West Shore Railroad tracks.

The idea of the pump storage plant has been favorably received by the majority of the local citizens.

In summarizing, the commission feels that in this particular instance it must, on balance, consider the need for this added facility development, and prefers to take the positive approach to insure that the esthetic, historical and recreational values of the area are protected as much as possible. In this we will endeavor to work with and expect the cooperation of both companies, as well as other interested civic and public groups.

LAURANCE S. ROCKEFELLER
Vice President, Palisades Interstate Park Commission
Bear Mountain, N.Y., June 19, 1963

[*The Central Hudson proposed plant at Breakneck Ridge was abandoned some time after this letter was written. Mr. Rockefeller disclosed that at the request of the Commission, Central Hudson transferred the land involved to the state and this became the nucleus of the 2,500-acre Hudson Highlands State Park which is now operated by the Taconic State Park Commission.—The Editor.*]

Nonexempt Status of Sierra Club

To the Editor:

Your June 17 editorial "I.R.S. and the Grand Canyon" overlooks some significant factors. If these had been taken into account, you might not have been led to the conclusions that our action "raises serious questions of fairness and due process" and that it "looks suspiciously like harassment and intimidation."

The Internal Revenue Service has the responsibility of administering the tax laws as they have been enacted by Congress. These laws, as they pertain to tax-exempt groups such as the Sierra Club, provide that an organization eligible to receive contributions deductible by the donor may

302

not devote a substantial part of its activities in attempts to influence legislation.

On June 9 the Sierra Club placed full-page advertisements in two of the nation's leading newspapers, *The New York Times* and the Washington *Post*. These advertisements contained a mass appeal for funds to help the Sierra Club fight a bill currently pending in the Congress, coupled with an urgent solicitation of public effort in opposition to the bill.

Thus the Sierra Club set in motion a nationwide campaign to influence legislation which could reasonably be expected to be vigorous and continuing. On the basis of these facts, some action on the part of the I.R.S. was clearly indicated.

The Sierra Club is listed in an I.R.S. publication entitled "Organizations Described in Section 170 (c) of the Internal Revenue Code of 1954." The action taken by the I.R.S. is predicated upon a long-standing exception to the general rule that a taxpayer is assured of deductibility of contributions to organizations listed in this publication. The exception, set forth in the introduction to the publication, is that this assurance does not extend to persons who are aware of an organization's activities which result in its disqualification to receive deductible charitable contributions.

Anyone who responded to the Sierra Club's appeal for funds on June 9 would obviously be aware of the club's campaign to influence legislation and, if the club were later determined to be disqualified to receive tax deductible contributions, would be denied tax deductions for contributions to the club.

Under the circumstances, the I.R.S. felt it was under a duty to warn the club and possible contributors of the consequences if the club were subsequently determined to be disqualified to receive tax deductible contributions.

The I.R.S. announcement emphasized that the merits of the Colorado Dam legislation have no bearing on application of tax law which the I.R.S. has the responsibility for administering. In fairness to all taxpayers and to all other exempt organizations, the I.R.S. is expected to act equitably and expeditiously without regard to the justification or popularity of the cause.

SHELDON S. COHEN
Commissioner of Internal Revenue
Washington, June 21, 1966

Tax Law Inequities

To the Editor:

Sheldon B. Cohen, the Commissioner of Internal Revenue, is right in what he says in his letter printed June 27. What is wrong is the law he administers.

Section 162 of the Internal Revenue Code of 1954 permits you to deduct in your income tax return business expenses if they are "ordinary and necessary." But the Treasury has ruled, and the Supreme Court of the United States, that even though they be ordinary and necessary, expenses cannot be deducted if made for the "promotion or defeat of legislation" or for "lobbying purposes . . . the exploitation of propaganda."

Let me illustate that: A donation to a group studying narcotic addiction would be deductible but not if the group opposes or supports legislation making addiction a crime. You may deduct what you give to a group working for the prevention of cruelty to animals, a laudable purpose, but not if you give to a group advocating the abolition of the death penalty, an equally laudable purpose.

Our laws control our lives every minute of every day. They are made by 51 legislative bodies. Very many of them badly need improvement. Anyone doubting that should read, every day, the editorial pages of *The Times*. Next to service in the armed forces in time of war the highest duty an American owes to his country is to try to improve the law by influencing legislation.

The bias against such influencing can be traced to a confusion. People equate open and honest advocacy of law reform with the bribery of lawmakers that was a great public evil from the days of the Yazoo scandal of 1795 through the days of *Credit Mobilier* and the early part of this century. Let us jail both the giver and the taker of a bribe whenever we catch them. Bribes, of course, never are income tax deductible.

But let us exempt from income tax the moneys our people give to him who urges law reform. We need that man. His voice cannot reach us unless we are free to help him spread his message.

ALBERT HIRST
New York, June 27, 1966

Protection of Russia's Lake Baikal

To the Editor:

Harrison Salisbury's August 1 news article on Lake Baikal, was an interesting and fairly accurate account. However, I would like to clarify some of the points made.

All the land and natural resources in the Soviet Union belong to the people. The people, therefore, take a personal interest in seeing that these riches are used wisely, without waste. The power of public opinion in that area has been demonstrated numerous times.

For example, strong public protest succeeded in stopping two projects which would have had harmful effects on nature—one was the Nizhne-Voizhskaya hydroelectric power station on the Volga River, the other was a dam for the lower reaches of the Ob River in Siberia.

Now the public is raising its voice again to protest the construction of a pulp and paper mill on Lake Baikal, despite guarantees from the State Timber Committee, which sponsors the project, that the plant's chemical and biological purification system will prevent any pollution.

Two leading newspapers—*Komosomolskaya Pravda* and *Literaturnaya Gazeta*—are also actively campaigning against the project.

Recently 36 leading scientists, artists and writers joined in denouncing this "mistaken project" and demanded that those responsible be made to pay for their gross errors and oversights.

As a result, the Government has set up a special committee of experts, headed by Academician Nikolai Zhavoronkov, to study the problem and draw up final recommendations. Under no circumstances will the pollution of Lake Baikal be permitted.

I would like to mention also that the U.S.S.R. Academy of Science is mapping out plans for a national park around Lake Baikal to cover an area of 15,000 square miles.

A. MAKAROV
Managing Editor, *Soviet Life*
Washington, Aug. 16, 1966

To Limit Function of Engineer Corps

To the Editor:

In your November 15 editorial "The Last Word" you correctly name the Army Corps of Engineers as the "perennial ally" of the sand and gravel companies, the real estate developers and others.

It is essential for national conservation that the authority of the corps should be limited to its true function—the maintenance of navigability. Historically the Engineer Corps was entrusted with control of navigable waterways because these were the natural (in fact often the only) highway, and thus vital to the Army's mobility.

This has led to the very sins of which your editorial rightly complains, for the corps now gives applicants permission to pollute and desecrate waterways just so long as these acts do not adversely affect navigability. That they destroy the breeding grounds of fish or change a beautiful stream or bay into an ugly one is something the corps does not take into consideration, in fact has no basis for judgment.

Undisputed examples are legion. A notable one: Reclamation of tidelands, marshes and submerged lands in San Francisco Bay may proceed by permission of the Corps of Engineers because the whole bay is a navigable waterway and this intrusion does not make it less navigable.

The law should be amended to require the corps to state when a proposed act will have no effect on navigability, In which case the issuance of the permit should pass to another department; Federal, state or local, as the case may be.

It is not entirely the corps' fault, though it will surely oppose any change in the law. Although it must ask the opinion of the Bureau of Sport Fisheries and Wildlife, it is not required by law to pay any attention to this opinion. The net result all over the country is just what your editorial says it is.

Congress alone is to blame and remedial action must come from Congress.

WALTER D. BINGER
New York, Dec. 1, 1967

To Conserve Wild Life

To the Editor:

This letter, although late in being written, relates particularly to your editorial of May 1 "The In Thing to Do"; but in general I write about the support you have, for a long time, given to the conservation of nature and related activities. I want you to know how encouraging this is, and has been, to those of us who are working intensively in conservation fields.

Personally, I feel that aside from human survival there is nothing more important than the conservation of nature and natural resources. (I have been concentrating my own attention largely on wild life and wilderness areas.) I say aside from human survival; but actually human survival is inseparable from environment, so it is pretty much one and the same thing.

It is good to feel the influence of *The New York Times* with us and behind us. My deep appreciation goes to you with this letter.

CHARLES A. LINDBERGH
Darien, Conn., June 3, 1968

To Protect Wildlife

To the Editor:

Despite the Senate failure to vote on the Endangered Species bill before their adjournment, public opinion now is growing at an accelerated pace for the protection of some of these animals plundered by fashion— notably leopard, cheetah, jaguar, ocelot, sea turtle, alligator and crocodile.

The public service and leadership of *The New York Times* has continued to enlighten a wide segment of the public. The support of the press generally, radio and television, are bringing the controversy into proper focus.

The World Wildlife Fund is continuing its advertising campaign to change a fashion trend, and the furrier is making a last ditch stand. Some have contended the regulation of the sale of animal skins should be controlled by laws in the country of origin; that basic wild stocks continue to abound; that some species are not listed as endangered by the International Union for the Conservation of Nature and Natural Resources.

307

These notions are contrary to the evidence. First, economic pressures and purchasing power in America render existing laws ineffective. Smuggling trade in many countries of origin and falsification of documents is still a common occurrence.

Close to home the American alligator offers the finest example of the problem. The excellent article in the current issue of the *Audubon Magazine* points up the facts. From experience, I know that poaching of alligators in Everglades National Park, in the world famous Corkscrew Sanctuary, in the Waukulla Spring Sanctuary, and other areas, continues.

Arrests by wardens are difficult, and conviction in local courts next to impossible. It is more difficult to protect endangered animals in the vast continents and countries where distance is a handicap, population sparse, incentive great, law enforcement impossible.

In South and Central America, Asia and Africa the unrelenting and ruthless killing is resulting in complete extermination of local animal populations, and the poachers go further in quest of their kill.

We look to the designer, fashion arbiter and merchant for cooperation in removing this threat. I am sure, as the evidence continues to mount, they will join in supporting our efforts.

HERBERT MILLS
Executive Director
World Wildlife Fund
Washington, Oct. 16, 1968

Nixon on Conservation

To the Editor:

Editorial encouragement by *The Times* might help direct the Republican Administration in the right direction in conservation. For example:

Nixon statements have mentioned the need to enhance the quality of life in America. Environmental quality is most certainly an integral part thereof, and thus should be argued as a basic Republican commitment.

Since the Republican party heavily represents the business community, increased constructive cooperation between conservationists and the business community should be encouraged. This would follow Nixon's suggestion for business community involvement in helping urban and racial problems.

308

Because of Mr. Nixon's concern over the high level of Federal spending he should do all he can to defeat boondoggles of the Bureau of Reclamation and the Army Corps of Engineers—such as the newly rumored Rampart Canyon Dam in Alaska, Hells Canyon Dam in Idaho, Red River Gorge Dam in Kentucky, and the incredible tree-cutting plan for the Rio Grande Valley here in New Mexico. Funds thus saved could go toward a stepped-up effort against air and water pollution, among other urgent crises.

RUSSELL D. BUTCHER
Santa Fe, N.M., Nov. 6, 1968

To Orbit Chemical Wastes

To the Editor:

Instead of anguishing about the utterly heedless plan to dump quantities of nerve gas and other barbarities into the sea, probably to emerge decades later to harass the whole living world (if it lasts that long), how about putting our interstellar know-how to practical use?

If the Soviets can get a vehicle into orbit around Venus six months subsequent to launching, why not dispatch one of our space vehicles, loaded with those unspeakable burdens, into infinite space, to travel endlessly without seeking an orbit, ridding our planet of these warlike monstrosities?

If we get anything back from outer space in reply, we will reaffirm that H. G. Wells was a prophet, and we'll be in a war between worlds—a far more rational thing than mankind against mankind.

STUYVESANT VAN VEEN
New York, May 27, 1969

Moon for Atomic Waste

To the Editor:

The letter by Stuyvesant Van Veen published June 4 regarding our disposal of atomic waste matter by shooting it off into space has the elements of a good idea. His suggestion that we simply aim the rocket to nowhere was, I am sure, delivered with tongue in cheek. With uncounted numbers of constellations in the cosmos there is a possibility of hitting a planet—one that may have life upon it.

I would suggest that we select a planet that we know to have no life upon it and create for it an artificial moon, made-up modules of atomic waste; a constantly growing moon as our use of the atom pile increases. We would, at least, be sure that our man-made pollutants would be doing no harm to any form of life.

The cost would of course be prohibitive—that is, unless we measure it against the cost of transporting the last sickly remnants of humanity away from a no longer habitable earth.

ALBERT KOTIN
New York, June 4, 1969

Price Tag on Pollution

To the Editor:

The increasing degradation of the earth environment is due in part to a deficient account system. A pure environment accounting system would put a monetary value on such crimes as the murder of Lake Erie, and would make it possible for society to find out the price of using chemical fertilizers and allowing steel mills to discharge waste into rivers.

We have national accounts and cost-benefit analysis for bacteriological warfare. Why cannot our economists devise a system that will put a value on pure air, pure water and so on?

As a start I would suggest calculating the cost of providing swimming pools for a quarter of the population of the Lake Erie watershed and putting this down as a part of the cost of ecological barbarism in the area.

OLIVER BELL
Chagrin Falls, Ohio, Sept. 6, 1969

Army Engineers' Dams

To the Editor:

It has long been apparent that the Army Corps of Engineers builds dams the way beavers build dams—moved by some inner compulsion, doubtless rooted in the genes.

Nevertheless, the corps is required, before converting another of our

310

vanishing streams or rivers into still water, to present an economic justification. In doing so, it estimates the costs of the project and also the economic benefits—the well-known cost-benefit ratio. For this purpose it now uses, as a bench mark, a rate of return of 4⅞ per cent, and this, I am informed, is a recent increase from a lower figure.

If this country is paying for the destruction of streams and the flooding of canyons in order to obtain benefits (however broadly defined) of no more than 4⅞ per cent on the capital invested, this country is being cheated.

The Federal Government is paying nearly 8 per cent for the money it borrows. Leading corporations are paying more than 8 per cent, and home buyers much more. The Corps of Engineers should be required to furnish cost-benefit estimates using 8, 9, and 10 per cent rates of interest in the calculation.

It's a fair bet that were this done, a lot of dams on the drawing boards would never be financed by Congress. It is even possible that the notion that building dams is not the only way to deal with the impact of flowing water on the environment would gain some ground in Congress and elsewhere.

MICHAEL L. HOFFMAN
Washington, Oct. 7, 1969

What Is Ecology?

To the Editor:

Definition: Ecology is the science which warns people who won't listen about ways they won't follow of saving an environment they don't appreciate.

L. G. HELLER
New York, April 2, 1970

Ecological Activists

To the Editor:

As one who has expounded ecology for years, I am somewhat suspicious of the sincerity of the young activists who have latched on to a new cause, environmentalism and ecology, and who propose to express their wrath and indignation at pollution and other man-made evils of our industrial-technological society.

I wonder if they are truly concerned or if this is merely another excuse to condemn, criticize or create incidents.

In addition to the waste and destruction attributed to profit-seeking industry, will they condemn the pleasure-loving and convenience-oriented public? Will they condemn the apathetic, uncivic-minded citizen?

Will they condemn the billions of dollars worth of purposeless vandalism inflicted on public and private property by their peers? Or will their activity consist of trampling and littering the Central Park meadows as has been done previously in the cause of voicing dissent? Or altering a bucolic environment as they did in Woodstock, making "beautiful scene" but being insensitive to the garbage heap that they created?

Last week some collegiate protesters purchased an automobile which they buried as a symbolic gesture of their resentment of the automobile and the evils of pollution. This is the type of theatrical which is absurd and wasteful.

Those who are truly concerned with the problem of ecology and environment act constructively. The important job is to educate the citizen and his legislative representative to create the changes for our survival.

WARREN A. KISCH
Yonkers, N.Y., April 6, 1970

Con Ed's Problems

To the Editor:

Consolidated Edison claims that its present difficulties in supplying power are the result of "conservationists" blocking its plans to build a pumped storage plant at Storm King, a five-year undertaking.

Five years ago the Second Circuit of Appeals heard and rejected Con Ed's argument.

For years the conservationists have advocated the use of a large number of gas turbine generators as an alternative to pumped storage. They have been used successfully by other large cities and have the advantages of being minimally disruptive to the environment while diversifying the risk of malfunctions.

Con Ed's current trouble is the result of poor design, maintenance, or both, causing the breakdown of the 1,000,000 kilowatt "Big Allis." By what magic would the utility avoid similar problems with the highly concentrated capacity of a pumped storage facility, especially since it would exist only to store power generated by, among others, "Big Allis"?

The nature of the opposition as stated by the utility omits a few names. The utility is being opposed in whole or part on Storm King by lawyers for the City of New York and the Palisades Interstate Park Commission.

Other utilities have criticized Con Ed on the Storm King project, on which it has fruitlessly spent $20 million, because it is so ill-conceived from a social, environmental and engineering standpoint that it has galvanized citizen opposition to all pumped storage plants.

Governor Rockefeller has suggested that gas turbines may be the answer to Con Ed's problems. The present crisis has brought this solution into sharp focus as the only one available to those truly trying to solve the problem in anything less than five years.

JAMES HAMILTON
New York, July 30, 1970

Power Plant Sites

To the Editor:

It is hard to find anything more chaotic than the utterances on the subject of electric power for New York of those who call themselves conservationists.

Since pumped storage hydro, nuclear reactors and fossil fueled plants are anathema, perhaps New York can be powered by a genie with a lamp.

Would a tunnel diagonally through a mountain really ruin the Hudson?

SHERMAN B. CARLL
Commack, L.I., Aug. 13, 1970

Nuclear Power and Thermal Pollution

To the Editor:

The Sept. 30 editorial "Threat to Waters" states that "The Atomic Energy Commission, for one, has the notion that in licensing nuclear plants it has no authority even to consider a threat of thermal pollution, though the act (National Environmental Policy Act) clearly enjoins all government factors in their decisions . . ."

That statement implies that the A.E.C. does nothing about protection of the environment from possible thermal effects. Such an implication is erroneous. It ignores the following facts:

The commission has, for many years, followed the practice of requesting comments from appropriate Federal agencies on the environmental and safety aspects of proposed nuclear power plants.

It has been a matter of A.E.C. policy to obtain comments from agencies having interest in thermal effects, such as the Fish and Wildlife Service, and to transmit them to the license applicant and to state agencies and to urge compliance with them.

In addition, in compliance with N.E.P.A., we have expanded our efforts and are publishing detailed environmental statements concerning nuclear facilities covering thermal as well as radiological matters. The comments from other agencies are included in those statements.

The A.E.C. now does have authority and responsibility under the Water Quality Improvement Act (the Muskie Act) with respect to nonradiological matters affecting water quality, such as thermal effects, to require the licensee of a nuclear power plant to provide a certfiication by the appropriate state or Federal agency that there is reasonable assurance he will comply with applicable water quality standards.

Unless this certification is provided the A.E.C. license must be denied or revoked. This certification procedure was established under the Water Quality Improvement Act in April of this year and was intended by the Congress to place primary responsibility for protection against adverse thermal effects from nuclear plants in the appropriate state or Federal agency having authority over water quality standards.

The A.E.C. is conducting research on thermal effects which will total $3.2 million in fiscal year 1971. We believe this kind of research, together with that carried out by other Federal agencies and by individual utilities, will provide the basis for sound technological decisions on what additional steps may be required to protect the quality of our waters.

I want to assure you that the commission is deeply concerned and vitally interested in protection of our environment. It is ironic that an agency which has gone to great lengths for many years to protect our en-

314

vironment should be told by *The Times* to "be made accountable for its decisions affecting the environment . . ."

JAMES T. RAMEY
Commissioner
U.S. Atomic Energy Commission
Washington, Oct. 2, 1970

Harassing Conservationists

To the Editor:

The recent decision by the Internal Revenue Service to re-examine the tax exempt status of those organizations employed in litigation is just another sophisticated cynical tool of political oppression used by the present Administration to protect its "private interest groups." It seems to be particularly aimed at those interested in conservation.

The record of the Federal Government in protection of natural resources is something on the outside of dismal. The record of the business community in conservation and ecology is less than the Administration's and is generally planned and budgeted for corporate public relations.

Therefore, when a group of competent, committed individuals decides that it is time to protect and act, not to study, it is regarded as a threat to the status quo, which it is, and the industrial lobbies, themselves tax supplemented, exert enough pressure to have the "ecology-conservation radical liberals" politically bludgeoned.

In view of the above, I must presume that a disastrous event, or fear of such an event, is the only thing which will move the Government to action. But then why should these problems be any different from all the other domestic issues confronting us which have been so cynically shelved?

DONALD FREEMAN
New York, Oct. 14, 1970

315

The SST

To the Editor:

Your sarcastic attitude in your Dec. 2 editorial "Downwind from the SST" indicates that although you are neither scientist nor economist you have the privilege of misinterpreting inadequate data to your own advantage.

Your scientists who claim that water vapor in the stratosphere will end the climate as we know it are most likely the same people who said the Westford space needles program would also pollute the stratosphere "forever." Why not suggest some controlled experiments? Or why not accept the launch of the early Saturns, which carried water loads and emptied them into the stratosphere?

As for the noise, I'm sure that engineers will develop a system that will make the noise no worse than existing jets. Research and development is still the only answer.

And lastly—do you assume that your airlines will not buy French, English or even Russian SST's if the competition warrants? Will you stop them from landing in this country?

Why not train your editorial prowess on the big business and the public utilities that pollute the rivers and air and get a Federal law passed with heavy fines and jail terms for the corporation heads. That would stop the mercury poisoning rapidly. A law to stop the soap companies and only allow use of bio-degradable products would also help.

ALAN S. GROSS
Lakewood, N.J., Dec. 7, 1970

The writer is deputy technical director of the U.S. Satellite Communications Agency.

Environmental Capitalism

To the Editor:

The main issue in the current SST debate is not financial. It is environmental. The SST can be built, but that is not the real problem. The real problem is what it will do to the ecology of the earth once completed.

Birds, flowers, trees, water, air, soil and even people are important—

each in its own particular way. How this plane would affect them is crucial. If we must err, let us err on the side of that which God has created.

I propose no funds whatsoever for the SST. However, this does not help the innocent Boeing employe in Seattle who consequently may be out of a job. Thus, I believe Boeing should be granted the $210 million for an experiment in environmental capitalism.

Let them use this money to rechannel their manpower into developing new ways of solving old problems: pollution, urban decay, technological waste. A company capable of creating an SST should certainly be willing to tackle such problems. In this manner no individuals will personally have to suffer for the common welfare of man.

JOHN L. WARREN
Dobbs Ferry, N.Y., Dec. 11, 1970

Alaska: Last Wilderness

To the Editor:

The United States Department of Interior is about to grant approval for a group of oil companies, including Atlantic-Richfield, to build an 800-mile pipeline across Alaska from the oil-rich North Slope to the ice-free southern ports.

This would mean placing a barrier, 100 feet wide, in the center of which would be a pipe carrying scalding hot oil across the fragile Arctic tundra. This shortsighted project would destroy the wilderness and endanger the unique wildlife. The Interior Department knows the scheme would be an environmental disaster and readily admits it. That makes it all the more tragic.

Here in the continental United States—which 200 years ago was carpeted with virgin forests, unique deserts and great plains—only 3 per cent of land remains in the wild state. The time has come for us to start caring about the last vestiges of our heritage before it is all gone.

Some people seem to feel that God created Alaska so that a handful of people could get rich quick but in fact 96 per cent of the state is Federal land and belongs to all of us. What those concerned with environment are saying is that we are rich enough to afford to worry about preserving our last wilderness and vanishing species.

Only if there is a strong public outcry will the Federal Government

317

find it possible to stop a greedy few from raping Alaska's land and exploiting its people. Alaska is our last chance.

Douglas LaFollette
Director, Wisconsin's Environmental Decade
Racine, Wisc., Jan. 16, 1971

Alaska's Pipeline Needed

To the Editor:

In commenting on the proposed Alaskan oil pipeline and its impact on environment, supposedly responsible, rational people have issued statements showing an incredible lack of perspective.

Some conservationists speak of the loss to us all of our wilderness heritage for the sake of the greedy few, which is a wild inversion of the number of beneficiaries of oil vs. tundra. *The Times* supports a Congressional decision in the pipeline matter, as if 535 semi-informed Congressmen could make a complex conservation assessment, involving highly technical and local factors, better than the local people (Alaskans).

With regard to benefits, the following aspects of a major secure oil source for the U.S. are just a few of the gains for all U.S. citizens:

Prevention of significant increases in United States gasoline, home heating oil and electricity prices due to imposed, astronomical taxes on crude by oil-rich countries (who wish to redistribute U.S. wealth unilaterally).

Protection of billions of United States dollars in foreign investments for oil-producing facilities currently without a United States bargaining alternative in the face of threatened expropriation.

Greater freedom to follow our own political ideals and ideas and choose our own friends, rather than having to bend to the whims of foreign, crude-rich political regimes.

Increased domestic standard of living (including significant environment conservation progress) for 220,000,000 people, uninhibited by energy or power shortages. Contrast this with the few thousands of people who just might visit Alaska and one small area of tundra in a decade.

With regard to the need for further political football games (Congressional or otherwise) prior to pipeline construction, consider the total land area and population involved. The pipeline (and road) covers about 800 miles by 100 feet, or a total of roughly fifteen square miles. Alaska

318

is about 586,000 square miles in area—which means that the pipeline will be invisible in at least 99.99 per cent of the state.

As to life on either side of the pipeline, it should continue unchanged, as it does on either side of the 1,200-mile-long Yukon River.

Further, the majority of Alaskan citizens and their local government favor the pipeline construction. The environment of 294,607 Alaskans (equal to the number of Staten Island residents but with an average of two square miles per person) is not likely to be best utilized and protected by non-Alaskan politicians sitting 3,500 miles away.

Let's cut the hysteria, bring the facts into focus and start this project (with appropriate conservation safeguards) which will benefit all U.S. citizens.

D. J. KAHN
Metuchen, N.J., Jan. 27, 1971

The writer is in the employ of a major oil company.

Objections to the SST

To the Editor:

Despite the fact that the President's Science Advisory Committee, the President's SST Ad Hoc Review Committee and the Environmental Quality Council have all warned against building the SST, the debate about the plane's environmental effects will rage for a long time. But something should be said about another side of the issue, the dollars and cents of the aircraft.

The British Overseas Airways Corporation has reported that it will be impossible to operate the Anglo-French supersonic Concorde economically. Not only will the plane lose money, but SST's may reduce airline demands for them by 70 per cent. This will force the developers of the Concorde to increase the $28-million price by 60 per cent just to break even. This price will probably cut demand for the aircraft more. At best, airlines would have to price tickets at twice what they would charge for a jumbo-jet ticket. At worst, the price hike will put the SST out of the reach of the airlines. (Editorial, March 8.)

How then can the American Government justify spending more on the plane? Claims that it will improve our balance of payments are based on sales abroad, and, using the evidence of the Concorde, foreign demand is not going to be too great. Interestingly, if the SST stimulates American travel abroad, it will actually hurt our balance of payments.

This month, Congress will make a final decision on the SST. If funds for it are defeated, it will be only because the American people have realized that the plane can cost them tax dollars and benefit them not at all.

DANIEL REISBERG
West Orange, N.J., March 8, 1971

XI • Revolt on the Campus

The American college campus, traditionally a refuge of reason, a community of scholars and a forum for the rational examination of the new, the unorthodox, became in the sixties the nation's battleground. Student power vied with university power; classes were closed, buildings seized, plants vandalized.

The war in Southeast Asia, the draft, unresponsive administrations, police on campus, the grievances of blacks and the alleged irrelevance of the curriculum triggered the campus revolt. It shocked the nation and brought violence and death to students at Kent State, Wisconsin and Jackson State.

Once accused of political apathy and prodded for a lack of involvement, the college student was now a threat to academic freedom and the democratic process. *Times* readers and the academic community reacted to this revolution with a Niagara of letters to the editor. Some are reproduced here from the time the Free Speech Movement began at Berkeley in 1964.

321

Berkeley Upheaval and Suppression

To the Editor:

In *The Times* of Dec. 12 Dr. Eric A. Walker, president of Pennsylvania State University, is quoted as charging that the recent controversy at the University of California was part of an organized campaign to embarrass American universities. He based this charge on a warning he received last March from the Federal Bureau of Investigation alerting college presidents to an "organized attempt using bogus students and bogus faculty members to divert the energies of students into channels embarrassing to our universities, using slogans like 'free speech' and 'civil rights' to make their goals."

I don't know just what is meant by "bogus students" and "bogus faculty members." All too often epithets of this kind are applied to bona fide members of the university communities who "rock the boat" and raise the specter of publicity that will disturb influential parties such as alumni and members of state legislatures.

I hope that the word "bogus" is not being applied to students and faculty members who are actively responsive to the larger social environment. Surely our campuses should not be isolated from outside influences, even from individuals who seek to enlist the energies and talents of our students and faculties for direct social action.

After all, it was only a few years ago that our university faculties and administrations were worried about the indifference of "the silent generation" to social issues. Now that students are getting less indifferent all the time, the talk, predictably enough, shifts to the problem of "irresponsibility" and to charges that students are excessively responsive to the influence of "outside agitators." We ought not to lose our perspective; the response of contemporary students to the challenges of the civil rights struggle and of the Peace Corps is reason for rejoicing.

I do not deny that the excitement generated by the activists on campus may be exploited by various interests, but our universities need not be embarrassed by this. We need only adhere to the standards of freedom of expression and openness to criticism that we affirm all the time. If universities are not to encourage freedom and openness, then we are in a bad way. And by freedom of expression I do not mean "freedom of expression provided that it is responsible." And by openness to the expression of criticism I do not mean "criticism is permitted provided that it is constructive." The test of a free society is its openness to the free expression of unpopular and even of abrasive opinion.

Furthermore, administrations of all sorts, universities included, almost invariably regard sharp criticism as irresponsible.

322

The best way to deal with any organized attempt to embarrass our universities would be to practice what we preach.

MALCOLM L. DIAMOND
Associate Professor, Department of Religion
Princeton University
Princeton, N.J., Dec. 20, 1964

All Losers in Berkeley

To the Editor:

I think that one can agree with Richard Abrams, whose letter was published on Dec. 12, about the inopportunity or stupidity of the University of California's withdrawal of what students and nonstudents had come to look on as an imprescriptible right to engage in political activity in the Bancroft strip, and yet still deprecate the actions subsequently taken by students and faculty to protest this withdrawal.

In order to situate the dispute in its context, one must keep in mind that the university is a public institution, and that as a consequence the administration has always had to balance the interests of the state and the taxpayers on the one hand, and the students and faculty on the other.

Up to this year it has performed this balancing act with some skill and has managed, by providing the safety valve of the Bancroft strip, to accommodate the needs of an increasingly active body of students and nonstudent hangers-on. Certainly the growing attraction of the Berkeley campus for militants and activists of all shades is proof that freedom was not being stifled.

The closure of this safety valve was a bad mistake. But the steps taken by the students to redress their grievance have, in my opinion, been far more injurious in their character and potential consequences.

For one thing, the issues of the dispute are by no means so obvious and one-sided as the so-called Free Speech Movement pretends. The obligation of the University of California to make its campus available for political action of any kind, even calls to violent and illegal measures, is a matter on which reasonable men may differ. For another—and this is the heart of the matter—reasonable men cannot differ reasonably under the pressure of riots, occupation of buildings, strikes, ultimatums and the rest of the tactics perfected in revolutionary situations and introduced for the first time in the United States into a university context.

Worse yet, the injection of foreign elements into the dispute—viz., the

323

Teamsters' Union, CORE—has aggravated the difficulty and represents a serious breach in the jealously protected autonomy of the university from outside or sectarian influences. There is no reason to assume that the force and outside pressure employed in this instance will not be turned, on some future occasion, to far more dubious ends.

In short, the Berkeley revolt represents potentially the most serious assault on the academic freedom in America since the McCarthy era.

In conclusion, I should like to point out the deleterious implications of this dispute for the University of California. I know personally of five or six faculty members who are leaving, not because of lack of sympathy with "free speech" or "political action," but because, as one put it, who wants to teach at the University of Saigon?

The net result, I fear, will be a sharp decline in public support for what was the finest state university in America; a rift within the faculty and the departure of some of its best members; and the persistence of suspicion and animosity in a world where suspicion and animosity have no place.

I grieve for the University of California; and I grieve for its students, who will be the real losers in the long run.

DAVID S. LANDES
Professor of History, Harvard University; Former Professor of History and Economics, University of California at Berkeley
Cambridge, Mass., Dec. 17, 1964

Extremism in Berkeley

To the Editor:

It is a strange commentary that the faculty of the University of California has unwittingly given its approval to the Goldwater Doctrine of which so many were so critical—that extremism in defense of what they regard as liberty is not a vice.

ROBERT WILSON, M.D.
Charleston, S.C., Dec. 22, 1964

Nixon Explains Stand on Ousting Genovese

To the Editor:

In accordance with the great tradition of *The Times* for complete and objective coverage of the news you might want to carry statements I made on the Genovese case which were omitted in *The Times* news story of Oct. 25.

Every American is for free speech and academic freedom. The question is how do we preserve that freedom?

We do so by recognizing and protecting the right of individuals to freedom of speech.

We do so by defending the system of government which guarantees freedom of speech to individuals.

Unfortunately, there are occasions—particularly in wartime—when the individual's rights and the nation's security come in conflict.

Justice Learned Hand summarized it best when he said, "A society in which men recognize no check on their freedom soon becomes a society in which freedom is the possession of only the savage few."

In his recent speeches in New Jersey, Robert Kennedy, by contending in effect that the right to freedom of speech is absolute and unrestricted, confused the fundamental issue involved in the Genovese case.

He charged that Senator Dumont's demand for Professor Genovese's dismissal was the same as Governor Barnett's demand that professors at the University of Mississippi who advocated integration should be discharged.

He completely missed the fundamental distinction between the two cases. No one has questioned the right of Professor Genovese or anyone else to advocate any controversial issue in peacetime.

The question in the Genovese case is whether a professor, employed by a state university, should have the right to use the prestige and forum of the university for advocating victory for an enemy of the United States in wartime.

The victory for the Vietcong which Professor Genovese "welcomes" would mean ultimately the destruction of freedom of speech for all men for all time not only in Asia but in the United States as well.

The question at issue, therefore, becomes: does the principle of freedom of speech require that the state subsidize those who would destroy the system of government which protects freedom of speech?

We are confronted in the Genovese case with this choice:

The responsibility of the state to protect the right of freedom of speech for an individual.

325

The responsibility of the state to defend itself against enemies whose victory would deny freedom of speech to all.

America's 20th-century war Presidents, Woodrow Wilson, and Franklin D. Roosevelt, were forced to make this cruel choice and in both instances they properly concluded that in wartime preservation of freedom for all the people must take precedence over the rights of an individual to exercise freedom of speech when it would serve the enemies of freedom.

Reports from Hanoi and Peking conclusively indicate that the demonstrations against our policy in Vietnam encourage the enemy, prolong the war and result in the deaths of American fighting men.

Our recognition of this unhappy truth does not mean that we suppress the views of all those who may oppose the war in Vietnam for ideological reasons.

But there is a point at which a line must be drawn.

I say as long as the demonstrators and those participating in teach-ins are acting in an individual and private capacity no action should be taken to curtail their activities.

But any individual employed by the state should not be allowed to use his position for the purpose of giving aid and comfort to the enemies of the state.

Where the choice confronting us is between the lives of American men fighting to preserve the system which guarantees freedom of speech for all and the right of an individual to abuse that freedom, the lives of American fighting men must come first.

We must never forget that if the war in Vietnam is lost and the victory for the Communists which Professor Genovese says he "welcomes" becomes inevitable, the right of free speech will be extinguished throughout the world.

RICHARD M. NIXON
New York, Oct. 27, 1965

C.I.A. in Academic Areas

To the Editor:

It is fashionable at the moment in some of the very best quarters to regard the C.I.A. as an untouchable, unclean thing with which no self-respecting and ethically pure academic institution should have any con-

326

tact. I submit that, on the contrary, for these institutions to refuse C.I.A. research contracts is self-defeating nonsense that is disadvantageous both to the academic world and to the C.I.A.

If the C.I.A. were to control the academic curricula or to report on the private lives and opinions of the students, or even the professors, one can see certain unpleasant and harmful consequences. But if the C.I.A. contracts to have a university report with complete independence on a question requiring research, we should welcome and encourage, not deny, the C.I.A.'s access to the source of objective information.

We should likewise welcome, rather than discourage, the opportunity offered to universities of applying to serious public questions—which presumably the C.I.A. staff cannot answer—the specialized talents of their available experts. In most academic areas experts become experts by working in their fields with real life problems; they rarely become experts solely through study and reflection.

Indeed, we have only to read the headlines—whether they involve automotive safety or foreign affairs—to realize that often only the practical result will tell us which is the duffer and which the expert.

What we need is more, not fewer, tests of academic theory, and the C.I.A. (or any other source) does the universities a service—as well as vice versa—in arranging for research on current problems.

Name Withheld on Request
Paris, May 10, 1966

Berkeley's Dissenters

To the Editor:

Your Dec. 4 editorial "Nihilism in Berkeley" distorts and confuses not only the origins, leadership and goals of the student strike at the University of California, but also raises serious doubts about the underlying conception of the nature and purposes of institutions of learning presupposed by the editorial. Since that conception is shared by the present university administration, it becomes all the more important to attempt to explicate and clarify its inadequacy. In doing so we shall also come to some understanding of the students' vision of what a great university should be.

There is no doubt that the cry of "nonstudent" has become for the university administration what "outside agitator" is to the anti civil rights movement. The insistence that university affairs be conducted by students alone, aside from its mistaken assumption that students now have an effective voice in the running of the university, ignores the nature of the "campus community" that the chancellor is so fond of invoking.

In fact, that "community" cannot be defined by possession of a registration card, but by a commitment to and involvement in the critical process of analyzing and evaluating the society, coupled with the belief that what one learns in an academic setting is meaningful primarily insofar as it is relevant to the crises which face us—whether in Vietnam, in the ghettoes of Oakland or the vacuum of middle-class suburbia.

The charge of nonstudent leadership becomes all the more specious when many of those against whom it is directed have been barred from the Berkeley campus by the very administration that now denounces them as "outside agitators." It is ironic that their expulsions were specifically for political acts which addressed themselves to the critical problems of student powerlessness in the face of an administration that is all-powerful.

In any case, the charge that the student demonstrations are led by nonstudents is part of a deliberate campaign by the administration to characterize student dissent as illegitimate. It is significant that the administration deliberately chose to arrest—or to cite—only nonstudents, and that they could find only six nonstudents among the more than 70 protesters sitting-in in the lower level of the Student Union Building (the area sealed off before the arrests) at the time. And, according to faculty members who were present during the events leading to the arrests, one of the nonstudents arrested did not speak at all and two others "participated minimally if at all" in the lengthy strategy discussions of the protesters.

Finally, the editorial indicates sympathy with the student protests at Berkeley two years ago. It should be pointed out—and this is made explicit by the student negotiation demands—that a major objective of the student strikers, including the so-called "nihilists," has been to initiate the institution of due process and student rights embodied in the Dec. 8, 1964, Faculty Resolutions which signaled the end of the 1964 dispute.

MARIO SAVIO
DAN ROSENTHAL
BETTINA APTHEKER
Strike Committee, University of California
Berkeley, Dec. 6, 1966

Student Activists

To the Editor:

I would like to take issue with Fred M. Hechinger's contention (Dec. 12 column on the editorial page) that student activists pose a threat to the independence of American universities. The fact is that American universities are not independent of politics; they are only independent of students. First, it is common for Regents or other governing bodies of universities to be appointed by political officials. These appointees will have a "liberal" or "conservative" bent as it pleases their Governor or State Legislature.

It is also common practice for State Legislatures to appropriate money to universities according to their "freedom" from left-wing professors. This has been the occasion of more than one political purge of university faculties; the case of the University of Washington in 1948 might serve as a good example of this process.

Second, not only are state universities political in this sense (and others relating to Federal Government) but they also try to be independent of students insofar as possible. The administrations and faculties not only tolerate increasing teacher-student ratios in the name of "freedom for research," but they also tolerate and promote far worse and clearly political threats to student rights. These include turning membership lists of student organizations over to Government agencies, and turning class rank over to draft boards, both without consulting the students on the matter.

Improvements in these matters have come about through the work of student activists, not through the benevolence of the faculties and administrations whose well-paid, privileged, and very political connections with Government-sponsored research rob them of the necessary independence.

ROBERT HALLAUER
Graduate Student
University of Chicago
Chicago, Dec. 12, 1966

Student Control

To the Editor:

In their letter published Dec. 15 Berkeley strikers Mario Savio, Dan Rosenthal and Bettina Aptheker seem to nurture a vision of today's university which is akin to the "community of scholars" of Paris, Oxford and Bologna in the 12th and 13th centuries. They assert that such a community extends beyond merely those who pay tuition to include the nonstudents so frequently referred to.

The problem of the nonstudent has plagued university authorities since those early times. The nonstudent represents a perversion of the true spirit of the university, for what he seeks is an escape from, not a means of understanding and grappling with reality.

In this community they envisage they expect peer status with the faculty so that they may sally forth from their sanctuary on matters of foreign policy, domestic sociology and class psychology. Considering the credentials of many faculty members who have recently held forth on such matters, these students may be equally qualified.

The point is, however, that this community cannot be one of equals. The often intellectually arrogant and narrow-minded students coming out of our "modern-oriented" schools are hardly ready to share the lectern with their professors. The atmosphere bordering on mental tyranny which followed the Berkeley coup of 1964 demonstrated that such student control as these writers have in mind is the very antithesis of true education, now as it was in Bologna in the 13th century.

WILLARD L. HOGEBOOM
West Islip, L.I., Dec. 15, 1966

Students in Politics

To the Editor:

The press is hailing the dove candidates for having brought students "back into the system." I disagree. It is the students who have brought the politicians back into the system—the system is achieving change in America. Were it not for student efforts and discontent about the war for the past two years, we probably would not be witnessing the rising public sentiment against the war that occurs now.

Nor are the student workers in dove campaigns primarily newly shaven students radicals. For the most part, they reflect the mass of socially concerned undergraduates who have not supported draft card burnings or anti-recruiter demonstrations, but who have agonized over the seeming futility of restoring hope in America. Now, in George Washington Plunkett's words, they have seen their opportunity and are taking it. They are showing what student power is all about.

Yet the public should understand the stakes. If electoral politics fails these students, this same group who knock on your doors in the spring will be the most disfranchised of them all. And for the disfranchised, resistance may be the only answer.

EDWARD SCHWARTZ
President
National Students Association
Washington, March 20, 1968

Student Activism at Columbia

To the Editor:

With the general tenor and purport of *The Times'* April 25 editorial on "Hoodlumism at Columbia" I am in full agreement. Yet it seems clear to me that this current example of student activism, seen in the context of a hundred examples daily across the country in all sorts of situations, calls for sharper analysis.

With brushfire rapidity, it has become almost the norm for any group to resort to direct and forcible action to obtain immediate, unconditional compliance (with amnesty automatically included) with its particular demands of the moment. In most cases, the normal democratic processes of election, representation, petition and discussion are ignored.

Decisions made by these normal processes are scorned and overridden. Persons and property are seized, normal activities are impeded or halted, the law is flouted and disrespect for authority is flaunted—without a shadow of legal right or political authority or even pretense of majority rule.

What is happening represents a direct and fundamental attack on the bases of our political order—a direct rejection of the principles and processes of representative democracy. Unless the history books have all been miswritten, this constitutes the first stage of revolution, in any age and in any country.

The meaning of this growing pattern of direct action must be urgently faced. That people are increasingly frustrated by the vastness of an administrative apparatus which has passed largely beyond the practical control of elected executives, elected legislatures and the courts, is quite clear. That this gives rise to real questions about the effectiveness and even the continued acceptability of the democratic system which we inherited must be frankly admitted. But that the timeless violence and chaos of government by the mob and "the streets" can be tolerated among us is not to be thought of for a moment.

These considerations must be troubling our political scientists in the universities, even though some of them seem to be so astonishingly blind to the direction and significance of developments that they reportedly encourage and support direct action on the campuses. We need their best thought, and urgently, to the devising of new political forms and imaginative adaptations of old forms, so that some measure of liberty and democracy can be preserved in the vast and complex society of today.

None of us should condone them as passing phases of impatience of this or that segment of the population with the pace of overdue social and other reforms. None of us should allow moral fervor of opposition to war in Vietnam or any other Government policy to permit disregard for the fever of this spreading illness among us.

All of us should remember and ponder the somber judgment of Mommsen in writing the history of Rome: ". . . when anyone able to command the streets for a few hours could impress on his projects the legal stamp of the sovereign people's will—then Rome had reached not the beginning but the end of popular freedom. . . ."

PERRY LAUKHUFF
Norwalk, Conn., April 28, 1968

Freedom at Cornell

To the Editor:

The authors of this letter are visiting scholars at Cornell University, one in the Society for the Humanities, the other in the English Department. Eleven days ago we took the step, perhaps unprecedented among visitors to a great American university, of announcing that we were suspending our teaching for the rest of the semester, although we would remain available to our respective students for private consultation.

Implicit in our invitations to Cornell were the conditions of free speech and personal safety that have normally obtained in the academic communities of the civilized world. In our judgment these conditions no longer obtained. We see no reason to change our decision; for although the situation at Cornell is today superficially calmer, academic freedom remains in jeopardy.

We advise our colleagues in other universities that the revolutionary "restructuring" now going on in several departments and in the government of this university, with the approval of the administration and many among the faculty and student body, threatens to destroy the intellectual standing of Cornell.

HAROLD BLOOM
Professor of English
Yale University
MATTHEW HODGART
Professor of English
University of Sussex, England
Ithaca, N.Y., May 6, 1969

Flight of Scholars

To the Editor:

By now it is well recognized that the reasons for the "revolt" on the campuses are many and complex. But regardless of its causes, it is often suggested that the current militancy may push American universities into a position similar to their Latin-American counterparts. Although this may be an exaggerated view, there is another trend, already visible and certainly on the rise. It is a distinct shift in prestige away from the traditional scholar, however defined (the good researcher, teacher or both), to those who get along well in the new environment; certainly to the instructors who in one capacity or another lead revolt.

In some ways this change is reminiscent of the appearance on the campus, over a decade ago, of the "money broker." At that time both prestige and compensation were shifted to those who were able to tax the financial resources of government and large foundations on behalf of the university. But the analogy cannot be carried too far. The "money broker" had to share his newly earned prestige with the scholar. He simply needed the latter to deliver his product so that he could get the next sizable grant.

333

By contrast the instructors who either lead or manipulate the new militancy do not need the scholar. Inadvertently or not, the scholar may gradually be pushed either to the few remaining calm universities, or out of academia altogether. Organized research institutions (such as Brookings) and perhaps industry, may come to sponsor most of the good research, and perhaps even carry out instruction at the doctoral level. That would be a sad day for universities in general, and for the many serious students who come there to get an education and prepare for a meaningful career.

MORDECHAI KREININ
Professor of Economics
Michigan State University
East Lansing, Mich., May 14, 1969

Role of the University

To the Editor:

Your distinction between political dissent by individual professors and students and the necessary political detachment of the university as an institution, is too simple. (Editorial, Oct. 7.) I agree that the university should not engage in day-to-day or year-to-year politics; but if a political situation happens to threaten the very principles of civilization, e.g. free inquiry, the humanities, or civil legitimacy, then it is of the essence for the university to take a stand.

Consider, for instance, if there were some extraordinary case of censorship against a university or even in outside society, the universities would have to protest it as institutions.

It is, of course, debatable whether the Vietnam war is such a threat to our civilization, but this hard issue cannot be avoided by a definition. In my opinion, the facts—the body counts, the defoliation, the destruction of a culture, the aura of illegitimacy of the whole enterprise—warrant closing the schools on Oct. 15.

PAUL GOODMAN
New York, Oct. 7, 1969

334

S.D.S. on Campus

To the Editor:
Has anyone ever stopped to wonder what the Students for a Democratic Society study?

ROBERT RUSSELL BENNETT
New York, April 4, 1970

Violence at Kent State

To the Editor:
President Nixon's cynical and hollow statement on the massacre at Kent State University is a disgrace to his office. There was indeed violence at Kent State, an extension of the same form of violence presently mistaken at almost every level of American government as some sort of solution.

It is the same violence which is destroying Vietnam and Cambodia; it is the same violence which is destroying the soul of this nation.

The real tragedy at Kent State was not Mr. Nixon's self-fulfilling prophecy but the simple fact that it is very easy for the repressive mechanism of deranged authority to turn from killing children in Vietnam to killing our own children. God help the nation which lives in fear of its young.

JAMES O'SHEA WADE
New York, May 5, 1970

'Purged' Scholar

To the Editor:
The tragic news of the last few days has touched me deeply, but none more deeply than the moving May 8 news account by Craig Whitney of the personal tragedy that befell Dr. Isador Rabi, a Nobel Prize winner, now retired.

It seems that he was attempting to enter his laboratory, the very place in which he had wrought some of the ideas which have profoundly affected mankind. But his way was "blocked by a group of young men

335

with arms linked across the door." I continue the quote from Mr. Whitney's account:

"Dr. Rabi tried to argue with them unsuccessfully. Exasperated, tears in his eyes, he tapped his cane on the granite step and said: 'What you are doing is wrong, and you are crazy. You are blocking my way. Do you want to fight with me? Would you fight with me?"

Dr. Rabi's offer of a fight was declined, and he finally managed to sneak into his laboratory when a workman was allowed to enter. On the sidewalk, "a group of 20 other students, who looked amused, were watching."

I am not a Nobel Prize winner, but as an ordinary social scientist I can suggest some answers to Dr. Rabi's queries. Dr. Rabi perhaps also wondered about the workman, but he need not have—it is clear that the workman, as presumably a nonthinker, was a safe person to be admitted to the laboratory.

The students, of course, did not want to fight with Dr. Rabi. They are firmly opposed to fighting and, in fact, to all forms of violence—so firmly, indeed, that they will make everyone go along with them. They are not "crazy" nor are they "bums," as others have suggested. They are very dedicated young men, perhaps willing to die for their ideas.

Why the "tears in his eyes"? Why, indeed? Does Dr. Rabi's memory reach back further than the empty minds of the smiling student onlookers?

I can only surmise, but perhaps he was thinking of other times, other places, some long ago and far away, when distinguished professors in great universities were not permitted to enter their classrooms or their laboratories, when the light of learning went out for much of mankind, when elite groups (often dedicated to the point of dying for their goals) preached their catechisms and made "demands."

And so many were spectators—and were amused.

PAUL K. BENEDICT
Visiting Scholar
Department of Linguistics
Columbia University
New York, May 8, 1970

Why Students Rebel

To the Editor:

Permit me to add one more perspective to the subject of student rebellion. The issue does not lie with the students—it is in their nature to rebel.

The issue lies with the Establishment (including university officials) and in its equivocal reactions to the demonstrations. What one senses here, and what is so frightening, is that so many responsible adults have had cause to agree with much that the students are trying to say. Let the Establishment put its house in order and it will have little to fear even from the extremists who are trying to knock it down.

The question in this and other areas of national disturbance is not, as the President says, simply one of law and order.

No revolution ever started where authority was in the hands of reasonable and responsible men. Violence, whether justified or not, is the last resort of people who have no other way to make themselves heard.

It is shocking that this country, which was born under these premises, should have wandered so far from its own heritage. Let us hope that it will not continue to do so.

STEPHEN S. DELAFIELD
New York, May 25, 1970

Student Revolt of the 30's

To the Editor:

The report of the President's Commission on Campus Unrest is possibly one of the most significant documents since World War II. It must be studied and implemented by all of us, if the nation's best features are to be preserved.

I was a student 35 years ago who was actively "unrestful" and the current report reminds me of the situation and the issues on the campuses in the 1930's. The activist organization was the American Student Union, called "leftist" by the conservatives because there were some members of the Communist party in positions of leadership.

The primary issues then were the rise of fascism in Germany and Italy and the threats of world war that were being ignored, it seemed to us by our elders, the ineffective national efforts to overcome the Depression; the lynchings and open repression of Negroes and the milder discriminations against Jews and Catholics.

337

It is worth recalling that part of the revolt on the campuses in the thirties was against installation of new R.O.T.C. units in colleges; against low pay for teachers, and in support of the struggle to unionize labor, which led to the Wagner Act and the National Labor Relations Board.

We rebel students of the 1930's can also take some of the credit for passage of the Social Security and unemployment insurance and minimum wage laws. For our elders in power were then, as we elders in power are today, relatively conservative and a step or two behind the consensus of the nation as a whole.

The similarities and the differences between the 1970's and the 1930's are significant. Resistance to change in the Establishment then encouraged us and activated and unified the nation. Hitler, Father Coughlin, Martin Dies, Ernest Weir, the Black Legion, Senator Bilbo, the America Firsters and Liberty League helped the student and youth rebellion and moved the nation forward. The formation of the C.I.O., the sympathy and support of people like Eleanor Roosevelt, La Guardia, Senator Robert Wagner and Albert Einstein defused the revolt and channeled it into relatively peaceful and constructive reform and action.

The new Presidential report will, I hope, be read by the Vice President, the Governor of California, the leaders of New York's Conservative party and A.F.L.–C.I.O. leaders, who should be able to recall those turbulent 1930's and the lesson of history. It takes two to make a conflict and it takes two to resolve one.

My sympathies are with the new generation. Many of their demands are both just and negotiable, while much of my own generation's resistance is unjust. We have, in reality, refused to negotiate or even listen, let alone react constructively, promptly or effectively on the reforms needed to defuse a civil revolution.

RANDALL B. SMITH
New York, Sept. 27, 1970

Indictment of Universities Examined

To the Editor:

Now that the election is behind us, we can take a dispassionate look at the implications of the indictments aimed at universities by some highly placed governmental leaders and politicians.

In trying to make a case that our institutions of higher education are riddled with dissent and led by a group of weak and ineffectual admin-

338

istrators, these spokesmen were neglecting the facts. Most campuses were entirely peaceful this fall. Nearly every institution of any size has well-developed plans to cope with violence and disruption should they occur.

But the problems generated by this fall's campaigns lie less in distortion of facts than in the further breach that is created between two great and interdependent sets of institutions—governments and universities—each of which must respect and cooperate with the other if the Republic is to prosper.

Governments are obviously our prime source of solution for the array of problems—social, economic, cultural—which must be dealt with in the decades ahead. No other instruments at our command can muster the power and the resources to deal with these problems.

The talents of the professionally and technically skilled are being called upon by governments, as never before in history, to participate in addressing all our urgent needs. Yet governments are utterly dependent on the universities for those highly skilled people whom they require, as well as for the production of new knowledge.

Creating the impression that universities are embroiled in chaos, that they are marginal institutions which threaten the welfare of the country, is hardly the way to move toward increasingly productive associations between government and the universities.

Anyone intimately connected with institutions of higher education agrees that considerable internal reform is required. Universities and colleges are now facing up to many issues which they have failed adequately to address in the past.

They have not been as interested in reaching the disadvantaged as should have been the case. They have been too bound by the disciplines; too constrained by tenure; too unwilling to broaden the base of university governance.

While they must never lose sight of their central educational role and of their responsibility to generate new knowledge, these functions must be carried out with a keener eye on the needs and nature of the "real world." Universities must be addressing these "reform" questions more actively than any social agency, including governments.

One of the surest ways to keep in contact with reality is for universities, in consultation with governments, to find new creative routes to exchanges of knowledge and experience. We must be innovative in developing arrangements which will allow government officials to share their knowledge with the campus. We must encourage faculty and students to relate their interests to the great issues with which governments grapple.

Over 20 years ago, Felix Frankfurter wrote: "That our universities

339

have grave shortcomings for the intellectual life of this nation is now a commonplace." This fact is still unhappily true. But great leadership both from the universities and from our public offices can help to identify the shortcomings and inspire the best, the most creative in all of us.

If such leadership is forthcoming, we can hope for an era of fresh creativity in the universities which will inevitably generate a like era in government.

JOHN E. CORBALLY JR.
Chancellor, Syracuse University
Syracuse, N.Y., Nov. 9, 1970

[*Dr. Corbally became President of the University of Illinois on Sept. 1, 1971. The Editor.*]

Campus View on Laos: Repressed Outrage

To the Editor:

I believe that the decision to invade Laos reflects another dangerous miscalculation of the mood on college campuses in this country. The full-scale invasion, followed by the statement from the White House that it is "not an enlargement of the war," is insulting to the intelligence and sensitivity of young men and women who are striving with all the encouragement that our academic institutions can give them to value truth, reject the spurious and expose the deceptive and the inhumane.

Students of social psychology, political science and history are not the only ones on our campuses who are aware of the artful uses of propaganda to cloak grotesque acts of inhumanity under the names of fatherland, peace, and Vietnamization.

In contrast to the reaction on the campuses to the Cambodian invasion last spring, students have not vented their anger over this latest escalation of the war. Instead, an uneasy calm pervades the campuses today. But it is just this uncertain mood that holds the greatest danger for miscalculation.

The feelings of outrage and despair that were expressed over the Cambodian invasion have been repressed, not expelled, since that time. The more deeply repressed those feelings become, the more violent the reaction could be if another nationwide protest were finally provoked.

The judgment that students now see the futility in launching another attempt to affect public policy through peaceful demonstration is probably accurate. However, the corollary to that proposition is not that there will be no response, but that the response when it comes will not be peaceful.

The verdict that the days of peaceful marches to Washington are over may be more of an apocalyptic judgment than assurance that continued enlargement of the war in Southeast Asia will be unprotested on college campuses.

On the eve of the Cambodian invasion, Mr. Nixon portrayed this nation as a thwarted giant needing to be aroused to a final test of will and fortitude. It is precisely this image which reinforces the conviction in so many of our youth that there can be no justice for the weak peoples of the earth until Goliath has been curbed or fatally wounded.

The feelings of moral revulsion arising from an unnecessary and barbarous war, compounded by the provocative campaign rhetoric last fall, the renewed bombing of North Vietnam and now the invasion of Laos can only lead to the further alienation of a large segment of this nation's youth.

Recently that alienation has been channeled quietly into utopian and quasi-religious life styles with the hope of transcending the whole sordid mess. But if the nostalgia for a radically different kind of life leads to the same frustration that has plagued most utopian movements, the possibilities for a more violently countercultural life style aimed at the institutions and values that seem to perpetuate Goliath will be vastly increased.

Mr. Nixon's rejection of the principal thesis in the Scranton Report on Campus Unrest, his apparent coolness to Chancellor Alexander Heard's counsel, together with the combative posture consistently assumed by the Vice President create the impression that this Administration has lost touch with the nation's youth and on occasion is willing to use the alienation to political advantage.

For a Government either to ignore or manipulate the nation's youth, even if the immediate calculations of "apathy" are correct, would be a far greater tragedy than any short-run tactical improvements of our military position in Southeast Asia could ever rectify.

GUILFORD DUDLEY 3D
Associate Dean of Students
University of Pennsylvania
Philadelphia, Feb. 10, 1971

341

XII•Space

Man's walk on the moon topped America's—and the world's—space achievements and opened up an exciting new era. The daring of the astronauts and the space program generally were both roundly praised and criticized. The new frontiers which space exploration put within man's reach may be of incalculable value, but letter writers raised serious questions about the nation's priorities as earth-bound man grappled with immediate, mounting problems begging for short funds.

Following President Kennedy's call in 1961 for greater efforts in space exploration, thousands of letters on the issue came to *The Times*. Most stressed these aspects; others raised the question of rules of law in outer space, the matter of liability in space, joint exploration efforts with the cosmonauts of the Soviet Union and lunar contamination.

Defining Air Space

To the Editor of *The New York Times:*

The thought-provoking letters of Prof. Quincy Wright (Nov. 23) and Prof. Leon Lipson (Dec. 23) raise interesting and highly important legal considerations relating to the concepts of air space and outer space which are involved in the question of the discontinued U-2 flights.

As Professor Wright points out, the hazard of aircraft falling on underlying territory and the danger of bombing have been a basic consideration justifying national sovereignty over air space. However, the definition and delimitation of "air space," over which national sovereignty is claimed, as distinguished from "outer space," which is open to all, should be determined not by what was feared in World War I or II, but by factors which are relevant today.

At the great altitudes where spacecraft escape from the rotating atmosphere of the earth the very measurement of space "above" a territory becomes impossible and even a theory of demarcation becomes controversial by its nature.

To permit sovereign space boundaries to extend outward from the globe like the spokes of a wheel, enclosing wider and wider areas, would be absurd beyond the earth's atmosphere. The national territories which may be endangered by any orbiting space craft are certainly not determined by whether or not such a craft is overhead in space, nor even by its direction and speed, but rather by the time and place of its controlled re-entry into the atmosphere.

In short, the hazard of an air or spacecraft falling upon underlying territory becomes either impossible or very remote as speeds increase above the velocity of sound and altitudes approach outer space. Aircraft, such as the X-15, which may be capable of operating at the altitudes of satellite orbits, are no more of a hazard to territory directly beneath them than are satellites.

Satellites and spacecraft, unless they burn up in the atmosphere, may also be expected to descend somewhere sooner or later, if not at a chosen spot by a signal from earth.

The Soviets have recently shown that they may try to control reconnaissance satellites even in outer space.

The Soviet Union has apparently based its protest against all forms of reconnaissance on the function, which is claimed to violate the United Nations Charter, and not on the ground that such satellites would violate sovereign air space. G. Zadorozhniy has recently stated that national sovereignty does not extend to the area "where an artificial satellite can fly freely without being forced to earth by air resistance." (Translated from *Stuttgarter Zeitung,* Nov. 11, 1960.)

According to this theory, Soviet satellites which are claimed to have only peaceful and scientific purposes would be legal, while United States reconnaissance satellites would be illegal.

Of course, the physical properties of the atmosphere at any given altitude would probably not be the only factors considered in setting a boundary between air space and outer space or in determining what activities are permissible in either zone. For instance, satellites carrying atomic warheads may well be prohibited altogether because of their obvious destructive menace, while unarmed satellites would be governed by different considerations.

The informative American Bar Foundation survey report on space law, with which I agree, has suggested the difficulties inherent in any detailed or comprehensive code. Nevertheless, in view of growing controversy over reconnaissance satellites and the launching of satellites into proper orbits with trajectories necessarily crossing above other nations, such as Cuba, the danger of long delaying at least an initial conference of scientists and lawyers on particular problems would seem to outweigh the admitted difficulties.

The space law controversy is not only a legal and scientific question. It threatens to develop into a major cold war dispute in which our space exploration program may possibly be enmeshed and our foreign policy suffer unless we actively work for reasonable and fair principles and procedures.

We must not let the future of space law be determined by *ex parte* statements which are not carefully examined by an impartial body of scholars.

ARTHUR R. DEAN
New York, Jan. 11, 1961

The writer, formerly Ambassador to Korea, was chairman of the United States Delegation to the United Nations Law of the Sea Conference.

Rule of Law in Outer Space

To the Editor of *The New York Times:*

The world community of jurists, lawyers and sociologists who have been devoting close attention to the problems and solutions of the rule of law in outer space certainly welcome Arthur H. Dean to their midst with the publication of his letter in *The Times* on Jan. 16.

I am most heartened that Arthur Dean should conclude his letter by pointing out that the problem of defining space jurisdiction is not only a legal and scientific question, but may well develop into a first-class international problem if not contained. He concludes by stating, "We must not let the future of space law be determined by *ex parte* statements which are not carefully examined by an impartial body of scholars."

The space law community, national and international, might well feel a little thwarted by Mr. Dean's obviously inadvertent remark concerning "*ex parte* statements." In 1952 the American Rocket Society organized a space flight committee which considered the entire ambit of space law problems and was composed of distinguished American scientists. The activity of the original committee was gradually taken over by a large number of new technical committees, including the space law and sociology committee.

The International Astronautical Federation, composed of learned societies from thirty-six nations, including most of the Iron Curtain countries, has held colloquiums on the law of outer space at The Hague, London and Stockholm.

The American Bar Association set up a committee on the law of outer space within the framework of the section of international and comparative law.

Mr. Dean has also overlooked the existence of the United Nations Ad Hoc Committee on the Peaceful Uses of Outer Space and, indeed, many other groups.

I must say it is quite disappointing to read Mr. Dean's citation of the comparatively ancient and altogether discredited references of the Russians, Kislov and Krylov, to the Russian claim that sovereignty extends over national territory endlessly and reaches out into infinity like the spokes of a wheel.

When the Soviet Union was the first to penetrate outer space on Oct. 4, 1957, the declarations of Kislov and Krylov were abandoned in favor of the theory of Zadorozhnyi.

Since then the principles of the freedom of outer space have been supported by the Soviet Union publicists Galina, Kovalev, Cheprov and the great Korovin himself.

346

The failure of lawyers to do the "bread-and-butter job" of examining international law, international treaties and the statutory laws of the nations of the world with respect to the jurisdictional aspects of airspace is the prime cause of confusion.

More than 70 nations, speaking individually through their Constitutions or statutes, have asserted their sovereignty over the airspace above them. The International Civil Aviation Convention adopted at Chicago in 1944 is the most recent multilateral expression on the subject.

Where exactly is that point which separates airspace from what is variously called outer space or cosmic space and, more important, which separates the realm of national sovereignties from a domain of international space law in the making? In all pertinent fields of science one must deal with median curves based upon an immense family of curves. As a practical guide for the space age, the weight of authority favors a measure of the sort I have termed the Karman primary jurisdiction line.

This line was suggested by Dr. Theodore von Karman and adapted by the writer on the basis of a diagram by Masson and Gazley of the Rand Corporation. An adaption of this diagram shows that the Karman jurisdictional boundary falls at approximately 275,000 feet (83 kilometers), where an object traveling at 25,000 feet (seven kilometers) a second loses its aerodynamic lift and centrifugal force takes over. The line may be changed somewhat as physicists and lawyers hammer out agreement as to where the aeronautical vehicle no longer may perform and where molecular oxygen dissociates and airspace no longer exists. But after all the data are reduced the boundary will not differ materially from the Karman line.

The principles we have stated receive most unexpected support. One example has been mentioned—namely, as a result of the far-sightedness of the law editors at Harvard the "doctrine of consent" was published and received world-wide approval. And now the Karman jurisdictional line has received the highly unlikely support of the International Sporting Committee of the Federation Aeronautique Internationale.

Officials of the Soviet Union and the United States, during October, 1960, at Barcelona, agreed that a line not materially different from the Karman (100 kilometers) would be the dividing line between airspace and outer space for record-keeping purposes. Maybe the hope of civilization rests with students and sportsmen.

ANDREW G. HALEY
Washington, Feb. 10, 1961

The writer is general counsel of the International Astronautical Federation and of the American Rocket Society.

To Save the Earth—Bound

To the Editor of *The New York Times:*

Something tells me that whatever the missile age and the astronauts mght be up to, John Doe and Richard Roe are going to remain earth-bound till the end of their natural days.

Commuters are abandoned these days to all manner of snarls, tie-ups, and inefficiency and obsolescence, while nothing seems too good for the spaceman in his rush to the moon. Let's hope mine is not the only voice to maintain that there is greater human value in spanning the distance between home and the office than that between the earth and the moon. (Would you rather be sure that the 6:07 you take gets you home without fail by 6:41, or would you rather orbit around the earth?)

What have we earthlings done to deserve such wanton abandon and neglect? Let a law be passed that makes it mandatory to spend a dime on improving the lot of the earth-bound traveler for every dollar spent on speeding man to outer space.

K. H. CHANG
Hastings-on-Hudson, N.Y., March 14, 1961

New Lexicon for Space

To the Editor of *The New York Times:*

With the advent of manned space flight, may I suggest the adoption of a new word—"abweight"—to replace the more cumbersome term "weightlessness."

EDWARD EARLY
Stamford, Conn., April 17, 1961

Value of Space Race Queried

To the Editor of *The New York Times:*

At this point in the space race Americans should begin asking: How many more billions of dollars are going to be wasted in a losing race? Suppose our initial attempt to send a man into orbit should end in failure? Is it worth the risk of the inevitable world-wide reaction?

Let us concede victory to the Russians and transfer the use of these vast funds to other great endeavors where we can show the way to the Russians and to the rest of the world. Elimination of starvation, eradication of disease, weather control, harnessing the power of the sun and harvesting the wealth of the sea are just some of the areas in which great achievements are possible to contribute to the benefit of humanity.

The space program should be continued to the extent necessary for defense preparedness only. Let the Russians boast to the world that they put the first man into orbit. If we put more bread into hungry mouths here on earth we will win a far more important race.

HERBERT GISSEN
Laurelton, N.Y., April 20, 1961

Space Exploration Backed

To the Editor of *The New York Times:*

During the last weeks since President Kennedy called for greater efforts in space exploration, and especially for manned exploration of the moon, various arguments have appeared in print arguing against these proposals. I believe that some of these arguments are false, and it would be unfortunate if decisions were made on false reasoning.

It is supposed by many that diverting the billions of dollars required for the space program to other projects regarded as more desirable would produce great progress or even definite solutions of important problems. Money procures suitable men and materials, but only if suitable men and materials are available.

It is my impression that substantially all men reasonably competent to attack the cancer problem, and many other medical problems, are adequately and even generously supported in their research. Appropriating more funds for this problem would accomplish essentially nothing more than is now being done.

Again, desalting sea water is suggested as an alternative to space research. This problem is being studied by many people because any acceptable process would be valuable commercially. Fresh water produced from the sea requires expensive chemical processing. Water for distribution in San Diego coming from the Colorado River costs 2½ cents a ton. It is just difficult to meet such a price by any known desalting process.

Space developments require men and materials more like those of the

349

airplane industries and the television and radio industries than anything else that comes to my mind. But airplane companies are anxious to do the space work largely because of a near saturation in the commercial and military aircraft needs.

We might divert space engineers to the automobile industry, but does the United States really need more automobiles? Isn't it likely that the effect of more effort in this direction would be to produce gaudier cars with more unnecessary power and perhaps of even less durability than we now have?

Some suggest that the space program is evidence of decadence. A decadent 20th-century society would build great estates, large, extravagant automobiles, garish vacation spots, etc. Possibly we show some signs of this, but promoting a vigorous space program is not decadent.

The Soviet Union is doing so also, and in spite of our very sincere dislike of many things it does, it certainly cannot be described as decadent. It is striving to win the approval of the world, while decadent societies care nothing about this.

Imagine the excitement of all people in our own country and everywhere else in the world on the day that men first step on the moon. The thrill that we knew when Amundsen reached the South Pole, Lindbergh flew the Atlantic, Hillary climbed Everest, will be insignificant in comparison. This age has produced the great knowledge of science and the greatest engineering feats of all time, and we can send men to the moon. At least some of us in the United States of America are aiming at the stars in a number of ways, and among these ways is the exploration of the moon and planets.

The fundamental purpose of space exploration is not only scientific investigation but adventure and achievement for all of us. The President can hardly have a detailed knowledge of scientific objectives, but he has a correct sense of the human and historical importance of space exploration.

HAROLD C. UREY
La Jolla, Calif., June 14, 1961

The writer was awarded the Nobel Prize in Science in 1934 for his discovery of heavy hydrogen. He is an authority on the composition of celestial bodies.

350

Space Program Deplored

To the Editor of *The New York Times:*

What a sad letter for a distinguished man of science to write! I am referring to Harold C. Urey's letter published June 25. It indicates a distorted sense of values, and a limited comprehension of human problems.

Several times he refers to the space exploration program as if it were desirable as a medium of public entertainment. He uses the words "excitement," "thrill," "adventure." He cites the exploits of Amundsen, Lindbergh and Hillary. Exciting, yes, but are these to be the measure of aspiration for the dedicated scientist? How much has society benefited by such efforts compared to those of thousands of nameless and obscure scientists in medicine and the humanities?

Knowledge is desirable from any source, for one cannot predict its potential spread of value. Yet its degree of importance as a guide to how we spend our resources depends upon its relevance to an area of human benefit.

Dr. Urey states: "It is my impression that substantially all men reasonably competent to attack the cancer problem, and many other medical problems, are adequately and even generously supported in their research." How far from the truth this is! Ask the American Heart Association, American Cancer Society, United Cerebral Palsy or any other voluntary agency.

Visit the hospital, rehabilitation center, homes for the crippled, blind, and the aged and see our children, our parents and the representations of ourselves in time or by circumstance. Ask these afflicted people whether they would have preferred the eradication or amelioration of the ravages of their impairment or a space exploration program.

Ask the young man excluded from a career in medicine or the humanities because of his economic situation, racial or religious prejudice or the poor quality of his schooling. In a society in which six-year-old children because of the color of their skins are "escorted" to school by policemen and in which disease, accident and aging strikes every single one of us and many prematurely, we are urged to devote our precious resources to thrilling the public and the immature scientist.

FREDERICK A. WHITEHOUSE
Garden City, N.Y., June 26, 1961

The writer is Director of Rehabilitation, American Heart Association.

351

Voyagers in Space

To the Editor:

As a long-time collector of moon voyages, I was delighted to learn from *The Times* of March 19 that Col. Aleksei Leonov scrupulously observed literary tradition when, after emerging from the capsule, "he did a slow-motion somersault in the wake of the ship, turned around like a man rolling in the snow, and finally stood stiffly on his head."

Three hundred and fifteen years ago an intrepid French space mariner had the same experience. Cyrano de Bergerac in his "Histoire Comique ou Voyage dans la Lune" (published *sans privilège* in 1650; authorized edition, 1656) made a somersault dive three-quarters of the way to the moon: "I found my feet turn over of a sudden, without any apparent jerk; nay, I had not perceived it, if I had not found my head loaden with the rest of my body."

Even in a grotesque position, Cyrano did not neglect to make scientific observations. He looked back between his legs at the earth he had left, which now "appeared to be like a large Holland cheese gilded."

Cyrano, by the way, was the first moon voyager to take off in a rocket-ship, quite without design on his part. A group of soldiers had fastened firecrackers and other fireworks to the flying ship Cyrano had made.

Edgar Allan Poe was one of several later writers who picked up the somersault idea from Cyrano, in "The Unparalleled Adventure of One Hans Pfaal," first published in *The Southern Literary Messenger* in 1835. He too made a somersault dive. The fact that "the *bouleversement* in itself was not only natural and inevitable, but had long been actually anticipated," had not prepared Hans for the experience of seeing his world literally upside down.

Not for the first time literature preceded scientific actuality, as imagination bodies forth the form of things unknown.

MARJORIE NICOLSON
Princeton, N.J., March 19, 1965

The writer is the author of "Voyages to the Moon" and a member of The Institute for Advanced Study.

'Firsts' in Race

To the Editor:

The advances in space exploration are breathtaking and exciting—man has entered an entirely new era. This can be compared to evolution, when the fish first grew legs to leave his medium, the sea, and adapt himself to the terrestrial environment.

Most unexciting and boring, however, is the United States–Soviet Union rivalry to be first at this or at that. What a waste: Brains, energy and money should be pooled for a combined effort. We (the people of the world) could accomplish more with less effort and duplication.

Does it really matter today whether Columbus was an Italian, Spaniard or a Portuguese?

THOMAS LEE BUCKY, M.D.
Weston, Conn., June 8, 1965

Military Implications of Space

To the Editor:

I enthusiastically join in the world's applause for the personal courage and valor of Majors McDivitt and White and for the splendid efforts of thousands who contributed to the success of Gemini 4. However I would like to add a dissonant word of warning to these celebrations.

The space race has grave military implications. A mature public analysis of this fact has been avoided by official Government sources and barely mentioned in the public press or in TV and radio broadcasts. In fact, it seems certain that the United States already has significant military space programs under way about which the American public has little or no knowledge.

Indeed, in the past decade the peaceful aspects of space exploration have been greatly emphasized almost to the complete exclusion of an analysis of its military aspects. This situation is akin to that of an ostrich with its head in the sand.

In recent months Generals LeMay and Power, after retiring from active military service, have publicly voiced their fears on this issue. They are to be commended for their candor, for we desperately need an adequate public analysis of this problem.

Moreover, in view of the continued deterioration of the United Nations as an effective instrument for the preservation of world peace and the continuous threat to that peace by the repeated violation of international law by nations both large and small, it appears that by 1970 there may not only be men on the moon but also nuclear weapons in orbit around the earth.

Our only hope in avoiding this tragedy and the increased likelihood of nuclear destruction is squarely to face the issue before it is too late.

RANDALL J. LONGCORE
Cambridge, Mass., June 9, 1965

Arms in Space Opposed

To the Editor:

While astronauts are trying to find out whether man can survive in outer space and aquanauts are trying to learn whether he can survive under water, perhaps a still more pertinent question is: Can man survive here on good old *terra firma?*

Much has been said of late about the 20th anniversary of the atomic age. Very little, however, has been said about the most amazing paradox with which mankind has been confronted for these past two decades. This is the overwhelming faith in the military to protect it at a time when militarism as a means of security is an obsolete institution.

With the ushering in of the atomic age it became apparent at once that the military could no longer protect either life or property. They could now destroy on an undreamed-of scale, but they were helpless when it came to protecting life and property.

Few wanted to believe this, and certainly not the military themselves or the big industrial components that support them. Give us time, they said, and we will come up with something that will again restore the balance between military defense and offense. In these twenty years billions have been poured into military establishments and scientific research for national defense. As yet the best these apostles have been able to come up with is a balance of terror neither neat nor delicate.

Dissatisfied with such a balance, President Johnson has now given the go-ahead to the Air Force for its much-coveted MOL project. This go-ahead signal simply gets out in the open what many of us had suspected for years—that much of this interest in outer space has been prompted by its military implications rather than by any genuine interest in bona fide scientific knowledge.

354

Although announced primarily as a defense measure, is there anyone in Washington naive enough to believe that the Russians will so interpret it? The probability is that the Bambis will be flying in the heavens long before MOL becomes a reality.

In the twenty years since Hiroshima there has been but one constructive measure that has been taken toward achieving a more sane world. This was the limited test-ban treaty of two years ago. Since then no positive action has been taken. It now begins to look as if this, too, might soon go overboard in the mad plunge toward insanity.

Spending some $50 billion a year as we are for defense, is it not time that we were asking ourselves whether we are really creating a mode of life—one could hardly call it building a civilization—that is, after all, worth defending?

NORMAN BOARDMAN
New York, Aug. 28, 1965

Military Use of Space

To the Editor:

Your Aug. 26 editorial is yet another example of the bankruptcy of military thinking. Terrifying and fantastic—indeed, manned orbiting "laboratories" are that. But are they really necessary?

Once again we are asked to silently acquiesce to a questionable military dictum—"If we don't, they will." Because Russia has the capacity to send up such armaments, why does it so logically follow that they will do so? It is we, not they, who have a three or four to one superiority in ICBM's.

How hollow, how hypocritical our pacific intentions must sound to the rest of the world.

By our action will we allow the Soviet Union any alternative but to respond in kind? Would not President Johnson's invitation to the Soviet scientists stand a much greater likelihood of acceptance if coupled with an offer of diplomatically exploring the possibility of not constructing such armaments?

The Administration's proposal can only increase the tensions of a world troubled enough.

DANIEL W. MURPHY
Washington, Conn., Aug. 26, 1965

355

Weapons in Space

To the Editor:

Daniel W. Murphy in his letter published Sept. 1 refers to your Aug. 26 editorial "Arms in Space" as ". . . yet another example of the bankruptcy of military thinking." Mr. Murphy continues, "Terrifying and fantastic—indeed, manned orbiting laboratories are that. But are they really necessary?"

In my opinion manned orbiting laboratories are necessary and represent military vision, foresight and preparedness. As President Johnson has so ably stated, "This program will bring us new knowledge about what man is able to do in space. It will enable us to relate that ability to the defense of America." I believe manned orbiting laboratories have the capability of adding important elements of strategic deterrence.

Our potential enemies being what they are, history has shown that they respect strength. I believe the Administration's proposal will increase that strength.

I. B. LASKOWITZ
Brooklyn, N.Y., Sept. 2, 1965

Space Program Upheld

To the Editor:

The Rev. Wesley Shrader (letter, Jan. 17) repeats the question, "Why this costly space race at the expense of medical and social progress?" As a former NASA scientist and presently professor of astronomy at West Connecticut State College I should like to answer.

The history of science and technology has shown that a continuing policy of pure research is necessary to insure vital advancement, inventiveness and progress, even though results are usually predictable and serendipitous.

Imagine, for example, the outcry against a lucrative research program into moldy bread. Yet today we have penicillin as one such freak accident. Consider all the space-age plastics, bonding agents, metallurgical break-throughs, etc., that developed from the designing of rockets alone, not to mention the growth of computer technology.

"Are we searching for greater security in civil defense?" Yes. That nation which first puts a ballistic missile station on the moon literally controls this planet. Naturally, we are not out to do this, but we wish to make sure no one else does.

With the population crisis and the eventual disappearance of many of our natural resources, planetary colonization leaves the realm of science fiction and becomes stark realism.

Thus, while it is true that this $3-billion annual expenditure could help to expedite the discovery of cold remedies and cures for cancer and arthritis, the chaotic situation this country would face with the dumping on the market of so many thousands of scientists and technicians would be far more catastrophic. Rather than a cosmic game indulged in by playboy astronauts, the space program will provide benefits unimagined from this viewpoint in time.

ROBERT F. WEIRAUCH
Danbury, Conn., Jan. 17, 1969

Lunar Contamination

To the Editor:

The debate over the hazards of contamination of the terrestrial environment by the impending manned lunar landing, a debate most properly encouraged by *The Times,* seems to have overlooked a troublesome aspect of the problem.

One source of contamination may of course be lunar molecular systems capable of damaging living terrestrial forms. The first of these to be exposed will be the astronauts themselves. Another source may be earth forms, deposited on the moon by previous unmanned landings and since altered by mutation. In either event, their effects are not predictable by any existing information. Previous exposure to lunar material has been to molecules which have had to travel in space from moon to earth, taking significant time to do so.

What information will be available to those responsible to allow them to decide whether an astronaut is experiencing a toxic effect of lunar exposure or an infestation or infection should he on the return journey fall ill, or deviate in an as yet unobserved manner from the expected limits of those physiologic parameters being measured, e.g. an unaccountable fall in blood pressure.

How will it be possible to decide, in the short time available, whether new steps need to be undertaken to avoid contamination of the entire terrestrial environment?

357

Is this problem so insoluble that it has been disregarded, or has its solution been arrived at in a fatalistic way by the very commitment to a manned landing itself? A decision not to return the capsule, on grounds of safety, is probably morally unacceptable.

The reasonable alternative, which it is probably not too late to undertake, is a project involving the exposure of a variety of terrestrial life forms, including mammals, to the lunar environment. This could be achieved by presently available technology, making use of unmanned capsules and lunar landing devices. It is possible that the economy of payload in an unmanned flight might allow the vehicle, once contaminated, to be kept in a lunar orbit for a considerable and biologically meaningful period while data from its experimental living systems is being gathered by telemetry.

On the basis of this data, decisions about returning the vehicle to earth could be made. And, in that event, the capsule could presumably be returned to NASA's laboratory in an unopened state, an arrangement which Dr. Philip Abelson (Editor, Science) properly pointed out might be prohibitively hazardous with a manned vehicle, however, large the risks of opening it might be.

If lunar landing and recovery are to be undertaken at all, then surely the living forms on earth merit this much by way of preliminary study of the unpredictable biologic dangers.

IRWIN H. KAISER, M.D.
Professor, Albert Einstein College of Medicine
Bronx, N.Y., June 22, 1969

Lunar Quarantine

To the Editor:

Your editorials, news comments and letters on the quarantine of astronauts returning from the moon are addressed to a fascinating and important issue of public policy. Above all, they highlight the absurdity of the efforts now programed as if they were intended to protect the earth from a tangible risk of global infection by lunar microbes.

In fact, no responsible official or scientific adviser believes there is such a risk. If there were, the response would have to be the cancellation of the entire manned lunar program. We would have to be able to destroy the "contraband" or send it back, measures which we do not contemplate for national heroes having accomplished an arduous and courageous feat.

It is impossible to say that the risk is strictly zero despite the fact that we have a great deal of information about the moon. It has no atmosphere, and under relatively close photographic observation shows no sign whatever of life. The theoretical risk is perhaps comparable to that of opening an oil well or bringing deep-sea cores to the surface of the earth. These materials are far more likely to carry exotic forms which have been separated from the main stream for millions of years. We face, and do not properly attend to, much larger risks in the importation of wild monkeys and other animals for use in preparing vaccines.

The quarantine exercise does have two functions: to protect the lunar samples from contamination by earthly materials, and as a dress-rehearsal for explorations of the planets. By pointing out the insuperable difficulties of managing the quarantine of planetary travelers, it may have done an invaluable service in our plans for the exploration of Mars.

Before we can properly plan how to protect the earth against possible infection from Mars, we would need the information from a much more detailed study of the planet by automated instruments than the Administration believed necessary for the Apollo program.

JOSHUA LEDERBERG
Professor of Genetics, Stanford School of Medicine
Stanford, Calif., July 7, 1969

Goals for 1976

To the Editor:

In 1961 President Kennedy committed this nation to putting a man on the moon in the next decade. Perhaps before this letter reaches you— the nation's postal system being what it is—we shall have achieved this end.

With the same kind of commitment of human resources it might be possible to set ourselves a worthier goal for, say, 1976, when we celebrate the bicentennial of the nation's independence. Suppose we set out to try and find a cure for cancer by that date; or to end hunger and malnutrition throughout the world? If that seems too tall an order, how about pledging ourselves to wiping out the ghetto and providing decent housing and education in our vast urban wilderness?

The possibilities are as endless as the needs and if it is prestige or triumph over the Soviet Union we are seeking, surely the accomplishment of even one of these would help to achieve that end. We might even recapture some of our national self-respect along the way.

On the other hand, maybe a moon shot is easier and more likely to succeed. Compassion cannot be computerized, and perhaps, as T. S. Eliot put it, our only monument is doomed to be ". . . the asphalt road, And a thousand lost golf balls."

BARBARA M. COLLINS
Jenkintown, Pa., July 14, 1969

Dollar Bills to Moon

To the Editor:

I was interested to see that the Apollo 11 crew will carry torn dollar bills to certify that the same men who went also came back.

In ancient times it was the custom of merchants to make an agreement for shipping goods and then tear it in halves. The ship master took one half and the merchant kept the other. Only if the two torn parts matched, could they be sure it was the same agreement.

This was called a *charta partita,* and the word remains in nearly the same usage today, when most marine chartering agreements are called "charter-parties."

A. B. PURBRICK
Pittsburgh, Pa., July 15, 1969

Comment on Mars

To the Editor:

In reference to Vice President Agnew's statement on July 16, that this country should now pursue a course to Mars, I have only one comment, "If you've seen one planet, you've seen them all."

ROBERT M. STEIN
Elmsford, N.Y., July 17, 1969

360

Space Race for Prestige

To the Editor:

One needn't be a harsh critic of the Kennedy Administration or Theodore Sorensen's utopian account of its space policy-making process (Special Supplement—July 17) to recognize that the decision to land a man on the moon within the next decade was hastily developed and ill conceived.

It should be recalled that the Apollo program commitment was secured in May 1961, a short month after the abortive Bay of Pigs invasion and Yuri Gagarin's flight around the earth. These two events combined to do considerable damage to American morale and to the reputation of a new Administration. It is thus not surprising to find that President Kennedy's memorandum for the Vice President (April 20, 1961) reproduced on the same page as Sorensen's analysis, emphasizes not the scientific or technological importance of prospective space efforts, but the rather narrow spirit of cold war competition and the urgent desire to find a compelling program which would regain Presidential prestige.

In this connection, the two key questions posed in that memorandum are worth requoting: "Do we have a chance of beating the Soviets . . . ?" and "Is there any other space program which promises dramatic results in which (sic) we could win?"

It is to be hoped that an exhaustive and calm national debate over America's spending priorities shall precede, and not follow, the next major Presidential space decision. For there is some danger that America's disappointment with political and military stalemate in Vietnam will encourage similar desires to gain short-run prestige and recognition in the space competition with Russia, at the cost of yet another postponement of the serious effort to come to terms with our nation's urban crisis.

REYNOLD LEVY
Charlottesville, Va., July 17, 1969

Nixon's 'Horning In'

To the Editor:

Your July 19 editorial "Nixoning the Moon" is superb. Nixon's horning in is a perfect example of utter tastelessness.

361

What would have happened if those brave, sweating astronauts hadn't made it?

I fear we have a President so lacking in humility it is frightening.

GERTRUDE MERTENS
Woodstock, Vt., July 20, 1969

Merit of Message

To the Editor:

In your narrow-minded, petty, partisan editorial of July 19, "Nixoning the Moon" you have missed the entire point and significance of the "moon conversation."

Man's walking on the moon merited more than a comment from the ever-present, anonymous voice of Houston Mission Control. It required words from our elected President, our highest spokesman, to say on behalf of all mankind at that very moment—"We are with you, we are proud of you; job well done."

CLARK J. WINSLOW
New York, July 22, 1969

Liability in Space

To the Editor:

Our magnificent achievements in space should not permit us to forget that there is still no viable international law governing liability for injuries and damage caused by space activities.

In June a small Japanese freighter was hit by wreckage from a Soviet spacecraft (news story July 5). The freighter was badly damaged and five crewmen were seriously injured. With the number of satellites now circling the globe and the extent of current activities in space, it is inevitable that there will be other accidents and perhaps very serious ones.

Efforts to reach an international treaty governing liability for space-caused accidents have so far been unsuccessful, and the United States is largely to blame. The key problem is whether or not there should be a damage ceiling. According to your news report our delegation to the legal subcommittee of the United Nations Committee on Outer Space, which is attempting to formulate a treaty, is insisting on a limitation of liability of $500 million. Interestingly enough the Russian delegation refuses to agree to any ceiling.

The United States should be opposed to any artificial limitation of damages. The position now being taken by our delegation is inconsistent with the strong opinions expressed by many Senators on damage limitations in international air law when the Warsaw Convention and the Montreal Agreement were being actively discussed, in 1966.

To the extent that artificial limitations of damages are imposed, the losses sustained in excess of those limitations are borne by the innocent victims of the accident. Even if the damage limitation is $500 million it will never have any practical effect unless the actual degree of loss sustained exceeds $500 million. If the current United States position is adopted, and such losses do occur, it simply means that individuals, or even countries, that sustain damage through no fault of their own, as a result of space activities, will have to bear those losses without compensation.

Thus, in this case, it is the Soviet position of opposition to any artificial limitations that is the proper one. Principles of liability for damage caused by space activities should be established before we have a major accident. Whether the accident is caused by an American spacecraft or one launched by the Soviet Union, the rules should be established in advance. The United States can make a significant contribution to the establishment of these principles now by changing its improper position on the damage ceiling.

LEE S. KREINDLER
New York, July 17, 1969

Ravished Moon

To the Editor:

The July 23 lead editorial ("Man the Polluter") expresses exactly what I felt when I read about the imperishable litter that man has left behind him on the moon. (I was reminded of my visit to the site of Rampart Dam on the Yukon—a beautiful spot now occupied by abandoned Nissen huts, scrap iron, rubber floats, etc.) If Shelley were writing today, he would have to revise those lines:

363

"That orbéd maiden with scrap metal laden
Whom mortals call the moon."

I'm afraid Diana has lost her virginity at last.

PAUL BROOKS
Boston, July 23, 1969

Identity with Human Race

To the Editor:

Nona E. Smith (letter, Aug. 9) thinks she cannot identify with the astronauts because she considers herself black. I identify with the astronauts, but only because they and I are human beings, and that would be the same if they were Japanese or Congolese or Javanese or Lebanese.

I cannot and should not identify with their achievement, and my son does not, because it is not my achievement. It would help a great many of those (in more ethnic groups than one) who are worried about their identity, if they would accept the fact that they are members of the human race, not of a subgroup hostile to all others; and that a sense of pride is not anyone's by right of birth, nor is it conferred on one, but is something earned by one's efforts.

LEO MILLER
New York, Aug. 9, 1969

Value of Space Study

To the Editor:

The triviality of the scientific returns from the man-on-the-moon program is finally becoming evident even to those—mostly non-scientists—who had been misled by publicity and by the play on popular imagination indulged in by Government and the mass media.

The moon rock samples, about which full columns of news are released by NASA, cannot even answer the few questions some geologists are interested in solving.

It is important that this be made clear because of the current discussion about big versus small Mars-landing programs—probably $3 billion a year for fifty years or $10 billion a year for fifteen years. This at a time when the Institute of General Medical Sciences of the National Institutes of Health has announced substantial cuts in new health-related research projects, news that has received much less prominence than any of the rock-news from NASA.

Even apart from the social benefits that American health research has been in the habit of delivering, such as polio, measles and flu vaccines and a hundred other medical advances, almost any one of the hundreds of projects that the National Institutes of Health cannot fund has intrinsic scientific interest at least as great as a trip to the moon—in terms of the number of intelligently concerned people and addition to human knowledge.

Technology, however sophisticated, is not science unless its goal is knowledge. Intellectual priorities are at least as important for human culture as socio-economic priorities, and both are being distorted by the space program.

It is time the American people were told frankly that the present space program is technically impressive, scientifically trivial, culturally misguided and socially preposterous.

S. E. LURIA, M.D.
Cambridge, Mass., Sept. 17, 1969

The writer, professor of biology at M.I.T., is a member of the National Academy of Sciences.

Home Front Priorities

To the Editor:

I suppose it is important to spend $14 billion on perfecting recoverable spaceships, but it seems to me that perhaps we should reconsider priorities such as schools, public health, cleaning up our environment and spend at least some of the billions on these necessities.

If the earth is not fit to live on, what's the difference whether we go to the moon or to Mars, and who will want to come back?

JULIA JOHNSON
New York, May 19, 1970

365

Index

371

372

Marshall, George C., 156, 284
Marshall, John, 225
Marvin, Langdon P., 186
Marx, Ruth N., 205
Mason, Robert S., 196
Matthews, Herbert L., 38
Maurer, Millicent, 82
Mayer, Henry, 79–80
Mboya, Tom, 93, 94
Mead, Margaret, 50
Means, James A., 196
Medina, Harold, 282
Mendès-France, Pierre, 53
Menezes, Ruth de, 97
Mertens, Gertrude, 362
Metropolitan Transportation Authority, 198, 200
Metzger, Paul, 198
Miles, Geoffrey, 189–90
Miller, Clyde E., 223
Miller, Leo, 364
Miller, Margo, 190
Mills, Herbert, 308
MIRV (Multiple Independently targetable Re-entry Vehicles), 133–34, 139, 142–3, 144
Mitchell, David, 57–8
Mitchell, John, 291–2
Mondale, Walter F., 224
Montagu, Ashley, 92
Morment, Alma C. J., 87
Morris, Howard L., 275
Morse, Sen. Wayne, 164
Mott, Stewart R., 245
Mowry, Aileen, 188
Moynihan, Daniel P., 102, 103, 217, 287, 294
Mundt, Karl E., 281
Murphy, Daniel W., 355, 356
Murphy, Frank, 183
Murray, Pauli, 73
Musicus, Milton, 201

N.A.A.C.P. (National Association for the Advancement of Colored People), 54, 74
Nagasaki, 107, 109, 132
Nash, Ogden, 195
Nasser, Gamal Abdel, 256–74 *passim*
Negroes, 37, 54–5, 67–104, 214
Nehru, Jawaharlal, 45
Nelson, Gaylord, 166
Neumann, John von, 111
New York City, 11–12, 15, 22, 74–6, 98, 188–205 *passim,* 231, 312, 313
Nguyen Cao Ky, 181–2
Nguyen Thi Binh, 181
Nguyen Van Thieu, 181–2
Nichols, Gen., 284
Nicolson, Marjorie, 352
Nixon, Richard M., 56–7, 60–1, 102, 135–41 *passim,* 175–82 *passim,* 203–204, 219–42 *passim,* 291, 294, 308–309, 325–41 *passim,* 361–2
Noether, Emmy, 21–22
Nolting, Frederick E., Jr., 170
North Atlantic Treaty Organization (NATO), 116, 137, 160, 259
Nuremberg Trials, 48, 147, 149, 169, 182

Oakes, John B., 7
Ochs, Adolph S., 3–4, 7
Oden, David H., 267
Oppenheimer, Fritz E., 257
Oppenheimer, Robert, 107, 192, 283–4
Ordway, Samuel H., Jr., 300
Orear, Jay, 265

Tran Thien Khiem, 181–2
Trevor, John C., 39
Trotsky, Leon, 26–8
Truman, Harry S., 154, 285, 298

Ulman, Joseph N., Jr., 205
United Nations, 29, 31, 34–5, 36–7, 112–37 *passim,* 159–80 *passim,* 248–69 *passim,* 344, 353, 363
Unwin, J. D., 232
Urey, Harold C., 350, 351

Van Buren, Martin, 205, 206
Van Name, Willard G., 299
Van Veen, Stuyvesant, 309
Vernon, Raymond, 90
Viereck, Peter, 153
Vietnam, 4, 41–2, 50–1, 52–3, 56–7, 58, 60, 133, 145, 163–67, 171–83, 220, 224, 326–7, 331, 334, 335
Villa, Pancho, 178
Vo Nguyen Giap, 52

Wade, James O'Shea, 335
Wagner, Robert, 338
Waite, Morrison Remick, 225
Wald, George, 59
Wald, M. H., 204
Walker, Eric A., 322

Wallace, George, 230
Wallach, Richard W., 202
Walser, Gladys, 112
Walter, Francis E., 288, 289
Warren, Charles, 212
Warren, Earl, 225
Warren, John L., 317
Warsaw Pact, 137
Watkins, Capt., 198
Weir, Ernest, 338
Weirauch, Robert F., 357
Weiss, Edward L., 201
Weisskopf, Dr., 107
Weizmann, Chaim, 31
Wells, H. G., 309
Westmoreland, William C., 182, 183
White, Edward H., II, 353
White, Harry Dexter, 285
Whitehouse, Frederick A., 351
Whitman, Walter G., 120
Whitney, Craig, 336
Whittlesey, Julian H., 195
Wicker, Tom, 85, 171
Wiesner, Jerome B., 117
Wilkins, Roy, 54–5, 87
Willrich, Mason, 138
Wilson, James Q., 103
Wilson, Robert, 324
Wilson, Robert W., 200
Wilson, Woodrow, 17–18, 178, 282, 326
Winocour, Jack, 250
Winslow, Clark J., 362
World Wildlife Fund, The, 307–308
Wright, Lord, 149
Wright, Quincy, 344

Xuma, A. B., 35